Breaking Ground

Breaking Ground

CHARTING OUR FUTURE
IN A PANDEMIC YEAR

Edited by Anne Snyder and Susannah Black

Mark Noll, N. T. Wright, Gracy Olmstead, Jennifer Frey,
Michael Wear, Danté Stewart, Marilynne Robinson,
Christine Emba, Tara Isabella Burton, Phil Christman,
Jeffrey Bilbro, L. M. Sacasas, Oliver O'Donovan, and more

The editors want to thank members of the *Comment* team, specifically Ray Pennings, Heidi Deddens, Jeff Reimer, Kathryn de Ruijter, and Leigh Harper as crucial teammates who made this book a reality.

Published by Plough Publishing House
Walden, New York
Robertsbridge, England
Elsmore, Australia
www.plough.com

Plough produces books, a quarterly magazine, and Plough.com to encourage people and help them put their faith into action. Plough is the publishing house of the Bruderhof, an international Christian community.

This book was created in collaboration with *Comment* magazine, a publication of Cardus. All essays were originally published on BreakingGround.us, an online platform created by *Comment* in 2020. Views expressed by contributors are their own and do not necessarily reflect the editorial position of *Comment* or Plough.

CONTENTS

SPRING *(March–May 2021)*

PREFACE

ANNE SNYDER AND SUSANNAH BLACK

HINDSIGHT IS TWENTY-TWENTY, or so they say. It will be many years, though, before we understand the new normal that the *year* 2020 has carved. As *Plough Quarterly*'s Peter Mommsen wrote while Covid-19 was tearing through North American hospitals in that first spring of felt apocalypse:

> In a time of crisis – whether a pandemic, a terrorist attack, or a war – people are quick to say that "things will never be the same." This comes from an understandable urge. Faced with suffering of such magnitude, our instinct is to find meaning in it by claiming it has shifted the course of history. In reality, while some things may change in the wake of the pandemic, most will not. This crisis reveals many truths, but in itself will not transform or heal or renew.

These were wise words, and the book you hold in your hands is a diary written in the spirit of their prudence. But it is also a record of human beings striving for humility before an onslaught of uncertainty and rapid adjustment – humility that is the necessary soil for hope to seed a more intelligent and humane future.

Comment magazine created *Breaking Ground* out of a sense that 2020 offered a *kairos* moment – an opportunity to recalibrate tired cultural values and ways of thinking, and to renew particularly fragile spheres like education, health care, media, and politics with a recovered moral purpose oriented toward our actual makeup as human beings, and toward serving the needs of the commons. Launching publicly just hours after the first memorial service was held for George Floyd, the project soon stretched to engage even more painful – and long-standing – realities of injustice than we had foreseen in the "mere" context of Covid-19. Urgent questions came at us like hail on a tent just pitched: How do our institutions preserve their ideals while pruning their habituated hypocrisies? Where are wise and courageous leaders we can look to for guidance and cooperate with in trust? Is it possible to have an honest reckoning with our sins as nations, and come out better and closer on the other side? Where are the bridge-builders, peacemakers, place-makers, and justice-builders working in appreciative tandem?

These longings, and the crises fueling them, were strained further by something that began to feel like an epistemological crisis. Forced into physical isolation for months on end, we all seemed to careen into magnified shadow. Years of intensifying political idolatry ruptured into in-group splintering and betrayal. Distrust of vested authority festered into conspiracy and new, totalist explanations as to what was really motivating what. The media sprinted to keep up with events and articulate their meaning, but most interpretations were weighted by partisan conviction and zero-sum moral narratives. We started to hate one another just a few shades more. We started to feel like we were going crazy.

So *Breaking Ground*'s task became still more basic. Our editorial team and the twenty partner institutions that supported us gradually realized that we couldn't just seek to equip God's people to serve the suffering in this chaotic season, but that we had to try to nurture a shared sense of reality for all, whatever our faith or politics. And we needed to do so without falling into the trap of faux-neutrality, mere proceduralism, and the perpetual postponement of the need to grapple with the question of the Good. We needed something stronger than civility.

This book memorializes that quest. *Breaking Ground* hosted a public conversation for one year between June 2020 and June 2021 – commissioning essays and hosting virtual events and podcasts inspired by the Christian humanist tradition to respond imaginatively to the year's public-health, economic, racial, and political crises. You'll find signature voices from the spheres of politics and policing, education and journalism, medicine and business, theology and science, philanthropy and technology, and the family and household too. You'll find students of history and exemplars of social solidarity. You'll find a space where complex truths have been aired in public, where conversation has been rigorous in its search for truth yet grace-filled in its respect for the human face.

The two of us discovered a friendship as we built *Breaking Ground*, a friendship born out of our shared desire for Christians and Christian institutions to be more confident in recognizing the resources they possess as goods worth offering to our broader society – an unparalleled anthropology and a this-worldly incarnational care directed and sustained by an eternal hope. We committed ourselves to creating a space that might be of service to all, Christian or not, and find ourselves now not just preserving a record of a historic time but also stewarding the seeds of a new public sphere.

This book is in one sense the annals of a harrowing year. But it is also, at least by implication, a set of proposals for that new public sphere, a set of schematics and prompts for the building of a true and strong commons. This is a period in which nearly every corner of society, secular and sacred, has been stopped short at the question of unity. That is not a question that can be solved from the outside, but has to be tried afresh from the inside. In our case, and in the case of the writers you are about to read, we and they have been animated by an encounter with a God who is alive and redeeming yet. Not everyone believes that, but that doesn't shake its truth. And we're tasked with living in, and seeking to help order, a world where those who do believe that and those who don't are our beloved family, our fellow citizens, and our friends. This book is an invitation, a recipe book, and a citizenship manual for the future that we now have to build, the garden that we now have to tend, in the ground that this past year has broken.

Yours,

Anne Snyder
Founder, *Breaking Ground*
Editor-in-Chief, *Comment*

Susannah Black
Senior Editor, *Breaking Ground*
Senior Editor, *Plough*

November 2021

SUMMER

Anne Snyder

Susannah Black

Mark Noll

N. T. Wright

Gracy Olmstead

Doug Sikkema

James Matthew Wilson

Patrick Pierson

Jennifer Frey

J. L. Wall

Michael Wear

Danté Stewart

Joe Nail

Benya Kraus

June 1, 2020

FOUNDING VISION

ANNE SNYDER

DEAR READER,

These are deeply disorienting times. Many of us are losing loved ones and livelihoods – to Covid-19, to racial violence and injustice. All of us are having to loosen our grasp on familiar rhythms and assumed futures. The institutional, economic, and social backdrop is a mess, and many of our vocations have been yanked into a violent gem-tumbler, the somersaults revealing little of where we're headed or how long we'll have to keep spinning.

Historically, change of this scope has created moral opportunity. The question is whether our societies harbor the discerning capacities to see it as such, whether they have the humility to accept it, and whether they enter the crisis with the baseline social and civic health required to do something about it – productively.

Welcome to *Breaking Ground*, a collaborative web commons created by *Comment Magazine* to inspire a dynamic ecosystem of thinkers and doers to respond to the needs of this hour with wisdom and courage. In a founding partnership with *Plough Quarterly* and seventeen other organizations, we've worked to create a space where the sacred lens might influence the wider conversation, where the painfully fragmented body of Christ might come together in humility and urgent calling, and where the ecumenical church with all her scars might be better resourced to lead – in service, sacrifice, and solidarity. If you see something of your hopes echoed here, please do get in touch. We are eager to build a big tent of collaborators.

Over the next year, *Breaking Ground* will convene world-class scholars and seasoned practitioners, artists and pastors, community-weavers and those made resilient by long-standing struggle to contribute original essays and participate in our podcast and virtual events. We will also celebrate and point you toward the work of those people, publications, and organizations that are providing particularly insightful moral leadership, weaving a broader tapestry that we hope will unearth an ecosystem that already exists but rarely sings as one.

This adventure officially begins the first week of June. All content on *Breaking Ground* – whether original or curated – is motivated by the following three needs:

1. **Seeing clearly and deeply:** What exactly is being revealed in this layered crisis? About society? About the state of our own hearts?
2. **Learning from the past:** How have plagues historically provided opportunities for new beginnings, new building, a renewal of institutions?
3. **Imagining the future:** What institutions need renewing now, and how might that happen? What might be born anew in this time, and how might God's people help in the building?

This is at heart a rethinking project aimed at community-building, one that seeks to offer a creative lens borne out of two thousand years of Christian social thought and the witness it has inspired time and again. It's never easy to imagine new wineskins, to say nothing of stitching and sewing them. But as followers of Christ we believe there is a model for living that still has power to orient our hope, perhaps even direct our steps. We hope you'll come along.

Humbly,

Anne Snyder
Editor-in-Chief, *Comment*

June 4, 2020

FROM ASHES

Renewing the World in an Age of Crisis

SUSANNAH BLACK

IT'S A STRANGE time to build.

We've lived through what seem to be many worlds since February. They come in quick succession, as the layers of the everyday have been, so painfully, peeled back to reveal stranger and more frightening landscapes.

Given that reality, how can we have the heart to begin a project? So many of the thoughtful policy analyses and cultural reflections of January seem hopelessly naive, aimed at a world so much more stable and tame than the one we live in now.

One of the things that this *Breaking Ground* project is meant to do is look, carefully, at where we are. Where, then, are we?

Well, in the middle of a pandemic, for one thing. Not at the top of our minds in the last few days, but that fact remains. And it's taught us some things. We've been isolated, physically, these last months, but the world before Covid-19 had allowed us to be isolated in other ways. We had thought that we didn't need each other, that our choices affected only ourselves.

But the first thing this epidemic did was reveal that as a lie. We are deeply embodied beings. And the first thing we did was respond, for the most part, to the call to socially distance as a way to

SUSANNAH BLACK served as the senior editor of *Breaking Ground,* and is an editor at *Mere Orthodoxy, Plough Quarterly, New Polity,* and The Davenant Press. Her writing has appeared in *First Things, The Distributist Review, The American Conservative, Mere Orthodoxy,* and elsewhere.

care for each other with our bodies. Given the reality of a virus that can live in the air between us, we can no longer look at questions of care and responsibility and even nonviolence in quite the same way. Voltaire famously said that "my right to punch you in the nose ends where your nose begins." But the method of transmission of the Covid-19 virus is a synecdoche for the fact that an individualistic, rights-based discourse that sees our responsibility as ending at the barrier of our own skin is profoundly inadequate.

We can see more clearly than at any other time in recent memory that this is a problem which must have a society-wide response; at the same time, however, what each of us chooses to do from day to day matters vitally. We can see vividly that wisdom in leadership matters, and that wisdom in "followership" matters too. We can see that both local networks of friends and larger political bodies are absolutely vital in helping us survive. And we can see that death is real, that it cannot be dodged, and that this requires a certain reckoning. We've been thrust into a mass *memento mori* moment.

We had thought that we were, perhaps, immune to the human condition: that death might have a technical fix, that politics might be brought down to a manageable level where neither real conflict nor real love had a place, that history might have drawn to a sort of stultified, if not entirely satisfying, conclusion, that questions about what lies beyond this life and about the mysterious nature of our selves might be . . . well, shelved, in favor of complimentary two-day shipping on our tchotchkes.

That is, very obviously, not the case. The metaphysical questions that we have always asked are very much alive: Is there a Good to which just laws, and their just and honorable enforcement, corre-spond, and against which bad laws and the abuse of authority may be judged? Is there a future for us, as selves, beyond death, and is there a possibility of true fellowship and loyalty in our lives together here, even if only an imperfect echo of something we hope for?

Can we hope for peace?

These questions have, in the past few weeks, been brought even more sharply into focus. I found myself, in the midst of the news about George Floyd's death and the protests, nostalgic for two weeks ago, when we had seemed to be united against the disease, at least:

simpler times. But we are now living after that murder, reminded once again of the fact that for many in our society, the pandemic is not the only thing to fear, and that the just peace which is the common good had been very imperfectly realized even before this latest pandemic. Police should be, are meant to be, the agents of true and harmonious civic order, acting to preserve peace by securing justice. In far, far too many cases, they have failed in this. The civil order that had felt pacified is not one that has been experienced as peaceful by many. Black Americans and others, not least those left behind by a runaway market, have often not experienced this land as safe, or as welcoming, or as theirs. They have not reliably experienced themselves as represented by the government; it has not, as effectively as it ought, borne their image into the public sphere; they have too often not been able to say, This is *our* government.

In a time like this, peace seems simply a hope. At the moment it is easy to feel as though, at root, the world simply is clamor and violence. Perhaps history has only ever been an ongoing, slowly-rolled-out tragedy of incompatible demands clashing by fire and flash grenade at night. Perhaps reality is not, after all, to be trusted.

—

Early on in the virus there was a common refrain invoked almost without thinking–namely, "When life gets back to normal . . ." But now, in view of all that's happened, what is the normal we will go back to? More lockdown? Unemployment? The fear of each other as carriers of disease? Our elders locked away in nursing homes, neglected, to die alone? This is not, we may think, the part of history we signed up for. And because we tend to have such short memories, it may seem as though there is no hope, no way forward.

That's why another part of the *Breaking Ground* project will be a consultation of our cultural memory. Our cities, our societies, have memories of pandemics, of war, of massive disruption. These are the things we read about in the Scriptures, in our history books. We have been, to a large degree, insulated from the reality of how the world is. But now, as we say the daily office or pray the Psalms, we find–I have found–a shock of recognition. Yes, the world the Bible describes is, simply, our world–complete with a natural world that we don't fully control, with injustice and civil strife; complete, too, with God's care for us, and his rule, and his audacious, militant challenge to the dominion of death. It's all real.

These are the times that test what we are and whose we are. Where is our allegiance? For those who claim to know Jesus, has our Christianity been a game, so that when the evils that we said we knew were in the world, and in our society, show themselves plainly, we are caught flatfooted? To say that we have hope, and love for our neighbor and for our enemy, and faith in God's goodness and power, when we are comfortable, is one thing. To call ourselves Christians in the thick of battle, when the world seems to have had its pretty veneer ripped off – that's another thing altogether.

That battle is joined, and it is against all the enemies of the human race: against disease and poverty, against the wrong in our society and in our own hearts, the greed that would measure human lives by lost corporate profits, the vicious callousness that would turn an arrest into a murder, the intemperance that would turn a protest, through the alchemy of escalation and retaliation, into a vicious cycle of violence, and perhaps above all, the cowardice and love of comfort that just wants it all to go back to normal, that tells us we shouldn't have to deal with this, that it's not fair, that somehow we can opt out of being where and when we are.

But this time is our time. This is our struggle, and we are called to walk though it together. In the face of the pandemic and all its myriad consequences, in the face of George Floyd's murder and our clashes over what to do and how to respond, we must not abandon each other.

—

In any successful political movement, the crucial element is solidarity. A group bound together in a good struggle that allows itself to be torn apart by factionalism, or by suspicion and resentment, or by ineffective leadership unable to address injustice, will fail. This past Sunday, we Western Christians celebrated Pentecost. "Lord, send out your Spirit," many prayed, "and renew the face of the earth." What Pentecost is is the inauguration of God's political movement here on earth. And the solidarity that we must have is solidarity among all the members of the human family.

That solidarity will be attacked. Every opportunity will be used to destroy the bonds of fellowship between those who ought to know each other as brothers and sisters: human beings, the sons of Adam and the daughters of Eve. What will be most sorely tested are the faith, hope, and love that prevent us from despairing that peace, that wholeness and health, will ever be ours.

It seems like a fanciful thing to ask for. Peace? What is it, even? Is it a cop-out? Is it entitlement to ask for peace or hope for it?

I think that that depends on what you mean.

We have no right to go back to normal, and we have no right to an existence without conflict. We have no right to be just left alone, to not need to ask questions about what justice looks like and where it has gone wrong. In that sense, we have no right to a peace that is pacification, that is an end to the conversation.

What we have instead is a calling, a duty, to fulfil our natures as the political and social animals we are, by learning to live in just and honest friendship with each other. It's not easy, because it does take realizing, if we're white, that we don't know what it is like to be a black person in America. It's all right that we don't: no one can inhabit another's life, and no one should. But again, we have the calling, the duty, to learn to live in friendship with each other: not by erasing difference or denying it, but by seeking the justice, the equity that gives to each man and woman what he or she is due. One of the things that we owe each other is listening ears, and the conversation that, through language, can lead us humans to true communion with each other. We don't get to opt out of that conversation, because we are part of each other's political community and each other's lives; because beyond America, we are families, ethnicities, nations that are given to each other to be part of the community of communities that is this world, called to paint a picture of the peaceable kingdom to come.

That peace is not a cease-fire, and it's not an uneasy coexistence. It is the rich and just common life that allows each man and woman to find his or her fulfillment in the common and, ultimately, joyful project of a harmonious polity. We need each other for this.

We cannot do it without each other. We cannot, finally, be ourselves without each other.

—

As we watched, all too able to believe what we were seeing, as George Floyd's breath was crushed out of him—as we watch, unable to believe what we're seeing, as our cities seem to be turned to places we can't recognize, and as just protest is in danger of being drowned out by the white noise of chaos and confusion—as we dread what retaliation will look like, picturing a cycle of escalation that leaves those cities wastelands—as we crave just and responsible leadership, the first thing we have to do is lament.

The virus attacked our bodies, the bodies of our elders and those weakest among us. The shutdown attacked our spirits and our hope, as savings—if there were any—dwindled, and as we all tried to see into the mystery of the future we had assumed would be more or less like the past. This murder, and what we have seen since the murder, reveal a society profoundly fragile, still riddled with racism and racial division, attacking itself like a body with an autoimmune disease. And I'm writing this on Monday night, when the president has just threatened to invoke the Insurrection Act of 1807, which will allow the military to be deployed against US citizens on US soil. You who read this will know better than I what will happen in the next several days. How can we even talk about the concept of a common good, of shared justice, of peace, when everything that comes across our screens seems to sneer at the idea?

But we are going to do just that.

It's a strange time to build.

But what we are building is, we think, one of the things needed right now: a media project and community that is an attempt at a wise response to an unprecedented time; a response that both accompanies readers and contributors through this time, and helps us think together about what might come afterward. Because the third major aspect of the *Breaking Ground* project is to imagine, and work for, a future that is profoundly better than that half-forgotten world of December 2019. This is an opportunity. To build this now is to take responsibility for the moment we are in, and to respond in such a way that, when we look back, we will see blessing, and see that we were able to be a blessing to others.

In 1977, Óscar Romero was appointed archbishop of San Salvador. At the time, El Salvador was a nation in violent upheaval: In response to long-term structural injustices in Salvadoran society, which was sharply divided between rich and poor, left-wing guerilla groups, supported by the Soviet Union and by other Soviet-bloc countries, staged incursions against the right-wing junta in charge, which was supported by the Carter administration in the United States; the government's death squads, in response, carried out kidnappings and assassinations on a large scale. Romero saw both the leftist groups and the government as his children to shepherd – baptized Catholics, they were, almost all of them, who may or may not have been practicing, whose practice may or may not have been a show of piety. He spoke to all, commanding repentance and forgiveness: a repentance and forgiveness based on acknowledgment of truth. And he was killed for this, by agents of the state police, murdered as he was saying Mass.

A wise and careful pastor, he found that his role was to observe and condemn patterns of injustice and oppression – but to remind his flock, too, of the need for personal holiness, loving obedience, and solidarity at every level. He was scathing in his condemnation of particular crimes by those in the government who ought to have been, *whose calling was to be*, the agents of God's just order in the country, but he refused to condone violence in response. He never for a moment lost sight of God's love for each person in his care, even when those persons could see in each other only the face of an enemy. He never held out forgiveness and reconciliation as easy tasks, but he never ceased to command them – for all. And he reminded his people, always, that this fruitful and honest unity of justice and peace in their country could only be the work of God himself.

"We are simply preaching the kingdom of God," he wrote, "which means pointing out sin in any human situation, even when the sin is found in political and economic situations. . . . Those who are in sin must . . . renounce all forms of injustice and selfishness and violence." But he wrote too that "there can be no freedom as long as there is sin in the heart. . . . What's the use of violence and armed force if the motivation is hatred and the purpose is to buttress those in power or else to overthrow them and then create new tyrannies?" he asked.

> What we seek in Christ is true freedom, the freedom that trans-forms the heart. . . . That doesn't mean accepting the situation, because Christians also know how to struggle. Indeed, they know that their struggle is more forceful and valiant when it is inspired by this Christ who knew how to do more than turn the other cheek, and let himself be nailed to a cross.

He knew the passion for social change, and saw in those who had it the seeds of a calling from God:

> This liberation is incomprehensible without the risen Christ, and it's what I want for you, dear sisters and brothers, especially those of you who have such great social awareness and refuse to tolerate the injustices in this country. It's wonderful that God has given you this keen sensibility, and if you have a political calling, then blessed be God! Cultivate it well, and be careful not to lose that vocation. Don't replace that social and political sensitivity with hatred, vengeance, and earthly violence.

He refused, under much pressure, to countenance violent uprising, just as he refused to keep silent and thereby countenance the violence done by the government. Peace for him was a rich and substantive state of being, not passivity, not pacification. "We want peace," Romero said over the radio on October 8, 1978, "but not the peace of violence and of cemeteries, not peace imposed or extorted. We want peace that is the fruit of justice, peace that is the fruit of obedience to God."

And he never lost sight of the fundamental task of the Holy Spirit: to create one holy people, one people who love each other with true, delighted, self-giving love, to present to Christ as his Bride:

> There is no longer distinction between Jew and Greek. There is no longer a privileged people and a marginalized people. All of us are coheirs in the mystery of Christ . . . in Christ all human beings are called to this wealth of God's kingdom.

We are members of the same body. . . . God did not make us to live dispersed and separated. We need one another. . . . All the members, each in its proper function, are members of the living body.

Our situation is not Archbishop Romero's—St. Óscar's, I should say; he was canonized two years ago. The situation in El Salvador, the breakdown both of civil order and of basic justice, was worse than what we are experiencing. So much more, then, can we take heart from his words; so much less can we think we have the right to disregard them. I have quoted them because I trust them more than my own, as I trust his wisdom more than my own, and because his gift of words across the decades points to one major aspect of this project:

Now more than ever, ressourcement is crucial: digging deep into Christian memory to find tools and ideas for how to respond to massive disruption and infectious disease, to injustice and the possibility of something like civil war, and how to think about, and build for, what will come after.

Because we can't go back to normal. We shouldn't. If this crisis is a kind of apocalypse, revealing a country that is a tinderbox, ready to burst into flame, we can't simply put the lid back on and pretend nothing happened. We have to build, but we have to build something better than what was here before. We need, at the very least, to try, to sow seeds for a just political economy based, truly, on the common good. We know that nothing good we do will be, finally, lost; and that every sickroom that's the site of honest lament or of the fever that breaks, every hospital that is a barracks against the dominion of death, every outpost of peace and justice and wholeness and friendship that we create is, in some way, part of God's kingdom. And we know that all this is enabled by that Spirit of love who, at Pentecost, revealed himself as flame, and who gave language to the disciples so that the divisions between the nations—and within them—might, finally, be healed.

June 4, 2020

WHAT KIND OF TURNING POINT?

MARK NOLL

Wᴡ HERE THE VIRUS abounds, so does pontification much more
abound. But thankfully so do scraps of genuine expertise, some
informed analysis, and a lot of common sense, keeping pace with
panic.

Occasional words of wisdom bob to the surface in the oceans
of commentary on the Covid-19 virus. Stephen Williams knows
something about crises after many teaching trips to Eastern
Europe and a long professorial career at the Union Theological
College in Belfast. He recently offered the sobering reminder
that much of the world's population lives every day with the kind
of uncertainties that the lucky few in developed economies are
experiencing only now because of the pandemic. (Think of life in
eastern Congo; Syria; northern Iraq; refugees in Turkey, Lebanon,
and Jordan; the Rohingya in Bangladesh; Uighurs in western
China.)

Another friend, Grant Wacker, was asked by his North Carolina
Methodist church to prepare a lecture on the pandemic historically considered. He did so by comparing today's unemployment
figures (as bad now as during the Depression, but that decline

MARK NOLL is retired as a history professor from Wheaton College and the
University of Notre Dame. His recent books include *A History of Christianity in the
United States and Canada* (2nd ed.) and, as co-editor with George Marsden and David
Bebbington, *Evangelicals: Who They Have Been, Are Now, and Could Be*.

lasted nearly a decade); today's death toll to the toll of earlier pandemics (much, much worse in the Middle Ages from the Black Death and in 1918–19 from Spanish flu); and today's death toll to the toll in America's various wars. (There have so far been more deaths from the Covid-19 virus than American fatalities in World War I; more than American fatalities in Korea, Vietnam, Iraq, and Afghanistan combined; but far fewer than in the American Civil War.) His conclusion sidestepped pontification entirely: "However the statistics cash out, God reigns; history is in God's hands."

Margaret MacMillan, a distinguished historian of British imperial history at the University of Toronto, has stated succinctly what many others have concluded when they look beyond daily demands: "France in 1789. Russia in 1917. The Europe of the 1930s. The pandemic of 2020. They are all junctures where the river of history changes direction." Surely MacMillan is correct. But where is the river turning, how fast, and in what direction?

THE IMPOSSIBILITY OF PREDICTION

It is simply impossible to answer such questions with any degree of confidence. Historians routinely disappoint interviewers who ask, "On the basis of your study of x, y, or z, what do you think the future holds?" The mumbled response usually includes something about how difficult it is to understand past events with unambiguous clarity, even with time to pursue documents and sift alternative assessments. How much more challenging to look ahead where there is no documentation and when antithetical predictions proliferate? Still more, because they spend so much time digging up material about past generations, historians know beyond doubt how rarely predictions actually forecast reality.

George W. Bush and Neville Chamberlain compete as prime examples. When Chamberlain returned from Munich in September 1938 to announce "peace for our time," informed opinion agreed that he had dealt successfully with Adolf Hitler. President Franklin Roosevelt spoke for many others in congratulating the British prime minister for this diplomatic triumph. In the moment, Winston Churchill's naysaying only reinforced his reputation for eccentric willfulness. Somewhat more skepticism greeted President Bush's speech aboard an aircraft carrier on May 1, 2003, with the bold banner in the background proclaiming "Mission Accomplished." Yet it would be months before trickles of doubt about the pacification of Iraq became torrents of dissent.

Misguided confidence in the ability to predict, and thereby control, the future has been perpetual. In the winter and spring of 1989, I was preparing for a summer visit to Romania, where for several years Wheaton College professors had offered courses in theological education for Baptist laymen and women. As part of the preparation, my reading included all I could find on the Soviet sphere of influence in the *New York Times*, *New York Review of Books*, *New Republic*, and several academic journals. Many articles highlighted serious difficulties in the communist bloc; none that I can remember predicted what actually came to pass in the second half of that year. Josef Tson of the Romanian Missionary Society was helping with our preparations; as a lonely voice he spoke with bold assurance about the imminent collapse of the whole Soviet system. Josef was not a figure to challenge directly, but I remember rolling internal eyes at such nonsense because I was informed by those who knew better.

The parade of predictions gone awry is endless. Responsible observers knew that the Continental Army under George Washington was nearing collapse as it huddled at Valley Forge in the winter of 1777–78. The Confederate South exulted in the certainty of independence secured after the first and second battles of Bull Run. In 1922 a Polish visitor to the United States published *Impressions of America*, a book explaining how Woodrow Wilson had brought about a new and better world. Konstanty Buszczyński also announced with great relief that "in defeat Germany will once more take its place in the civilized world." The election of Barack Obama in 2008 meant that the nation's long racial trauma was at last coming to an end. The stock market's strength in January 2020 assured a bonus for pensioners' Required Minimum Distributions in 2021. As Woody Allen is supposed to have once said, "If you want to make God laugh, tell him about your plans."

THE IMPERATIVE TO PREDICT

But is it really so pointless trying to predict the unpredictable? Probably it is, if the predictions are spoken with assurance, if they are meant to end rather than stimulate debate, or if they are taken as infallible mandates for immediate action. If, however, they are advanced with humility, in order to think more carefully, and as respectful suggestions to discern possibilities, maybe they have a place. Above all, if trying to figure out the future clarifies present conditions, present duties, and present responsibilities, then maybe the effort is not entirely pointless.

Rusty Reno, the editor of *First Things*, recently wrote that "in the coming months, we need to think about what the crisis has brought out of darkness into the light." That injunction, because it focuses explicitly on what can be known, along with its implied encouragement to plot future steps with care, points in the right direction. That right direction is to concentrate on what responses to the current crisis reveal about ourselves right now. In looking ahead, it asks what can be learned for immediate purposes from earlier responses to similar situations. Such questions certainly involve preparation, but they lead in the here and now to self-examination, self-assessment, self-criticism, and even self-redirection.

Policymakers try to discern the right government responses to the crisis, and the rest of us chip in. My own admittedly partial grasp of the past, present, and future possibilities of American health care inspires the hope that the Covid-19 virus might accomplish what Harry Truman, Richard Nixon, Mitt Romney (when governor of Massachusetts), Hillary Clinton, and even Barack Obama could not bring off – a more universal health-care system. Historical responses to much more localized health crises give wing to that hope. In 1910, when Tommy Douglas was six years old, he emigrated with his family from Scotland to Winnipeg. Soon thereafter Douglas faced the amputation of a leg, but a local surgeon donated his services and the limb was saved. A generation later during the Depression, now a Baptist minister and leader of the Cooperative Commonwealth Federation in Saskatchewan, Douglas witnessed children dying because their families could not pay for medical treatment. Another generation on in 1962, and with much help from many others, Douglas as the Saskatchewan premier secured legislation that guaranteed doctor and hospital service for all. Within ten years all of Canada followed suit. Lessons from a painful past plus persistence eventually paid off. Legitimate questions remain, but from that point in Canadian history, later crises in health care, including the current pandemic, have raised serious issues concerning how, what, and where, but not who.

But, for almost everyone, even those in positions of authority, policy decisions going forward remain less existential than character decisions. To encourage the latter decisions, the past offers a luminous cloud of witnesses.

In mid-March, Bruce Hindmarsh found himself in a contemplative mood as his airliner flew high in the skies above Greenland. He was returning to home base, Regent College (Vancouver), after a sabbatical in England was abruptly terminated by the virus. Mix a historian in a contemplative mood with a long flight and a battery-powered laptop, and the result, in this case, is a brief but edifying reflection, "Coronavirus and the Communion of the Saints." How did Christian believers in other times react when facing crises like the world now experiences? Many times, it appears, they rose to the occasion. Gregory the Great (pope, 590–604) presided over a church very much in crisis, not least from the plague that carried off a third of Rome's population during his tenure. His response mingled prayer with attentive care to the sick, refugees, and the poor. (Gregory's treatise, *The Book of Pastoral Rule*, remains good reading for those today who are called to the care of souls.) He managed to commend (and practice) contemplation while carrying out an extraordinary range of active duties that included dispatching the missionary to England who would become known as Augustine of Canterbury. Centuries later, St. Francis disregarded rules for social distancing to attend, clothe, and even embrace the lepers who lived close by in enforced isolation. "Because Jesus became poor and outcast for our sakes," Hindmarsh summarizes, "Francis saw each leper as an icon of Christ crucified."

More centuries on, as the plague ravaged central Europe, Elector Johann the Steadfast ordered Saxony's sole celebrity (and chief money-spinner) to flee for refuge into the countryside. Martin Luther disobeyed the order. Instead, he remained behind to open his own home as a hospital-of-necessity and to inform a correspondent: "There are battles without and terrors within, and really grim ones. . . . It is a comfort that we can confront Satan's fury with the word of God, which we have and which saves souls even if that one should devour our bodies. Commend us to the brethren and yourself to pray for us that we may endure bravely under the hand of the lord . . . be it through dying or living."

Hindmarsh takes care not to leave his historical reflection up in the air as if to champion a mindless spiritual heroism: "The strange thing about this new communicable disease today . . . is that the Christian instinct to care for the suffering and embrace the outcast means, at least initially, doing the opposite" of what Gregory, St. Francis, Martin Luther, and other self-sacrificing believers have done. "Instead of physically embracing the sick and dying, Christian charity means protecting the vulnerable from the deadly, silent transmission of the coronavirus. . . . Social distancing is now one of the ways to love our neighbor, at least initially." His admonishment for the present concludes, "We must be especially creative to find other ways to bring the love of Christ to the suffering and the outcast."

The message from noteworthy historical exemplars might be read as encouragement to pray the psalms more existentially – to take words from the page as the staff of life: "God is our refuge and strength, a very present help in trouble" (46:1). "You shall not fear the terror of the night, or the arrow that flies by day, or the pestilence that walks in darkness, or the destruction that wastes at noonday" (91:5–6). If such prayer leads to deeper love of God coming to expression in a purer love to neighbors, the future will not thereby take care of itself. But it should not paralyze or terrify, whatever comes.

The necessary balance in Hindmarsh's historical reflection came from his sober recognition that the past provides as many warnings as encouragements. The Black Death that ravaged Europe from the mid-fourteenth century, and from which the continent did not recover for more than a century, remains a prime case in point. That health crisis produced among Christians a great outpouring of conspiracy-mongering, desperation, fingerpointing, despair, violence, and self-flagellation – all, except the self-flagellation, responses we have witnessed during the current outbreak. The scapegoating of Jewish communities – as in the two hundred Jews incinerated at Strasbourg during one day in 1349 – remains a permanent scar. This scapegoating reinforced the pattern that Luther would also strengthen when as an old man he turned ferociously on the Jews.

Research of my own has led me to another time and place, when a health crisis stimulated responses with particularly notable effects. In the fall of 1793 yellow fever decimated Philadelphia, then the United States's largest city and also its temporary seat of government. The poignancy of the occasion for present consideration includes the wider context. In the early 1790s the denominations setting the religious course for the new country were making unusually strong demands for ending the American slave system. Together, national Presbyterian and Methodist assemblies, along with many local Baptist associations, had gone on record appealing for all but immediate abolition.

In September and October 1793, the disease descended with a speed and a fury anticipating the worst of what virus hotspots of our day have experienced. Within six weeks a sixth of Philadelphia's population perished (about five thousand out of thirty thousand). A city historian has captured some of the distress: "The hospitals were in a horrible condition; nurses could not be had at any price: to go into a house in which nearly every bed contained a dead body, and the floors reeked with filth, was courting death in its most dreadful form."

As President George Washington, the Congress, and the city's wealthier residents fled to the countryside, a few prominent citizens stayed behind. The nation's best-known physician, Benjamin Rush, became the Anthony Fauci of his day. He led the fight with a regimen of increased sanitation, bloodletting, and calomel (a mercury compound). While bloodletting and calomel were actually counterproductive as treatments for many diseases, they had some positive effect against yellow fever. Other Philadelphians criticized Rush for not simply trusting God to end the epidemic; some blamed the outbreak on refugees from an ongoing revolution in Saint-Domingue (Haiti). Rush replied that God intended natural evils to be met with natural remedies, as well as with prayer.

Because Rush also believed that African Americans possessed a natural immunity, he asked the city's black leaders, William Allen and Absalom Jones, to enlist their community for tending the sick and sanitizing homes and streets. Jones would later found the first African-American Episcopal congregation, while Allen became the propelling force behind the nationwide African Methodist Episcopal Church. Blacks were in fact not immune, as the death of about 250 of their small number showed. But with Allen and Jones in the lead, and with very few leaving the city, African Americans sustained a great share of the city's nursing, cleaning, and burying.

In a word, black altruism during a crisis seemed for the moment perfectly positioned to move the ideals of the nation's founding ("all men are created equal") closer to reality.

The scourge came to end in late October when (as later epidemiologists concluded) an early frost killed the mosquitos responsible for transmitting the disease. Almost immediately, an energetic young printer capitalized on the moment to publish *A Short Account of the Malignant Fever, Lately Prevalent in Philadelphia*. Mathew Carey had recently immigrated to the United States from Ireland. As a printer of great energy and market savvy who knew how to cultivate influential connections, he had already published the country's second complete edition of the Bible, and the first to be commercially successful. This Bible was a Douay-Rheims translation for the nation's tiny Catholic population, but within a decade he would also become the country's leading publisher of the much more popular King James Version.

Carey's report did commend Allen and Jones for helping during the epidemic, but he also went out of his way to highlight black malfeasance, especially when he described black nurses as extorting huge sums for tending the sick and criticized others for looting: "Some of them were even detected in plundering the houses of the sick."

Allen and Jones took immediate steps set the record straight, but the damage had been done. When they responded to Carey with their own pamphlet, subtitled *A Refutation of Some Censures*

Thrown Upon Them in Some Late Publications, they acknowledged a few instances of abuse. But most of their rebuttal recorded specific names, places, and actions where African Americans, despite danger to themselves, selflessly served the city. One recorded the efforts of "an elderly black woman" who nursed a white householder back to health and, when asked about payment, replied "a dinner master on a cold winter's day." "And thus she went," continued Allen and Jones, "from place to place rendering every service in her power without an eye to reward." They also published a balance sheet showing that the city's black organizations had spent nearly twice as much money to provide coffins and burial services as they received in official and informal payments. Carey – from his pamphlet – was about the only Philadelphian who made money out of the yellow fever.

But because Carey's work circulated much more widely than the riposte from Jones and Allen, his response to the health crisis played a small part in reversing the trajectory of the churches against enslavement. Much else was involved, but by the end of the decade, the movement of Enlightenment and Christian principles propelling equal rights for black citizens stalled. In other words, Carey's exploitation of yellow fever deepened the furrow of racial prejudice that black Americans, along with a few white supporters like Benjamin Rush, were trying to redirect. On questions of equal access, equal opportunity, and opportunities for equal service, it would be more than a century and a half before the nation returned to where Philadelphia had been in the fall of 1793.

The warning from the macro (Black Plague) and micro (yellow fever) is the same. Put in terms for today, strengthened character in response to the coronavirus is the best preparation for the future. It may contribute to the kind of positive outcome that Margaret MacMillan hopes for: "Future historians . . . will analyse the choices that individual countries and the world made. Let us hope the story shows the better angels of our nature, in Abraham Lincoln's words: enlightened leaders and publics creating together sane and inclusive policies, and strengthening our vital institutions at home and abroad. The alternative story will not have a happy ending."

But, historically considered, it is just as possible that responses to the pandemic will reinforce the disparities and the evils now being "brought out of darkness into light." For better and for worse, the influence that Christian communities may exert on policy decisions in the future depends on character decisions in the present.

THE IMPORTANCE OF WHAT WILL COME

It is certain that the circumstances of the past along with actions taken in the present will determine the course of the future. That course will be set in considerable measure by channels dug in the past, about which historians can provide some insight. But those who work directly at understanding the present will do much better than historians in recognizing how past channels may be redirected by crises like the one we are passing through.

For myself and for believing communities, I'm not aware of a better historically informed analysis than a book published a decade ago by the sociologist James Hunter, *To Change the World: The Irony, Tragedy, and Possibility of Christianity in the Late Modern World*. Because Hunter's judgments are more reserved about the future than much of current punditry, they speak more clearly to the present. For North Americans, this book is more relevant now than when it first appeared.

Hunter's title drips with irony as he describes the historical propensity of Protestants to dream big dreams (think the American social gospel, the United Church of Canada, the post–Jimmy Carter American Christian Right). As a responsible social scientist, Hunter devotes many pages to showing that, by comparison with the funding available to institutions that dominate North American intellectual life, self-defined evangelical and Catholic institutions provide minuscule support for culture-building structures. Yet he also contends that for those who want "to change the world," mistaken conceptions create even greater problems than insufficient funds. In particular, the "market populism" so characteristic of evangelical Protestants, which looks for change from individual actions thrust haphazardly into a supposedly free market of ideas, almost completely misunderstands the incremental accumulation of power and the massive funding that usually determine cultural authority.

Although published before the recent intensification of religious and political partisanship, Hunter's analysis has never been more pertinent, especially the suggestion that efforts by religious groups to influence political culture have resulted in political culture shaping them. In his view, "the whole-hearted and uncritical embrace of politics by Christians" of whatever ideological stance has all too often meant accepting "a culture that privileges injury and grievance, valorizes speech-acts of negation, and legitimates the will to power." For Hunter, this cultural captivity is particularly tragic because it abandons the essence of Christian witness. Following in a long line of prophetic voices, he insists that when believers put their all into shaping the future, they betray the faith itself. In his thought-provoking conclusion, he points to the path God chose in becoming incarnate for humanity in Jesus Christ as the only path for those who honor Christ to live faithfully in the world of late modernity.

Practically, Hunter urges believers to set aside big dreams for big arenas, and instead pursue "a theology of faithful presence." He means taking small steps to strengthen existing institutions, building positive relationships with those closest to hand, and treating local challenges as the primary venue for Christian witness.

Transposing the message of Hunter's sober book to the present makes for one responsible way to think about the future. If leaders act with humility and guard against abuses of power, if they give up the delusion that efficiency, technique, and publicity can master events infallibly, their long-term policies may actually benefit from this short-term crisis. More immediately relevant for most believers, if character during these parlous days is strengthened by a new identification with the cross on which their Savior suffered, they will make this hour a turning point toward the good.

June 4, 2020

GOD AND THE PANDEMIC

N. T. WRIGHT

PERHAPS THE MOST vital question of all, and one that should be near the top of serious conversations at the highest level between church, state, and all interested parties, is how we move back toward whatever the "new normal" is going to be. Some people have expressed the pious hope that when this is all over we will have a kinder, gentler society. We shall pay our nurses much more. We shall be prepared to give more in taxes to support health services. We shall celebrate our emergency services, our delivery companies, and all the people who have looked after us.

I wish I thought this were true. I fear, however, that as soon as restrictions are lifted there will be a rush to start up again such businesses as we can – and, in all sorts of ways, that is quite right and proper. We are told on all sides that the economic effects of the lockdown are already catastrophic and could get worse. The problem is then quite like the tragic decisions that leaders face during a war: think of Churchill during the Blitz, deciding whether to sacrifice that unit for the sake of rescuing this one, and whether to send coded messages to the enemy that will make them bomb those houses instead of these public buildings. At the time of writing we have been concentrating entirely on "staying safe" – at a massive cost in terms of bankruptcies, unemployment, and social malaise.

N. T. WRIGHT is one of the world's leading biblical scholars, with numerous published books. He is Professor of New Testament and Early Christianity at the University of St. Andrews, and was formerly Bishop of Durham in England.

Certainly if the debate is conducted between those who see death as the worst of all possible results and those who see economic ruin as the worst of all possible results the end product is likely to be an acrimonious dialogue of the deaf.

If all this is approached purely pragmatically, as though the machinery of state were, well, machinery, rather than the wise working interrelationship of fully alive human beings, the result will be predictable. The weak will go to the wall again. Someone needs to stand up and read – perhaps not the riot act, but Psalm 72. This is the list of priorities that the church should be articulating, not just in speech but in practical proposals to go at the top of the agenda:

> Give the king your justice, O God,
>   and your righteousness to a king's son. . . .
> May the mountains yield prosperity for the people,
>   and the hills, in righteousness.
> May he defend the cause of the poor of the people,
>   give deliverance to the needy,
>   and crush the oppressor. . . .
>
> [The righteous ruler] delivers the needy when they call,
>   the poor and those who have no helper.
> He has pity on the weak and the needy,
>   and saves the lives of the needy.
> From oppression and violence he redeems their life,
>   And precious is their blood in his sight.
>   (Psalm 72:1–4, 12–14)

This too could be mocked as wishful thinking. But it is what the church at its best has always believed and taught, and what the church on the front lines has always practiced. In the early days of the church, the Roman emperors and local governors didn't know much about what Christianity really was. Yet they knew this strange movement had people called "bishops" who were always banging on about the needs of the poor. Wouldn't it be nice if people today had the same impression?

In all this, I return to the theme of lament. It is perhaps no accident that Psalm 72, setting out the messianic agenda that puts the poor and needy at the top of the list, is followed immediately by Psalm 73, which complains that the rich and powerful are getting it their own way as usual. Perhaps that is how we are bound to live: glimpsing what ought to be, then struggling with the way things actually are. However, the only way to live with that is to pray with that; to hold the vision and the reality side by side as we groan with the groaning of all creation, and as the Spirit groans within us so that the new creation may come to birth. What we need right now is someone to do in this challenging moment what Joseph did at Pharaoh's court, analyzing the situation and sketching a vision for how to address it. We urgently need statesmanlike, wise leadership, with prayerful Christian leaders taking a place alongside others, to think with both vision and realism through the challenges that we shall face in the coming months. It could be that in the days to come we will see signs of genuine new possibilities, new ways of working that will regenerate old systems and invent new and better ones, which we could then recognize as forward-looking hints of new creation. Or perhaps we will just go back to "business as usual" in the sense of the same old squabbles, the same old shallow analyses and solutions.

If we simply sit and wait to see, and wring our hands either because our churches are locked, or our golf clubs are shut, or our businesses have been put on hold, then it is all the more likely that the usual forces will take control. Mammon is a very powerful deity. Our leaders know what it takes to appease him. If that fails there is always Mars, the god of war. May the Lord save us from his clutches. If we are to escape those dark forces, we must be alert to the dangers and actively, prayerfully taking other initiatives. The garden is far less likely to grow weeds if we have been planting flowers.

It isn't for me to tell church leaders, let alone leaders of other faith communities, how they ought to be planning for the coming months, what they ought to be pressing on our governments. Yet those of us who watch and wait and pray for our leaders in church and state must use this time of lament as a time of prayer and hope. What we hope for includes the wise human leadership and initiative that will, like that of Joseph in Egypt, bring about fresh and healing policies and actions across God's wide and wounded world:

O send out your light and your truth;
    let them lead me
Let them bring me to your holy hill
    and to your dwelling.
Then I will go to the altar of God,
    to God my exceeding joy;
and I will praise you with the harp,
    O God, my God.

Why are you cast down, O my soul,
    and why are you disquieted within me?
Hope in God;
    for I shall again praise him, my help and my God.
    (Psalm 43:3–5)

June 4, 2020

IN A TIME OF PANDEMIC, "HEALTH IS MEMBERSHIP"

GRACY OLMSTEAD

IN HIS POEM "East Coker," T. S. Eliot writes that "the whole earth is our hospital."

Eliot is referencing "Adam's curse": the death and sin which resulted from mankind's fall in Genesis 3. But the line seems particularly affecting amid our current Covid-19 global pandemic. From continent to continent, we are facing the visceral reality of death, quarantining of individuals, and collective fear of infection. The whole earth is indeed our hospital, and we all are in desperate need of healing.

In his essay "Health Is Membership," Kentucky essayist, farmer, and philosopher Wendell Berry suggests that individual health cannot ever be divorced from one's larger membership with the earth and its various communities. Therefore, as we remind ourselves of the curse and its implications, we must not just turn inward – but also toward each other, toward community. Health, Berry suggests, requires re-membering: resisting a culture that "isolates us and parcels us out."

But how does this apply to our current moment, in which we are all, in fact, physically isolated and segregated from each other? How do we begin to deal with the spiritual, physical, economic, and

GRACY OLMSTEAD is a writer whose work has appeared in *The American Conservative*, the *New York Times*, the *Washington Post*, and elsewhere. She was a 2015 Robert Novak Journalism Fellow and is the author of *Uprooted: Recovering the Legacy of the Places We've Left Behind*.

communal devastation caused by the Covid-19 virus? What ought we to *remind* ourselves of, and what ought we to *remember* in a more communal sense, going forward?

Berry wrote "Health Is Membership" approximately twenty-six years ago. But its prescriptions and condemnations are well-suited to our own complex, troubling moment.

Berry first considers the root of the word "health" itself, which stems from the same Indo-European root as "whole." Health, then, is literally "to be whole" – but this wholeness cannot and should not be attributed to individuals in isolation. Health-as-wholeness must have larger implications: "not just the sense of completeness in ourselves," Berry argues, "but also . . . the sense of belonging to others and to our place."

Full health rejects the division and disintegration of culture, community, and ecology. It rejects the separation of family from family, as well as the specialized view of the self that severs body from soul – or even parts of our body from other parts.

Yet we often like to see the various parts of our world as separate entities: churches, nuclear families, schools, grocery stores, office buildings, hospitals, assisted living centers and nursing homes, apartments and townhouses all subsist in detached zones. Beyond all this, there are the shared parks and forests, rivers and streams, roads and gardens, which we see as lovely and important, but rarely view as "ours." We approach our world like a machine: divorcing ourselves from every other part, pulling apart the various strands in the tapestry.

Most approve of this segregation, thinking how well we have "streamlined" society. But we cannot reclaim health without considering practices that hurt those beyond and around and underneath us: in the soil, the water, the air, the neighbor's house, and beyond. Modern thinking on health "excludes unhealthy cigarettes but does not exclude unhealthy food, water, and air," Berry writes. "One may presumably be healthy in a disintegrated family or community or in a destroyed or poisoned ecosystem." But reality, of course, is far more nuanced and interconnected than this definition allows.

Scientific American reported, shortly after the Covid-19 virus began to spread across the world, that it is indeed a "destroyed or poisoned ecosystem" that makes our world especially vulnerable to viruses of this nature.

"[A] number of researchers today think that it is actually humanity's destruction of biodiversity that creates the conditions for new viruses and diseases like Covid-19 . . . to arise," author John Vidal wrote. "In fact, a new discipline, planetary health, is emerging that focuses on the increasingly visible connections among the well-being of humans, other living things and entire ecosystems."

It has taken us approximately three decades to catch up with Berry. But we are beginning to realize that he is right. Our world is interconnected and interdependent – much like a body, as Berry describes in his essay "The Body and the Earth": "Body, soul (or mind or spirit), community, and world are all susceptible to each other's influence, and they are all conductors of each other's influence," he says. "This is a network, a spherical network, by which each part is connected to every other part." Indeed, Berry suggests that we could compare our world to a circulatory system: disease in such a system "tends first to impair circulation and then to stop it altogether."

It is interesting here to think of Covid-19, and the often strange, unpredictable, full-body impact it can have on those who suffer from it – from one's toes to one's lungs, symptoms have been sporadic, severe, and unpredictable. The frustrations it has posed to our health-care system are likely increased by the fact that our system is extremely specialized, and likes to view the body as a machine with disparate parts, rather than as a whole in which all affects all.

But the entirety of the Covid-19 pandemic has served to remind us that our health is predicated on each other's: individuals grappling with anxiety and depression while shelter-in-place orders continue surely have felt their dependence in a new, sharp way. Parents seeking to work full-time, homeschool, and provide 24/7 care of their children are realizing their need for community assistance and support. The elderly, divorced from the rest of society in specialized nursing homes, are both at increased danger for this virus, and the most likely to suffer from intense loneliness. Children required by their schools to complete lessons online are cut off from the natural world and spring weather beyond their front doors, chained to a screen until their assignments are complete.

Here, too, Eliot's statement—"the whole earth is our hospital"—rings true. It is not just because we share a fallen, broken reality. It is also because the health of each piece of this world affects every other piece. To lack empathy, care, or love for one part of our world facing destruction is both selfish and unselfconscious: it reveals that we believe we are somehow separate from the fate of our fellow creatures, or of our shared earth.

The prevalence of this attitude has become especially clear as resistance to Covid-19 health recommendations or shelter-in-place orders has escalated. Thinking of the world reductively, or in a radically individualistic way, makes it easy to put individual rights, freedoms, or inconveniences before collective health—because we think of ourselves as isolated and autonomous, rather than as parts of a whole.

The wearing of masks, therefore, is derided as cowardice by conservatives who suggest wearing a mask is more about political correctness or personal fear than it is about safeguarding the vulnerable. This complaint is part of a larger narrative on the right which suggests that we should not sacrifice our own comfort or freedoms in order to protect a minority of immunocompromised or elderly individuals.

But this, too, is a reduction of health—or rather, a sacrifice of it in the name of individual comfort. It is important to note that the decimation of our economy through the last several months is indeed a problem, and indicative of the fact that every piece of our world is deeply connected. But the fragility of our economic system should not call on us to ignore the needs of the sick—to further sever or reduce our definition of wholeness or prosperity.

"The parts are healthy insofar as they are joined harmoniously to the whole," Berry writes. Putting economics before community, before health, is not the answer—even while ignoring economic unhealth and fragility is not the answer. "Healing . . . complicates the system by opening and restoring connections among the various parts—in this way restoring the ultimate simplicity of their union."

An economic system that can only profit from the ill-health or destruction of bodies is itself sick, and requires healing. An American food system predicated on the horrific treatment of slaughterhouse workers, farmhands, and delivery-truck drivers desperately requires reform. We should not live in or tolerate a system that forces us to sacrifice the health of the few, the voiceless, or the disenfranchised for the comfort or health of the many. It is true that we live in a broken, fallen world in which triage is a necessary reality. But the curse is not our only reality. There is hope – because there is love. And love, Berry suggests, is what steers our world toward real health.

"I take literally the statement in the Gospel of John that God loves the world," he writes. "I believe that the world was created and approved by love, that it subsists, coheres, and endures by love, and that, insofar as it is redeemable, it can be redeemed only by love. I believe that divine love, incarnate and indwelling in the world, summons the world always toward wholeness, which ultimately is reconciliation and atonement with God."

Health is wholeness, Berry says. But this wholeness, when and where it exists, is not the fruit of some mere intellectual exercise or expertise – it is the result of love's dogged efforts to redeem, defend, and protect. Love is the answer to a reductive health-care system – and it is crucial to safeguard all those whom our world sees as disposable.

"To the claim that a certain drug or procedure would save 99 percent of all cancer patients or that a certain pollutant would be safe for 99 percent of a population, love, unembarrassed, would respond, 'What about the one percent?'" Berry writes. "There is nothing rational or perhaps even defensible about this, but it is nonetheless one of the strongest strands of our religious tradition . . . according to which a shepherd, owning a hundred sheep and having lost one, does not say, 'I have saved 99 percent of my sheep,' but rather, 'I have lost one,' and he goes and searches for the one."

Our struggles with the Covid-19 virus are far from over. But our attempts to find healing in days to come will not be limited to a vaccine. They must be deeper, wider: taking into account all the multitudinous severances which suggest that our world needs wholeness and love. The virus has revealed the fragility of our food system, the way efficiency has broken down health and resiliency. We've seen how broken our nursing homes and eldercare systems really are – evidenced in a horrific amount of deaths. The spread of the virus in prisons should show us, once again, how urgently we need prison reform. And the very existence of the Covid-19 virus shows us that the diversity and health of our ecosystems need to become more important than the temporary benefits created by logging, mining, and other systems that deteriorate or destroy the earth.

But just as important, perhaps, will be individual acts of quiet fidelity on behalf of the voiceless or vulnerable – the one percent Berry refers to. Perhaps even as larger reforms appear daunting or distant, there are efforts each of us might make to heal and restore broken connections. Henri Nouwen has suggested that Christ is a "Wounded Healer" – the Savior who, even now, redeems our brokenness and offers healing. But he adds that through Jesus, we ourselves can become wounded healers: "Those who do not run away from our pains but touch them with compassion."

Even in this dark and difficult time, such healing is taking place. Within our hospitals, it's evidenced in the nurse who faithfully holds the hand of a dying patient until his last breath. It's displayed in the priest who died after giving his ventilator to another sick individual. It's visible in neighbors who regularly offer free food or diapers to those in need, local townspeople who are donating to food pantries, and churchgoers who are providing food to needy families, parents with newborns, or to the sick. It's evidenced in the abundant growth of victory gardens, the letters sent to nursing home residents, and the widespread surge in community-supported agriculture support.

None of these steps, by themselves, represent a perfect return to health. None of them can fully fix problems of systemic injustice, which lead to larger trends of ill health in our country. But they are a beginning. They reflect a realization that we are indeed part of a membership, and that our health is therefore predicated on more than our own physical resilience. To be healthy, we must acknowledge – and love – the entire web of life we are part of.

The world may indeed be our hospital. But if so, each of us can be a "dying nurse," in Eliot's words: seeking to bear each other's burdens, drawing our whole broken earth toward wholeness.

June 10, 2020

THE ATMOSPHERE

The Most Formative Aspect of School

DOUG SIKKEMA

WHAT IS IT about certain homes that draws us in? You know the homes I'm talking about. They possess a magnetism that makes us want to stop by and then linger just a little longer. Usually it starts with the people and how they make us feel as if *we* were just what *they* needed. Sometimes it's an arresting collection of art, or literature, or plants, or music that invites us into new worlds. These homes always seem bigger on the inside. Or perhaps it's the promise of thoughtful, stimulating fellowship; you know the world will be more capacious afterward. Whatever the case, such homes draw us to them because they possess an *atmosphere* in which we are easily, unguardedly our best selves. Perhaps yours is a home like this. Perhaps you want it to be.

One of the biggest mistakes we can make, though, is to think such homes are just happy accidents resulting from the right people with the right amount of disposable income and *joie de vivre*. This is rarely the case. Wealth and opulence, for instance, are almost never clear indicators of a healthy atmosphere. A home stocked with the nicest things guarded by a cold miser who wants nothing touched repels us. Conversely, there are homes with very meager furnishings yet rich in the wit, wisdom, and warmth that are signs of a life in abundance. There are also cranky curmudgeons who are more of a

DOUG SIKKEMA is an assistant professor of English and humanities at Redeemer University College and an aspiring gentleman farmer.

delight to be around than some outgoing, charismatic narcissists who make us want to escape at any chance we get. Creating a healthy atmosphere for our homes is a complex amalgam of cultivating our characters while curating our possessions, disciplining our attitudes while forging our relationships.

Over the past several months, many of you must have attended closely (more closely than you ever wanted) to your home life. What are the rhythms of your day? What are, to use Tish Harrison Warren's delightful phrasing, the "liturgies of the ordinary" around which time and routines become patterns of meaning for your family? What ideas and principles guide you? I hope one of the silver linings of our sheltering in place will be the unique opportunity it affords us to think seriously about the places in which we shelter. The homes we make will make us. Are we paying attention?

Our homes will also make our children. So while many of us bemoan that we have become unlikely homeschool parents – Lord knows I've almost suffered an aneurysm explaining sentence diagrams – the truth is we've always already been homeschooling, whether we like it or not. The home is our first school. This is not to say that curriculum and pedagogy don't matter – they do! – but your home's atmosphere applies the constant force under which you and your children take shape. It's in the food you cook, where you come together to eat it, and how you clean up afterward; it's the clothes you wear and where you choose to buy them; it's how you get up, get to work, and wind down; it's how you yell at one another and forgive one another and cry and laugh and sing; it's in who comes through your home and shares a handshake or a meal or a night's stay; it's in how you talk; it's in how you talk about others; it's in your tone of voice; it's in the rhythms of prayer; it's in the budget. We are social animals. From the moment we emerge into the world and into families and homes we did not choose, we are being enculturated in how to talk, how to think, how to behave, how to love. Our education starts the minute we enter the world. It starts at home.

SILENT FORMATION

I've been a teacher for over a decade now and have taught in the primary, secondary, and postsecondary sectors. I've come to believe that this rather elusive concept of *atmosphere* is arguably the most formative aspect of education that almost nobody talks about. When we do talk about it, it's more descriptive than aspirational, let alone strategic. Despite lofty mission statements and value propositions and brand campaigns, many schools at all levels spin their wheels revamping delivery methods, innovating curriculum maps, or sharpening student-experience metrics without attending to the interstitial, in-between spaces where most of the real student-formation is happening. We know students need their advanced calculus class, but do we think they need a tech-free lunch commons? And what will we do about it?

The nineteenth-century British school reformer Charlotte Mason was a vocal advocate for home education (and might just be the unlikely friend we need in these times). She maintained that "education is an atmosphere, a discipline, a life." To be clear, what Mason is arguing is not that the home must be pristine and worthy of a *Home & Garden* feature essay. Hardly. Listen to how Mason describes the value of the home's atmosphere for a *good* education:

> We all know the natural conditions under which a child should live; how he shares household ways with his mother, romps with his father, is teased by his brothers and petted by his sisters; is taught by his tumbles; learns self-denial by the baby's needs, the delightfulness of furniture by playing at battle and siege with sofa and table; learns veneration for the old by the visits of his great-grandmother; how to live with his equals by the chums he gathers round him; learns intimacy with animals from his dog and cat; delight in the fields where the buttercups grow and greater delight in the blackberry hedges. And, what tempered "fusion of classes" is so effective as a child's intimacy with his betters, and also with cook and housemaid, blacksmith and joiner, with everybody who comes in his way.

Victorian prose and sensibilities aside, Mason's vision is intriguing. The home as an "educational institution"—a phrase Mason would cringe at, no doubt—is not some sterile, constructed environment disembedded from the messiness of sibling scraps, baking, intergenerational drop-ins, domestic chores, animals, or explorations into the countryside. In other words, it should not be a separate thing from home life because school is meant for the home. Children do not learn at home *despite* these so-called interruptions; they learn *by* them.

When we return to our regularly scheduled programming, it would be helpful to think a bit more about the relationship that our homes have with our schools as co-laborers in the job of child formation and cultural transmission. If schools are, arguably, extensions of the home, have the past several months revealed anything to us? In so many ways we have become conditioned to think that the school is an extension of the state or of industry or some contraction of the two.

While Mason has had some dedicated followers who continue to show another way to school, the overwhelming majority of our Western schooling takes its cues from the entertainment-industrial complex. Even in smaller Christian private schools I've been shocked by how much of the language belies a co-option by these hegemonic forces of our late-capitalist society. Principals, with the encouragement of their boards, understand themselves to be CEOs; parents are referred to as clients and customers without shame; student feedback is feared by teachers and administrators alike because they know how such consumer reports drive policy decisions; student happiness at all costs makes discomforting experiences like manual work or poor grades or even discipline increasingly improbable. I once heard a principal of a Christian private school, without irony, excitedly talk about plans for a new school library construction project that "will feel just like a *Starbucks*!" Such an atmosphere will shape students in certain ways. Education is always the transmission of a culture, but are we aware of just what – or whose – culture we are transmitting?

"The child breathes the atmosphere emanating from its parents," Mason wrote, "*that of the ideas which rule their own lives.*" We might add that children breathe the atmosphere of their schools which are the ideas that rule teachers, administrators, boards, and parent communities. Schools would do well, when we return, to gather their community of parents – who are ultimately *co-teachers* – and think about the type of atmosphere they want for their schools, understood as extensions of the home. What benefit would classroom chores bring? Does it matter what our students wear? How might intergenerational relationships be meaningfully forged? Where does our food come from and who cleans it up? What formative role does the time "between" classes play? Is there space to explore the neighborhood and learn the names of local flora and fauna? Is that a priority? Are the teachers the sorts of people students want to be around outside of class? Are students the kind of people we want to be around outside of graduation?

Atmosphere is not a choice. Every school will have one. The question that falls on us is, Will we take the time to understand ours and create the conditions in which our students will thrive? Not as entitled consumers or epicures-in-training, but as children who have a well-furnished imagination, dependable and virtuous characters, grit, attention, and well-ordered affection. And while schools might be very good at curriculum vision and pedagogical delivery, they often fail in cultivating a healthy educational atmosphere for two very different reasons, both of which I've seen firsthand as student and teacher.

The first school I'll call Jupiter, which, at one of its lowest points, would have students get off the bus only to be met by a vice principal who would hand out little slips for uniform infractions. Untucked shirts, non-uniform socks, brand-name undershirts, or kilts that flirted dangerously above the acceptable knee line would warrant one of these little pieces of paper. Slips were given throughout the day too, for all kinds of other misdemeanors: being late to class, talking out of turn, running in halls. In an attempt to discipline students, the leadership of Jupiter opted for a "three strike" policy of sorts. Three slips led to a detention, three detentions to a suspension. In its arguably well-intentioned attempt to curb a rather undisciplined school body, Jupiter created an atmosphere that was oppressive, anti-authoritarian, and filled with suppressed (and not-so-suppressed) anger. Disciplined students follow rules, but it turns out that a rigid, fearful observation of those rules does not a great school make. It ignites rebellion.

In another school we'll call the Moon a completely different approach was taken for discipline. Words like "restorative justice" buzzed through the staffroom and administrative offices and there was almost no punishment or consequence for any student behavior. Class start times were suggestions and students rolled in at their convenience, uniform compliance required constant reminders, and the use of phones and other distracting devices in and out of class was so pervasive teachers had to build in "text times" so students could relieve their device anxiety. The Moon's motivation for this arguably "lax" approach was to better prepare children for an adult world where the structures of buzzers, detentions, and constant teacher and principal attention simply does not exist. If children are going to be punctual, courteous, and diligent, the Moon leadership maintained, we should embody it but never enforce it. This choice created a particularly different atmosphere from Jupiter's, but neither was conducive to life.

My hunch is that schools that take the heavy-handed, top-down approach of Jupiter crush students under their oppressive atmospheres. School culture that is not allowed to grow organically will wither. The Moon, however, held children so loosely, they floated away from its well-intentioned lunacy. A school culture must be organic, but administration must delineate the bounds in which this growth occurs.

What if there were a third way our schools cultivated an atmosphere, one where children belonged and felt at home? What if there were a school atmosphere in which children thrived because it felt a bit more like a home that was made for them? Imagine with me a school, I'll call it Earth, where the atmosphere not only tethers one in place but also gives life. It's a place people want to be. The school is run by a principal who is the first student. She considers herself a shepherd of young souls, guiding teachers and students to delight in what's true, good, and beautiful. The library is carefully stocked with beautiful, living books that furnish children's imaginations with some of the most worthwhile things ever written or thought. There are old chairs and pillows to relax in; most of them were donated. The hallways are not littered with flickering screens, and students are not permitted to have cell phones at the school at any age, not because the school is technophobic or outdated, but because they share a love for the child's attention and would do anything to nurture it. Mothers and fathers frequently drop by to help in the classrooms or on the schoolyard. They often bring along their younger children and the occasional grandparent. Children are taught to stand when a guest enters and to look adults in the eye and to give them a firm handshake. There is a garden where students grow vegetables, and each student is given a chore to help clean the school. Mornings are patterned by school-wide liturgies where ancient catechisms are memorized, prayers are offered, and songs are sung. The curriculum is rigorous; homework is rare. The school is restful.

Some of these are obviously aspirations, and perhaps ones you might not share. That's okay. But the point remains: atmospheres need not be accidents. Parents, boards, teachers, and administrators can create the conditions for a healthy school atmosphere without overtly controlling it or simply letting it run its own course. When we return, I would love for townhalls, board and parent nights, and community meetings to take place in order that more people can feel empowered to shape the culture of *their* schools. School is not simply a state or commercial activity you pay for, drop off your kids, and call it a day. Education is the transmission of a way of life, your way of life. When this is over, let's talk about what we have learned about our home culture, warts and all, and then let's start to shape the types of spaces that continue to bring us together when coming together is possible once again.

June 17, 2020

VERSE LINES WHEN THE STREETS ARE ON FIRE

JAMES MATTHEW WILSON

SEVERAL WEEKS AGO, I was speaking with a friend of mine about the disruptions to everyday life wrought by the coronavirus pandemic. As it happens, he is a C. S. Lewis scholar and is one of those people who excites envy in me with his punctual efficiency. He's the sort of person who can get his girls off to school in the morning, turn on a dime and for a couple hours to his work, take a break for some other duty, and then get right back to business. For those of us of a more Oblomovian character, who can only gradually rise to any effort after much contemplation, and who no less reluctantly set it down and turn to other things, such an ability to switch hats at the tolling of a bell appears almost supernatural.

And yet, several weeks into the age of quarantine, he confessed that, yes, he could still do such things as were required of him, but no more. He now found himself sitting, listless, sullen, at his desk, his mind distracted by the great vacancy in time that had opened up. It must have felt a bit baffling for him, he who had read so often before Lewis's classic sermon "Learning in War-Time" and yet now found himself, in the breach, almost powerless to profit from it, when the time was most ripe.

JAMES MATTHEW WILSON is an associate professor of religion and literature in the Department of Humanities and Augustinian Traditions at Villanova University, and the poetry editor of *Modern Age* magazine. Dr. Wilson is the author of eight books, including *The Hanging God*; *The Vision of the Soul: Truth, Goodness, and Beauty in the Western Tradition*; and *The Fortunes of Poetry in an Age of Unmaking*.

I have not spoken to him since the streets were lit aflame in Minneapolis, and then across the country, including, at this hour, midtown Manhattan. I do think I have, however, come much closer to his own vexed condition. The times are an ugly, violent spectacle from which it is nearly impossible to turn away. To those who look on in grief, anger, and horror, I can only say I have joined you.

Our age has for long been suffering from a syndrome of frenetic, empty time, wherein we keep ourselves in a state that is, at once, occupation without concentration and distraction without rest. We have already grown used to a nearly perpetual scrolling-through of interesting stimuli, to none of which do we fully surrender our attention. We thus feel busy but vacuous, enthralled but disconnected. That was more or less our habit. And then came the virus. And then came the spectacular murder of George Floyd by police. And then came the riots. All of which serves in its way to justify our frenetic half-attention, because at least thereby we are bearing witness to the unraveling of our society. If there were ever a time in which we might justify playing the role of passive spectators, this must surely be it.

But this cannot be the last word. Just as Lewis insisted that the activities of human culture – the telling of jokes, the combing of one's hair, and above all the "search for knowledge and beauty" – will carry on during wartime, and indeed should, even when the country is at war, so, now, do I propose that these things must continue in our day, even as some of us may fear we have passed beyond a state of emergency to the end of things. In fact, with Lewis, I propose that we need to do some such things even more concertedly *as if* the end times were already here. Disease, disorder, and riot are reminders to us of the mortality and fragility of all worldly goods and that the way to live most intensely and richly, here in the world of our history, is to live every moment as if it were a window into the immortal and the eternal.

Lewis's sermon concludes that the dead of war are themselves a memento mori that helps us live more consciously for eternity. The empty waiting of quarantine, the chaos of policing gone wrong, and the frantic spectacles of riot ought themselves to remind us that we are only living well when doing so with conscientiousness, concentration, and attention – all of which I would gather into one word, contemplation. To contemplate is to see, or enter into, the enduring wonder and infinite depths of an object; what is a unity and so, in that sense, limited, in fact proves an unbounded fullness in which we may linger.

I argued some years ago, in a book called *The Fortunes of Poetry in an Age of Unmaking*, for the art of poetry as the fine art of contemplation par excellence. All the fine arts propose to make something that is a good in itself and for the sake of beauty. In this they are concrete, finite reminders of our true natures. The dead of war remind us that we are mortal and so must live for eternity. Works of fine art (as opposed to applied art), because of their intrinsic goodness, which is also a specifically spiritual goodness, in an analogous way are reminders of eternal life itself.

It has been the central and most precious knowledge about human beings, since even before Plato and Aristotle gave us language to express it, that we are, in our essential nature, made for the contemplation of the eternal. This is the basis of human equality, as Simone Weil observed, and a clue to our divinity and immortality, as Blaise Pascal contended. But contemplation comes in diverse forms: the supernatural contemplation of the Christian and the natural contemplation of the philosopher, to begin with; and then, there are the more distant analogical forms of contemplation, such as the concentration of the craftsman or artist at work; the free, somewhat dreamy contemplation of a loved one across the dinner table; and, among all these, the contemplation of the work of art.

Poems stand out from these other objects of contemplation because poems have historically drawn from all of them; given them form, focus, and expression; and indeed become themselves occasion for such contemplation. The poetic is in this way unusually capacious and comprehensive. In my attempt to explain why, in *The Fortunes of Poetry*, I argued that poetry can essentially be defined in terms of four *M*s. First, because a poem comes to be through the cooperation of an otherworldly inspiration and the technique or skill of the artist, it is our paradigm for all *making*. Second, because it draws together all that has been or may be known and must not be forgotten, and gives it form, poetry is a mode of *memory*. Hesiod so well understood this that he celebrated Mnemosyne as the mother of the muses.

Third, because a poem also gives concrete, finite expression to truths that may be otherwise ineffable, it has, in its essence, the element of *metaphor*. Every poem, in its metaphoric aspect, reminds us of a great truth about reality as a whole: everything is multiple and self-transcending. Everything bears within itself a myriad of meanings, irreducible and ordered among themselves, so as to be, as Dante once observed, polysemous. And, fourth and finally, because it is the measuring-out as verse that makes it memorable (mnemonic) and because that ordering of language metaphorically expresses, at the microcosmic level, a sense of the greater order of the world, the macrocosm as a whole, poetry is essentially understood in terms of *meter*.

This kind of making, composed of memory, metaphor, and meter, is a human and finite thing. It is a thing made to be good in itself. But, in contemplating that good-in-itself, we cannot help but sense that aspects of reality that infinitely transcend it are darting in and out of its shadow. Furthermore, while it is a material and made thing, we sense immediately that it is so only in virtue of the life of the spirit. By words, as Aristotle once said, one mind communicates the fullness of its life to another. The poem discloses not only the richness of the world in small compass but also the way in which even material things serve our lives as great adventures of mind, spirit, and communion.

A poem is therefore a limited and specific reality that rewards our extended concentration. To read a poem is not to engage in the highest form of contemplation, but such reading does prepare the soul for it and, moreover, does so in a way that reminds us that contemplation is a thing of leisure, an activity whose foundation is expressed in the modest phrase "It is good that this thing should exist and that I am here to see it."

In Lewis's sermon, he felt obliged not to confuse the contemplation of scholastic learning with the awed devotion of the saint. Matthew Arnold's substitution of the stuff of "culture" for actual religion was a fresh and dangerous memory. In our time, however, we need the experience of poetry to remind us of our natures; this mode of contemplation is distinct from, but also preparatory for and complementary of, the highest contemplation to which our souls are called for their fulfillment. The lyric poem that exists in itself and for its own sake prepares us by way of analogy to know the one who exists as the good of all and solely by his own aseity. This is not to reduce poetry to a useful good, a mere exercise in service of the genuine article; it is merely to say that its proper goodness reflects and resonates with the most important activity of our lives and that this mystery is one we err to pass by or overlook.

Let me discuss just three poems that help us understand the role poetry plays as a finite good that manifests, and draws us toward, the infinite: one by Czesław Miłosz, one by Christina Rossetti, and, finally, a sonnet by Sir Philip Sidney.

When I read Czesław Miłosz's earliest poems, I see a minor and undirected talent. As he came into maturity in the Warsaw of the 1930s, however, the shock of the Nazi invasion and, after the Second World War, the Communist takeover of Poland forced him – against his own instincts – to become a poet of the national conscience. One exemplary poem, "A Book in the Ruins," from 1941, admirably suggests what that entailed. The poet describes entering a library "caved in by a recent blast":

> And above, through the jagged tiers of plaster,
> A patch of blue. Pages of books lying
> Scattered at your feet are like fern-leaves hiding
> A moldy skeleton, or else fossils
> Whitened by the secrets of Jurassic shells.

Curiosity about what has been destroyed "compels" the poet to enter, just as found shells would excite the paleontologist to study. But to pick up one of the books is to discover a lost world, "distant" and "sleepy," yet elegant, one in which a woman slips out of the ball to meet a lover in an overgrown bower. Other worlds with their sententious wisdom "erupt" from other pages, such that the "immortality" of books seems to instruct and even exist for "the present." Still another book, telling of Daphnis and Chloe, has been shredded by an exploded grenade; the poet addresses Chloe herself, whose "breasts / Are pierced by shrapnel." We turn away from her eternal beauty wounded by history to see workers at noontime, who have stacked heavy tomes amid the ruins as a makeshift table for their lunch.

Miłosz suggests that we need old books especially in wartime. We need to know there is another world beyond the flux of devastation, and to feel its visitation upon us even as we stand in rubble. The poem takes this need as its subject, however, and this may tempt us to think that only an emergency could justify poetry, as if it must be one more tool of which we make use as we pass through the wreckage of history. For this reason, I would have us turn to a less explicitly occasional poem.

Christina Rossetti's "A Pause of Thought," even by its title, hints that what is most important is what stands outside the normal, quotidian train of our activities. The poem describes the search for some elusive good – "that which is not, nor can be" – and the heartsick agony of hope frustrated. In the first two of its five quatrains, the poet doubts and waits. In the third, she imagines resignation and peace only to cut it off abruptly with the contradictory, metrically short line that ends each stanza: "Yet never gave it o'er."

The agitation grows, until the fourth stanza casts us into the fundamental choice every person confronts in life: to live in the "peace" of complacency with the present, or to suffer on in yearning:

> Sometimes I said: It is an empty name
>   I long for; to a name why should I give
>   The peace of all the days I have to live?—
>   Yet gave it all the same.

In *A Secular Age*, philosopher Charles Taylor describes the modern mindset as having an "immanent frame." He means this primarily in terms of what we acknowledge as true or knowable, but it has a moral dimension as well. Rossetti, a pious Anglo-Catholic in an increasingly "pagan" and secular literary society, must have had her faith and her hope routinely called into question simply by the patronizing expressions of those around her. The only thing resisting her own conforming to that world of immanence was the stubborn discontent of unfulfilled faith itself, which left her "alike unfit / For healthy joy and salutary pain."

What seems most important about her poem, however, is not the summary of a spiritual predicament it carries to us, but the way her lines shape and give form to it. In each stanza, three pentameter lines narrate her condition, before the fourth, trimeter line unravels all that thinking, as with, to quote again, "Yet I gave it all the same." The form of the poem expresses the immanent drama, but with a stable structure that speaks not merely of her own tenacity, but of the permanence of the impossible hope to which she clings. Every poem is a manifestation of such permanence precisely in and through its form. Because its form is dramatic, and leads us from thought to thought, it thrusts us into the spiritual drama of living in a world of change and doing so in dynamic response to a truth beyond all change.

Rossetti's poem, like Miłosz's, contrasts the lively flux of the present with the everlasting of the literary and the divine, and proposes to us, almost as explicitly as I just have, that poetic form brings the permanent into our evanescent lives so that we may contemplate it, be nourished by it, be transformed, and so live in some sense more wisely and fully. But the real test of such a claim, it seems to me, lies in whether poetry can do such a thing purely in virtue of what is essential to it, that is to say, its metrical form. And for this reason, I want to conclude with Sonnet 31 from Sidney's *Astrophil and Stella*.

The poet and critic Yvor Winters once dismissed Sidney as a technically accomplished but superficial poet. When Sidney writes of poetic inspiration, he seems himself to be a secular character, on Taylor's terms. In many of his poems and in the *Defense of Poetry*, he eliminates the nine divine muses as the source of poetic inspiration and relocates it in the "immanent frame" of a woman's beauty. But is there not something of the eternal present even in the form of this otherwise worldly poet?

The sonnet begins with a fell conceit: the moon appears sad, as the poet is sad, and so he queries whether the moon has been pricked by Cupid's arrow for a lady and then refused her love, just as Sidney has been:

With how sad steps, O moon, thou climb'st the skies;
How silently, and with how wan a face.

> What, may it be that even in heav'nly place
> That busy archer his sharp arrow tries?

Sidney is trifling here. In the next quatrain he explains that the only basis he has to judge the moon thus is his own "long-with-love-acquainted eyes." He asks the moon if there, as on earth, to be constant is deemed mere stupidity, or rather, "want of wit." But wit has several senses. Raw intelligence, to begin with, and, in our day, a humorous cleverness. In between these two is the classic English meaning: the whole poetic faculty that can draw the disparate things of experience and put it in striking, surprising order – to give it form.

Consider the wit here, where, in the first line, the heaviness of Sidney's accent climbs syllable by syllable, from the weak "With" rising to "sad steps," dipping a bit in calling to the moon, before finishing on the strong sentence stresses on the verb, "climb'st," and direct object, "skies." There is a different kind of "dip" in the second line, as Sidney pauses to find one, then another, expression to describe the moon's climb. And, then, the exasperated ejaculation of "What"! before plunging into a long question whose anguish is rung more loudly by the question's own improbability. Have you been pricked by Love, too, moon?! Three decades later, King Lear would ask a storm raging over England if it was upset because it had ungrateful daughters. Shakespeare may have found the source of his apostrophe here, in Sidney.

The poem ends with a rather worldly-wise and sardonic question: up in heaven, do they call "ungratefulness," by which he means his beloved's refusal of his love (what some might call chastity), "virtue"? But what merits contemplation in this poem is no aspect of its content, but the form by which it manifests that content, the use of meter to bend the voice and give a shape to the whole. It is the meter, the subtle rise of accent across the first line and the other modulations beyond it, that leads us upward, not so much the explicit invocation of the moon.

It is through form that the poem becomes an object befitting our contemplation. In staring into it, as one might stare into an icon, we find a stasis that nonetheless reveals depths – syllable by syllable, figure by figure, layer by layer – over which we may linger and ourselves fall still. That this finite object has meaning and implications that extend beyond it to many things is in itself a great source of interest and delight, but what I am trying to convey is that the poem itself merits remaining the focus of our attention.

To puzzle over a poem, to see how it fits together, there on the page before you, or spoken in the air about you, is to discover a finite analogue of the infinite, a small intrinsic good that, again, reminds us, in its formal perfection, in its little self-sufficiency, of the aseity of the divine. Even when a man has been killed, when order has with its heavy boot unleashed disorder, even when the streets are on fire, the humble poem is a reminder that there is a peace that transcends this world. Even when there is an emptiness all around us, it discloses a certain plenitude sufficient for the day, not because of what it says, but because of the very act of its saying.

June 26, 2020

CHRISTIANITY AND THE SOCIAL QUESTION

PATRICK PIERSON

WE ALL KNOW something of where we are: staggering under the weight of the most devastating pandemic in more than a century, massive unemployment, a long-overdue reckoning with slavery, and an election year that is bound to get worse before it gets better.

Amid the anxiety, anger, and fear, however, emerges a peculiarly hopeful unsettling, a laying bare of what is, and a recognition of the great chasm that remains between *what is* and *what ought to be*.

More than a century ago, Dutch theologian and statesman Abraham Kuyper found himself in a similar place. Struggling with the social dislocation introduced by the Industrial Revolution, Western Europe faced runaway inequality between the bourgeoisie and working class, with the latter falling prey to increasingly dire working conditions, untenable wages, and widespread exploitation at the hands of "the new aristocracy." Seeking to chart a way through the morass, Kuyper convened the inaugural meeting of the Christian Social Congress to deliver a lecture called "Christianity and the Class Struggle."

Surprising to some, Kuyper's lecture offered little in the way of pragmatic legislative changes or technical policy innovations to counter an increasingly fractured social ecology. To be sure,

PATRICK PIERSON is a writer and speaker based in Atlanta, Georgia. You can follow him on Twitter at @plpierson and find his latest work at patrickpierson.co.

the perceived oversight was not driven by a disregard for such activity – Kuyper labored as an activist and social reformer for decades, and eventually served as Dutch prime minister from 1901 to 1905. Rather, Kuyper recognized that the visible signs of social breakdown all around him were merely by-products of a sociopolitical order incommensurate with the social needs of his time.

Part social commentary, part neo-Calvinist manifesto, Kuyper's speech argued that Dutch society's glaring social inequities – widespread use of child labor, dangerous working conditions in Europe's rapidly expanding manufacturing sector, rampant inequality, public health crises in overcrowded working-class neighborhoods – were directly tied to a liberal social order "planned only according to [the] whim and caprice" of self-seeking, atomized individuals. As such, Kuyper's point of departure was profoundly, if somewhat paradoxically, immaterial. Ultimately, Kuyper realized that the discussion of means must, necessarily, be preceded by a vision of the desired end.

British philosopher Isaiah Berlin captures just this idea at the onset of his famous essay *Two Concepts of Liberty*:

> Where ends are agreed, the only questions left are those of means, and these are not political but technical, that is to say, capable of being settled by experts or machines like arguments between engineers or doctors. That is why those who put their faith in some immense, world-transforming phenomenon, like the triumph of reason or the proletarian revolution, must believe that all political and moral problems can thereby be turned into technological ones.

Put differently, Kuyper and Berlin's contention is that, where the ends are agreed on, the questions of "how to get there" are decidedly simple. The challenge, then, is to offer a compelling vision for a shared life together commensurate with human flourishing and the common good.

—

For the past three decades, conversations in the public square have focused almost exclusively on the means; with the fall of the Berlin Wall, liberalism stood alone, the undisputed victor of a centuries-long struggle for sociopolitical hegemony. History had, in the words of Francis Fukuyama, found its end. The unrest and disquietude of our current moment, however, has stirred a number of voices – both right and left, irreligious and religious – to return to the social question, with public discourse devoting less attention to the means of material and technological progress and instead engaging in a reimagining of the foundational principles that bind our lives together as a social and political community.

Indeed, the common thread running through the various sociopolitical challenges of our current moment is the decidedly collective, communal nature of their successful resolutions. Take, for instance, the Covid-19 pandemic. From AR-15-bearing protesters descending on state capitals to widespread refusals to wear face masks on public transportation, the era of quarantine has revealed just how resistant Western liberalism is to the notion of denying self for the sake of the community. And yet a successful response to the pandemic is predicated on the will of the community to act for the good of all its members – as it turns out, we're only as strong as our weakest link.

Or consider the tidal wave of protests set off by the callous, cavalier police killing of George Floyd. While books on white fragility and anti-racism soar to the top of best-seller lists, beneath all the social media posts and self-education campaigns lurks this truth – righting the wrongs of slavery and racism that run all the way to the roots of Western culture will require a collective rebuilding that extends much further than individual reflection and personal reform. And a fundamental reimagining of our social architecture and its attendant institutions is a fundamentally collective endeavor.

Kuyper – whose own legacy on race is complex and troubling – realized just this problem. As a principle for sociopolitical ordering, liberalism promised to unmoor the self from the strictures and confines of place, family, culture, and creed, thereby ushering in an era of unrestricted personal freedom and, with it, human flourishing. This loosening and dissociation, however, came with costs, the most fundamental of which Kuyper himself recognized:

> The French Revolution destroyed that organic tissue [of mutual aid and interdependence], broke these social bonds, and finally, in its work of atomistic trifling, had nothing left but the monotonous self-seeking individual, asserting his own self-sufficiency. . . . This is the pivot on which the whole social question turns. The French Revolution, and so, too, present-day Liberalism, is anti-social, and the social need which now disturbs Europe is the evil fruit of the individualism which was enthroned with the French Revolution.

To be clear, Kuyper's disaffection was not with the French Revolution and its associated ideals per se—elsewhere, he acknowledges the Revolution's "appalling necessity," arguing that the state of affairs made such a reaction "inexorably necessary." Instead, Kuyper's critique is grounded in a clear-eyed realization of liberalism's logical end—namely, that liberalism is fundamentally unable to serve as an ordering principle for our social life together because it is, in the purest sense, antisocial. Put differently, liberalism's boundaryless ennoblement of expressive individualism is fundamentally incompatible with the renunciation of self that collective social reimagining requires. Once ultimate authority is placed in the autonomous self, the possibility of any and all collective claim-making is functionally eradicated.

The liberal sociopolitical system created, as it were, a world in which "the law of the animal world, dog eat dog, became the basic law for every social relationship." The result?

> But, alas, the "equality" of which men had dreamed turned out to be an even more shocking inequality; and instead of the promised "fraternity," they received a revised version of the fable of the wolf and the lamb.

For Kuyper, following liberalism's appeal to its logically consistent conclusion simply replaced one form of arbitrary oppression (the crown) with another (the socially and economically fit; those best able to make their way under the liberal milieu of individual competition). The result was a society that betrayed the very foundations of the French Revolution and produced an oppressive, inequitable, unjust society that represented the archetypal antithesis of Liberty, Equality, and

Fraternity. In due time, liberalism produces a society of persons whose only shared cultural project is a collective genuflection before the primacy and preeminence of the untethered self. The result is an atomistic society devoid of mutual aid, in which every man is pitted against his brother – Hobbes's "solitary, poor, nasty, brutish" state of nature has become a reflexive, self-fulfilling prophecy.

—

"No justice, no peace."

These four words define the times in which we live. The collective social conscience of Western culture finds itself unsettled. Something is amiss. In the words of Kuyper, "Every tie-beam and anchor of the social structure is disturbed."

Made poignantly and acutely aware of the inequities that continue to pervade our shared social architecture, people are looking for answers. The rallying cry of justice is found on the lips of urban social activists and suburban soccer moms alike, and a growing spirit of communal-mindedness has emerged. In the midst of our hyperindividualistic age, we've begun to realize that the challenges we face are too great – the wounds and hurts too deep and real – to forge ahead alone. And so an opportunity emerges. As Kuyper put it, speaking of his own times,

> serious doubt has arisen about the *soundness of the social structure in which we live,* that in consequence public opinion is divided as to the type of foundation on which a more appropriate and more liveable social order may be built. . . . Only this one thing is necessary if a social question is to exist for you: that you realize the *untenability* of the present situation, and that you realize this untenability to be one not of incidental causes, but one involving the very *basis* of our social association.

These words should speak to us. Only when the fissures and fractures of a social architecture begin to emerge is it possible to embark on a process of reimagining the structure altogether. This is where we find ourselves.

To be sure, in many ways it feels like an odd time to build. To create. To repurpose, reimagine, and restore. But such is our call. So where do we begin?

First, we must acknowledge that our life together is shaped by an understanding—whether implicitly or explicitly—of what ought to be. In the words of philosopher James K. A. Smith, we are, first and foremost, desirers. Our thinking—the means, as it were—emerges only once the end has been conceived. We must offer an alternative vision for our collective life together, one that recognizes the inviolable dignity of the individual without dissociating that individual from the broader community within which she finds her home. Liberalism, after all, sought a more just and equitable social and civic culture not by offering a more compelling vision of our shared communal life, but by decoupling the individual from the collective altogether. Any sort of meaningful attempt to rebuild our fractured social ecology must begin with a vision of the common good that embraces, rather than scorns, the need for mutual aid and codependence. In the words of Kuyper, we are an "organic body," not an "aggregate of individuals."

Second, while a reimagining of our shared social architecture may begin as an intellectual or philosophical exercise, we must remember that it is also a thoroughly material, incarnational practice. What begins in the social imaginary must find its embodiment in the life of the polis.

> The beauty of a love springing up from God in you displays its radiance not in this, that you allow the poor Lazarus to quiet his hunger with the crumbs that fall from your overburdened table, for all such benefaction is more like an insult to the manly heart which beats also in the bosom of the poor man; but rather in this, that just as you, rich and poor, sit together at the Communion table, so likewise you feel for the poor man as for a member of the body, and so too, for your servant or maid as for a child of man, which is all that you, too, are. To the poor man, a loyal handshake is often sweeter than a bountiful largess. A friendly word, not spoken haughtily, is the mildest balsam for one who weeps at his wounds. Divine pity, sympathy, a suffering *with* us and *for* us, that was the mystery of Golgotha. You too, from fellow-feeling, *must suffer with your suffering brothers.*

Renewing the social order requires a traversal of the schism between self and society. The present social malaise is not a problem out there – it's a problem in here. To build something new, we must shoulder the burden together, renouncing liberalism's unbridled exaltation of self-efficacy for an otherworldly vision of a sociopolitical order that embraces suffering for the sake of advancing the common good. ❧

July 2, 2020

POLITICAL WISDOM AND THE LIMITS OF EXPERTISE

JENNIFER FREY

IT HAS BEEN exactly one hundred days since my ordinary life ceased to exist and I began to navigate the landscape of a global pandemic. Although this seems like a natural point for a moral philosopher such as myself to pause and take stock, I find myself fighting intellectual vertigo instead. Given the dramatic nature and dizzying pace of events over the past two weeks, and the sudden shift of focus from fighting the natural evil of the Covid-19 virus to fighting the twin social evils of systemic racism and police brutality, I feel unmoored. The crisis accelerates and changes in ways that outstrip my capacity for analysis.

As my own philosophical work focuses on the nature of right practical reason and how it depends on virtues of character, our pervasive and persistent failures in this regard stick out.

On the one hand, there is the widely shared tendency to engage in what I call *motivated partisan thinking.* Such thought subordinates concern for truth to political ends, leaving us with a distorted vision of reality built on arguments made in bad faith. On the other

---

JENNIFER FREY is associate professor of philosophy at the University of South Carolina. She is also the host of the philosophy, theology, and literature podcast *Sacred and Profane Love.* She lives in Columbia, South Carolina, with her husband, six children, and a bunch of chickens.

hand, it seems safe to say that we – especially our political leaders, government experts, and members of the professional-managerial class – have lost sight of the distinction between practical wisdom or prudence and mere expertise, with disastrous results.

The problem of how to reason well in a crisis is not only political but also deeply personal. We have all experienced the anxiety and self-doubt that comes from the complete disruption of our normal, everyday lives. One way to address this is simply to remember, as best we can, how we got here.

WHAT JUST HAPPENED?

I can still vividly recall early March when I began to hear from fellow academics in Italy about the virus spreading there like a wildfire. A close friend in Rome was adamant that I needed to pull my kids out of school and stop all social engagements. But the urgency of his advice was completely out of step with my own social environment. I was still teaching, multiple universities were expecting me to come to their campuses to give lectures, and the public schools remained silent about Covid-19. Should I cast aside all social expectations and take my friend's draconian advice? Was he alone practically wise?

When we make practical decisions, we always (at least implicitly) bring our particular circumstances under our general conception of how to live well. We do this without noticing it, because our practical reasoning draws on our stable habits – of mind and character, but just as importantly, of our social customs and routine. I don't have to deliberate about my morning espresso, how or when to greet strangers, or whether to get my kids ready for school. But in novel circumstances, our habits do not necessarily serve us well. To compound the trouble, we find ourselves with no exemplars of right reason to imitate and no inductive reservoir of past experiences to draw from. In my own case, otherwise normal decisions felt suddenly fraught, my deliberations tinged with self-doubt.

Soon enough, decisions were being made for us, in the name of public health. Classes were canceled and then moved online. The older children began to be homeschooled – and what a wealth of drama is buried in that use of the passive voice. Our city went into lockdown, and then our state quickly followed suit. Our family understood that we would need to make great sacrifices for the sake of public health: no Masses, no gathering with friends or family, no trips to the park, no sports or public events. We adjusted our reasoning to match our new reality—we supported the lockdowns. In fact, we supported wearing masks long before the experts came around to common sense about them. Health and safety became our foremost ends, followed by the well-being of the children, with our own work coming dead last. Our world constricted, and with it, so did the space and shape of our practical reflection.

As far as lockdowns went, we were privileged. South Carolina was far less draconian than other states, for one thing, but we are also a large and cohesive family who enjoyed our newfound time together: all eight of us. My husband and I have secure jobs, and our home has ample outdoor space. Other Americans were not so lucky. Many small-business owners watched in horror as a lifetime's work dissolved in a matter of weeks. Tens of millions were losing their jobs and, with them, their health insurance, while those in the service economy were risking their lives so that the rest of us could keep ourselves comfortable, fed, and entertained at home. Many could not visit dying loved ones in the hospital or bury their dead. Parents of disabled children could not get them their therapies, while children of elderly parents struggled to deal with problems that fell below the threshold of "necessary" care. For many, the lockdown was a full-blown mental-health crisis. Yet any complaints or small attempts at relief—such as family drives or walks on nature trails—were widely condemned and punished. My own neighborhood had its own self-appointed scold who drove around in a golf cart threatening to call the police on those not sufficiently socially distanced. Solidarity was in short supply when it was needed most.

LOCKDOWN BACKLASH

Anti-lockdown animus was swift and largely from Red State America. Calls to reopen the country for business became louder as the lockdown continued. Scattered protests of the lockdown began to emerge across the country. The protesters were largely white, people from communities who were suffering tremendous economic losses without (at that time) experiencing significant spread of the coronavirus. They were mostly small and peaceful – despite some obvious outliers, such as the notorious protest in Lansing, Michigan. Here in my own city, many of the protesters were small-business owners who felt their voices were not being heard.

In general, Blue-Staters largely favored expert-recommended lockdowns and treated public opposition to them with contempt. Public health experts were some of the loudest in their condemnation of these acts of civil disobedience as irresponsible, showing a cavalier disregard for the lives of others. Red-Staters, in insisting that the cure was worse than the disease, downplayed the risks of the virus and complained that the personal sacrifices that Americans were being asked to make were too costly. Many pointed out that there are other social factors that contribute to negative health outcomes, such as poverty, loneliness, social isolation, stress, anxiety, and depression, conditions that the lockdown was clearly exacerbating in great numbers. Their concerns were dismissed by our expert class.

THE MURDER AND WHAT FOLLOWED

This political dynamic continued until late May, when George Floyd, a black resident of Minneapolis, was senselessly and mercilessly killed by a white cop in broad daylight. As Floyd's murder followed closely on the heels of the racially charged killing of Ahmaud Arbery in Georgia – whose apparent crime was jogging while black – and Breonna Taylor in Kentucky, long-simmering racial tensions suddenly boiled over all across the country. People took to the streets in the tens of thousands, venting their legitimate anger and frustration and demanding the recognition that black lives matter, begging law-enforcement officers to stop killing black people. Several protests across the country descended into violence, looting, and the destruction of property, though most remained peaceful. The riots were complex, with many different groups participating for varied reasons; though most Americans both on left and right were able to distinguish the riots from the protests in their minds, some —on both left and right—seemingly, could not, equating support for one with support for both. Despite widespread acts of police brutality against protesters, the protests not only persisted but also grew in size and number.

Almost overnight, Covid-19 became a subsidiary plague, and concerns for it were taken to be a threat to concerns for racial justice. The response of public health experts underwent a stunning gestalt shift. It's not just that public health experts were silent about the risks associated with these protests, whereas before they were quite vocal about them. In many instances they vocally downplayed them in order to endorse and encourage people to join the protest movement, and to do so *as a matter of public health*. That is to say, they used their considerable authority as public health experts to encourage acts of civil disobedience on a massive scale *as effective public health measures* in the midst of a deadly pandemic that disproportionately kills black people.

For example, in an open letter signed by more than a thousand experts that was circulated widely, it was claimed that "the way forward is not to suppress protests in the name of public health but to respond to protesters' demands in the name of public health." One might be forgiven for thinking that public health experts were now claiming that abolishing the police was an urgent matter of public health, since "white supremacy is a lethal public health issue" and therefore "our first statement must be one of unwavering support for those who would *dismantle*, uproot, or reform racist institutions." Suddenly, our expert class affirmed that not only do social determinants matter, they matter far more than the obvious risks of further spreading a deadly plague for which we have no effective treatment or vaccine. Furthermore, the letter baldly states that public health experts were correct to oppose anti-lockdown protests and *must* support anti-racism protests. This amounts to public health experts weighing in, as health experts, on the political questions of who gets to exercise their free-speech rights during a pandemic and why.

What do we make of this? Is there nothing to their claims? Certainly, systemic racism is a social determinant that helps to explain some of the differential health outcomes within black populations here in the United States. I have discussed these racial disparities and their causes extensively in my medical-ethics classes, where we have analyzed some of the relevant literature together. As a philosopher teaching medical ethics to future health-care workers, I strive to help my students to see that their future patients are more than bodies or vectors of disease – they are human persons, with spiritual and social as well as physical needs; their social environment has a great impact on their prospects for health. Public health experts are correct to point out the social aspects of human health.

Still, the statements of the public health experts overstepped the mark by quite a lot, and for a very particular reason: What counts as an instance of white supremacy, what economic and political structures and institutions need to be "dismantled, uprooted, or reformed," what acts of civil disobedience ought to be tolerated and which actively sanctioned by the state are well outside the sphere of epidemiological expertise. Experts are not political leaders, and they are not, in any formal way, called on to exercise political prudence, except inasmuch as we all are as citizens. And the questions of how to respond to the protests are philosophical and political questions. To address them requires political prudence. It is hubris of a high order for our expert class to pretend otherwise and to render sweeping judgments about which group should be afforded free-speech rights and why.

EXPERTISE, PRACTICAL REASON, AND PUBLIC TRUST

As might be expected, Red-Staters responded to these statements with scorn, lambasting experts for blurring the lines between sound science and partisan politics. Some public health experts responded by saying that "science is an inherently political activity." Such statements are not only false but deeply unwise, since they further erode the already fractured trust between many Americans and the expert class. Expertise is in fact a genuine good, and is essential to sound political decision-making: it is simply that it is not itself constitutive of that decision-making. Moreover, public health measures are only effective if there is trust in the experts who issue them, and that trust is undermined when it seems as though those experts' guidelines are being applied in politically motivated ways.

However, just as unelected public health experts have no business deciding political questions, we must not reduce medical expertise to value-neutral scientific inquiry either. The truth is far more complicated.

The expert is someone who has a certain kind of education, training, and experience relative to a certain narrow domain of knowledge. She is typically credentialed to practice her expertise and is given authority relative to the domain in which her knowledge operates. Some forms of expertise are theoretical, which means their authority derives from their reputation for a certain domain of knowledge. If you have a question about the Civil War, for instance, you should consult a historian of nineteenth-century America who has spent her career trying to understand it.

But other kinds of expertise fall in the realm of art or practical skill, which concerns not mere knowledge but the ability to produce certain goods in accordance with associated techniques. A skill involves the possession of a unified body of practical knowledge and reasoning. Skill is an intellectual habit—a stable disposition that makes one ready to act in ways that are ordered to the realization of the end internal to it. If you need to have your pants taken in, you should not consult a fashion historian, but a tailor, since he has the habits of practical knowledge and reason necessary to do this well. He knows not just about sewing, but *how to* sew.

Medical expertise, broadly speaking, is also practical expertise. It concerns the realization of health, which is a human good. Doctors aim to understand the human body in order to bring about health in individual persons. This habitual knowledge is practical because it involves seeing how to realize a good. They know *how* to heal.

Epidemiologists aim to understand the factors that determine the presence or absence of disease and disorders, as well as how diseases and disorders affect society at large. They study populations rather than individuals, in order to guide effective public health policy with the goal of promoting, protecting, and preserving individual health within specified populations. An excellent epidemiologist has mastered the art of identifying, containing, and eradicating disease – not just as a matter of satisfying his curiosity but in order to restore health to a population.

In order to underscore these points about the sort of practical reasoning that defines expertise, let us consider two different sorts of mistakes an expert might make. The first is a failure of expertise, which is always a failure to apply the techniques necessary to attain the desired end. So, suppose an epidemiologist gets the rate of transmission of a virus wrong, because there were factors of transmission he failed to put into his model. He may be faulted for this, qua expert.

But now let us imagine an entirely different scenario. Imagine an epidemiologist who intentionally makes a faulty model because he thinks that humans are the real virus and nature must be protected from them. He wants to use his expertise not to bring about health but to spread disease. But here we do not fault him qua epidemiologist. (In fact, it would take epidemiological brilliance to fake a model that would be convincing enough to fool everyone.) Rather, we fault him as a human being. That is, what he has done isn't a failure of expertise but a failure of prudence, or right practical reasoning about how to live a good human life. Our fanciful thought experiment demonstrates that prudence is not an expertise but a virtue. It is a disposition not to produce certain goods but to be good and live well in an *unqualified* sense.

The expert should always be wary of overstepping the bounds of his own expertise. The Civil War historian might be passionately committed to promoting racial justice, but it would be hubris for him to think that his credentials make him qualified to lead anti-racist movements. To execute that work well, he would need a different sort of training and experience, which would create different habits of judgment in him. It is sometimes possible for one person to harbor these different sets of training and to be able to appropriately switch between these different habits of judgment. But it is quite difficult, and rather unusual, to be able to do both equally well and without letting the habits of mind of one discipline inappropriately overtake the habits of mind of the other. Similarly, the epidemiologist *in his role as an epidemiologist* should not pretend to have the expertise to weigh in on which of our social institutions needs to be dismantled, when, and why, or whether politicians should encourage or permit protests. This is a question of political prudence, which depends on political experience and a sound vision of what generally constitutes the good life for all citizens. Moreover, these are issues that deserve robust political debate, and need to be subject to democratic processes. Protest is part of that, as an exercise of free speech. It is an exercise of political prudence and authority, however, to make tough calls about when to limit that speech in the name of public health.

POLITICAL PRUDENCE AND THE COMMON GOOD

So what is political prudence? It is not another form of expertise, but an intellectual virtue that enables a political leader to judge, in the particular, changing circumstances of life, what laws, orders, or policies will promote and protect this common good. That is to say, it is not a mere shift of topic, but a different kind of practical reasoning altogether, one that is directed to the common good of all citizens, and therefore dependent on the virtues of good character.

When I use the term "common good," I do not mean to invoke the public goods often referenced by economists, which are non-rivalrous and non-excludable goods subject to the tragedy of the commons, like fresh air or clean water. Rather, I mean the common good in the sense one finds it in the Aristotelian philosophical tradition. Following Aquinas, we can say of the common good that it is common to our nature as human beings to seek and enjoy; that it is noncompetitive, which means it is not diminished in any way by others' pursuit or enjoyment of it; and finally, that it is participatory, which means that it is a good that is such as to be brought about and enjoyed with others. I can enjoy a piece of birthday cake by myself; I cannot enjoy a birthday party by myself, because the "party" part is the pleasure in being with others I care about to celebrate the life of one of them.

For someone to possess political prudence, she must possess a correct vision of the good life that all citizens can participate in equally. She must not only know what sorts of generic goods constitute the common good, but she must also grasp how these goods are hierarchically arranged in a well-ordered human life. For part of wise political judgment is seeing how to prioritize different goods in various, changing circumstances. Obviously, health will be given an unusual priority during a plague, but our political leaders will need to weigh the good of health against competing goods, like economic stability and racial justice. A wise leader can hold more than one good in his mind at once, and act to promote the common good by balancing those generic goods, seeking to realize them all, as much as possible, in their time and in harmony with each other. Wise citizens can do this, according to their own roles in the polity, as well.

Talk of a robust vision of the common good sounds illiberal to some ears, but this is so only if we are confused about the relation between the general and the particular. At a high level of generality, there is widespread agreement about the goods of human life and how they ought to be generally ordered within a well-functioning society. Virtually everyone agrees generally that health is a basic human good that needs safeguarding and also that health is not the highest good we seek. In addition to shelter, food, and security, most people agree that humans have spiritual needs: we seek to find meaning and purpose in our lives and a connection with goods that transcend ourselves. We agree about the need for the pursuit of knowledge, for the dignity of work, of family and friends, recreation, art, play, and contemplation. Our political battles all tend to be at the level of particulars—what practices best instantiates these goods and what specific means will best realize them in just and equitable fashion. These political disagreements ought to be settled by democratic means and through various processes of democratic debate.

In order to know when and why to risk public health, a leader must make recourse to her general conception of the common good and apply it to the particular circumstances at hand. To do this is to step outside the proper bounds of mere expertise—medical or otherwise. A wise leader will rely on experts for sound advice and policy, but in the end the political decision must be made through an exercise of political prudence—especially when the circumstances call for swift and decisive action.

Political prudence, like all prudence, requires the virtues of good character, which develop over time and are the result of a very different form of education than any expertise. Cowardice, lack of self-discipline and patience, dishonesty, pride, greed, and other vices distort our ability to know what to seek and avoid in particular, changing circumstances of private and public life. Right now, above all else, we need our political leaders to have the courage to speak the truth about the reality of our current situation, regardless of how the truth affects their political prospects or their political goals generally The truth is, the virus has not ended; it's accelerating, and it has no regard for justice. The truth is, systemic racism and other structural inequalities persist in this country and are heightened, and revealed, by this pandemic. And the truth is that tens of millions of Americans are suffering in myriad ways and want and need their voices to be heard. We need to seek political solutions to these stark realities. But we will need political wisdom as citizens, and we will need leaders with political wisdom, to address them. This wisdom will draw on expertise, but cannot and must not be reduced to it.

A crucial feature of prudence is foresight. Aquinas argues that the prudent man can grasp the future in light of both the present and the past, by a process of comparison. Of course, this takes experience and the ability to seek good counsel from others. Prudence includes the ability to foresee the likely effects of one's actions (or inactions) and one's policies.

FORESIGHT AND THE EFFECTS OF PROTESTS

We know the *likely* effects of gatherings that last for hours or even days, with a great deal of shouting and without any hope of social distancing, and that is further spread of a deadly virus. It is very difficult to directly measure cause and effect in this, of course, and the results of studies are still coming in. At this point, the picture isn't clear. Accuracy and honesty in data collection, interpretation, and reporting are absolutely crucial.

Here in my own city of Columbia, South Carolina, Covid-19 cases are up 30 percent—a terrifying jump. Four of the principal organizers of the anti-racist protests have announced that they have now tested positive for the Covid-19 virus and are encouraging the many thousands who protested over the past two weeks to get tested as well.

This result is entirely predictable and very worrying. For, although only 27 percent of South Carolinians are black, they make up 36 percent of the current confirmed Covid-19 cases and 46 percent of its confirmed fatalities. These terrible facts put considerable pressure against the experts' claims that mass protests are a critical tool for increasing public health within black populations in this particular moment of intense vulnerability.

We do not know, yet, with certainty, how the protests have or will affect the spread of the virus. We can hope that they do not increase spread at all. But that seems unlikely. That is the fierce reality of a virus that does not care about the reason you are gathering, and that reality must be faced. It is the role of experts to bring that reality before those politicians and citizens making their own prudential judgments, so that it can be fairly weighed; so that that evil can be balanced with other goods that may be accomplished. The Black Lives Matter protests were a legitimate response to a horrific national tragedy, and one that I support. They have brought about some positive changes in our country already. But the question of whether to protest is always a matter of prudence, both personal and political. It is not, and should not be, a matter for the experts to decide.

In this moment of unrest, uncertainty, and suffering, we need humility, compassion, and solidarity. We need to recognize that our fates are tied. Our crisis has exposed our structural injustices, but it has also exposed the lack of good character of much of our political leadership. Imagine if we had leaders who could unite us around a shared vision of the common good in this moment of division, anxiety, and fear; who could call us to grow in solidarity rather than give in to our darker impulses to scorn and judge; who could call us to sacrifice humbly for the sake of one another, to protect and look after each other. Imagine if they could set aside their partisan differences in order to work together for the common good. I think we are all painfully aware that we are all too often lacking such leaders when we need them the most. Prudence has been in short supply.

During the first month of lockdown, when my insomnia and anxiety were peaking, I rewatched the Steven Soderberg film *Contagion*. The film tells the story of a deadly pandemic that kills millions of Americans, spread by respiratory droplets, brought to the United States from Asia. The heroes of the film are the experts and diligent researchers who heroically direct policy and fashion a vaccine in record time. Politicians are noticeably absent from the narrative. There are eerie similarities in the film to our current moment, but its central message – that expertise and scientific rationalism will save us – seems wildly out of touch with our present reality.

The truth is that experts will not save us – our problems are much bigger and deeper than they are equipped to solve. We need wisdom. The time to demand it, in our leaders and in ourselves, is long overdue. ⁘

THE HABITS OF EXILE

J. L. WALL

If I had the power I would provisionally close all synagogues for a hundred years. Do not tremble at the thought of it, Jewish heart. What would happen? Jews and Jewesses without synagogues, desiring to remain such, would be forced to concentrate on a Jewish life and a Jewish home. The Jewish officials connected with the synagogue would have to look to the only opportunity now open to them – to teach young and old how to live a Jewish life and how to build a Jewish home. All synagogues closed by Jewish hands would constitute the strongest protest against the abandonment of Torah in home and life.

—Rabbi Samson Raphael Hirsch

My PARENTING GROUP, to say the least, wasn't buying it. How can you actually raise Jewish children without the anchoring spaces and events of a synagogue? And how could Rabbi Hirsch – credited as the founding figure of modern Orthodox Judaism – have even imagined it? As the father of an infant, I was already the outlier: everyone else's children were old enough to be in school, already used to socializing with other Jewish kids their age on Shabbat mornings, now in need of supervision at home from parents also expected to keep working full-time.

J. L. WALL is an essayist, poet, and teacher living in Michigan. His writing has appeared in *First Things, Modern Age, Kenyon Review Online, University Bookman, America,* and *Arc Digital.* You can find him on Twitter at @jl_wall.

Hirsch's words, I found, offered a way to express what I'd already begun to feel in the first few weeks of the coronavirus lockdown, as the paragraph above circulated through Jewish institutions and we, in hard-hit southeast Michigan, watched the case numbers tick steadily upward.

Without a synagogue, I found myself falling into a different, more daily rhythm of Jewish practice, one still anchored by Shabbat but grounded in more broadly repeated actions: laying tefillin in the morning; counting the fifty days of the *omer*, the period between Passover and Shavuot, each night; taking five minutes in the afternoon for virtual text-study with the rabbi. The routines of Jewish life changed but didn't disappear. Centered exclusively on my home, they're what Hirsch called for.

The detailed rules of traditional Jewish observance – its many prescriptions and proscriptions – account for a large part of this. So too does the perspective learned from Judaism's history of creative response to exile from the places and practices with which Jews have grown familiar.

I'm aware that what I'm about to describe doesn't have perfect analogues in Christian life – and I'm not presumptuous enough to suggest what useful ones might be. But this coronatide is a period of exile: from churches and synagogues, from schools and clubs, from workplaces, from friends and family. For all of us, life in our own homes begins to feel like something of a miniature diaspora. These are conditions and feelings with which Judaism has grappled for millennia.

—

As stark as this season's realities may be, they're not as drastic as the change that was Hirsch's starting point. His call for a Judaism without synagogues comes in an essay discussing the month of Av, the late-summer portion of the Jewish calendar marked by the destruction of the First and Second Temples. The month's ninth day – Tisha B'Av – is one of fasting and lamentation. The week preceding it, for traditional Jews, resembles the period of shiva, mourning for a close relative. Tisha B'Av marks a radical break in Jewish history: from pilgrimage and sacrifice to prayer and study;

from a central, national house of worship to local centers, often in competition. To talk about Av is to talk about the period in which Jews were cast out of all that was familiar about Jewish worship.

Yet Hirsch suggests voluntarily reenacting this break on a smaller scale. Sudden decentralization, he holds, is what the Jews of nine-teenth-century Germany need. In part, this is Hirsch's response to the early Reform movement, which he believed outsourced religion from the home to the synagogue, effectively limiting Judaism to one day a week. And he feared something similar was beginning, despite continued surface-level observance, in Orthodox Jewish families as well. The places and times of Jewish life were becoming too clearly distinguished.

Jewish observance consists largely of making such distinctions: between pure and impure, kosher or *treyf*, Shabbat and the work-week. The Hebrew word *kadesh*, to sanctify, means more literally to separate or set aside. Shabbat in particular is made holy by being set apart and distinguished from other days; in the closing *havdalah* ceremony on Saturday nights, Jews bless God for allowing us to make this distinction and for separating the sacred (Shabbat) from the mundane (the rest of the week).

But there's a danger in this to which Hirsch was attuned. A century later, Rabbi Joseph Soloveitchik, one of the leading figures of American Orthodox Judaism, would frame it as the distinction between "religious man" and "Halakhic man," referring to the difference between one who follows a religious sensibility and one whose life is ordered according to the strictures of Jewish law. He has no time for the religious outlook in which "the temple stands at the heart of religion." Synagogues and religious schools are "minor sanctuaries," but the "true sanctuary is the sphere of our daily, mundane activities."

Both Hirsch and Soloveitchik discuss (through different vocab-ularies) a defining feature of modernity's secular age, what Charles Taylor refers to as the "immanent frame": a way of perceiving the world that values the natural and material over the transcendent and supernatural. Too much focus on the synagogue, too much emphasis on observing a single, time-bound aspect of Judaism – and the six days of the regular week aren't merely "mundane," but secular; God and transcendence are not sanctified in the Sabbath but *circumscribed* within it.

W. H. Auden put the dilemma more conversationally in the closing section of his 1942 Christmas oratorio, "For the Time Being." As the pageant ends, its narrator returns readers to the period of mundane time: life between the crucifixion and the resurrection, when "The happy morning is over, / The night of agony still to come; the time is noon." This "Time Being," he writes, "is the most trying time of all," a period defined by "bills to be paid, machines to keep in repair, / Irregular verbs to learn, the Time Being to redeem / From insignificance."

Halakhic man, not bound to the place of worship or focused on achieving transcendence, has something to teach us – Jews and Christians alike – about how to deepen and sustain faith in our own virus-driven exiles from church and temple.

—

The exile we've been living in since March is more extreme than Hirsch's thought experiment. Precisely those pillars of community that he would let stand in place of the synagogue are also closed off: schools and study groups, welcoming guests to share meals, many forms of charitable work in the community – beyond the nuclear family, everything embodied has been proscribed. It's not just that we can't go to synagogue or church and must now spread out the behavior that defines that day across the full week. Even as the workweek starts to blur into a weird sabbatarian pause from what once was normal, we're cut off from the actions that once defined the Sabbath itself.

It all feels like the opposite of *kadesh*: Shabbat and holidays set aside, out of reach, while the weekday work is to infuse the most mundane, repeated, and niggling tasks into habits infused with religious meaning.

In Jewish communities, this is particularly jarring. The need to pray in community is common to Jews, Christians, and others, of course – but Jewish tradition makes it quite clear that private prayer should be avoided. Without a minyan, a prayer quorum of ten, central portions of the liturgy can't be recited. In a time of mourning, it's especially difficult and poignant that this applies to the Kaddish, which most Jews have been unable to recite for family members lost years ago and those lost more recently.

But the English word "prayer" obscures a distinction between two different kinds of Jewish speech-acts: *avodah* (or service) and *bracha* (or blessing). *Avodah* defines communal prayer; *brachot*, though integral to *avodah*, are not limited to it. Certain blessings require a community – sometimes three, sometimes ten – but most are meant for the individual.

Moreover, many *brachot* are said over actions that have no inherent religious quality – for deeds that seem at home in Taylor's immanent frame: blessings on wearing new clothes; on washing hands; on urinating; on smelling fruit, flowers, trees, or anything fragrant; on seeing lightning; on hearing thunder; on seeing the ocean; on seeing the trees budding at winter's end; on seeing a secular academic, the president, or the Queen of England; on encountering a rare animal; on hearing good news – and the news of a death.

Brachot demand intentionality, the awareness that one does something not necessarily *because* one is a Jew, but *as* a Jew, with the knowledge that there is transcendence which may not be visible but exists nonetheless. The Talmudic tractate *Berakhot*, which discusses prayer and blessings, is included in the section devoted to *Zera'im*, or seeds, otherwise devoted to agricultural laws. Among the many explanations offered for this quirk of organization is the idea that *brachot* are the seeds of Jewish life: a way to grasp and sanctify mundane acts by setting them, at least momentarily, outside their immanent frame.

The difference between the sacred and the mundane, on this account, lies in the form of attention we grant everyday acts; Judaism's web of laws creates opportunities to do this. Even in my frantic, nervous rush through the grocery store, I have to pause, from time to time, to check to make sure what I'm buying is actually kosher: a small moment, yes, but a Jewish one, and one that carries over to the kitchen as I cook, and to the table as we eat. When I pass from room to room in my home, I see the *mezuzot* on the doorposts; when I go outdoors, I know that my clothing, the knit *yarmulke* I've finally taken to wearing regularly, will mark everything I say or do as something done by and as a Jew.

—

And then there's simply walking.

Almost every Jewish community has a "Shabbos park" – a public, outdoor space where families gather on Saturday afternoons, after shul and lunch and possibly a nap, to let the kids play together and the parents socialize (or nap). What I didn't realize, until my daily lockdown constitutionals took me past our park midweek, was how clearly this space is mapped into my mind as the Shabbos park: each visit, now, recalls the spirit of that day. Somehow, just going there is in itself a Jewish act.

This isn't something I could have deliberately created – certainly not in the days after the rushed week of email conversations and synagogue updates that restricted and eventually canceled our community indefinitely. It was built, through slow accretion, by years of habit: all those Saturdays I've spent walking to the Shabbos park, walking through the neighborhoods around it, walking to the houses of community members for meals, for a drink, to play board games, to sit and talk. And walking, of course, to synagogue.

The physical constraints of Shabbat observance mark the day as holy – but also provide the most condensed example of how Halakhic man transforms the mundane while making a home in it. There's no inherent difference between Saturday and the rest of the week. All that changes is behavior in my control: that I can't drive or ride in a car, turn on the lights, cook, walk outside the boundaries of the *eruv* (the area in Jewish neighborhoods that symbolically extends the private domain of the household into public areas, allowing activities forbidden in public on the Sabbath); the time I have to read with my wife or play with my daughter without glancing at the clock. All these have marked my Saturdays as Sabbaths, and a decade of walking similar routes to and from this synagogue has marked the spaces I pass through as somehow Jewish.

That my mental map of the city has been formed around walking to shul isn't enough to sustain religious practice, of course: it provides just enough of an echo to remind the families still gathered, six to ten feet apart, in the Shabbos park, that by being in *this* park we're still marking Shabbat, remembering it and guarding it. But it does highlight the ability of repeated action to mark the mundane as religious – or, more rightly, to highlight and draw out the sacred from within the mundane.

This, ultimately, is the goal of the myriad laws and regulations that define traditional Jewish life: not to control or constrain the individual, but to mark each action as, in some way, defined by recognition of God's truth. "Halakhic man," Soloveitchik writes, "apprehends transcendence. However, instead of rising up to it, he tries to bring it down to him. Rather than raising the lower realms to the higher world, halakhic man brings down the higher realms to the lower world."

And I suspect it's also true of the many small habits of Christian life and prayer, those items of mundane life and overlooked charity that are easy to ignore – or let slide with the promise that you'll make sure to perform the public, communal deeds from which we've been exiled. "Halakhic man" might be a Jewish concept but has his Christian counterparts as well. What Hirsch sought and Soloveitchik described is more than a set of behaviors – it is a particular way of paying attention to the world and oneself, produced and sustained by habitual repetition, that transforms the mundane without seeking to escape it.

—

One day, of course, all this will be over: we'll go back to our churches and synagogues and sing without fear of spreading a virus. But I know from the rhythms of synagogue attendance on a university campus that the feeling won't last: renewed commitments, fueled by the quest to see old friends, almost always fade.

What we'll face then as Jews and Christians, as communities of religious believers, will only be a seemingly less urgent version of the task we already face with houses of worship closed. Auden, of course, describes it well: "Back in the moderate Aristotelian city / Of darning and the Eight-Fifteen," we'll look around and mutter aloud, "It seems to have shrunk during the holidays. The streets / Are much narrower than we remembered; we had forgotten / The office was as depressing as this."

"Holiness is created by man, by flesh and blood," Soloveitchik writes; the time being is redeemed through routine, through practice, through ritual. In a small way, we're all now sharing in the bewilderment of Jews from the first century suddenly without the Temple, forced not merely to adapt but to develop and embrace ways of sacralizing that already existed. For them, it was study, prayer, a reimagining of the Sabbath table set with candles, challah, and wine as a homebound version of the Temple itself.

For us, it can be something less drastic but no less essential: taking on the mindset of the Halakhic man, developing the habits and routines of a Jewish or Christian home, understanding prayer not merely as service, worship, or request, but as blessing – the incorporation of ways to break through the immanent frame into our daily lives. Not just to notice the cracks where transcendence breaks through, but to make them ourselves.

July 10, 2020

A POLITICS WORSE THAN DEATH

MICHAEL WEAR

THIS YEAR, our politics has been riveted by death. The Covid-19 virus has been a blunt reminder of a truth we try so desperately to avoid: that death is coming for us all. Yet the solidarity that might be inspired by this knowledge has been challenged by the renewed realization that death is not colorblind in America, whether it comes to the racial disparities of the pandemic or the deadly violence against black people at the hands of the state. What do we do when death comes to our politics? Whose death matters in our politics?

Of course, death has always been tied to politics. In fact, some would argue that politics itself is a response to death, and our desire to ward it off. Violence unto death has been an engine of economic development. Violence is so pervasive in political affairs that the development of tools of violence so extraordinary as to ensure the annihilation of entire communities of people have been hailed as victories for peace. It is conventional wisdom among much of the foreign-policy establishment that the threat of violent death as a result of nuclear warfare is an acceptable and wise tool for peace and protection. Many are reckoning with the fact that, as a society, we have made a similar bargain domestically: the ever-present specter of death for some at the hands of law enforcement is an acceptable cost for the security we believe violence provides for us.

MICHAEL WEAR is the founder of Public Square Strategies and co-author of *Compassion (&) Conviction: The AND Campaign's Guide to Faithful Civic Engagement*.

This violence is necessary, some think, because they never anticipate that it will fall on them. This violence is acceptable because it
happens only with the legitimacy we grant it, not by our own hands.

Framed in such striking terms, I am tempted to judge this
bargain quite harshly. Indeed, I am tempted to judge us harshly for
making it. But perhaps such a judgment is too easy. It is difficult
to count deaths averted, especially in such a violent world. What
violence has been avoided because of the deterrence of the nuclear
bomb, or of the death penalty? If physical death is not just inevitable
but an imperative, perhaps our politics needs to plan for it, to consider it, to redirect it as long as possible. One feels vulnerable even
expressing such doubts, but what hubris to refuse to even consider
the utility of the nuclear bomb or the electric chair, even if you seek
to abolish both, as I do. Perhaps the nuclear bomb has saved my life.
Perhaps lethal injection has saved yours. Might ending either only
lead to misery of a different sort, death by other hands? How do we
weigh these possibilities? Whose death matters?

In a discourse centered on privilege, it's tempting to draw a
clear dividing line between the powerful and the downtrodden on
questions of death and violence. We might assume that only the
powerful are content with such "necessary" violence, and that the
downtrodden would do away with it if they could. But the powerful
often fly above death, unaware it lies just beneath the cover of the
clouds. The downtrodden can view death as a matter of practicality,
a potential source of order and safety, however unreliable, amid
chaos.

But here is the real distinction: For death to come to the powerful, it almost always has to come for the powerless first. To reach
the palace, an opposing army must first make its way through the
slums. The deaths of the powerful are often everyone's deaths. For
the unnoticed and unnoteworthy, death comes like a thief in the
night. A fundamental privilege, certainly, is the privilege to stave
off death, to die knowing every appropriate measure was taken to
protect your life.

A pandemic like the one we are enduring now cuts through these
typical divides. While the burden of the Covid-19 virus has not fallen
equally on all, it is striking how it has forced a kind of solidarity. It

is easy to mock celebrities complaining about stay-at-home orders while they sip cocktails in their exotic swimming pools, but I can't really think of anything other than Covid-19 that has forced me to adjust my life, that has also forced bank CEOs and movie stars to adjust as well, particularly over such a sustained period of time and over such a geographic spread. The powerful sometimes have unique reasons to fear death because of their power, but Covid-19 has caused powerful people to fear death simply because they are human. There is a certain unity in this.

For a moment, at least, it seemed as though we were ready as a country to meet the moment. A Pew study in March found that 89 percent of Americans were following news about Covid-19 very (51 percent) or fairly (38 percent) closely. In April, an overwhelming majority (80 percent) of the American people supported stay-at-home orders, knowing and bearing their cost.

This pandemic has brought governance, especially state and local governance, back into the center of a politics dominated by personality, identity, and movements. I was struck on a recent walk as I passed by a series of local government signs urging me to protect myself and others. Local government, which mostly fades into the background in my life, is now brought to the fore. A March NBC/ *Wall Street Journal* survey showed about three-quarters of registered voters had confidence in state and local government to deal with the outbreak of the virus. Congress, which has evaded responsibility for much in recent years, actually acted to pass a significant, if flawed, relief bill on a bipartisan basis. Perhaps the pandemic would prove that some seemingly intractable political problems were not so intractable after all. This is the story I would love to see and tell.

Instead, while we should not ignore the bright spots, I do not believe death has jolted us out of anything. Yes, we have had a politics riveted by death this year, but death has exerted little discernible discipline on our political dysfunction. Rather, our politics has proved capable of forcing even death into its mold.

—

In March, Rusty Reno, the editor-in-chief of *First Things*, decried the "sentimentalism" and "false god" of saving lives. His article was widely panned on social media, and easy accusations of pro-life hypocrisy were called forth. In May, on Twitter, Reno shared his view that the "mask culture" was "fear-driven" and that wearing a mask is a "mark of cowardice." This, too, was not received well on social media.

There is a kind of pseudo-Christian narcissism that places on others its own embrace of calculated risk in determining death's value. We've all seen the folks at protests who claim they're okay to be out in public because God will protect them. Or the Ohio legislator who invoked the "image of God" as depicted in the human face specifically as the reason he would not wear a mask, and asked, "Is the role of government to protect us from death, which is inevitable? Or is the role of government to radically protect our freedom and our liberty?" Many of us recognize these kinds of sentiments as irresponsible. But perhaps we simply lack theological insight? Perhaps we lack the faith of Christian bravado? Are we not supposed to "reject death's dominion" as Reno called for us to do?

In the eighth chapter of Matthew, we're told that while Jesus was teaching, a crowd began to surround him, and so Jesus told his disciples that they would take a boat across the nearby lake. Before they could leave, a teacher approached Jesus and said he would follow Jesus wherever he went. Jesus indicated to the man what he was volunteering for, a life on the run. One of Jesus' disciples asked to bury his father before traveling on with Jesus. Jesus replied, "Follow me, and let the dead bury their own dead."

"Then," Scripture tells us, Jesus got into a boat and his disciples followed him. "We'd better do what he says," they might have said. "He's been worth following so far," they might have reasoned, the implicit question hanging in the air.

The passage continues,

> Suddenly a furious storm came up on the lake, so that the waves swept over the boat. But Jesus was sleeping. The disciples went and woke him, saying, "Lord, save us! We're going to drown!"

> He replied, "You of little faith, why are you so afraid?" Then he got up and rebuked the winds and the waves, and it was completely calm.

The men were amazed and asked, "What kind of man is this? Even the winds and the waves obey him!"

As Dallas Willard suggested in a talk, Jesus is not just reproaching his disciples for fearing that the boat would sink, but for "their thought that if their boat were to sink it would be the end of the world." In other words, he reproaches them for their overriding fear – of danger, of physical harm, of death – fear to the point of the diminishment of their faith.

At another point in Jesus' ministry, he had been sent word that someone he loved in Judea was sick. Jesus told the disciples who were with him that the sickness would not end in death, but would be an occasion for God's glory. After two days, Scripture tells us, Jesus said that they were to return to Judea. Jesus' companions reminded him that he had almost been killed the last time he was in Judea, but he told them Lazarus had died and he was going to see him. Martha and Mary, whom he also loved, were there as well. Andrew told the other disciples that they were to follow Jesus to die as well.

When Jesus arrived in Bethany, he was greeted by Martha, who expressed utter confidence that Jesus had the power to prevent Lazarus's death, and that "even now God will give you whatever you ask." Jesus tells Martha her brother will rise again, but Martha gives Jesus an out: "I know he will rise again in the resurrection at the last day." This understanding of physical death seems like precisely the kind of faith Jesus wanted from the disciples on the boat.

When Mary saw Jesus, she fell at his feet, and told him, "Lord, if you had been there, my brother would not have died." Scripture says that when Jesus "saw Mary weeping . . . he was deeply moved and troubled." Jesus asked to be taken to Lazarus, and it is when those who had gathered told him "Come and see, Lord," that Jesus wept. He would, of course, raise Lazarus from the dead. And Jesus and his disciples would not die that day, as the disciples had worried.

In the passage of Scripture describing Jesus' greatest miracle, and his supreme confidence in his Father, Jesus is described as "moved" multiple times, troubled, weeping. What was it that led Jesus to rebuke his disciples on the boat but to weep with those mourning the death of Lazarus?

When confronted with death, when is the proper Christian response to proclaim, like Paul, "O death, where is thy sting?" and when is it to weep, to mourn, to try to avoid death or turn it back?

There is a passage in Scripture where Jesus is talking with Simon Peter about death. The way a person interprets this passage can be an indicator of what they think about God and how God views death. Jesus, who had risen from the dead, had joined several of his disciples on the shores of the Sea of Galilee and made them breakfast. After they were fed, he addressed Simon Peter, who had denied that he knew Jesus three times prior to his crucifixion.

> When they had finished eating, Jesus said to Simon Peter, "Simon son of John, do you love me more than these?"
>
> "Yes, Lord," he said, "you know that I love you."
>
> Jesus said, "Feed my lambs."
>
> Again Jesus said, "Simon son of John, do you love me?"
>
> He answered, "Yes, Lord, you know that I love you."
>
> Jesus said, "Take care of my sheep."
>
> The third time he said to him, "Simon son of John, do you love me?"
>
> Peter was hurt because Jesus asked him the third time, "Do you love me?" He said, "Lord, you know all things; you know that I love you."
>
> Jesus said, "Feed my sheep. Very truly I tell you, when you were younger you dressed yourself and went where you wanted; but when you are old you will stretch out your hands, and someone else will dress you and lead you where you do not want to go." Jesus said this to indicate the kind of death by which Peter would glorify God. Then he said to him, "Follow me!"

I am afraid many of us read this as a story of Jesus shaming Simon Peter, reminding Simon Peter of his betrayal and then giving Simon Peter his punishment. Instead, I believe this is a story of reconciliation, of Jesus assuring Simon Peter of his love. By telling Simon Peter how he will die, he tells Simon Peter that he will be with him, that even in death Simon Peter will never be abandoned by Jesus. It's a tender moment, not an alpha moment, just as when Jesus tells Thomas he may put his hand into Jesus' pierced side. This was not to shame Thomas, but to help him believe. We so often put ourselves in the center of the drama, when Jesus was always thinking about others.

Jesus' life testifies to a concern for the lives and physical deaths of others, even as he was on his way to his own death. He told his disciple to put away his sword, and healed the ear of a man who would take him to his death. Bearing his cross, he looked at his mother and the "disciple he loved" and thought of how his death would leave them, and entrusted them to each other's care. On the cross, he asked that his Father forgive those who put him there. On the cross, as a thief feared his own death, Jesus spoke through anguish to offer consolation and salvation.

—

Our political culture is sick with self-expression and a self-interested pursuit of power that masquerades as civic contribution. This sickness is not as developed for most Americans as it is for its greatest purveyors, but that is part of the problem. Many Americans are so fatigued with the political atmosphere that their attitude to politics boils down to self-satisfied rejection. There are many who become so exhausted by a culture intended either to convert them or grind them down that they become limp in their convictions.

There was no widespread outcry for stay-at-home orders and restrictions to be lifted. As of late May, 83 percent of Americans were concerned loosening restrictions would lead to a second wave of infections. They were betrayed by elected officials, yes, but that explanation is both insufficient and a practical dead-end. Those elected officials were simply more certain they would be held accountable by special interests and a vocal, active, and organized fringe than they would be by an exhausted, disengaged majority.

Our political problem is not simply a function of those who haven't thought about their own deaths, but of those who aren't motivated by the death of others. Our political problem is that we have a system that requires tremendous energy to be heard, and a citizenry that cannot find the energy, resources, and will to be heard. At some point, we must question the conventional wisdom that the stratification and sophistication of media, including social media, has been a neutral democratizing force, and instead ask whether it has empowered and incentivized unrepresentative voices at the cost of a representative politics. We should ask the question now, while we still can, before we become so limited by the extremes in our politics that we can't imagine there are any other options.

Watch the Republican governor of North Dakota plead through tears, marshaling great rhetorical tools of persuasion, that citizens not assume a person wearing a mask in public is sending a political message of antagonism but consider that they might have a five-year-old at home who is at risk of death if they are infected with the Covid-19 virus. How can our politicians gain trust and respect as experts when our politics is so stupid? When a governor of a state has to explain to grown adults, citizens, that they should prioritize the safety of vulnerable children over their discomfort at the sight of a mask, I'm not sure a mere change in political leadership is sufficient to the challenge. No, our political narcissism is now institutional and systemic, and deeper reform is needed.

Why is the primary response our political system can muster to a man dying at the hands of police in Minneapolis the rejection of the Confederate flag, which apparently required nine people dying in a church basement in Charleston five years earlier for South Carolina politicians to finally agree to take it down from the state capitol building?

Here is where federal reform that would actually be responsive to the millions who have protested following the killings of Ahmaud Arbery, Breonna Taylor, and George Floyd sits today: Senator Mitch McConnell charged Senator Tim Scott with drafting legislation without Democratic input in the Senate. Speaker Nancy Pelosi held a vote on legislation drafted only by Democrats that they knew had no chance of becoming law. Democrats in the Senate refused to negotiate with Senator Scott, contending his bill was not robust enough. That assessment is valid; I agree with it. But I would also note that Senator Scott's bill includes provisions Democrats believed were important enough to include in their own bill.

It is now doubtful Congress will pass any legislation in response to the clear injustice that has grabbed the attention of the people. Correction: Juneteenth is still on the table. What a predictably American way to commemorate a history of racism in this nation, to respond to black death with kente cloth and a holiday.

How is inaction preferable to insufficient action? With political will so fleeting, the attention span of politicians and the people so short, can we really afford to wait until another election, in the hope that we'll be more empowered, not less, come January? Is this political gamesmanship commensurate with the moral gravity of the moment?

Our politics can muddle any clear intention. You see, the political insiders tell us, it is really for the best that we don't pass any federal reforms now, when there is political will to do so. In order to pass federal legislation addressing police brutality, the best course of action is to raise money for political campaigns that will promise to pass reform, and also raise money for the advocacy groups that will ensure those politicians we elect will pass reforms. What's the cost of waiting? We won't know for sure, because the national database of police use of force that is in Senator Scott's bill that Democrats won't negotiate on, which is also in the Democrats' bill, won't see the light of day until the right tragedy meets the right expression meets the right constellation of politicians who are in power to take the right amount of credit for the reform.

The expressive drives American politics right now, at least when it comes to the terms of debate. When the American people actually get to vote, like in the Democratic primary, it's more of an even contest.

One reason our politics is now so driven by executive action and legal balancing tests is that this mode of "governing" is sustained by personalities. Once a bill becomes law, that's it. That work is done, and there is no more symbolism to extract from it. The expression is expressed. Once it is law, the debate over it is dead. A new debate might emerge, but that debate now must consider a new feature. A new word has been spoken, and it stands on its own. How frustrating that is for those who prefer to talk without ceasing, without ever really saying anything at all.

—

It is exhausting – this political culture that responds most readily to those who find in politics an ultimate arbiter of meaning, who view politics as a forum for their inexhaustible expressions—but if anything is to change, the exhausted must choose to act. As citizens, we hold an office we cannot leave vacant. As Christians, for those who are Christian, we must identify the harm our politics is causing and the harm our politics is unwilling to rectify, and recognize that our capacity as citizens paired with our obligations to our neighbors require us to act. Our actions might prove insufficient, but in a pluralistic democracy like ours, we are not held accountable for outcomes but inputs. Ideally, all citizens can come to the public square fully as themselves. This is not in contradiction to the idea that citizens, and especially Christians, ought not come to politics only for themselves as individuals. Our political participation should be grounded in our perspective and our convictions, yes, but our political convictions are a different thing than merely our personal preferences, affections, interests, loves, and hatreds made public. This is not relativism; it is discernment. And the Christian faith offers tremendous resources for our actions in a pluralistic society, and for the society we live in itself. We must act for the good of our neighbors, the good of our politics, and hope that, by the grace of God, our actions accomplish some good.

For this to happen, we, the exhausted, must institutionalize. We must coordinate. We must invest. We are exhausted because we shout into the wind with no plan, alone, and are disappointed when the wind does not return to us with a reply. Politicians cannot respond to incentives that are never presented to them. Institutions respond to those who are active participants in them, not silent bystanders who express their displeasure through cold shoulders and disappointed scowls.

The exhausted must know what they believe, and actually believe they have something to offer the public. They must affirm truths, not just sigh when they hear falsehoods.

The exhausted must recognize they are exhausted because politics is demanding from them what it does not deserve, and distracting them from providing what it needs. When we refuse to grant politics' claim as a source of affirmation and forum for unmediated self-expression, we'll have space and energy to view politics as a forum for the mediated pursuit of the common good. This pursuit will be healthier once we acknowledge that our political convictions, our convictions about how to advance justice and affirm human dignity in our politics, are imperfect and prudential. We pursue right as we see it, but we assume we could be wrong, and therefore our political participation will always be tinged with enough ambivalence that we can act in politics with integrity, and treat those with whom we disagree with dignity.

The exhausted must stop looking to politics for motivation, and find their motivation elsewhere. Politics cannot be the source of our action, only the object. We must refuse politics' claim as ultimate, while also refusing to cede politics to those who make an idol of it.

We must die to our ourselves, to our nonsensical desire for a politics that is just our own, so that we can see and act in politics as it is, in a way that is free to reflect concern for others as well.

On the night before his death, Reverend Martin Luther King Jr. called for something like this, what he called "dangerous unselfishness." He told those gathered about the good Samaritan. Here, he sought to empathize with the priest and the Levite who passed the man on the other side of the road. He imagines not just cold indifference, ignorant, but that the priest and the Levite were conflicted.

> And you know, it's possible that the priest and the Levite looked over at that man on the ground and wondered if the robbers were still around. Or it's possible that they felt that the man on the ground was merely faking. And he was acting like he had been robbed and hurt, in order to seize them over there, lure them there for quick and easy seizure. And so the first question that the Levite asked was, "If I stop to help this man, what will happen to me?" But then the Good Samaritan came by. And he reversed the question: "If I do not stop to help this man, what will happen to him?"

What King describes here is the moral paralysis of refusing to address the injustice in front of us because of uncertainty about what would follow. I am not advising here a reckless politics; I have already cautioned about a dogmatic politics that fails to consider the potential costs of pursuing a particular agenda. But you will notice that dogma is rarely accompanied by a concern for others' interest and perspective. The issue here is not whether citizens and policymakers should react recklessly to whatever injustice seems most pressing without concern for the consequences. The issue is whether we allow *the possibility of unintended consequences that would more directly affect ourselves* to override whatever motivation we might have to alleviate an injustice that more directly affects someone else. Does the mere imagining of harm falling to us prevent us from intervening in a real injustice we know is happening today?

—

In April, a story circulated about the Catholic Archdiocese of Chicago. Priests had stepped forward to volunteer to offer final rites to dying coronavirus patients. Some hailed their actions with similar language as was used to praise those who defied convention to wear a mask. Here, too, were people who weren't going to let fear over a virus get in the way of doing something they wanted to do. But, of course, the nature and context of what these priests did is far different. Their confidence in Christ was not used as justification to act in a way that put their neighbors at risk. Quite the opposite – it was because of their security in Jesus that they had the freedom to sacrifice in the service of others who faced death. "Though I walk through the valley of the shadow of death, I shall fear no evil. For you are with me." Christians never welcome death on its own, for this is a very rejection of life. But to walk where death might be in order to follow God – like David, like the disciples following Jesus to Judea even as they did not understand what would happen or what Jesus intended – this is to embrace life to its fullest.

I have been thinking about one death in particular over these past few months. Rev. Joseph Echols Lowery helped found the Southern Christian Leadership Conference (SCLC), served as its vice president under Rev. Martin Luther King Jr., and served as the SCLC's third president. The SCLC is arguably the most powerful, explicitly Christian organization for human rights and justice in the history of this nation. Lowery was there in Montgomery for the bus boycott. He was the person who presented the demands to Governor Wallace from the "Bloody Sunday" march. He was one of the principal American voices against apartheid in South Africa. He delivered the benediction at President Obama's first inaugural, and was awarded the Presidential Medal of Freedom in 2009.

In his book *Bearing the Cross*, David Garrow wrote of Lowery that he was "the most prominent survivor" of the civil rights movement, "the human and symbolic link going all the way back."

Lowery died on March 27, 2020. Had he passed during any other time, the city of Atlanta would have been consumed with honoring this man even more than it already has. (A street is named in his honor, and Atlanta's mayor ordered flags at half-staff in the wake of his death.) Had he not passed during a pandemic, he would have been honored as Billy Graham was, laid in honor at the capitol. Had he passed during the presidency of any person with the slightest sense of history, of honor, Lowery would have been honored from the Rose Garden, perhaps — with some expression of gratitude and recognition from the president of the United States.

I knew Lowery, and had the tremendous blessing of spending significant time with him over the last twelve years. My personal sadness over his death has mingled with a public sadness. I have been quite sad that Lowery's name has not been on everyone's lips. I have wondered where the inexpressible mourning will go, as I believe it must go somewhere. The dead always leave a trace.

There's a story about Lowery that has helped me.

The run-up to Bloody Sunday in March, 1965, was a difficult season for King. He was physically tired. He was tired of fundraising. He was off the highs of the Civil Rights Act, but he was now back in Alabama, where his first major action took place a decade earlier. The FBI had notified him of the most serious threat on his life up until that point, and had urged him to take much greater precautions in his travels. Malcolm X had been assassinated. Jimmie Lee Jackson had been murdered.

It was Jackson's funeral that brought King to Alabama on March 3. (Bloody Sunday was March 7.) Jackson was murdered by an Alabama state trooper during a peaceful, nonviolent protest for voting rights. He was a civil rights activist and deacon in his Baptist church. Garrow describes the scene:

> King returned to Alabama on Wednesday to attend Jimmie Lee Jackson's funeral. He preached at the memorial service and led a procession of some one thousand mourners through the rain to Jackson's grave site. The constant death threats and the reminders of Malcolm's and Jackson's violent ends, had put King in a morbid state of mind. As the march started out for the cemetery, King beckoned SCLC board member Joseph Lowery to come with him. "Come on, walk with me, Joe. This may be my last walk," King remarked in a bantering tone that did not conceal the concern underlying it.

"Come on, walk with me, Joe. This may be my last walk."

Might we consider our political participation less as an opportunity to express and advance our personal interest, and more as an opportunity to come alongside those who face death, those whose backs are against the wall? Will we walk in our politics without thinking of only ourselves, but the death and injustice around us?

There was a time when Jesus' "soul was overwhelmed with sorrow to the point of death." He went to pray, taking several disciples with him, and asked them to keep watch with him. They could not. While Jesus stared death in the face, the disciples slept.

I know many of you are exhausted. We are exhausted because we believe our life is our own, and that politics is ours to manage and control. But in politics, as in all things, our call is to be faithful. To stay awake. To walk with those who face injustice. To stop obsessing over our feelings, our interests, our tribe, and to consider that politics in a pluralistic society just will not work if that is what guides us. Clearly, we see that now. We can trust in Jesus in the political realm, like any other. Jesus, whose death matters. Whose life matters.

ALRIGHT

DANTÉ STEWART

I look then at the silly walls
Through dark eyes in a dark face—
And this is what I know:
That all these walls oppression builds
Will have to go!

I look at my own body
With eyes no longer blind—
And I see that my own hands can make
The world that's in my mind.
Then let us hurry, comrades,
The road to find.
> —Langston Hughes, "I look at the world"

N—, we gon' be alright
N—, we gon' be alright
We gon' be alright
Do you hear me, do you feel me? We gon' be alright.
> —Kendrick Lamar, "Alright"

AS A KID, I grew up in the Pentecostal church. The kind of church that was caught up in the rapture of Spirit-filled moments: Sister Debby shouting Psalm 23 before testimony service, Bishop Thorton's

---

DANTÉ STEWART is a writer and speaker. He is currently studying at the Candler School of Theology at Emory University. You can reach him at www.dantecstewart.com.

yell, Deacon Black's off-key singing that somehow always made someone shout because it was sung from deep honesty, humility. There was something about this space, this gathering of the "left-out ones" in society, that was incredibly transformative for me.

I was one of those kids who had a deep respect for the preacher. When the sermon was on the way to its crescendo – what Black folks call the *whoop* – I would imitate him. I would grab the Martin Luther King fan my mom had sitting beside me, rip off Martin's precious and stern face, throw my hand on my hip as I moved my oversized jacket, and I did it: I was caught up in this moment of ecstasy. While in this moment of lostness, you couldn't tell me that I wasn't preaching to my own congregation. There I was, young, preaching, free. Maybe that was the meaning. Maybe that was where I found my deep love for justice, blackness, liberation. *Dreams.*

I often think about those years, especially now that I'm older. The Pentecostal church. The people. The intimacy. Why were they so caught up in praise? What was it about this space that did that? What was this sort of mysticism? I don't know if I know the answers to that, but I do know that something struck me more than anything: the *joy.*

I wonder if today this is a part of what we are missing – narrating joy. As we are living in what Professor Elizabeth Alexander calls "the Trayvon generation," she writes that we know the stories of violence visited on Black flesh, that "anti-black hatred and violence were never far." We understand what white supremacy will do to us: It will kill us. Slowly. Violently. Publicly. It is, as Langston Hughes writes, the walls oppression builds. Sturdy. Seemingly impenetrable.

It forces us into resilience. It is not normal. No people should be *forced.* There is a certain type of depression that descends upon those forced to deal with the tragic conditions to which Black people are subjected in this country. In this moment of struggle, it becomes critical – I would even say spiritual, moral, and political – to narrate and normalize Black joy in the face of brutality.

Blackness as a place of joy in this moment is not simply found in public protest, bodies being on the line, baby girls screaming "No justice, no peace!" It is also found in a moment of intimacy. Even as protest is still going on, reading *this* moment, reading ourselves as the site of joy is revolutionary. It is not simply resistance; it is also power.

"The intent here is not to disregard these terms," Kevin Quashie writes, "but to ask what else—what else can we say about black culture, what other frameworks might help to illuminate aspects of works produced by black writers and thinkers?"

This brings to mind Kendrick Lamar. I've been playing "Alright" on repeat. There is something profoundly joyful, even powerful, about being all right in the midst of brutality. It is hope. It is Black joy in an anti-Black world. Alexander reflects deeply on the meaning of Lamar's ode to freedom—an epistle of love, of liberation. She writes, "'Alright' has been the anthem of many protests against racism and police violence and unjust treatment." It is spiritual for my generation.

The young one flying in Lamar's video is "joyful and defiant, rising above the streets that might claim him, his body liberated and autonomous." To be free is not simply an affirmation but a living expression, a discipline, a practice, a dance. It is profoundly spiritual.

Then things change: a police officer raises a finger to the young man in the sky and pulls the trigger.

The one flying falls—like Maya Angelou's caged bird—and lands. "The gun was a finger; the flying young man appears safe," Alexander writes. "He does not get up." In the end of what she calls "this dream," the young one opens his eyes, smiles. Death? No. Life. "Black celebration," Alexander concludes, "is a village practice that has brought us together in protest and ecstasy around the globe and across time." Joy is a weapon of love. Blackness is beautiful, free. Powerful. Lovely.

Alexander reminds us that Black creativity was born out of response to an anti-Black world. To stand in the face of danger, to hold on to one's imagination of a better world, to hope in the midst of unbearable social suffering, to remember one's dead in a world that forgets—these become *gospel* to a people bent and broken. "Theology cannot, must not," M. Shawn Copeland writes, "remain silent or complicit before the suffering of a crucified world and the suffering of God's crucified people." Creative responses to such suffering, the Black artist's imagination, "evokes our integrity, calls us to responsibility for one another, calls us to entrust our lives to the dangerous Jesus."

In this moment, there is a profound intimacy. The beauty of this moment shows that suffering is not the total image. This is a moment of faith. What is compelling is the unexpected glimpse we get of the inner dimensions of public bravery – the willingness to rise again. There is something about Lamar's song and image that calls out to us to sit still and be brave; it calls us to quiet anticipation of something beyond brutality. But the call to quiet is not resignation to the chaos or confusion of life. It is a call to radical faith in the midst of darkness. It is a call to joy. It is joy, as Malcolm X would say, "by any means necessary."

This serene moment tells a story. Inside of this song are the hopes, the dreams, the freedom of those bound. It is joy unspeakable. Mary's Magnificat has become our own: He has brought down the mighty from their thrones, and lifted up the lowly. He has kept the promise he made to our ancestors. The Black body is loved by a God who stands in Christ with us in a loveless world, in the midst of tears, rage, death, oppression – a God who promises to shepherd us, strengthen our resolve, liberate the world to beauty. For that is the Christian story. "The Christian story," Eboni Marshall Turman shares, "is that despite the coming of death, there is resurrection, there is life. There is an afterword. There is joy. That is Black joy."

This joy is love in a dance with reality, humanity. It is the complex and complicated relationship with hope, a tragic but necessary one if it is to be what it can become – beautiful. If there is resistance, it is resistance found in the quiet places of our interior lives, the space where the divine reaches out to us to rest our weary bodies. When Jesus says that those who come to him will find rest, I often wonder what rest looks like for bodies suffocated in the brutality of white violence and racial terror. Is Jesus' rest a sort of apathy to our dignity?

No. He must have meant that rest is both achievable as well as a noble journey – a journey of deep meaning, ultimate concern, and hope-filled compassion. It is a journey that is able to hold in one place our rage, our hopes, our failures, our pain, our love. It moves beyond seeing life – Black life – as one focused ultimately on whiteness and its violence, as if whiteness can save us. It cannot. It will not. The news is not good; it is hell. No. This joy sings in a world in which one is bound. It dances. It is free.

It's like the freedom of the Black body that Baby Suggs speaks of when she preaches in Toni Morrison's *Beloved*: "Here in this here place, we flesh; flesh that weeps, laughs; flesh that dances on bare feet in the grass." It's the taste of liberation that the spirituals speak of when they sing, "Freedom, oh freedom / Oh freedom ova me!" even though freedom is at a distance. It is Lamar smiling after rising again, asking us, "Do you hear me, do you feel me?" Such a question is not meant to be answered; it is rhetorical. It is a reminder that *we gon' be alright*. Flesh – Black flesh – gon' be alright. These are both sorrow songs and lyrical protest, the spirituals and the blues.

As Alexander writes of her sons (and us), "They are beautiful. They are funny. They are strong. They are fascinating. They are kind. They are joyful in friendship and community. They are righteous and smart in their politics. They are learning. They are loving. They are mighty and alive." They are us, we are them.

We continue to struggle because we are free – even if we're bound. Our very public protest for our freedom is beauty. If beauty, as Fyodor Dostoyevsky noted, will save the world, then our Black is beautiful. It is profoundly spiritual. Black joy in an anti-Black world is revolutionary.

Maybe the Pentecostals I grew up around knew something: It is a journey that does not end. Many of the old Pentecostals have gone on, and I'm not a kid anymore. But they left me with something: They left me the power of joy. They left me knowing that the unexpected is possible.

These Pentecostals knew that we come from a long tradition of Black people who refused to accept the tragic belief and practices of white supremacy – the belief that we are second-class citizens, that we deserve exploitation and punishment, that we deserve disrespect and death, that we must be respectable and cater to the demands of whiteness. Finding joy, though it may be elusive, becomes a great spiritual, moral, and political task in each generation. They knew each day, it begins again.

It is this refusal, this courageous act of imagining a world that has never been, that has kept us going. It is impossible for a people to endure such gross injustice without dreaming a little. Yes, people speak of King's dream of '63. But since then, for us, it has been a nightmare. Yet we refuse to stop dreaming. It is our dreams that allow us to imagine the possible, to be critical of the present, and to press toward a future in which love and justice are the guiding principles of a more perfect union, a real democracy.

In this vision to shape a new world, a sort of resurrection, it is our artists, healers, and revolutionaries that we need. In their creativity, our artists keep hope alive by exposing the myths and keeping us planted in reality, but dreaming of a day when life is made new. In their willingness to mend that which is broken, our healers take us to the place where people are wounded and broken believing that which is lost can be restored again. In their willingness to deconstruct the oppressive, our revolutionaries keep our eyes on the social suffering of God's creation, showing us the way of solidarity to break the bonds of segregation, violence, and showing us how to build a life together that is just. To affirm one's worth – not simply in the eyes of God, but also in the eyes of our society – is to scream from our souls, "Black Lives Matter!" It is to imagine the possibility of a future where Black life is not only present but also powerful. As Robin D. G. Kelley writes, "We must tap the well of our own collective imaginations, that we do what earlier generations have done: dream."

Our tapping, affirming begins again each day: Black. Brilliant. Beautiful. It is our dreaming. Dreaming for ourselves and our children. We must remember: what we have endured does not tell of our worth, as James Baldwin would say, but it tells of others' inhumanity and fear. In this moment of reconstruction, I believe with Baldwin that "though we do not wholly believe it yet, the interior life is a real life, and the intangible dreams of people have a tangible effect on the world." How we dream today determines the world we see tomorrow. I just pray to God that we can dream again.

When you experience such inhumanity, the language of hope must be reimagined. It is not a celebration. It is not a theory. Nor is it even a point. It is a practice, a muscle, a discipline, a profound commitment to one's future beyond resistance. It is to have in one's body, in its movements, in its place, that which we dream of.

Hope is not content with the world as it is, as if it is the world that God wants. Hope, at least for us, has been the willingness to never give up on ourselves, God, or even our country. At every moment in history we have given up so much for a place and people who have not loved us back. At every moment in history, our people have had a deep love for this country. This country is ours—flaws and all. That we are still here is not a testament of the moral goodness of America, this type of passionate pursuit of a more democratic world. No. It is that Black people have been willing to stare in the face of white supremacy, anti-Blackness, economic injustice, and the tragic belief experience of second-class citizenship, and have the will to survive in spite of it.

I recall artist Whitfield Lovell's series "Kin" capturing this reality. Lovell, embodying the role of a revolutionary healer, puts in full view the complexity of Black life in America. In the series he pairs his subjects with "found objects, evoking personal memories, ancestral connections, and the collective American past." History, memory, and humanity meet.

In the painting *Our Folks*, you see only the young man's face, no body. It is vintage. It is a story of a time long past but still remembered. His face, resolute, elegant, strong. In his eyes, you can almost see the pain; you feel the piercing gaze as if there is something to be uttered but never mentioned. Around his neck are American flags, a sort of emblem. Worn like jewelry one has not asked for. They are everywhere. Worn, but not choking him. The sites of memory or a memorial of people like him who have long been forgotten. But also, worn as a sign of love. His face, still resolute.

He has Langston Hughes's dark face, dark eyes. He looks at you. Stares, even. You look back. There is intimacy, connection even. I know that look. I have felt that from time to time. The look of anger, wanting to tell of what has happened, but what others see is the country, its goodness, its shiny medallions around one's neck. What story does this young man's eyes tell? There is no grin. Or is there? I look again. This time. I see more than rage. I see more than resistance. I see more. I see him. I see him in all of his dignity. I see myself. I see us. I see our endurance. We both know what we have gone through in this country. But we also know who we are. We know that there is joy. Yes, there is struggle. But there is joy. We both know that there is more to us than what this country has done to us. So he looks back at me; he smiles. I smile too. No, our smiles will not protect us. But we are alive. Life is wide open to possibility. That is hope.

The final word on Black life is not brutality but brilliance, beauty. We see the world; our eyes are no longer blind. We look at our bodies, our hands, and create the world that's in our mind. A world where Blackness is boundless. Love is supreme. For us, it is not only resistance—it is resurrection. The final word? *Alright.* Do you hear? Do you feel me?

WHEN PLACE BECOMES PARAMOUNT

JOE NAIL AND BENYA KRAUS
IN CONVERSATION WITH ANNE SNYDER

Lead for America was founded to try to stem the tide of cities and towns losing talent, soul, and collective pride. It recruits recent college graduates who are game to do the often unpopular thing: return home. A lot of the places where these fellows hail from are considered forgotten. Lead for America refuses to let that be the final story, providing a paid, two-year fellowship that encourages proximate, culturally humbled, and empowering service at all levels of local government and civil society. Breaking Ground's founder, Anne Snyder, sat down with two of LFA's founders to talk about this budding movement and that evocative yet strangely elusive good in modern America: home.

ANNE SNYDER: Tell us a little bit about your origin story. What's the inspiration behind Lead for America? What fundamental problem were you trying to solve?

JOE NAIL is the chief executive officer of Lead for America and one of its co-founders. Before starting LFA, Joe – a UNC Chapel Hill grad and Kansas native – helped found and manage several nonprofit initiatives, including FairEd and the UNC Institute of Politics. Joe also previously served one year as a Congress Bundestag Scholar in Germany, where he first worked in local government.

BENYA KRAUS is a co-founder of Lead for America and the executive director of Lead for Minnesota. A Tufts University graduate hailing from Bangkok and Minnesota, Benya combines her experience as a board member with Amnesty International USA and local community work as a former Minneapolis Urban Scholar to convene local stakeholders around a framework for community development.

JOE NAIL: I grew up with two examples of people participating in public service. My dad works for the military, and my mom is a nurse. So I was around folks who were dedicating their lives to public service before I even realized that was a specific career trajectory.

There have been two big inflection points in my life. One was when I was turning fifteen years old. My dad, who was working as a military contractor, was given an ultimatum: his job was in jeopardy unless he deployed to Afghanistan for a year.

I'd grown up as the middle child of five kids. I'd never really had a position of family responsibility, but all of a sudden my dad was away, my older brother was starting college, and my older sister has a pretty severe intellectual and developmental disability.

So all of a sudden, I started asking questions: Why is it that we don't have the sort of professional care that we need for my sister? Why is it that my dad's deploying to fight in this war that a lot of people may not think actually needs to be fought any longer? And it was really during that year that I started seeing the intersection of public institutions and community. There are these huge public decisions that felt like they were being made in a black box – we don't have a great social safety net for people like my sister; more troops are being deployed – and I could see them for the first time affecting my family in profound ways.

And had it not been for neighbors, community members, et cetera, rallying around us, we would not have been able to get through that year. So that was a fundamental shift in thinking about what I wanted to do with my life. I'd wanted to be an engineer; I was very introverted. But I started thinking that maybe I wanted to do something public-service oriented.

The second moment that led me to Lead for America was leaving high school. I, like many people growing up in Kansas, thought the narrative of success was leaving and never coming back. I did not apply to any colleges in Kansas; I only applied to colleges on either coast. I was dead set on leaving. But I did a year in Germany on a Congress-Bundestag scholarship before starting college. And it was during that year that I started becoming dedicated to the concept of homecoming. I started feeling like I needed to take seriously the things that had allowed me to get to where I was, and I felt an obligation to give back in some way. I felt so far away from home, and at the same time I was thinking through Germany's history of persecution of people like my sister just seventy-five years ago, while I had a front-row seat to see how they're grappling with welcoming a million-plus refugees. It was inspiring.

So I had these two personally and professionally galvanizing moments of being able to see the intersections of public institutions, homecoming, and community-building. And as I was getting through college, I tried to surround myself with other people who've had similar realizations, who had similar goals and aspirations. And I saw the same thing happening over and over again, which is that for many students, those core convictions were only growing over the course of college. But colleges and universities were providing essentially no pathways for people to act on those convictions: no one was encouraged to go home; everyone was supposed to go to the star cities.

It seemed like this was a tragedy on a massive scale, depleting our communities and essential institutions of the most critical resource we have, which is dedicated people.

ANNE: Benya, what inspired you about this mission?

BENYA KRAUS: I met Joe right after I had signed on the dotted line for a two-year commitment to a corporate law firm out in Boston. Lo and behold, here's this guy sliding into my inbox with a one-pager idea saying, Why go to these star cities when you know your heart is connected to a different place? And here was my opportunity.

Home for me – it's a little bit more complicated. I was born and grew up in Bangkok, Thailand. My dad worked for the United Nations. We actually moved around quite a bit. But he is one of nine siblings who grew up on a sixth-generation family farm in Waseca, Minnesota, which is where I'm calling in from now.

We have deep ties to this community, but I grew up untethered. Home and family I loved, but I didn't grow up valuing how deeply important that was. I had a brother who struggled with mental health and addiction; home in many ways is a pretty scary concept for me. A lot of my life was wanting to go elsewhere and to get out. And I went to school out in Boston to study international relations; I was expecting to be living a similar path of moving between cities for the rest of my life. I was on a search to try to understand what my community was, and to somehow carry that with me, until a challenging family situation brought me back to Waseca one summer, and I was reintroduced to this community.

It's a real community, about ten thousand people. In the nineties, a federal penitentiary was established here, and by many Google searches, we were a community in decline. But I was introduced to a lot of things that you can't find via Google searches. There were pockets of possibility everywhere around me.

And yet I felt very lonely in my search to find my way back to Waseca, to find my place. There was a lot of pressure: my family had struggled financially, and my brother's mental health and addiction problems were taking their toll. I felt that I needed to be the one to sustain us, to be the capable, strong one.

And I thought that what capable and strong meant was working at this very prestigious brand-name law firm. I lasted there for about two months, until I realized that there was a deeper pull both to place, to Waseca, and to this problem, this systemic problem: if I couldn't find my way back, many others couldn't either. And what does that mean for the future of our democracy? What it means is that our country is being pulled into two very different Americas: the America of those who leave, and the America of those who stay.

ANNE: What you describe sounds like a conversion into a whole new (and also ancient!) set of values. Has LFA been an easy sell for today's twenty-one- and twenty-two-year-olds? Or a hard sell? What kind of person is drawn to it?

BENYA: We knew there was this innate desire because we had felt it, but a year ago when we first launched, we didn't know which communities or which people we were going to be supporting through this hometown fellowship. We put out this open call and wound up getting eighteen hundred registered applicants. Going into year two, we've received over three thousand registered applicants nationally. We reviewed that first round of applicants in three days, and I remember every single hour of those three days: we were poring through these personal stories and narrative videos of people describing their story, and the story of their community and describing how they intersect. And we had to google a lot of these places – they were not well-known. That was both humbling and exciting: it's clear that we were not alone in our own desire to go home. I think there's a growing movement of young people who are recognizing that there's more to life than the corporate law firms in Boston or New York. There's a hunger to go home – but to go home with purpose, not just to end up back there.

JOE: We have two dynamics that heighten the appeal for those young people who might already be interested. One issue is that the current job market is much more limited than it has been previously. So you see not just with programs like ours, but with all sorts of national service programs, applications increase and decrease in direct correspondence to the tightening or loosening of the job market. And I think the other dynamic is of course coronavirus, and what that's meant for the need that people feel to move home, to be back at home for extended periods of time, often for the first time in a long time.

There's so much happening in the world; things are so unpredictable and fragile: What is my place in this community, within my family, within my street? How can I contribute? How do I distribute medicine or food to elderly folks in my neighborhood or in my hometown? What do I do with the inequalities I'm seeing in how the virus is hitting? How can I be a part of fixing this, in these home places where things are hardest? These questions naturally lend themselves to more people thinking about homecoming or staying in their home communities. But it also presents a unique opportunity for us to be able to perhaps give language or voice or purpose to underlying longings that people may have had for a long time, but then they didn't have the time or space or proximity to actually realize they were there, to respect them.

ANNE: It's almost like you're riding a wave and providing young people with language and a new moral map to understand a different conception of value and belonging.

Benya, you talked about your initial couple months in the corporate law firm. I'm about a dozen years older than you two, but when I was graduating, my peers were very interested in "saving the world," whatever that meant – it was the phrase du jour in commencement addresses all over the land. But the sense of local orientation you're describing was not part of that calculus. And then at some particularly elite schools, there was a status-seeking pecking order, a promise that you're going to find your belonging in an amazing job at an amazing firm, but that that was pretty much the only option to make good on your tuition. Your value and your sense of how you fit into a broader whole had almost nothing to do with place in either case.

I'm struck by a shift toward finding your roots in a much more meaningful, physical, tangible set of relationships. A world of placeless status versus long-term relationships in a geographically defined area sound like two very separate moral systems.

It's also interesting that the values of homecoming, of localism, have often been enshrined in our ideological discourse on the conservative side of the political spectrum: the historically minded intellectual conservatives who love Edmund Burke and Michael Oakeshott – to say nothing of Wendell Berry and the more romantic agrarian thinkers. There's a sense on the part of conservatives that "we are the people who believe in local control and local problem-solving and federalism." But while you strike me as very respectful of that tradition, you seem to be scrambling the usual ideological and demographic categories in terms of who you're attracting and inspiring to return to their hometowns. How intentional has that been? How have you thought about ideological labels around home, roots, the local?

JOE: You use the word "scrambling": that's a really appropriate word. Not just on an organizational level, but also on a personal level. I gave you the personal anecdotes of how I came to want to get the organization off the ground. But what I didn't say was that directly before starting Lead for America, I was having this existential crisis. I was thinking, what do I want to do in the world? What's my place and where can I actually contribute? And so I made this list of what I thought were going to be the seventeen biggest challenges over the course of the twenty-first century. How do we address ecological devastation? How are we going to deal with the development of artificial intelligence? How do we align that with human values? How are we going to avoid nuclear war? Big, big challenges.

So one of the things that we're doing with Lead for America is placing people in local and state government institutions, because if we're going to address any of these challenges, or the current challenges of the racial reckoning and coronavirus, we need to have effective public institutions to be able to address them at scale.

Ideologically, that's pretty traditionally liberal, as opposed to, say, conservative or leftist: We need really effective public institutions. We need people at the local level, sure, but also at the state and federal level. And if we place people at the local level, that's going to be an incredible grounding. People's first experiences can be proximity to serving their closest neighbors and community members. But we also want people who trickle up to the state and federal levels after having had this grounding experience at the local level.

What's been interesting in all this is that as I've had more proximity to the sorts of conservative thinkers you've been talking about, plus change-makers themselves on the ground and our own fellows, I've had my own ideological orientation scrambled. I come from a conservative family. I went to a very liberal institution. But as time goes on, I find myself identifying more as a conservative now than when I started LFA. The reason for that is that as much as you can see the incredible potential of these governmental and public institutions, ultimately, if you don't have the relational foundation and a strong civic fabric, it doesn't matter. Civil society is at the core, even before government. You can provide great schools and economic resources and whatever else, but there still might be this huge chasm of meaning and purpose that you just can't throw dollars at or throw institutional resources at to fix. I worry about us looking at things like childcare, for instance, and thinking that the solution is going to be institutionalizing that more and more, removing care from family and neighborhood structures.

So these are the tensions, but it's good to feel them. There's incredible merit that both sides are bringing to the argument. We have so many fellows who are thinking, okay, I can't make a difference right now at a state or federal level, but I can very much make a difference at the local level. They're coming to see the importance of those Burkean intermediary civic institutions. I think it's been really grounding. But I also recognize the limits of some of those conservative thinkers you mentioned: they don't have the entire picture.

So I've come out of these first couple years stewarding LFA with a lot more humility. These things are so incredibly complicated. When you start diving into some of these issues, you need to come away with a lot of humility about your place in these things: a conviction that, yes, there's a lot we can do, but if you're looking to line yourself up with "left" or "right," neither one of those positions is going to be complete. And if we don't have that healthy tension, both within our community and more broadly across the country, we're never going to make the sort of progress we want to make.

BENYA: It's really interesting to be building Lead for America in partnership with Joe, because we come from different family backgrounds and experiences. I grew up in a more liberal-leaning immediate family, but there's a lot of conservatism in my extended family. And I grew up in a mixed-race family too, and I grew up abroad: in order to get along, I needed to make a lot of space for very different cultures and rituals and norms, and I always had to negotiate those, at every family dinner. There was a lot of cross-translation that needed to happen. I was always trying to reach something capacious: How can we hold it all? And I was always attentive to the way that one side of myself, or one side of my family, might not be held or protected or safeguarded in the same way that the other half might be. I was always aware that my mom and my dad experienced American life quite differently.

I'm not sure what side of any political line that puts me on, but a guiding question in my formative years was, why is it so hard to be fully me? Why is it hard to have my full self seen – my mom fully seen and also my dad fully seen? I did go to a very liberal university as well, and there, in ways that are different from when I'm in Waseca, I also had the experience of not all sides of myself being fully seen. There was always this push and pull.

I am now back in Waseca and I'm building out our next state affiliate, Lead for Minnesota, in my hometown. When I first came back, I went on this listening tour all across the state of Minnesota – thirty small towns in thirty days. And the board of Lead for Minnesota is largely made up of people who gave me their couches or spare bedrooms while I was on that listening tour. I've gotten to know them on a really intimate level; the mix of people who are guiding the creation of Lead for Minnesota is quite varied. Vanessa Goodthunder is bringing an Indigenous perspective: she was also a homecomer; she came back to her reservation and built the first ever Dakota integrated language center and daycare center.

And then I have another good friend, Bruce, who's come home, and he's on the same land that his parents and his grandparents were on as farmers in Redwood Falls, in southwest Minnesota. And it's so interesting hearing their stories – both of them – hearing their ability to speak to our mission, to the importance of homecoming even with totally different lived experiences. They can speak to why investing locally and starting where you live is the greatest impact that you can have. And it's really interesting, too, that, especially now I'm back and rooted in my small town, I have learned so much more about commitment to place from my uncle – he'll take me around our farm and tell me about how our great-great-great-aunt Clophia came in – that's the history to which we are tethered. And I think how incredible it is to feel that deep sense of care – I have to care about this place because so many of my ancestors have been here too.

It's not the same, but these are similar threads to what Vanessa is talking about when she speaks about her Indigenous history with her land: there's that thread of commitment. But it brings in those who are not from here: my mom is from Thailand, but she's coming to Waseca. She's part of a growing immigrant community here in Waseca. And it makes me wonder how we can also share the potency of that commitment to place with people who might not have a great-great-great-aunt Clophia, but they still have the capacity, if they're invited, to care about that place so deeply as well. And a lot of these solutions to the problems that we run into are not really about politics – not partisan politics, not the politics of left and right. It's about, what does Waseca need to thrive?

There are so many creative solutions: sometimes those require public institutions, sometimes they require our church stepping up, sometimes it requires remembering that redistribution of wealth and resources and love doesn't always have to come through a government program: this sharing of what we need with each other can be something that we as communities actually practice and do every day.

I've felt that as I've changed, and learned about my place and my context within it – well, sometimes those changes fall along the fault lines of conservative and liberal values, but most of the time, I don't think they do, at least in the ways that we as a society have come to use those labels, and the judgments that we put on them.

ANNE: "How can we share the potency of the commitment to place?" What a lovely way of framing a viable way to navigate the complexities of pluralism today; that's the American hope right there.

Do you think anything is problematically missing from the "go local, go home" trendlines – whether rhetorical or lived?

BENYA: I think especially in small towns, we can struggle to make space to talk and really grapple with larger, often unpleasant realities of power imbalances, of the darker sides of history. There is this beautiful small-town pride, pride of place, and as a country, we'd be better if we all had that sense of local ownership to which our identity is tied. But what can be challenging is that if there is truth being told that does not fit the narrative of that pride, of the good community, it can be hard to hear – there's this sense of, "What do you mean? I've experienced this community in a way where my neighbors have *absolutely* cared for me, I *do* feel safe walking around!" That experience is real. So to hear someone who might not have that experience because of their racial or religious identity, if they differ from the dominant identity in that place, it can come across as very personally devastating, like a gut punch – "What do you mean? My community isn't that way?" And those are really tough feelings to have, but I think they make us stronger, more resilient, as we have those conversions, as we're honest about the reality of all these experiences, and work through to a sense of pride that is also humble and can change.

Some time ago, my uncle took me on a walk through our farm and we stood on top of Blower's Field, which is the highest point on our family farm. He talked about the generations that have stewarded this land before us. I am intentional about using the word "stewardship": what I've learned from farming is that to do it right, you have to be planning for the future generations. One version of what happens when you have a conversation like that is that you hear about your ancestors on their place, and your takeaway is that this land is mine and I'm going to do everything I can to preserve it.

But what I have actually learned from my family and from so many farmers across Minnesota is that this land is not necessarily mine. It is for future generations. It is for my community, and I have the blessing to hold on to it now. But how can I seed it, how can I sow seeds into it, so that when it is time for harvest, whoever comes after me has way more to harvest?

I think for our small towns to survive for that future harvest, we need to be sowing seeds that allow more people to be able to come and harvest the goodness of that land. And as you think about great-great-great-aunt Clophia as you stand on Blower's Hill, if you look closely, you'll also see that there are dart heads from the Native people that were here before. So that is there too, when I stand on Blower's Hill: it's a place of genocide, of people whose ability to steward their land was taken away. And that is a hard, hard history that does not fit neatly into the true and beautiful story of my family being stewards to the land. But I have to hold the violence of that narrative too. And we do have to tell those truths if we are to be better stewards moving forward.

ANNE: I love the pasture images that you're using: you're speaking both literally in an agrarian context and figuratively. A number of years ago, I found myself drawn to communities that had this porousness about them. They were open to outsiders, they were open with their way of life, but they were also culturally rich and morally thick. We're suspicious of Winthrop's phrase these days, the "city on a hill," but these places were like mini cities on a hill: communities filled with light. They cross all sectors and different ways of life. So as I studied these kinds of luminous organizations and social collectives, a phrase hit me: within each of them, there's at least one shepherd, a community shepherd. One who tends. One who is trusted.

I do think of you guys as building an army of community shepherds. The metaphor sounds aggressive, I know, but there is an element of war here – a war on social isolation, on disenchantment, on complacency, on distrust. There's such dire need for what you're offering. But then there's the shepherd element: someone gentle and tender and protective. I think we need to consider the possibility that these kinds of people will not just be honored quietly, which is usually how it should be, but perhaps recognized more publicly, even, some of them, paid full time to do that tending role, that place-based, long-term-committed, carefully attending role. How does that strike you? Does that resonate with LFA's ultimate goals?

JOE: You mentioned Wendell Berry earlier. I've had long debates with other LFA team members and friends about what, from the perspective of community and village life, were the best times to be alive. I've lived for extended periods of time in villages in Sierra Leone and Indonesia, and I don't want to romanticize the incredible inequities in economics and opportunities between countries. Obviously what we've done so successfully in the Western world is to build incredible wealth.

But there's a cost. And part of that cost is that so much decision-making is out of your hands, and the proximity that you have to basic questions is really reduced. Where is my food coming from? Where's my water coming from? Where are my clothes coming from? If something goes wrong, do I go to a neighbor?

Am I building relationships? Or is the experience the impersonal one of filing an unemployment claim or filing an insurance claim? We've been so effective as a society at being able to meet these sorts of challenges by systematizing our response to them. But the messy, slow, deliberative process of relationship-building has been sacrificed on the altar of efficiency and interchangeability.

It's a real boiling-the-frog thing. I don't think we realized until very recently that we actually have a relational and a social capital problem. But now, all of a sudden, we're starting to see some real cracks in the livability of our system. It's no longer possible for a family to subsist on a single wage-earner's income. We no longer have direct proximity to our neighbors. We're now surrounded by more people who are like us, but people no longer feel comfortable having their kids walk to and from school together. All of these small changes ultimately make a big difference. And the cat's out of the bag—we can't just pretend that we're just going to reverse everything and go back to a village life, an agrarian lifestyle.

So then you start thinking, okay, how do we use the tools that are at our disposal, the tools that have already proved effective in addressing some of our challenges and eliminating suffering? There are some basic economic tools that we might still be able to employ. For example, in Elizabeth Warren's book *The Two-Income Trap*, she talks about the need to strengthen families by having either the mother or the father be able to provide for the family on a single income, so that we are not all so incredibly stretched all the time, so that we're not outsourcing the raising of our families, so that we have the energy, as families, to be active community members. We need to recognize that raising a family in that way is actually incredibly valuable, not just for the family itself, but for the community and for society as a whole.

So how can we get there? Well, obviously there are proposals around universal basic income, there are proposals about child care, but it also just boils down to us doing a better job at the family and community level of inculcating those values and those skills of family living and community living, holding up as people to emulate those who are doing the hard and really important work of community-weaving. How do we make these the celebrities, the superstars? As a national culture, we've celebrated people who are achieving extraordinary success while sacrificing building the deep relationships that are necessary for fulfilling sustainable human lives, embedded in family and community, and that success often leaves them feeling empty.

Until we stop and think about what our economic structures are rewarding, until we start being thoughtful about what stories and lives we raise up as "the good life," until we take into account aspects of the good life that go beyond pure classical "achievement," I think we're going to struggle.

We need to be humble about this. There's not going to be any one-size-fits-all solution. We have to address some of the economic indicators. Absolutely we should have more national service programs. We should have a network of community shepherds whose full-time job is to build the relational foundations of these neighborhood bonds. But ultimately it's also a lot about culture and what we actually signal as being really important.

ANNE: Let's wrap up by talking about the whole person. Our mutual friend Mack McCarter defines a whole person as someone who is both competent and compassionate. And then there is what I often say, which is that a whole person has matured into full integration: head, heart and helping hand.

I think we all yearn for this, to be growing, integrated people throughout our lives. But what's extra special is that a whole person never operates alone. By definition, they are interdependent with others; they're contributing to sowing and to bearing and to reaping the fruits of a whole community. How are you promoting that wholeness in your fellows? What are the rituals and the webs of support that help them develop both the qualities of character and the relationships that are necessary to help them be whole?

BENYA: A huge piece of the Lead for America experience is the rich training we provide, and all the support structures we've put in place. We've found ourselves building on a lot of Indigenous practices. We've drawn from the Anishinaabe idea of the Grandfather Teachings; we've focused on the image of balance, of the interweaving of things that sometimes seem to be at tension with each other. The heart of convergent leadership is trying to exist at the convergence of work that we do on ourselves and the work that we do in and for our community. We weave those into a practice of service and of a search for possibilities. We also have four pillars that we focus on, which are interconnected: foresight, innovation, service, and justice. We have a network of mentors who our fellows learn from, and we find that helping fellows balance their work is really important: you might have someone who's really strong on innovation, but we need to strengthen and balance that with service, which calls you to be proximate, to be grounded.

The more we can expose fellows to the deep tensions and sometimes contradictions of ways of knowing and doing and building community, the stronger their practice becomes.

JOE: One of the simplest concepts we have is that we encourage people to not always see relationships or mentorships instrumentally, through the lens of "How do I get to a specific place?" but rather treating them as an end in and of themselves. Service at its very best decenters the self: you put something else—your community, your faith—at the center. You say, you know what? It's not about me. Rather, I need to ask how I can be of service. I don't think that we can do that at a systems level or in national politics if we don't do that on a daily basis in terms of our practices and our habits.

No matter what we do, we're going to be interacting with so many people who don't have any transactional value to our own needs and wants. We need to commit to seeing their value, because you can't shortcut character: you really need to see others as this immense, impossible-to-define source of value. That's the challenge: How do we really live into that concept of loving our neighbor? How do you have that not be a slogan but rather something that at each and every moment, each and every day, in each and every interaction, that is the thing you're holding on to and using to guide your interactions?

ANNE: On that note, I want to thank both. You each embody what it is to be and pursue wholeness, not just as individuals, but towards the commons. I wish you every success in that long endeavor.

BENYA: It's people like you, with all the work that you put out into the world, who have paved the way for us to have language to be able to describe so many of these things.

JOE: Truly, thank you. It's been a pleasure.

AUTUMN

PATRICK TOMASSI

AMY JULIA BECKER

JEFFREY BILBRO

MARILYNNE ROBINSON

CHERIE HARDER

JOEL HALLDORF

IRENA DRAGAŠ JANSEN

KATHERINE BOYLE

L. M. SACASAS

JAKE MEADOR

JOSHUA BOMBINO

CHELSEA LANGSTON BOMBINO

PORTLAND

On the Ground

PATRICK TOMASSI

ON A HOT Tuesday evening in the end of June, I sat at the desk in my upstairs bedroom and discussed the current political situation with a couple of my former students over Zoom. The sounds of the neighborhood – crickets, car horns, and people chatting – drifted in through the open window next to me. Suddenly, an amplified voice joined the other sounds – "This has been deemed an unlawful disturbance. Disperse immediately" – so loudly that I thought it was coming from the neighbor's backyard. I closed the window, and we put the conversation on hold to find out what was going on.

My house is near the Kenton neighborhood in North Portland, a few blocks from the building that houses the Portland Police Association, the union that represents police officers in Portland. That night was the first time I realized there were protests in my area.

Soon, Portland's protests were the focus of national and international news, after federal law enforcement was sent here to protect the federal courthouse. I started getting texts from friends in other parts of the country – "Are you okay?" "What's it like?!" Liberal friends wondered if we were being rounded up by the Gestapo. Conservative friends wanted to know if Antifa were burning our houses down.

PATRICK TOMASSI is a teacher and writer in Portland, Oregon, his native city. He helps organize the annual New York Encounter and is a contributing editor at *Veritas Journal*.

But if it had not been for the disrupted Zoom call, I would hardly have known from my experience that there was civil unrest at all. Even relatives who live here were getting their information mostly from social media or the national news. After a family argument over whether downtown was in fact a "war zone," it became clear that I would need to find out for myself.

THE JUSTICE CENTER

On a Sunday evening two weeks later, I arrived at the Justice Center around eight o'clock. A crowd of a few hundred stood in front of the building while an older black man with a megaphone addressed the crowd. He spoke about police brutality, and told demonstrators not to light the place on fire. "This building holds black people who have not been convicted of a crime," he said. "Think about who you're hurting if you burn it down." When he was finished, he handed the megaphone to a teenager who told the crowd about the racism he experienced in his rural public high school. Between the speakers, members of the crowd started chants of "No justice, no peace!" and "Black lives matter!" Around me, more people were arriving, carrying gas masks, shields, and goggles. A man walked around writing the number for the National Lawyers Guild on people's arms in Sharpie. After a brief lull, the energy of the crowd picked up again. The "Wall of Moms," then in their second or third night and before the strange coup that occurred within the organization, were marching up the street to join the crowd, wearing their signature yellow and carrying sunflowers. They formed lines and linked arms in a large square, boxing most of the protesters inside.

I had come to the demonstration hoping to interview black protesters about what they thought. But I was finding that there were virtually no black people in the crowd. While I was asking a woman from the Wall of Moms to do an interview, another woman walked up. "Ask a black person!" she told me in frustration. I looked around. "I want to—do you see any?" She paused for a moment, then walked off. The mom decided not to be interviewed. Every now and then, a chant of "black lives matter" would begin again.

An announcement came from the federal courthouse next door. "This is the Federal Protective Service. Do not attempt to breach the fence. If you do, crowd-control measures will be used." The Wall of Moms crumbled on that side, and the entire crowd rushed to the fence in front of the courthouse. A white man in a bulletproof vest pulled down his gas mask to start a chant of "All cops are bastards!" A couple people tried to drown him out with a counterchant of "black lives matter," but gave up. The chants got louder.

An hour later, I found the older black man who had been leading the protest when I arrived. He was standing with his back to the fence, addressing the protesters who were crushing in on all sides. Cans and pieces of trash were being hurled over our heads at the courthouse. "Stop trying to start something!" he shouted. "What does this have to do with black lives?" An older white man was listening to him, nodding his head. The rest of the crowd was ignoring him. A white woman with an army surplus helmet leaned past us to scream "Fuck you!" several times at the federal police.

The white man grabbed my arm. "Do you want to talk about white privilege? Do you want to see white supremacy? *This* is white supremacy," he said.

THE PORTLAND POLICE ASSOCIATION

A month later, a man crashed his car near a protest in downtown Portland. In a moment that was captured on video and shown repeatedly on the news, he was kicked in the head multiple times by a protester, leaving him unconscious. The next night, I went to a protest in my neighborhood. The flier promoting it read "No cops. No prisons. Total abolition." When I arrived at Kenton Park, where the protest began, the air was thick with pot smoke. People milled around in the dark and talked with friends, relaying stories of being chased and gassed by police and federal officers. But the energy and excitement of a month ago was absent.

Much had happened in the intervening month. Tensions had built between federal law enforcement and protesters. Protesters broke windows and set fires on government property. Footage compiled by the *New York Times* showed federal police detaining people in unmarked vans, using teargas, and beating an unarmed and stoic veteran with batons. The protests had grown from hundreds to over ten thousand people, centered on the federal courthouse. After public spats between city and state officials and the Trump administration, the federal officers had been removed from the city, replaced by state police. Then they, too, had been removed. Protesters saw these as victories, signs the movement was succeeding. But members of Portland's black community had begun to more vocally condemn the co-option they were seeing in the protests. The president of the Portland branch of the NAACP referred to what he saw as "White spectacle." It was part of a longer-term pattern. Over the past four years, some have claimed, white far-right provocateurs have targeted Portland and been supported by, or at least inconsistently challenged by, the police; they have been met by primarily white protesters, including some from far-left groups such as Rose City Antifa, and interactions between far-left and far-right groups have often ended violently. The culture of protest here is deeply rooted in the history of the city, and it sometimes feels as though the city has chosen itself as a stage on which to play out the nation's strife.

Just before the crowd began to march, I spoke with the leader, a tall man who identified himself as Matthew. He told me that his goal for the evening was "to be as annoying as possible." He believed that this was needed to get the community to wake up and join the cause. Matthew related the methods of the current protests to those of the civil rights movement. "If you look back at the pictures and see what's going on between the hoses, the dogs, the beatings – that was not a pretty thing because everything [the civil rights activists] were doing was highly illegal." The illegal actions at recent protests, he said, were not so different. He told me that the black leaders who had spoken out against what they were seeing at the protests did not really understand what was happening.

By my headcount, roughly 95 percent of the protesters were white. Matthew and others told me that the whiteness of the protest was reflective of the city's demographics. Portland is indeed very white, but not as white as the crowd – according to the US Census Bureau, 77 percent of the population is white, and only 6 percent is black. And historically black North Portland, where this protest took place, has more black residents than other parts of the city. While the early protests in Portland were very diverse, the ones that I attended were disproportionately white, even by Portland's standards. None of the protesters I spoke to would acknowledge what appeared to be evident: Portland's black community, not just its leaders, was largely absent.

Matthew made an announcement over the megaphone, and the crowd headed down a side street toward the Portland Police Association. Neighbors stood on the sidewalk, videoing the crowd. A couple of local faith leaders prayed over the protest as it passed. Then a chant began somewhere behind me: "What do we want? Justice! When do we want it? Now! If we don't get it? Burn it down!"

Despite the rhetoric, the energy of the crowd remained fairly low. Someone next to me commented that chants needed to be faster. When we arrived at the PPA building, cars had blocked off the street in both directions. Protesters crowded close to the building initially, but when the police didn't materialize they spread out in the open space, smoking, talking to friends, and milling around. A handful of people graffitied the building or attempted to pry off the plywood that had been used to board up the windows. Chants started and fizzled out sporadically. A man bought a couple of boxes of doughnuts at Heavenly Donuts, a twenty-four-hour shop across the street from the PPA building, and brought them around to the crowd. "It's hard being out here," he told me. "These people are out here every night." He said that the people who own the doughnut shop are good people who need the business. "And who doesn't need a sprinkled doughnut when you're trying to change the world?" There were no speeches. Someone plugged in a speaker and started to play a recording of a black woman talking about what it's like to be black in America. Few appeared to be listening. I had the sense that we were all just waiting for something to happen, waiting for the enemy to arrive.

When Joey Gibson, the Irish-Japanese leader of the alt-right-adjacent group Patriot Prayer, by that point a well-known figure in Portland, showed up, it was like someone had turned on the lights. "Do you stand by what happened last night?" he asked through a megaphone he had brought, referring to the attack on the man who crashed his truck. "Go home, Joey!" the crowd responded, following him across the street. Several people held up their phones to livestream the action. Someone threw a Slurpee, which missed Gibson and hit the windshield of a car. A voice from below me and to the left screamed, "Don't touch him!" and a woman tore off through the crowd in her wheelchair, placing herself between Gibson and the rest of the protesters.

"Do you stand by it?" Gibson asked the crowd again. "No," the woman responded. "It should never have happened." After a couple minutes, Gibson walked away from the crowd, covering his eyes with his hands. Apparently someone had maced him. The woman in the wheelchair found water and helped him get the mace out of his eyes, while a few people stood by livestreaming the encounter. At one point, a Latino man walked up and told Gibson that "your racist ass needs to do something." "I'm darker than you!" Gibson responded, holding out his arm. They yelled at each other for several minutes, the other man at one point calling Gibson "a Japanese white fellow that's darker than me."

The woman in the wheelchair was Amanda Siebe, a disability rights activist from Portland. I spoke with her after she finished helping. Gibson get the mace out of his eyes. As we spoke, she smoked a cigar. "The last thing I wanted was more violence," she told me. "If we turn to violence, then the movement is dead. We can't let that happen." She said that Gibson had come to the protest hoping to get hit, so that that would be the headline, and she wasn't going to allow that to happen. She said she felt safe doing what she did, because she knew that the protesters had her back. Although Siebe is white, for her, the protests are personal. "Justice, equality, and dignity aren't necessarily racial things," she told me. "Half of those killed by police are disabled." This number comes from a 2016 meta-analysis; the study notes that in most of these incidents, that disability is psychological or cognitive. If one adds in those who are under the influence of drugs or alcohol, the percentage rises to 81 percent, one study has shown.

I asked Siebe about the lack of black people at the protest. "That reflects our city," she told me. "If you look around what you see here is a lot of people using the white privilege that they have to try to make change for the black community." Siebe said that there were not more black people because of the risk of interacting with the police. "At some point we have to step up as white people and use that white privilege to help protect people."

KENTON PLAZA

A couple of weeks before the protest I attended in Kenton, the businesses along Denver, the main street, began using the road for outdoor seating. The restaurants and coffee shops had been hit hard by the pandemic, and welcomed the opportunity to rebound. The Kenton Business Association raised nearly $15,000 on GoFundMe to convert the space. The approach is called lean urbanism: adapt a space that has been car-focused to make it people-focused, with imagination but with minimal infrastructure changes. It's the same kind of adaptation that cities around the world have made to the virus: suddenly, everywhere is a sidewalk café. City officials placed barricades at the ends of the street to pedestrianize it. Parking spaces were cordoned off and picnic tables with umbrellas set up in them. Residents and local artists painted a colorful pattern over half the road to give it the feel of a plaza, and restaurants set up tables and chairs. Posies Bakery and Cafe, Swift & Union, Po'Shines, Kenton Station, Casa Maya, Fino: local places, working out ways to pull through the crisis, working out ways to keep themselves afloat and keep the neighborhood alive.

Shortly after midnight later that week – it was early in the morning on August 9, on the seventy-third consecutive night of the protests – protesters managed to set a small fire inside the Portland Police Association building, right down the road from the plaza area. It was the second time protesters had done this – as reported by the *Oregonian*, they had punched a hole in the plywood that the police association building had nailed up over its door, and set debris ablaze just inside. Several minutes after this happened, the police declared the gathering a riot, and dozens of officers began pressing the crowd back, using pepper spray and rubber bullets. Protesters retreated as far as the pedestrianized strip along Denver, and barricaded the road more than it had already been barricaded by the city, piling up picnic tables and wooden road signs. Then they lit trash cans on fire, and tossed the stencils that had been used to paint the street on top.

It's important to stress that not all protesters were involved in this—others want no part in this violence. But from what I have seen and what others who were there have told me, the arsonists were drawn from the crowd that was at the PPA building. These night protests are smaller than the largest of Portland's protests from several months ago—there are usually a couple of hundred people per night. But at this point, daytime protests have mostly stopped. What is left is night after night of a similar pattern: the situation between protesters and cops becomes more and more heated until a protester does something bad enough for the cops to declare a riot and attempt to clear everyone out—often with teargas and other such methods. Between May 29 and August 27, the police have declared twenty-three riots and twenty-two unlawful assemblies. You'll hear it over the loudspeaker, after things get hot enough each evening: "This is the Portland Police Bureau. We're declaring this a riot. You need to leave the area to the west. If you do not leave the area, you may be subject to use of force to include crowd-control munitions, pepper spray, or teargas." The Portland Police Bureau has put out a much-publicized video explaining what constitutes a riot. They order those who are peacefully protesting to leave, after the declaration is made. Usually, some people do leave. Those who don't put on gas masks and prepare for conflict.

That night, the fires were put out by business owners and residents of the Kenton neighborhood, in an effort led by Terrance Moses and a few others. Moses owns a computer repair shop in Kenton called TECH NET EZ. He is also the chair of the Kenton Neighborhood Association and belongs to the Kenton Business Association. He is on the neighborhood board supporting the Kenton Women's Village, a tiny-home-model transitional housing project managed by Catholic Charities, and runs a nonprofit that collects trash and provides food and clothing for houseless neighbors in North Portland. Moses went out after midnight with others to try to prevent the Kenton Plaza from being destroyed.

When Moses, who is black, moved to Kenton twenty-six years ago, it was a black neighborhood that was safe and affordable to live in. Things have changed, though: the house across the street from him is now worth half a million dollars. He has watched as members of the black community in Kenton have been priced out, and now hears some white people argue against efforts to create affordable housing.

I spoke to Moses outside his garage, where he runs his nonprofit. We stood next to the truck and trailer he uses to distribute food and clothing. Large signs with George Floyd's face and captions of "I can't breathe" and "8:46" adorn three sides of the trailer. Moses said that, when the protests began in May, he thought, "Finally, someone's standing up. Something's going to be done." He had been silent about the unfair treatment of black people by law enforcement for too long, he said. The protests emboldened him to become vocal.

But early on, he started to see things take a shift. The protests stopped being about black lives and started being about other agendas. "To see businesses get their windows smashed and stuff burnt up—that's not what black folks are looking for," he told me. He said that black people want to be recognized as human, to receive equal treatment under the law, to be given the same rights and the same treatment that white people enjoy.

When the protest moved into the Kenton Plaza, where many of the businesses are owned by people of color, Moses was one of the first people there. He ran buckets of water from the pizza shop to put out the fires. Picnic tables from a restaurant had been turned upside down and tossed onto the flames. "What's so sad about it is that as fast as we put it out, they would relight them," he told me. "They were relighting them as we were there trying to put them out. Now that doesn't say *anything* about Black Lives Matter or coming together in solidarity or support. This is just destruction for the sake of destruction—and out in front of seven people of color's businesses right here." Those businesses are his computer repair shop, three restaurants—Po'Shines, Casa Maya, and Derby—a corner store called the Triple Crown Market, a smoke shop, and—Portland being Portland—a weed shop.

"This is how you support us?" went on Moses. "By setting our businesses on fire and destroying the property? Most of the west side of Denver is people-of-color-owned businesses—those are what were getting trashed. It's infuriating to see them come down there and chant Black Lives Matter, throw stuff in the fires, set fires, tag buildings – 'No Justice, No Peace!' – in the name of BLM. You say that, but you're tearing up all these businesses that are black- or people-of-color-owned."

Moses said what he wants from the protests is simple. "Stop and listen to us. Don't keep telling us how you want us to be. Let us tell you what we need. Don't assume what we need and just run with it." ✴

IS GOD ANTI-RACIST?

AMY JULIA BECKER

OUR CHURCH SITS atop a hill in a little town in western Connecticut. Our population is fairly typical of a rural church – we skew toward members over the age of sixty, and we see about fifty people in the pews on a given Sunday morning. There are the "church widows," who only appear to have husbands on Christmas and Easter. There are the people with predictable prayer requests: Jodi always has a friend with a physical ailment; Bea always has a concern for a population in need somewhere far away. Everyone else fills in with various aches and pains of the body and spirit. On Sunday mornings, we pray together. We worship together. We eat the bread and drink the cup and try our best to care for one another.

We span the gamut of professions from plumber to accountant to teacher to hedge-fund manager, lawyer to writer to masseuse. Our church membership is almost entirely white, just like our town. Some of us are passionate progressives while others are fervent conservatives. Still, we typically adhere to a common understanding not to bring our political leanings into the sanctuary.

But after George Floyd was killed in Minneapolis and demonstrations erupted around the nation, our pastor asked whether we

---

AMY JULIA BECKER is a writer and speaker on faith, family, disability, and privilege. She is the author of four books, including *White Picket Fences: Turning Towards Love in a World Divided by Privilege*. A graduate of Princeton University and Princeton Theological Seminary, Becker lives with her husband Peter and three children, Penny, William, and Marilee, in western Connecticut.

wanted to make a public statement to name the injustice of his death and express solidarity with the protesters. After some discussion, our church council (of which I am a member) decided not to say anything. We have never made a statement about national events in the past, and our church members would certainly feel divided about how to respond. Why provoke controversy now?

In our church community, as in many predominantly white churches across the United States, the issue of how Christians should respond to our current moment of reckoning with a history of racial injustice has bubbled to the surface of our collective consciousness. What tools do we have at our disposal?

If we look to our culture, there are two bandwagons inviting us for a ride. There is the wagon of individual responsibility that denies systemic racism in the present moment and celebrates our nation's founding as a land of freedom and opportunity. And there is the wagon of anti-racism, which advocates for lifelong participation in the work of undoing the harmful systems and structures on which our nation was built and by which we still operate. Some Christians have chosen one or the other. Many others feel quietly uneasy before the limits of both options, but can't quite explain why.

The Scriptures warn against thoughtless acquiescence to the world's norms du jour. At the same time, they and the historical witness of the church encourage Christ's disciples toward discerning political and social engagement in whatever land they inhabit, made all the more urgent when questions of human dignity are at stake. Faced with the dueling temptations to ignore political "issues" on the one hand and to baptize every current of popular opinion on the other, it is incumbent on those who follow Jesus to learn how to bring the scriptural, spiritual, and social resources of his gospel truth to bear on the political and cultural moment in which we live, including that which we've simply inherited. What might Christian moral reasoning and reform look like in this complicated hour, and how do we recover these depths in our churches, practices, and broader public conversation?

THE WORLD IS BORROWING THE CHURCH'S LANGUAGE. DO WE REMEMBER HOW TO INCARNATE IT?

Our nation is publicly wrestling with racism and injustice in a way we have not seen since the 1960s. Confederate monuments and symbols are toppling. Icons of consumer culture like Aunt Jemima and Uncle Ben are being reconsidered as companies take a critical look at their brands. Anti-racism training is on the rise.

In the midst of these attempts to shift cultural norms in almost every sphere of our public life, many Americans find themselves leaning on spiritual concepts to frame the need for broad-scale change. The institution of slavery is referred to as "America's original sin." Popular books on the topic of racism lament the harm it does to the "soul" of America, and point to the "angels" and "demons" of our collective nature. Even social critic Ta-Nehisi Coates, an atheist, resorts to religious language, calling for "a spiritual reckoning that will lead to a national renewal."

Our world is crying out for real-world pathways to address what even the secular culture acknowledges as a spiritual problem. While American culture does not acknowledge Jesus as Lord, it has been nonetheless touched by a Judeo-Christian vision of human dignity that still finds expression in both our celebration of personal responsibility and our more collective movements for social justice. It is not an accident that the richest language our public prophets have to move civic hearts toward a vision of equality stems from those Christian leaders and preachers who led the movement to abolish the institution of slavery, as well as those who led the civil rights movement a century later. These leaders worked in the social and political spheres with a distinctly biblical understanding of human sin and human dignity. They embodied both the love and the courage of Jesus to advocate on behalf of the most vulnerable, to reject political systems of oppression, to pray for and forgive their enemies, and to turn the other cheek in the face of violence.

Unfortunately, many Christian institutions in America have not modeled this boundary-crossing care, instead bearing the scars of racial discrimination and segregation. As Michael Luo has recently written for the *New Yorker,* American evangelical Christianity has a "white supremacy problem." According to Luo, in contrast to progressive secularists and Christians who are people of color, most white evangelicals see no relationship between the history of racial discrimination in our nation and the treatment of African American men and women in our society. Luo quotes Robert P. Jones, whose book *White Too Long* further documents this relationship between white American churches and racist ideology and practice. According to Jones, "If you were recruiting for a white supremacist cause on a Sunday morning, you'd likely have more success hanging out in the parking lot of an average white Christian church – evangelical Protestant, mainline Protestant, or Catholic – than approaching whites sitting out services at the local coffee shop."

I'm pretty sure I count as an "average white Christian," and I desperately want those words to prove untrue. But after President Trump was elected back in 2016, and Christians seemed even more divided than ever about racial justice, I accepted an invitation to fast and pray one day a week about justice, mercy, and healing across our nation. I thought it would be a time to pray for all the people "out there" who needed help and healing. Instead it became a time for me to see my own sin in this area. I saw my own sense of cultural superiority. I saw my own hard heart in the face of the suffering so many of my brothers and sisters were experiencing. I had not behaved as though my black and brown brothers and sisters in faith were part of the same Body, and that if they were in pain, by extension, so was I. It took me decades to connect the prophetic writings in the Bible about justice to the plight of men and women wrongfully imprisoned in our country. I saw conversations about racism and injustice as peripheral to the primary work of evangelism, which is to say, preaching a gospel of personal salvation from sin.

Before we can engage with integrity, compassion, and effectiveness in the public square, we need to apply the truths of Scripture and biblical theology to our own lives and institutions. We need to take a hard look at the legacy of passive and active complicity in racist practices, so that we can lament, repent, and forge a path of restoration and renewal.

Many American Christians are late to the cultural action when it comes to political and social advocacy on behalf of marginalized people, and we have lost much credibility when it comes to offering a moral vision of social healing. That's not to say God's redemptive action hasn't been visible. Black Christians have been leading this work for hundreds of years – tracing back to the prophetic witness of Frederick Douglass and Harriet Tubman, through the courageous faith put into action by heroes like Rosa Parks, the Rev. Dr. Martin Luther King Jr., and Congressman John Lewis, and continuing today through the faithful work of activists and scholars like Bryan Stevenson, Dominique Gilliard, Lisa Sharon Harper, Natasha Sistrunk Robinson, Jemar Tisby, Esau McCaulley, and so many more. What would it look like for white Christians to follow their lead, to listen and learn, and to link arms in shared commitment to the bloody body of Christ, the regenerative power of his wounds, and the promise of a resurrected humanity?

Although Jesus and Paul did not speak in contemporary language of racism or anti-racism, they both offer a shockingly inclusive vision of God's ongoing work to bring the peoples of all nations, all ethnicities, and all sectors of society into the same family while maintaining their distinctive identities. Paul's letter to the Ephesians is devoted to the idea of unity in Christ, and applying his words to our day exhorts believers to engage in work to dismantle historical and contemporary racism within the church and the society at large.

According to Paul, God intends to be Father to all – both Jew and Gentile: "The mystery of the gospel . . . [is that] the Gentiles are heirs together with Israel." It doesn't seem remarkable to us now that non-Jewish people are welcomed into the family of God. But to Paul, and to any Jewish listener in his day, this message is at best "mysterious" and at worst a grave offense. Indeed, salvation history up to that point had traveled through a people commanded by God to be separate, to stand apart. But the advent of Christ introduces a most scandalous invitation: All nations who had previously been cut off from Israel are now welcome to enjoy that most intimate of all possible relationships – that is, the family of God. The mystery of the gospel is that the love of Jesus Christ pierces through our social hierarchies, and the practices, systems, and prejudices that have maintained those social divisions. God's family – both Jew and Gentile together, both white and black together – is called to live out that work. Unity among diverse believers is a mysterious and beautiful indication of God's Spirit.

REVISITING THAT WHICH IS "TOO POLITICAL"

As stated earlier, our culture offers two ways to respond to the inequity we see all around us: an ethos of individual opportunity and hard work, and an ethos of systemic change to power structures currently known as anti-racism. Christians have an opportunity to acknowledge the truth inherent within both of these responses while at the same time living out and offering a distinctive, gospel-centered vision of redemptive possibilities.

The gospel is a story of humble, sacrificial love overcoming the cosmic powers of sin and death. It's a message that includes the personal nature of both sin and salvation, *and* extends beyond. White American Christians have typically been baptized – literally and intellectually – into a purely individualized understanding of who and what Christ was sacrificing himself for. And this is not a complete error. It is vital that we honor the radical Christian turn to uphold the dignity and worth of every human being – to think first as personalists. History is littered with dangerous examples where this *imago Dei* of the individual was made subservient to the collective. And indeed, it's part of the irony of American history that one aspect of our very exceptionalism as a country stems from a Christian understanding of individual dignity as undergirding our founding documents, an understanding that has played no small role in shaping salutary pursuits of justice throughout much of the world.

But when Christians only attend to the rights of the individual, we end up segregated from one another, with a privatized faith divorced from the public square. We fail to live out Jesus' invitation to all the nations and all the peoples to feast together at the banquet table of God. And we become complicit in perpetuating systems of injustice.

Scholar Jemar Tisby has documented the history of this complicity in his book *The Color of Compromise*, starting with missionaries who made agreements with plantation masters to tell enslaved people only about the personal transformation offered by Jesus, but not the implications of the gospel for their social liberation. Missionaries often decried the treatment of enslaved people. Still, those same missionaries knew slaveholders would not allow them to preach if their preaching would result in their converts advocating for freedom. In Tisby's words, "European missionaries tried to calm the slave owners' fears of rebellion by spreading a version of Christianity that emphasized spiritual deliverance, not immediate liberation."

Centuries later, the "white moderates" highlighted by Martin Luther King swam in this same stream when they urged King to wait patiently rather than agitate for voting rights. Today, this complicity in racism persists when white Christians refuse to consider the historical and structural causes of ongoing racial inequities. Again, Tisby demonstrates the rift between Christians of different racial backgrounds: "Sixty-two percent of white evangelicals attribute poverty among black people to a lack of motivation, while 31 percent of black Christians said the same. And just 27 percent of white evangelicals attribute the wealth gap to racial discrimination, while 72 percent of blacks cite discrimination as a major cause of the discrepancy."

Christians in predominantly white churches today will continue this pattern of complicity unless we address the problems of our individualized gospel. But does this mean we should join today's anti-racist movement?

There are a range of viewpoints here. Taking Ibram X. Kendi's definition, anti-racism is support of policies that undo the harm of previous injustices and provide equal opportunity for all racial groups in the future. Conversely, racism is support of policies and systems that, intentionally or not, oppress one racial group and elevate another. Another way to frame it is to see anti-racism as active opposition to racist behavior and policies. Throughout the Old Testament, the God of the Israelites includes and welcomes the foreigner, the ethnic "other." Jesus was opposed to racist behavior and policies. Paul was opposed to racist behavior and policies. The broader arc of the Old and New Testaments reveals a God fiercely committed to justice and healing. By the time we get to the closing symphony in the Book of Revelation, John gives a supernatural vision of that multiplicity of voices and identities and cultures coming together to worship the Lamb that was slain, the healer who wipes every tear from their eyes.

Black Lives Matter has become the most visible advocate of anti-racism, and Christians have disagreed about whether to support a movement with roots in Marxist ideology and assumptions about family and sexuality that contradict a traditional Christian perspective. But these concerns can also serve as a convenient way to sidestep the call to expose injustice both within the church and outside of it. In light of the gospel imperative to work toward overcoming social divisions, Christians need to be less afraid of anti-racism, and consider – scripturally and in conversation with diverse siblings in the faith – what a Christian fragrance would bestow. "Christian anti-racism" will not look the same as its secular cousin. In fact, if we are willing to face our own history of segregation instead of unity and our ongoing complicity in racism and injustice, we will be able to offer an invitation not only to racial healing but to salvation as well. A Christian understanding of anti-racism goes further than an active opposition to injustice and oppression. Christian anti-racism is the work of living out God's beloved community.

THE WAY OF THE CROSS

As our secular prophets have noted, America is in the midst of a spiritual crisis when it comes to our racial divisions. The church can offer language, practices, and beliefs to equip people to heal, but only if we are willing to face our own history of segregation instead of unity and our ongoing complicity in injustice. In his book *J-Curve: Dying and Rising with Jesus in Everyday Life*, Paul E. Miller asserts that Christians who follow Jesus are called to follow him into suffering and death and then be raised up by God. It's a motion that looks like the letter "J." Miller suggests that there are three ways we enter that J-Curve – suffering, repentance, and love. A suffering J-Curve happens when evil comes to us. When we have done nothing wrong, and we suffer illness or injustice, we are nevertheless invited to walk with Jesus toward the cross and hold out hope for resurrection. The black church in American has emerged out of this type of suffering.

A repentance J-Curve happens when we recognize our own sinfulness. Here we follow Jesus to the cross as we die to our own self-centeredness and the harm it causes to us and to others. We suffer whatever consequences come from the humiliation and pain of sin exposed. And we wait for the Spirit of God to bring resurrection. Many American churches have an opportunity right now to repent of our complicity in racist practices throughout our history, even as it will mean painful, perhaps even humiliating exposure of our sin, even as it feels like a hopeless descent into death.

The third type of J-Curve is a love J-Curve, when we choose to lay down our lives out of sacrificial love for others. Again, we follow Jesus to the cross until that same love leads us to glory. American churches with historically and predominantly white populations need to learn how to lament, repent, and take loving action to heal social divisions and advocate for justice. Only then can we bear credible witness to the full gospel of dying and rising with Jesus Christ.

The church has both the language and doctrine of sin to help us understand the comprehensive and collective nature of the cosmic brokenness, oppressive systems, and evil individual choices that have led to our social divisions. We have the practices of lament and confession that offer ways for individuals and communities to mourn our participation in the injustices and brokenness of the world. We have been invited into the life of Jesus, a life of dying and rising again, a life of sacrificial love on behalf of others, a life that includes suffering and humiliation before it leads to joy and peace. Our theological understanding of society can equip us to expose injustice and seek to rectify it in the public sphere with grace and truth rather than shame or rage.

My own Christian practice has been shaped by decades of participation in faith communities that have offered solace to my soul but that have been disconnected from active engagement in bringing justice, peace, and joy to our land. But I am starting to learn how to ask questions and seek answers alongside diverse fellow believers when it comes to education, criminal justice, and affordable housing and fair zoning laws, to name a few. I am broadening the scope of theologians and lay church leaders who inform my thinking rather than continuing to depend solely on the perspectives of older white men. Jesus' inclusivity and Paul's "mysterious" gospel that breaks down social dividing walls have convinced me that I need to relearn and enlarge my understanding of sin and salvation while bearing public witness – in word and deed – to the reconciling, healing, empowering, loving work of Jesus.

Despite the earnest questions many Christians are currently asking about how to participate in undoing systemic racism in our churches and our country, the history of predominantly white churches suggests that the disparities and injustices between black and white communities will never heal. Nearly sixty years after Dr. King first said it, Sunday mornings remain one of the most segregated hours of the week, and that ecclesial divide is also reflected in the disparities in how white and black Christians vote and speak out in the public square. But the history of the people of God suggests that the Spirit will work among fallen, stubborn, sinful people just like us. In this moment of reckoning, white Christians have an invitation to repent of our complicity in racist structures, follow the lead of our black brothers and sisters, and engage anti-racism in the public square from a distinctly Christian perspective that upholds human dignity.

In my own church context, we did not make a statement after George Floyd died. But our pastor did invite members to read and discuss Tisby's *The Color of Compromise*. We joined other local churches in a webinar about racial injustice and the harm of social divisions and inequities. In our weekly Bible study, we've made a commitment to apply every passage of Scripture to both personal and social concerns so that the Word is living and active for our individual lives and our broader society. These are small steps—and even they are controversial—but they have led to small next steps, like people speaking up about politics in a way they wouldn't have before, calling a local police department to talk through police reforms in their town, and attending a nearby city's prayer gathering for repentance and justice. It's entirely possible that small steps like these are wholly inadequate. It also seems that these might be mustard seeds of faith, with which God can grow something surprisingly large and new. ✤

September 29, 2020

GOING DARK

JEFFREY BILBRO

To go in the dark with a light is to know the light.
To know the dark, go dark. Go without sight,
and find that the dark, too, blooms and sings,
and is traveled by dark feet and dark wings.
                    —Wendell Berry, "To Know the Dark"

IT WAS A normal July evening in the summer of Covid. I was sitting on the back porch reading while our five-year-old daughter read to herself in the hammock. My good friend and the chair of my English department texted to ask if he could stop by, and a few minutes later he pulled up in our driveway and sat down. I wondered if he'd received word from our administration about the fate of our colleague, the only member of our department who didn't yet have tenure. Jack told me that yes, our colleague would be cut in January, and that on top of this, my own position would end in May. Then he began crying. I sat there in disbelief. My daughter came over and began asking "Mr. Jack" what he had been doing. She prattled on about her day—overjoyed to have someone other

JEFFREY BILBRO is an associate professor of English and the editor-in-chief of *Front Porch Republic*. His research interests focus on theology and environmental ethics in American literature, and he's written several books, including *Loving God's Wildness: The Christian Roots of Ecological Ethics in American Literature*; *Wendell Berry and Higher Education: Cultivating Virtues of Place* (co-written with Jack Baker); and *Virtues of Renewal: Wendell Berry's Sustainable Forms*. He writes on a wide range of topics. For more information, visit www.jeffbilbro.com or follow him on Twitter @jeff_bilbro.

than her family to talk to after months when such opportunities were scarce. The squirrels continued to scold each other in the trees. Jack responded kindly to my daughter. And I just sat there, not knowing what to say.

As the news sank in, a knot of fear and anger and anxiety settled in my chest. I knew that millions of people had lost their jobs in the last months, most, like me, through no fault of their own. I knew I had time to look for gainful employment, unlike many who got two weeks' notice. I knew my chance of landing on my feet somewhere was fairly good. But none of that knowledge helped much. And the sense that higher education itself was imploding intensified my sense of vertigo.

I have been disabused of any pretensions to clarity about the future. Covid's apocalyptic gesture – its unveiling of complacence and injustice and decadence – has had this effect on many of us. But institutions of higher education have been famously stable (or infamously stuck in their ways), and as a professor with several books and the respect of my colleagues and students, I thought I was largely immune from the pandemic's immediate effects. I knew the next five to ten years would be difficult ones for my university, but I thought I knew roughly what the future held for me career-wise. I thought my next steps were fairly well illuminated. I had built my house upon academia's rock: I had tenure.

In the days that followed, I began to grow acclimated to the dark. The knot of tension dissipated. I slept well again. And I gained a new appreciation for the wisdom in Wendell Berry's poem "To Know the Dark." When we go into the dark with a light, we don't actually learn what the dark is and what mysteries it holds. We remain insulated in our bubble of light. For me, the light that shone along my professional path has been extinguished. I am now going dark. And as Berry testifies, I have found that the dark too blooms and sings. As the news slowly spread, colleagues at my institution and from around the country wrote kind and encouraging notes. People I had never met wrote to say they appreciated and valued what I've written. Former and current students wrote long emails and letters of gratitude. I felt like Tom Sawyer walking into his own funeral.

There is a grace too in having the extrinsic motivations for scholarship and learning stripped away. I had recently finished reading Zena Hitz's *Lost in Thought*, and now I was newly struck by her celebration of people who pursued knowledge in adverse circumstances. As she concludes, "Failure is perhaps the best-trod route to inwardness," to pursuing wisdom for its own sake. Having the extrinsic goods associated with learning radically pruned back can be profoundly clarifying. Whether my loss of these goods is temporary or permanent, this pruning forces me to ask why I want to seek understanding, why I am motivated to read and write and teach and question. Do I engage in these activities to earn the respect of my peers, the admiration of my students, or a salary increase from my institution? Or do I pursue them because I have taken Solomon's advice to heart and genuinely believe that "wisdom is the principal thing"?

Hitz draws on a distinction that Augustine makes between *curiositas* and *studiositas*—which she defines, in turn, as a love of spectacle or a dedication to seriousness. If our desire for knowledge is motivated by a love of spectacle and entertainment and external rewards, then we will cease to learn when the cord is pulled and the lights go out. Yet the studious soul is, at root, an amateur, someone who learns from love. Even in the dark, even when lost, the amateur follows beauty's faint murmurs, its dim glimmers, along the "way of ignorance" toward truth. As T. S. Eliot writes,

> In order to arrive at what you do not know
> You must go by a way which is the way of ignorance.
> In order to possess what you do not possess
> You must go by the way of dispossession.

Even those of us who have—or who had—the privilege of earning a paycheck for learning and teaching have always done our real work for love, not money. In being dispossessed of external rewards, I have been reminded that, as Hitz demonstrates, "contemplation in the form of learning" is a human good open to all, not just professional professors.

Yet the darkness in which I now find myself is not merely personal. It is also a darkness regarding the future of my institution and the broader landscape of educational institutions, particularly those historically dedicated to the liberal arts. When my friend Eric Miller wrote to offer me encouragement, he said that "being in Christian higher ed (and I'm sure it feels like this everywhere that isn't draped in Ivy) these past ten years is like being in a shrinking universe, with coordinates that have gone suddenly missing, as if the cosmos itself is vanishing. It's eerie." And now there is also a plague.

My sense of the surreal was heightened when, just three days after the Zoom call with HR officially informing me that my position was being cut, I received word that a collaborative grant I had helped lead had been accepted. Our group would receive $30,000 to convene conversations about the future of the liberal arts in higher education. In our proposal, we expressed hope that the coronavirus pandemic and the ensuing summer of protests might be a positive inflection point: "Higher education has been in crisis for decades now, and perhaps this moment will be apocalyptic – unveiling its disorders and laying the groundwork for a renewed commitment to the liberal arts." This possibility seems less likely to me now than it did just a few weeks ago. The future looks bleak for a genuine commitment to the liberal arts at the institution I have served for eight years. Many of the faculty members who were dismissed taught in our core curriculum: two from English, three from Theology, one from Art. And these cuts came in addition to ones just eighteen months ago that targeted English, Art, and Drama. But perhaps in this season of darkness and uncertainty institutions will be forced to ask hard questions about their purpose and mission. My university will no longer be the lead institution on this grant, but these conversations will go forward, and my hope remains.

The night I found out my position had been eliminated, I was hosting one of a series of Zoom seminars I'd arranged for the summer. I'd asked several colleagues to lead a discussion on how their discipline might respond to the Covid-19 pandemic. That evening, the brilliant art historian Jonathan Rinck – who had also found out hours before that his position had been cut – led a wide-ranging survey through what he called "apocalyptic art," art created during times of plague and war. He spent some time reflecting on Picasso's famous *Guernica,* which was painted in response to the bombing of civilians during the Spanish Civil War. Near the center of the painting, a bare light bulb appears as the pupil of an eye. It seems that some forms of light provide a false sense of clarity, a kind of apparent clarity that is, in fact, deadly.

The round of layoffs and closures sweeping higher education is not at all equivalent to the literal deaths and dismemberment justified by the pursuit of wartime objectives. But both acts may be guided by the same enlightened logic. All too often the logic of spreadsheets and metrics leads administrators to believe that they must destroy a university in order to save it. Yet perhaps if some institutions close and others drift away from their missions, new institutions, perhaps new forms of institution, might rise to carry on anew the enduring work of wisdom. Zena Hitz, for instance, is launching the Catherine Project to foster discussions of great texts, and there is an increasingly robust network of online magazines that seek to guide their readers in the pursuit of truth – *Breaking Ground* and its sponsoring institutions are certainly in this category. During this season of sifting, those of us who find ourselves institutionless may indeed uncover new aspects of our proper work.

Indeed, while *apocalypse* refers to an unveiling, it may be that some forms of unveiling entail shuttering – closing institutions, turning off the lights, going dark. In such darkness, we are forced to stop, take stock, and then learn to go ahead without sight. As Berry writes in an essay, "It may be that when we no longer know what to do we have come to our real work, and that when we no longer know which way to go we have come to our real journey. The mind that is not baffled is not employed. The impeded stream is the one that sings." I am still in the dark. I have no answers about what the future might hold for institutions of higher education. I have no answers about where my family and I will be living in a year and what work I might be doing. And yet by going dark, I am coming to know the dark and to know that it too blooms and sings. And I am learning to hope with Berry that the darkness might make not only fear, but also grace, more palpable. ✳

October 16, 2020

STORY, CULTURE, AND THE COMMON GOOD

MARILYNNE ROBINSON
IN CONVERSATION WITH CHERIE HARDER

How do we create a home and community in a fractious world? Award-winning novelist and essayist Marilynne Robinson sat down—remotely—with Cherie Harder of The Trinity Forum for a wide-ranging livestreamed conversation on the art of writing as a means of exploring truth and engaging the questions around learning to live well and love others. What follows is an edited transcript of that conversation.

CHERIE HARDER: It seems an especially fitting time to discuss story, culture, and the common good when our shared sense of the common good is challenged; our common culture is increasingly marked by divisiveness, anger, and alienation; and many of our public conversations are tarnished by snark and by ugliness. The writings and works of our guest today stand as a powerful and poetic challenge to this fractiousness and offer an illumination

MARILYNNE ROBINSON is a novelist and essayist. She has received numerous awards, including the Pulitzer Prize for Fiction in 2005, the 2016 Library of Congress Prize for American Fiction, and the National Humanities Medal in 2012, awarded by President Barack Obama for "her grace and intelligence in writing."

CHERIE HARDER serves as president of The Trinity Forum. Prior to joining the Trinity Forum in 2008, she served in the White House as Special Assistant to the President and Director of Policy and Projects for First Lady Laura Bush. Ms. Harder has contributed articles to publications including *Policy Review, Human Events, Harvard Political Review*, and various newspapers.

of the beauty of the ordinary and fallen world. They stand as a summons to think more deeply, see more charitably, and accept the invitation to wonder, mystery, and grace.

Marilynne, it is a delight to have you here.

MARILYNNE ROBINSON: It's a great pleasure to be here.

CHERIE: It seems that one of the recurring themes of your work is beauty. There is an element of both reveling in and revealing the beautiful that seems to characterize so many of your novels. But you recently wrote, "Beauty, as a conscious element of experience, as a thing to be valued and explored, has gone into abeyance among us." Why do you believe that the exploration of beauty has gone into abeyance, and what have we lost as a result?

MARILYNNE: My thinking about that actually was a response to teaching literature to writers and having them tell me that when I talked about something wonderful, like in *Moby Dick* or something, as "beautiful," it was the first time that they had heard "beautiful" applied to literature. Which is just stunning—just amazing. Here is the great prevailing art of our period, and I just couldn't believe that the way that literature is talked about has become so deeply a kind of form of sociology that aesthetic categories were dismissed in discussing it. I think that you find in any good writer that beautiful language is arising. It's something that is done for emphasis. It's something that indicates that a degree of focus has been achieved. I don't think that you can read good literature successfully if you exclude the beautiful as a consideration always active in good writing.

CHERIE: So much of what is beautiful does depend on our perception. You have probably one of your most beloved characters, John Ames, say that "wherever you turn your eyes the world can shine like transfiguration. You don't have to bring a thing to it except a willingness to see." You've said similar things in your own voice as well as your character's voice, which I am betting evokes no small amount of wistfulness in many of your readers who would deeply like to see the same luminous beauty that you do. How does one learn to see?

MARILYNNE: By looking, basically. I consider the primary privilege of being a human being as a universal privilege of being able to watch light fall on things, watch vegetation live in the world in the complicated ways that it does. The shimmer, the effulgence, all these things are simply there to be seen, whether or not people choose to look at them—whether they relegate too many things to the category of ordinary or meaningless. That's the original choice. But if you are interested in the nature of the experience of life on this planet, then very quickly all sorts of things begin to present themselves to you as mysteriously beautiful. Discovered beauty: no rarefaction or falsification, but the thing itself.

CHERIE: You mentioned once that as a child, a teacher told you that "you have to live with your mind your whole life. You build your mind, so make it into something you want to live with." Then you said, "Nobody has ever said anything more valuable to me." How did you build and furnish your own mind?

MARILYNNE: I was a bookish child, as I have mentioned in other contexts. I was very systematic about reading books that I knew were good—people like Dickens and Mark Twain and Robert Louis Stevenson. Sometimes I read very far over my head but nevertheless with the idea that I was giving myself something of value as a result of the effort. I'm sure there are lots of ways that people could have taken that teacher's advice. But for me, it was all books for a very long time.

CHERIE: C. S. Lewis once tried to encourage readers to read an old book for every new one, but you've gone further and read almost exclusively old books. What prompted you to start that practice?

MARILYNNE: I am always trying to put together what I find to be a credible model of the world, which is no easy thing. But the major valuable questions that have come to me have usually come from the fact that I've studied something historically in a way that makes me question present accounts and question them very deeply.

CHERIE: You've been writing a fair amount recently about democracy and the common good. At one point you call democracy the logical and inevitable consequence of religious humanism. What do you see as the connection between the two?

MARILYNNE: There are things that seem to me true because I reinforce them from other kinds of awareness or learning. I'm of course very, very struck by the unique brilliance of a human being, which is something that we tend to disparage, demean, utterly fail to notice. By my understanding, every person lives out a beautiful, complicated, inaccessible-to-other-consciousnesses sort of parable of life, and it is sacred. The intrusions or the deprivations that refuse to acknowledge this tend to take political forms of totalitarianism. Democracy, in any conceivable future as far as I'm concerned, is the only way that we can possibly honor the fact of the brilliance, the importance, of every human life and human awareness.

CHERIE: I was thinking back to a remarkable interview you did with President Obama in 2015. The two of you talked about what you saw as the basis of democracy: the willingness to assume well of other people. You warned against what you called "the idea of the 'sinister other.'" We are certainly in a period when there are media, social media, political, and ideological forces all intensifying tribalism and reinforcing the idea of a "sinister other." How does one cultivate, both on a personal level and on a cultural level, an appetite for a truer and more charitable story?

MARILYNNE: I think we have some obligation to support each other in this, not simply to support each other materially but to teach, and to preach, and to write. To do these things that are the addresses of one sensibility to others in a way that is respectful, that is generous, in its assumptions about the mentality of the reader. Speaking as a former teacher of writers, there is a pervasively low opinion of the general public. That means that what is said to the general public as culture—as popular culture, especially—is often less worthy, less good, than it would be possible for the same people who made that culture to produce if they proceeded more optimistically about what their audience would accept and be engaged by. I think we condescend horribly to one another. It's always a form of self-congratulation if you can think badly of other people. But it's very, very destructive.

CHERIE: You coined a memorable phrase in your work *Absence of Mind*: "the hermeneutics of condescension," which you describe as the idea that earlier generations were somehow either intellectually, or socially, or morally beneath us. Where does this chronological snobbery come from?

MARILYNNE: I think one of the major sources of it is that we teach history very badly or teach it hardly at all. People don't realize that when Shakespeare was alive, he walked across a bridge that had human heads on pikes displayed there for the birds to eat. The very steep upgrade of civilization (in terms of many things) is to be recognized, perpetuated, protected. But people don't know enough about the past. They idealize it – "That's when people were right-minded" and all the rest of it. In fact, it was savage in many ways.

We're looking all the time now at slavery, but that was one of the major forms of brutality in the human past. And we weed out the fact that there were people who hoped for something better, and worked toward something better, and risked or spent their lives trying to improve things. We could look to history for models about having things be better than they were – you know, the end of cruel and unusual punishment and so on. We don't do that. We simply obsess on the fact that things were worse and act as if we had some sort of role in making our lives very much less grotesque.

We need models. We need to figure out what reformers did when they created effective reforms. You have to look into the dark past to see that there were people in the dark past who were trying to make the world less dark. The fact that, for a while at any rate, with any luck, we are able to enjoy, by world standards and by historical standards, a humane civilization, granting all its faults – that was the work and thought of nameable people, nameable movements. And at this point, we absolutely need examples of humanizing influences that take hold and work. We're losing the sense of that.

CHERIE: Unlike many modern contemporary writers, you are a fan of John Calvin, Jonathan Edwards, and the Puritans. What sparked your excitement over their work and thought?

MARILYNNE: I really do think that the reason I have so much more interest in Calvin than other people who speak about him is that I've actually read him. One of the things that's very irritating about the general conversation, no matter how lofty it is in terms of its intellectual claims, is that it's often based simply on some kind of word of mouth that passes down through the generations. Calvin is a beautiful writer. He is a beautiful thinker. I think that much of the best subsequent philosophy (people like Descartes) comes straight out of Calvin.

I was aware of Jonathan Edwards because I went to a college in the Northeast. I was assigned an essay of his when I was a sophomore, and there was a beautiful footnote in it talking about the fact that reality is unaccountably re-created moment to moment and comparing it to the effect of light. That was very important to me, because everything else I was hearing – Darwinism, behaviorism, Freudianism – all of these things were different forms of a very unattractive determinism. Conventional ideas of God, that he was omnipotent and so on, would be disallowed by these determinisms that said, basically, we were not free to act; God was not free to act; it was all sort of an organic mechanism. When I read that note of Edwards's, it gave me a new model of reality. Edwards rescued me out of the deprivations of what we've called "modern thought," and I have been reading him in light of that ever since. He's a wonderful thinker. He's called the greatest philosopher born on the North American continent, and he is. He deserves his reputation.

CHERIE: You noted once that one of the things that comes with a Calvinist outlook is that you are always confronted by the question: What does God want from this particular situation? I'd be curious how you go about engaging with and wrestling with that question in your own life.

MARILYNNE: It's a question that doesn't recur all the time in the same forms. When you encounter someone, you look at them with the idea that they are sent to you by God, with the intention that you should react to them with that understanding – in effect, the way Calvin describes it, they become God, because they are his emissaries, no matter who they are. So, the idea is to understand the human situation in this profound way: What would God want from this moment? It is not that I should protect myself or that I should prove that I'm more intelligent or richer than the person I'm encountering. You know that those are not the answers God wants. The question is how to respond to the holiness and the vulnerability, or whatever is presented to you in the presence of another person. Also, any moral question that you encounter in life, even things like avoiding waste and extravagance or taking reasonable care of your health or anything like that—in these kinds of questions, what does God want of you? It's a question that is applicable in really any number of circumstances—in all circumstances.

CHERIE: We're going to turn to questions from our viewers. Our first question: "Do you believe that beauty is something we are simply struck with, or is beauty something like a capacity that we can grow in and hone?"

MARILYNNE: I think without any question you can enhance your own capacity for seeing beauty, or for seeing the deeply implanted character that beauty has in the existence of things. I always like the fact that mathematicians and scientists call a theory "beautiful" if they think it's plausible. Or "elegant." I think that that's a kind of model that we can carry over into all kinds of perceptions of things.

CHERIE: "Given the extreme concern about cultural appropriation today, what do you say to writers who want to write from the perspective of someone from a culture not their own—for example, a white man writing from the perspective of a black woman?"

MARILYNNE: If you do it well, I don't think anyone should object—if you make a full use of your understanding. It's a risk. You might seem insensitive. You might seem very ignorant. But that, in a way, is a risk that anybody takes writing fiction. I don't think there's anything inherently wrong in the effort to understand someone unlike oneself. I think that actually we're supposed to do that. To be afraid of making the effort seems to me just to entrap us all in a very narrow experience.

CHERIE: Another viewer would love to hear about your thoughts on the civil unrest we are experiencing now in America.

MARILYNNE: I find it very encouraging—truly. All sorts of painful things have become obvious. At the same time, it goes against the grain of expectation in a way that makes people conscious of what they expect and want and demand. It's a perilous moment that we're in at the moment. I've never seen such crazy times in my life, but I do think that the balance is probably on the side of a restoration of American democracy.

CHERIE: "It would seem that beauty should be persuasive, but the current fad is tending toward intentional ugliness. Do you agree, and if so, what do you believe we can do to reverse it?"

MARILYNNE: You know, with Walt Whitman, he would be writing about things that other people have seen as ugly until he wrote about them. There's a way in which a good writer can look at an amazing variety of things and discover a unique capacity for beauty in very unanticipated places—which is a broadening of everyone's experience. That's a very good thing. Ugliness for its own sake, I imagine, would be a project that would exhaust itself fairly quickly. There's a kind of refusal to acknowledge that people in general like to participate in what is interesting or what is beautiful. They like to engage art at that level. It's an insult or a conscious intentional deprivation to oppose that, to deny that.

CHERIE: "What challenges do you find as a Christian and as a writer who writes in the secular world?"

MARILYNNE: I have found absolutely no problem with that. Zero. I think one of the strangest things that happens is that many people who consider themselves Christians consider themselves strangers in the world—in the sense that if people found out what they really thought or believed, they would be ridiculed, or something like that. I made the test. I've been very forthright, and I think I have been as gently and fairly read and reviewed as any writer that I know of. That's part of what bothers me. We entertain these very negative assumptions about people in general. And actually, people restrict their own work, their own imaginations, because they're afraid. Christian people say to me, "Weren't you afraid about writing about a minister?" No. I'm not going to choose what I write about on the basis of some imagined fear. If my book had been banned and ridiculed and I'd been tarred and feathered, that's just the chance you take when you write a book. But there's something very, very wrong when so many people who claim to be religious people act as if they have to hide out, as if their understanding of things couldn't support daylight. That's just appalling to me.

CHERIE: Actually, our next question is also on fear: "You write about fear and claim that it's not a Christian habit of mind. What do you have to say about our current climate of fear? How does a Christian respond to the fears around the pandemic and civil unrest?"

MARILYNNE: We're just living in a kind of condensed form of human life. People have always had to deal with pandemic or plague or whatever. People have always dealt with unrest. We're not habituated to it because we've been very fortunate. But that doesn't mean that we're exempt from what people have lived through time out of mind. I think we can make a little appeal to our own sense of dignity to keep the anxieties that we have in perspective – which is not to say that they're easily solved. It's simply to say, all generations have dealt with difficulty. We don't have a special pass that will exclude us from it. What we have to do is make the best of it.

CHERIE: "Especially amid sharp cultural disagreement, how do we cultivate our minds and hearts to see the truer and more charitable story of individuals and not the 'sinister other'?"

MARILYNNE: I think that people basically have to fall back on their own resources. It's one of the reasons that I wish that we would talk about people who have done well in other generations and not assume that because they coexisted with things that were flagrantly evil they themselves must have tolerated evil. We know from our own experience that what you would choose to live with, what you would choose to see done around you, is not necessarily something that you determine or can have much impact on. I think you have to talk to yourself. Think through things. Attempt the imaginative extensions of compassion and circumstance. It would be nice if there were some solution that we could fall back on, but we're not offering ourselves good solutions these days. People are so enthralled by contentiousness that virtually anything can become a storm of contentiousness. With anger, and with contempt, and all these things, the excitement carries the behavior away from what was really the issue in the first place. It destroys the possibility of a conversation. When you are invited into one of these micro-storms, it seems to me that you could say, "No, actually, I have to go read a good book." Because we're not doing ourselves any good with this habit of antagonistic controversy. It just is not truthful.

CHERIE: Thank you, Marilynne. I'd love to give you the final word as we close out.

MARILYNNE: I think that one of the things that is interesting about the human situation is that we have a sort of unlimited capacity for generosity. Whatever you do, if you do it well, is an act of generosity toward anybody who would feel the benefit of your generosity, and that means any work that you do at all. It certainly means any artistic work that you do. We have that capacity to create society around us by acts of generosity toward the society. And, of course, the repayment of that sort of choice is very clear. You can make the society you want to live in. For many people this is not a tolerable model because they don't like the idea of giving something up, even with the possibility of having it returned – like the bread upon the waters. Nevertheless, if you accept a discipline of generosity in every circumstance where the word could come up – whether it's generosity of imagination, generosity of seriousness, actually putting good thought into everything that you do – that's my advice. That's what everybody ought to do. ✼

October 21, 2020

A TALE OF TWO EVANGELICALISMS

JOEL HALLDORF

I LEFT SWEDEN for the United States in the summer of 2000, and arrived in the middle of a captivating election cycle: the race between George W. Bush and Al Gore. I was a young Pentecostal, and my newfound friends mostly belonged to the evangelical camp. We shared theology, and the globalization of evangelicalism had made sure that we sang the same songs and read the same spiritual writers. But politically, we were worlds apart. I had never before met Christians who defended the death penalty or desired a stronger military. And little did I know that the Bible could be read as supporting welfare cuts.

I have been back many times since, and during several elections – but the conversations have not become easier. In fact, the distance now seems so wide that we can barely begin a discussion on political matters. Back in the early 2000s, our divisions concerned financial and foreign policy. Today, white evangelicals are a key voting bloc for Donald Trump, whose populist politics horrify most Swedish evangelicals. The populist equivalent in Swedish politics are the Sweden Democrats, who, like Trump, desire a more

JOEL HALLDORF is associate professor in church history at the Stockholm School of Theology. He is author of several books on evangelicalism, modernity, and politics, most recently *Pentecostal Politics in a Secular World,* which delves deeper into the topic of this essay. He contributes to several newspapers and magazines in Sweden, where he lives with his wife and children. He can be found on twitter as @joelsh.

homogenous society. But although they give Christianity a prominent place in their vision, they have been rejected by evangelical voters.

This is a riddle I have been trying to solve for decades: How can those whose theology and spirituality are so similar hold such widely different political opinions? There is a sense, especially among theologians, that differences between churches ought to have theological explanations. That is, after all, what should guide churches as well as individual Christians. But in this case it is not enough to explain the differences. Instead, we must look for the answer in the histories that shaped, and continue to shape, evangelicalism in Sweden and the United States.

DEMOCRATIC AVANT-GARDE

When Alexis de Tocqueville set sail for the United States, he was not convinced. It was the early 1830s, and he was on his way to a young nation that was experimenting with democracy. Tocqueville, like most intellectuals since Plato, saw it as a high-risk project. His philosophical misgivings were compounded by the fact that his father had barely survived the French Revolution, strengthening his suspicion that egalitarianism would lead to disintegration and chaos, before ending in tyranny.

But his visit left him impressed. Tocqueville toured the nation for almost a year and concluded that the Americans seemed to have pulled it off. This was due to what he famously labeled "the art of associating" – their untiring practice of small-scale organizing: clubs, congregations, and associations. This fostered democratic virtues and shaped citizens able to achieve democracy on a national level. He was particularly fascinated by the churches that spread all over the nation, founded as it was on the idea of religious freedom. They contributed by preaching and practicing solidarity and patience, virtues necessary to sustain a democracy.

The story of democracy in Sweden begins in a similar way, albeit a century after the inauguration of democracy in America. Here too the art of associating was vital for the development of democracy – and evangelicalism was instrumental in fostering it.

But it took time. In the nineteenth century, Sweden was one of Europe's least democratic countries. Religious freedom was established only in the 1860s, and before that evangelicals were fined, imprisoned, or ostracized for their convictions. When the first Baptist congregation was founded, in 1848, it had to be done in secret. But this congregation was the very first democratic association in the country.

With religious freedom came a rapid growth of evangelical denominations – or free churches as they are called in Sweden, in contrast to the established Lutheran state church. This changed the political culture, for most evangelicals formed democratic associations. As a grassroots movement these free churches fostered civic virtue through the art of association. Many evangelicals also became involved in national politics and worked diligently for democratization, particularly religious freedom and other liberal reforms.

The free churches belonged to the democratic avant-garde of Swedish modernity. They introduced the organizational forms that the other popular movements – the worker's movement and the temperance movement – would copy: democratic associations with protocols, budgets, and membership rolls. In Sweden it took until 1921 before women were given the right to vote in parliamentary election. By then they had already had this right in evangelical denominations for seventy years.

PROGRESSIVE EVANGELICALISM

During the nineteenth century, evangelicals in Sweden and the United States had similar political instincts. As the late historian Donald Dayton and author Marilynne Robinson have both shown, large parts of evangelicalism in this era were politically progressive. They spearheaded the fights against slavery, economic injustices, and discrimination against women.

This is a sadly neglected chapter of American church history. The famous revivalist Charles Finney is mostly remembered for his revivals on the East Coast in the 1830s. But it is a less-known fact that he preached that personal salvation must be tied to social justice. "Revivals are hindered," he wrote, "when ministers and churches take wrong ground in regard to any question involving human rights." His revivals inspired the founding of Oberlin College, the first university to allow not only women but also people of all colors to study together.

But the United States was politically very different from Sweden, and seeing this will help us understand the political differences between evangelicalism that would eventually develop in these two countries. For while the United States was founded as a democracy – albeit a flawed one – Sweden was still in the late nineteenth century a monarchy with a parliament open only to the well-off. In order to be elected or even vote in elections, you had to own property or have a certain income. In 1896, a mere 6 percent of the Swedish population had the right to vote – figures in neighboring Norway and Denmark, as well as Great Britain, were almost 20 percent. Furthermore, Sweden had established a reputation as one of the most economically unequal countries in Western Europe.

To change this, a massive political mobilization became necessary – a struggle to replace the old regime of king, state church, and nobility with a democratic and more equal society. Evangelicals were part of this mobilization. They joined hands with liberals and Social Democrats and fought against the conservative establishment to shape a modern nation with democratic rights and economic justice. Evangelicals wanted society to imbue those democratic values and practices that they had come to take for granted in their churches. As the political scientist Lydia Svärd concludes, "For people who had gotten used to voting in their congregation, temperance association, or local union, it was a natural thing to seek the right to vote in state and municipalities."

Evangelicals' political instincts and historical circumstances placed them firmly in the liberal camp. They were pro-democracy and pro-solidarity, but against revolution. They wanted to change society through reform, and were highly involved in the process of doing so. In 1908, forty-three evangelicals had seats in the second chamber of the parliament, and the majority of those (twenty-five) belonged to the Liberal party. This meant that 20 percent of parliament and almost 30 percent of the Liberal party were evangelicals.

Those are substantial numbers given that evangelicals at the time made up 5 percent of the population.

A few Social Democrats were radical Marxists who rejected religion of any kind, but most were ready to join hands with evangelicals for a common cause. Accordingly, liberals and socialists could work together for democracy and economic justice, united against a common enemy: the conservative establishment.

SWEDISH EVANGELICALISM IN THE TWENTIETH CENTURY

The struggle for democracy and economic solidarity shaped Swedish evangelicalism into a liberal, left-leaning political movement. This identity was strong and enduring. In the 1956 election, 58 percent of the evangelicals voted for the Liberal party (*Folkpartiet*), which was more than twice the figure for the party in the general election (24 percent). The second largest party was the Social Democrats, with close to 30 percent of the evangelical vote. The Conservative party gained 10 percent of the evangelical vote, a mere half of the support among the general electorate.

The politics of Swedish evangelicalism changed somewhat in the 1960s, when Lewi Pethrus, leader of the Pentecostal movement, founded the Christian Democrats. Pethrus was culturally conservative, and wanted to halt secularization, particularly of schools and entertainment. But he was still in favor of progressive economic politics. In their first official political declaration, the party began by affirming its "appreciation and respect" for the welfare state, and declared that it was ready to "wholeheartedly support and develop it further." They described unions as "indispensable," and warned against fiscal and corporate centralization. Pethrus, a theologically conservative Pentecostal, emphasized his whole life that "Christianity and social justice are intimately connected."

Swedish evangelicals were skeptical of socialism, not social justice – even when that justice was mediated through state-sponsored welfare. Polls from the late twentieth century show that Swedish evangelicals continue to be against the death penalty, and for welfare, migration, humanitarian aid, and the environment.

Compared to secular voters, Swedish evangelicals are more engaged in environmental issues, more supportive of migration and humanitarian aid, and more critical of military export.

White American evangelicals tend toward the opposite in all those issues. They are, as we shall see, shaped by another and very different story.

THE GREAT REVERSAL IN AMERICAN EVANGELICALISM

In the 1960s a young evangelical named Donald Dayton began his studies at one of the movement's colleges. All around him, the world was changing: the civil rights movement marched against racism and students took to the streets to protest the Vietnam War. But nothing of this reached his college. Here, politics peaked when the students protested the ban against TV on Sundays.

It was, Dayton thought, like living in a bubble.

Like so many in his generation, he felt squeezed between the progressive spirit of the age and an evangelical movement that wanted to preserve the status quo. He had to choose between evangelical piety and political involvement, and – again like many – he picked the latter. He moved to New York City, started attending black churches, and began his studies at Columbia University. He was saying farewell to evangelicalism.

But as he was working on a paper at his new university, he discovered that what seemed then a rather complacent movement had radical political roots. Evangelicals had fought hard against slavery, protested discrimination against women, and championed economic justice. But somewhere along the way that had changed, and Dayton would spend his life trying to explain what had happened.

Historian George M. Marsden later labeled this change "the Great Reversal": the rejection of progressive politics, including support for welfare through state politics – and in some cases even skepticism of private or church-sponsored charity. In the early twentieth century, the branches of evangelicalism in Sweden and the United States were moving away from each other politically. They swam in different waters, and were carried away by different currents. In America there were neither landed nobility nor state churches. Democratic rights, including religious freedom, were already in place. Accordingly, there was no need for political mobilization where evangelicals joined hands with liberals and socialists in order to overthrow a conservative establishment. The strong alliances that shaped Swedish evangelicalism – and for that part much of European evangelicalism – never took place in the United States.

Further, the state played a different role in their political imaginations. In the story of Swedish modernity, the democratic welfare state transformed an unjust and elitist society into a more just one. But the founding myth of United States is not a story about freedom through the state, but freedom from the state. There is a strong anti-statist theme in American politics and culture, which has its roots in the flight from the oppressive Old World and the struggle against British rule. This theme was baptized by Puritans, and later evangelicals, who saw it as part of the divine destiny of the United States: to be a shining beacon of freedom to the world. In this story, the state is associated with the oppressive structures of the Old World and should be kept to a minimum. Freedom is that pristine moment when the pilgrims arrived or the birth of the Republic, when the British yoke was broken. Welfare is seen as an unsound expansion of the state – something that undermines individual thrift and responsibility, and is financed by taxes that rob people of the freedom to do what they please with their money.

From these narratives came two developments in the early 1900s that pushed American evangelicals even further away from progressive politics. The first was the modernist-fundamentalist conflict. During this period, the social gospel movement emerged, uniting liberal theology with an emphasis on social justice. In response, Reformed theologians formulated a series of pamphlets titled *The Fundamentals: A Testimony to the Truth* in order to establish the nonnegotiable basics of Christian dogma. Soon, evangelicalism became firmly entrenched in the fundamentalist camp. According to the logic of theological battles and bundling, they had to firmly reject whatever the other embraced, including social justice. Marsden argues that "the factor crucial to understanding the 'Great Reversal' is the fundamentalist reaction to the liberal Social Gospel after 1900. . . . By the time of World War I, 'social Christianity' was becoming thoroughly identified with liberalism and was viewed with great suspicion by many conservative evangelicals."

Swedish evangelicals also rejected liberal theology; this movement was never strong enough to pose a real threat to them. Liberal theology was something distant, a sign of the corruption of already failing churches, and evangelicals did not fashion their theological identity in opposition to it. Swedish evangelicals did not have to choose between conservative theology and progressive economic politics.

But in the United States, this either/or binary became even more entrenched after World War II, when American identity was formulated in opposition to the Soviet Union. Now communism and socialism become the great enemies: they were not only anti-Christian ideologies but also pressing existential threats to the nation. While 30 percent of Swedish evangelicals voted for the Social Democrats in the 1950s, in the United States this was the decade of McCarthyism and the Red Scare. Some evangelicals connected the dots and claimed that the progressive politics of the social gospel were inspired by communism and stood in opposition to the divinely sanctioned American spirit. State welfare was anti-Christian as well as un-American.

These are two very different stories, and they go far to explain the differences between me and my American friends in 2000. I was the product of an evangelical movement tied to political liberalism, with an emphasis on social justice. In US history, a number of intersecting themes had moved them in a different direction: the anti-statist impulse shaping American culture and a theological battle that led to paranoia over social gospel and the Cold War fear of socialism. For them the state was no natural ally, but rather an obstacle to overcome in order to become free. In my history, the modern state was what guaranteed freedom from unequal and undemocratic structures.

In the end, the strongest argument I met was not political but moral. Evangelicals then dreamt of placing a born-again Christian in the White House. This reflected the tactics of the Religious Right, who wanted to elect Christian men to political positions.

But two decades later, this has changed. Donald Trump is no model of piety, and his politic are of a different kind. In Trumpism, the state plays a bigger role as protector of what is described as a "traditional" American way of life against the threatening forces of secularization, pluralism, and migration. This is a new chapter in the story of evangelical politics.

THE TURN TO POPULISM

The alliance between white evangelicals and the GOP was formalized in the 1970s through organizations like the Moral Majority. During this period a number of Supreme Court decisions perceived as secularizing – particularly the legalization of abortion – drove evangelicals into politics. They were motivated by a desire for a stronger Christian ethics in society and a fear that state regulations would interfere with their own institutions.

From Ronald Reagan onward, evangelicals had the sense that the Republican Party listened to their case and supported their cause. They were granted access to presidents and prominent politicians. In 1980, 65 percent of white evangelicals supported Reagan, and by the time of George W. Bush the figures approached 80 percent. But despite the fact that the Republicans controlled the White House and both houses of Congress from 2003 to 2007, very little changed in terms of the core issues that motivated evangelicals. Disillusionment started to spread. Pastor and subsequent Trump supporter Robert Jeffress recalls,

> I remember very well back in 2004, being on a conference call with religious leaders and how disappointed they were with George W. Bush, and how they felt like he had just really misled us. . . . I don't want to disparage him at all, but what came out of that eight years? A $7 trillion war in the Middle East.

The Republicans seemed either unable or unwilling to make good on their promises. Change continued to accelerate in a way that made many evangelicals feel increasingly left behind. In 1997, a quarter of the population identified as white evangelicals, but two decades later that figure is down to 17 percent. Religious pluralism is growing, and so is tolerance of divorce and LGBTQ rights. Some evangelicals worry that these developments will lead to regulation of their own schools, hospitals, and other institutions. They sense the contempt from the liberal cultural establishment, which views them as bitter people who "cling to guns or religion," as Obama infamously put it.

The liberals are after them, and Republicans seem unable to protect them. This feeling is the context for evangelical enthusiasm for Trump. After forty years of constant defeats, evangelicals were ready to try something else. A Christian character might be good for much but not, it seems, for winning battles in the cultural war. Sure, Trump is a brutal, crude strongman – but he is *their* brutal, crude strongman. The now disgraced Jerry Falwell Jr. articulated the new strategy in a tweet:

> Conservatives & Christians need to stop electing "nice guys." They might make great Christian leaders but the US needs street fighters like @realDonaldTrump at every level of government b/c the liberal fascists Dems are playing for keeps & many Repub leaders are a bunch of wimps!

Evangelicals worry about cultural, religious, and demographic changes. Historian John Fea argues that this worry reflects a fear of losing their own privileged position in the nation. His colleague Thomas Kidd similarly claims that evangelical politics is rooted in a desire to return the nation "to a nostalgic past of Christian cultural establishment while exhorting individuals to reject mere cultural Christianity and to be born again." Trump seemed strong enough not only to protect evangelicals from the state interventions orchestrated by liberals but also to return the nation to a more homogenous Christian past.

SWEDEN: THE REJECTION OF POPULISM

In Sweden, the political rise of populism is manifested by the Sweden Democrats, a nationalistic party that made it into parliament in 2010 with 6 percent of the vote. In 2014 that figure doubled to 13, and in 2018 they became the third-largest party, with support from 18 percent of Swedish voters. The party wants to limit immigration and

protect what they describe as a traditional homogenous Swedish culture. Christianity is important in their nationalistic project, and they
see the church as a central part of the national identity. This desire to
return to a Christian, more homogenous past clearly mirrors Trump's
political vision.

Given the fact that Sweden is one of the world's most secular
countries, one would expect that a party which highlights the role
of the church would attract many evangelicals. But instead, evangelical voters are among the most reluctant to support the Sweden
Democrats. For two decades, the number of evangelicals doing so
has been between one-third and one-half the total number of voters
to do so. The reason is that Swedish evangelicals are repelled by
the populist rejection of migration and pluralism. Political scientist
Magnus Hagevi concludes that "individuals who are regular free
church goers tend to have comparatively positive opinions toward
refugees and toward Sweden as a multicultural society."

Behind this openness are of course theological convictions, but
again, the wider political context seems to be an important factor.
In this case the fact that Swedish evangelicals have been a minority
since the beginning is significant. The fight for religious freedom
was, as we saw, central to the original political mobilization of the
nineteenth century. During the 1900s Sweden became a secular
country with a Lutheran state church, which further underscored
the minority status of the free churches. As a minority, they
depend on a state that accepts religious pluralism. The embrace of
this principle has led evangelicals to argue for tolerance of other
religious traditions – including Islam. Polls show that evangelicals
are more open to a multicultural society than the average Swede,
and that they oppose bans of religious building such as mosques.

It seems like churches that are at arm's length from power and
the cultural mainstream are in a better position to develop the
Christian virtue of hospitality. As a majority religion intertwined
with the state, Christianity often becomes more rigid, less hospitable,
and at times hostile – even to other Christian minorities. Pluralism
is seen as a threat, since it might mean that Christianity will lose its
privileged position. In contrast to this, a minority can never expect
to set the rules for any encounter. Instead they must find ways to

negotiate and live with difference. Accordingly, they become well equipped to live as a creative minority in a pluralistic society.

This explains why Swedish evangelicals are less threatened by immigration, pluralism, and the growth of Islam than are their US evangelical counterparts, to say nothing of the Swedish secular majority. To a minority, pluralism is not the big threat. In this case, diversity is a step up from the traditional homogenous secular-Lutheran society. It levels the playing field, and makes clear that there is no neutral ground, only competing perspectives. The development of what Jürgen Habermas called the post-secular society is a welcome development to a minority. Swedish evangelicals are aware that any attempt to homogenize the culture would marginalize them.

EVANGELICAL POLITICAL THEOLOGY

This historical sketch does not cover every factor shaping the politics of either Swedish or American evangelicalism. The latter has also been formed by multiple wars and the heightened patriotism in their wake, strong businessmen, and deeply unresolved issues pertaining to race. White evangelicals did to a large extent sit out the civil rights movement, and since the Civil War they have rarely been in the frontline for the struggle against racial injustice. This is something the movement needs to reckon with. The fact that Donald Trump's xenophobic remarks have not deterred evangelical voters, but according to some scholars is part of their attraction to him, makes the problem even more acute.

Interestingly, the political attitudes of Swedish evangelicals are similar to those of African American evangelicals. They too tend to oppose the death penalty, support humanitarian aid, and embrace social justice. Swedish and African American evangelicals share the experience of being minorities in their respective nations: the first in the shadow of a secular-Lutheran mainstream, the other of the WASP culture. This is another indication that sociological and historical circumstances strongly shape evangelical political theology.

The conclusion of this cannot be, however, that minority status leads to a "good" politics, while being in the majority – or expecting to be—is always problematic. Instead, it is better to note that both positions come with temptations as well as possibilities for faithful witness. The political theology of Swedish evangelicalism has many deficits. It has tended toward individualistic pietism, and has not reflected enough on what it means to build institutions shaped by a Christian political imagination. In its embrace of the welfare state, it has too readily accepted being sidelined on matters concerning *caritas*. It has neglected public debate and not built institutions that safeguard the formation of intellectual representatives of the movement. In all these matters, American evangelicalism has been stronger—and sometimes also more faithful.

But one inevitable conclusion from the stories told above is that there is no straight line from evangelical theology and spirituality to one particular political identity. This is an important insight given the growing homogenization of white American evangelical political identity. The intertwining with the Republican Party has gone so far that the term "evangelical," as Kidd notes, has become "fundamentally political in popular parlance." Mark Labberton, president of Fuller Theological Seminary, concludes that "evangelical" has "morphed from being commonly used to describe a set of theological and spiritual commitments into a passionately defended, theo-political brand." "Evangelical" names a white, self-identifying Christian who votes for the Republicans but does not necessarily go to church.

This means that theology has succumbed to ideology, and the church to a political party. In the age-old combat between state and church, white evangelicalism has de facto lost its independence. In tying themselves to Trump, American evangelicals not only reduce their faith to ideology but also make their future dependent on a political project. There is an ominous parallel here to the secularization of Europe, which to a large extent was a political reaction against churches that were perceived to be politically corrupt. For the state churches were allied with the old political order, and defended the monarchy against the growing demands of democratic reform. The religious establishment picked the wrong side, with the result that being pro-democracy meant being anti-church. In countries such as England and Sweden the evangelical movements, which were Christian as well as pro-democracy, made it possible to combine Christian faith with progressive politics. But when this was lacking, as in France, it resulted in rampant secularization.

The alliance between the established state churches and the monarchy gave these churches access to the halls of power, but when the political winds shifted they found themselves supporting a regime that lacked legitimacy. There are similarities here with what seems to be going on in the United States. Already there are signs that people – especially young people – who reject Republican politics also feel inclined to leave the church. American secularization might arrive a century later but for the same reason as in Europe: as a reaction against the politicization of the church.

Today, America is characterized by a political polarization that seeps into all aspects of life: culture, the universities, workplaces, and even family dinners. In this moment, the church needs to look at what has been its main political mission throughout history – namely, to keep the peace and, crucially, to *embody* peace. As historian John Bossy has noted, the liturgy and practices of the church in medieval Europe were designed to foster peace and friendship in a world where struggle, conflict, and war always seemed close.

This does not mean abandoning politics. Rather, one expression of such a politics would be to create spaces where people of different convictions are able to gather and explore a unity that is not based on political agreement. But this demands that Christians, instead of using politics as a theological shibboleth, listen – though of course not uncritically – to what has shaped individual convictions. For behind each conviction lies a story, and knowing it often leads not to consent but to some kind of understanding. But reductionism is always a temptation: to reduce individuals to their political convictions, and the church to a branch of a certain party. Withstanding it demands a richer anthropology, a deeper understanding of the church as the body of Christ and a realization that the political mission of the church is to work for unity. Not to keep quiet, but to keep the peace. ✢

November 3, 2020

OBSERVATIONS OF A NEW CITIZEN

IRENA DRAGAŠ JANSEN

I BECAME A CITIZEN of the United States of America on September 11, 2020. Every heartfelt expression of congratulations by friends, family, and acquaintances was almost always followed by a cheery admonition: "You can vote now!" Each reminder of my political responsibilities chipped away at the monumental amount of joy and relief I felt about becoming an American citizen. I was not looking forward to voting. I wanted to continue observing. My observation deck seemed a much safer and much more comfortable place than a looming voting booth.

For I have been observing the United States from various viewpoints my whole life. First, I observed America from a far-off distance, as a girl growing up in a Christian family living in a Communist country in Eastern Europe. American westerns, soap operas like *Dynasty* and *Dallas*, pop and country music, basketball, and American guests visiting our small local church all provided windows into this distant country that seemed at once unattainable and familiar.

This America we observed was the land of prosperity and endless possibilities. If you had courage and determination, you could

IRENA DRAGAŠ JANSEN conducts program and resource development for non-profits and social enterprises in Europe and the United States. A survivor of the Yugoslav Wars, she is currently writing a semi-autobiographical book exploring the power of art and faith, *Path Stops for the Middle*. Irena lives in Arlington, Virginia, with her husband Scott.

make anything happen in America. It was the land of John Wayne and Tina Turner. The playground of Michael Jordan and the Dream Team. Hollywood royalty and Texas oil dynasties. In America, you were free to be a Christian and not be persecuted or marginalized for it. You were free to follow any religious practice for that matter, or none at all. This land embodied freedom, and it shone brightly from far away. But my family and I were happy to observe and admire it from a distance. We still had a life in our own country, where we were rooted in a particular history, community, and faith.

Then in the 1990s, war ravaged my newly independent country of Croatia. My family and I became displaced when our hometown was occupied by enemy forces and we had to flee to the free part of our homeland. As we navigated the loss of our home, our possessions, and the devastating loss of life, we tried to comprehend a way through and forward for our family, our country, and the whole war-torn former Yugoslavia. Throughout all this, we paid close attention to what America was doing, or not doing, in regard to our dire situation.

America cares. America engages. We knew that. Our history books were filled with stories about World War II, the Allied Forces, and our own resistance movement. I remember my parents telling us stories about Marshall's eggs – their nickname for a staple in the food supplies that America provided in the aftermath of that old war. Now, in this new war, we all expected America to care and engage again. Every country in the region wanted the United States of America to side with them, to help them, to fight for their cause, and fight against their enemy. I felt for America. It was a tough position to be in. If the United States engaged, they were certain to make one side happy and the opposing side upset. If they did not, the whole world would be upset with them for not helping. And whatever America chose to do, they would of course be accused of acting out of self-interest.

THE VIEW FROM INSIDE

While still a displaced person, I got to see firsthand what this global protagonist was about when I spent four years as a college student in California. This, too, was the result of Americans caring and engaging—both on an organized level (through a scholarship at the university) and an individual level (one family's initiative and generosity). When I got off the plane at the Los Angeles airport that August evening, I stepped into a curious journey of having to reconcile the America of movies, humanitarian packages, and air strikes to the reality of America on its own turf.

America had giant cars, enormous freeways, and an almost endless number of variations of any single item. I spent a lot of time and energy trying to choose a toothpaste, or contemplating my options for a simple piece of toast at a restaurant. Upon closer inspection, this country did indeed seem to be a land of possibility. Perhaps too much of it. I called it "the curse of the possibility." I wondered, just because something was possible, did it need to be done? A supersized meal, a bigger house, a better car, another loan?

Once immersed in American culture, I realized how easily misunderstood America was by those observing from the outside. Upon closer inspection, a non-monolithic United States of America emerged: There was America's heroic history, but also its dark history; there were uniquely American issues that were still not resolved; there was division. The West Coast versus the East Coast, and the flyover middle. The North and the South. The rich and the poor. The Republicans and the Democrats.

And Christians were divided too. Not only were there dozens, maybe even hundreds, of different church denominations, but Christians were divided politically as well. I remember offending my professor and her husband when I innocently assumed that because of their Christian beliefs they supported one political party. I think it was at that dinner party when I first decided that when it came to political discussions, I was best suited to observe, not participate.

When I returned to Croatia after college graduation, I observed my native country making a transition from Communism to democracy, and from socialism to capitalism, all while dealing with the aftermath of the war, and the ethnic tensions still simmering. I compared our long and rocky transition process to the already established American political and economic system, discussing it with my American friends during my visits back to the United States over the course of the following thirteen years.

I found myself wanting to both encourage and warn my American friends. I would hear complaints about the United States from within, and I became aware of a growing fascination among American young people with alternative forms of governmental and economic systems. Having had the experience of living in two different political and economic systems, I could see the advantages and the downsides of both. I knew the Grand Experiment in democracy had created a good thing. A really good thing! Even though it was imperfect, it should be recognized for all its good characteristics, and it was worth refining – not replacing.

And there was another thing. Americans were used to living in a country whose public policies, political-party platforms, government-imposed laws, and moral values invoked Christian beliefs and values. It was a messy and often incomplete rendering, but Christianity was, by and large, not a cultural foe. This, too, seemed to be changing. There was a growing concern among some American Christians that the country they had assumed friendly to their beliefs was turning against them, and many began expressing fear. I thought back to my parents and how they had managed to live a vibrant and authentic Christian faith in a country whose political system and moral values did not represent their Christian and personal values and beliefs. They passed on this hopeful, remnant way of living to my siblings and me. I attempted to encourage my American friends out of that conviction and experience.

And then, ten years ago, I took yet another flight across the ocean. Holding the hand of my new American husband, I landed on the East Coast. I was now going to get a different view of the United States of America, that of a permanent resident. And even though my perspective was different, my modus operandi remained the same: I continued observing.

Much to the chagrin and frustration of my American husband, family, and friends, I would not engage on the issues defined by America's two political parties. Except on the rare occasion when I would ask questions, offer a few observations, and/or play devil's advocate, I refused to choose sides. I was giving myself, a foreigner, time to survey the land. Not being able to vote provided a good excuse. And vote I could not – not anywhere. For the past ten years,

I could not vote in Croatia because, even though I was a Croatian citizen, I was not residing there. I was not able to vote in the United States because, even though I was a permanent resident, I was not a citizen. My civic duty was limited by the laws of each land, and I happily accepted this reality as it created a sanctuary from which I could safely observe.

But I was not a detached bystander; I was an interested spectator with skin in the game. I was a student of American history and was familiar with historical issues this country had faced, which also shaped its present strengths and struggles. I witnessed and sought to understand the changes occurring on various levels of American society. I partook in many conversations about America and even shared my observations. I was, however tenderly, letting my roots take hold in this new country of mine. I planted myself into my new village and I cared for it. The village generously cared back.

What I had known to be true before was now confirmed. Americans care, and Americans engage – both internationally and domestically. While I had been a witness to and a recipient of their international care and involvement, once living here, I was deeply impressed by the vast number of organizations and initiatives (both governmental and private) that existed with the sole purpose of helping with international issues and needs. This is not the norm elsewhere. Almost with the wonder of a child, I began to observe how much Americans cared and engaged domestically too. As someone who had grown up in a Communist country, I knew that civic engagement was not always encouraged or even allowed among citizens, and I knew well how long it took to learn and develop civic responsibility even when it was allowed. I was a complete novice. But for Americans, young and old, this was a way of life.

During this tenure as an interested spectator of the United States, now from within, I had deep peace. I kept thinking back to my parents and our Christian family and community, the ways in which we managed to live with peace and hope, keeping our eyes on Christ while navigating the dangerous waters of living as Christians in a Communist country. We paid the price for it, but we knew our true allegiance was to the heavenly Kingdom. I even gave a talk here in the United States about heavenly citizenship versus earthly residency. I clung to this heavenly citizenship while I navigated the waters of not fully belonging to any earthly country, even as I continued to puzzle out the riddle of my evolving passport identity.

DISILLUSIONMENT AND PRESSURE

But as time passed, my continued observations of my new place of residency started fostering some frustrations. I was appalled by how much public and private discourse forfeited the rules of logic, and how many people resorted to the use of logical fallacies in their discussions and public addresses. It infuriated me when speakers used logical fallacies assuming that I, the listener, would not recognize them and would therefore be convinced by their faulty arguments. At times, they would be limited to simple but still harmful civic sermons based on either a wrong premise or hammering home an incorrect conclusion. Hasty generalizations were on the rise, leading to easy stereotyping, overstatement, and exaggeration in settings both intimate and mass. Distractions were deployed constantly as a way to avoid answering difficult questions. False dilemmas were presented more times than I could count, trying to force me to ignore that there were in fact more options than the limited ones offered. But most blatant were the ad hominem, the personal attacks that replaced arguments and invoked hypocrisy in the opponent in order to distract from the argument. It scared me how often this worked and produced the desired effect on the audience—in personal conversations, in charged street demonstrations, even in polished speeches on Capitol Hill.

As the political and social atmosphere in the United States became more heated, I grew more disturbed by the prevalent use of double standards. Each side, political or ideological, would choose a convenient "measuring stick" on their opponents, without applying the same set of measures to evaluate their own side. Ethical codes fell victim to an unequally applied measuring stick. Double standards on the issue of tolerance became so blatant that I was afraid America was becoming desensitized to it.

Most disappointing, Christians were not exempt from these pitfalls. They increasingly grew more polarized in their support of one of the two political parties. I watched aghast as they fell to either side of the widening schism. They seemed to be allowing their political leaders to frame their way of thinking about problems and solutions. I had no answers, but I had plenty of questions. Where was biblical problem-solving? Why are Christians allowing the political parties to make them think that there are only two packages of solutions to the issues America is facing? Why are Christians allowing their allegiance to a political party to determine their identity? Why are Christians not identifying problems and creating solutions that rise above the boundaries of visibly cynical political parties?

And then there was the issue of voting. What I heard communicated to me was that voting was my most important task as a citizen, and the future hinged on my voting choice. More specifically, by voting for president, for one single human being, I was deciding what my and everyone else's future in America was going to be. In addition to helping decide the future of the nation and every person in it, my voting would also determine what kind of a Christian I was, or if indeed I even was one at all. The explicit and implicit force of these messages alarmed me.

Then, as I was pondering all these disturbing developments, something shocking happened: I slowly started sliding toward one political party's platform. My support of one side's values and approach to solving issues crept up on me. The annoyance with the other side grew stronger. I slowly began connecting my personal safety and the country's well-being to the electoral victory of one political party and its primary candidate.

And I lost my peace. I became perturbed. The fuel of fear ignited anger within me. I felt as if I was being swallowed by a storm that I had stepped into when I abandoned the safety of my spectator's boat. The voices creating this tempest were infuriated and infuriating, enraged and eloquent. They were concerned, and they cared. But most of all, these voices were loud. Enveloped by my own fear and anger, I could not hear past them.

I craved the return of my peace. I started processing what was happening to me by furiously documenting my confusion and fear. I would talk to close friends about it and then retreat back to untangling the individual strands of my observations, which had formed into the knot of my angst. It all felt very much like wrestling. Like Jacob. With God.

Except, unlike Jacob, I invited other people into my wrestling match. I continued honest discussions with trusted friends and family members who were also eagerly searching and grappling with similar questions. I decided to limit my exposure to those voices that I knew would cause me distress and fill my head space with loud and forceful – but not always true – messages. This included news and social media. My palate needed cleansing. I also knew I had to put myself in the path of truth and wisdom. Choosing the correct *path stops* while I journeyed through the middle of this troubled season was imperative. I talked to my parents and asked them to tell me of times past and present, and their ways of living through them. I read history and sought lessons learned by those long gone. I watched online lectures and conversations by those living now who sought dialogue and offered hopeful perspectives and solutions. I listened to Bible readings. I signed up for weekly spiritual exercises called *Space for God* to help me create just that – space for God. When I got sick and my husband was gone on a work trip, I spent two weeks alone in my house listening to hymns and worship music, crying out to God to help me.

And God answered. Coiled together with the strands of my angst, I found the beautiful if delicate strands of hope and peace. I began to realize that the moment I lost my peace was when I took my eyes off Christ and put my hope in the victory of a political party promising to keep me safe. I began to realize that my trust should never have wavered from the One who addresses the root of all human problems and gives us eternal hope and ever-present help. I knew that there might be long-lasting and significant consequences to either side winning. But I have lived in a difficult environment before, and God was faithful and present in it. If it should come to that, it is possible to stay true to one's faith and beliefs even when there is a price to pay. I should not anchor my life in the circumstances around me, but in the One who remains the same; whatever happens.

And my peace was restored. It is a delicate bird, a true "thing with feathers – that perches in the soul," much like Emily Dickinson's hope. It needs constant tending.

Even though I had realigned myself with the heavenly Kingdom, I still had my earthly residency to live out well. So, how then should I live? Asking that question was the genesis of the answer. I realized that framing the conversation and posing the correct questions, instead of just reacting, is where I wanted to start.

FIRST THINGS FIRST

So, how then do I want to live–before, during, and after each election? I want to have compassion for other people's concerns, cares, and fears, regardless of what side they are on. I want to listen to hear. I want to look for common ground. If we look closely, all of our stories are the same, not, in fact, opposite. We all want to be safe. We all fear we are not, or will not be, if certain things happen. The fuel of fear ignites our actions. The fuel of fear can consume us, and our actions start to mirror the actions we condemn when they are committed by the other side. The face of my enemy is my own face.

How do I want to live, before, during, and after elections? I want to learn–glean insights from those dead and alive, from history and the present times. I want to search for and be inspired by those people who share their convictions with gentleness and kindness, and help and support those who create initiatives and solutions by bringing people together. Convictions include and invite in. Accusations exclude.

However, it is November 3, 2020, and one question remains: How should I then vote? After all, I am not just an observer anymore. After researching, reading, listening, and talking to people on both sides, I will decide the best I can. And I will cast my vote knowing that it is important, but also confident and assured that it is not the most important nor the only thing I can do. I can choose to place my hope in God and his everlasting presence. I can choose how to live. I can choose how to see and treat others. I can love my neighbor. I can get involved and contribute. Because Americans care and Americans engage. And I am one of them. ✤

EXODUS

The Ironies and Finalities of Being on Top of the World

KATHERINE BOYLE

Remember not the former things,
  nor consider the things of old.
Behold, I am doing a new thing;
  now it springs forth, do you not perceive it?
I will make a way in the wilderness
  and rivers in the desert.
                    —Isaiah 43:18–19

ON THE DAY the sun didn't rise in San Francisco, the early warning signs came through the screen. The 6:30 a.m. Zoom always requires unnatural light, making the outlines of faces fuzzy. The natural morning light, combined with the "Touch Up My Appearance" feature on 2020's preferred video conferencing system, hides the marks of age and sleeplessness that most of us seek to mask. But by nine o'clock, the fluorescent light was still dominating the screen, and the darkness outside our windows had turned to infernal orange.

The scientific explanation for our sunless day in September is pretty dull. Clouds of soot from the largest California wildfire in history intermixed with the Bay Area's perennial fog, turning the usual sepia hue of dirty global cities into an apocalyptic blood-orange

---

KATHERINE BOYLE is a venture capitalist based in San Francisco.

sky. Though Twitter blamed the hellscape on far more menacing forces, the direct cause of our Blade Runner Day was mostly carbon clinging to the blue-light hues while letting the red pierce through.

If we were more like ancient peoples, many joked, we would assume the gods were enraged. We'd be running for the hills to escape their wrath, or at least head straight for our prepper bunkers. That we are unlike ancient people is actually the only myth, as this is exactly the exodus that is happening in Silicon Valley right now—and will continue for the next few years as true believers deliver themselves from this promised land.

It's time to build, yes. But it's also time to leave.

The battle over tech's supremacy has been waged and all of our premonitions came true: we wanted flying cars and got vertical take-off innovation hubs from every car maker in America. Software has not only eaten the world, but feasted on your screen-weary eyes. It has swallowed your children, your church, your bank, and your politics, and somehow it all feels inevitable. That these feats of human progress – of instant connectivity in a now homebound world – became the scapegoat of our time is another symptom of the era's end, cueing the quiet exodus of builders who had bigger aspirations than the same-day shipping that keeps our households afloat.

Now, Silicon Valley is witnessing a reckoning, but it's not the long-awaited one predicted by the New York press, or the antitrust bonanza that Washington longs for because too many people seem satisfied getting their news from Facebook. The reckoning is more of a realization that tech exceeded expectations and somehow squandered the fruit of its own garden, and that a city on a hill that could have supported so much innovation was not Florence in the Renaissance nor the Athenian academy with MacBooks. Rather, it became a government-sponsored needle exchange, a haven for the homeless and forgotten that put government's paralysis on display downtown on Market Street.

San Francisco had four times as many deaths from overdose this year as it did from the Covid-19 virus.

2020 is not the great reckoning predicted in the Book of Revelation, despite the fires, the plagues, and the wailing on Twitter. It is the resignation and determination of Exodus, of a dogged people packing up U-Hauls and fleeing this frontier state to seek an even newer, more eternal world.

———

The computer revolution of the late twentieth century has yet to be named as an epoch, but we can assume that nomenclature will begin in the coming years, alongside the battle for what it all really meant.

What we now call our "technological age" was supposed to be a full-throated and enduring argument for the future, not unlike previous epochs in history that pushed art, science, philosophy, and religion forward in dizzying ways that run counter to ordinary time. The Enlightenment. The Renaissance. The French Revolution. These movements now sit as categories on our bookshelves with clear beginnings and ends, and more importantly, clear hubs and cities of frenetic building that drove the ethos forward. Many books assume that contemporary critics or philosophers were blissfully ignorant of the unraveling of their revolutions, but we should not assume that contemporaries did not feel the same twilight setting. The figurative orange skies always creep in before dawn.

Which brings us to the supposed death of Silicon Valley, a fate that has long been predicted but with data now finally catching up. San Francisco apartment rents in 2020 have deflated by 20 percent after an up-up-and-away decade that made the city truly unlivable. Home inventory has reached a fifteen-year high in a city blighted by restrictive housing policy that makes construction cranes as miraculous as stumbling upon a burning bush. The growth in online sales-tax collection, according to the *San Francisco Chronicle*, is the lowest of all counties in the state of California. And public tech companies, such as Pinterest, paid upward of $90 million to break their leases in downtown San Francisco. Some would argue this is a clear end to Bay Area tech dominance, while others would point to the many new unicorns that popped up this year despite the once-in-a-century pandemic. No one's living here, yet somehow the companies are still growing.

Silicon Valley doesn't really have cultural critics to weigh in on whether this era is officially over, but we do have venture capitalists. And our Nostradamuses are telling us that change is afoot.

Do we really need this office? The founders all have left.

Their entire partnership is now living in Montana. It's only a two-hour flight away!

Denver seems like a good option, but Reno has no state income tax.

The weirdness of this exodus is that it is not driven by fear. Technologists weren't *really* driven out by plague or fire or San Francisco's insatiable need for higher tax revenue. Those ills were always apparent, and yet people stayed to carry the torch.

The exodus of tech's true believers may be that the covenant is finally fulfilled. That when America – along with the rest of the world – met its darkest hour and turned inward, the technology that was long ridiculed as frivolous or dangerous led us to relative normalcy. The Zooms. The *Tiger Kings*. The Signal chats. The Slack jokes. An election news cycle that plowed ruthlessly forward on Twitter. Though inconvenient, mothers and fathers set their children in front of screens to occupy them for *just* long enough to survive a terrible year. And maybe, just maybe, the same-day-shipping racket that made Jeff Bezos the richest man alive was actually a feat of human genius that held the country together when public infrastructure and the social fabric were fraying at the seams. Perhaps our lowly software revolution was actually the fruition of a long-held California dream, when the physical world forced us inside and virtual life prevailed.

For that triumph, the nerds can now smell the impending scapegoating of their success. And like so many of history's prophets and heretics, those who believe most fervently in the promise of technology are beginning their long march away from the Valley.

And they will substitute the virtual world for the physical space that once defined this movement. Silicon Valley is no longer a place, they'll say. It's a way of being, of building, and the latest embodiment of belief in human progress. And it's spreading faster than the viruses and the wildfires and the apocalyptic threats that mire our physical world.

Silicon Valley is over. The exodus is just beginning. ✤

THE SKILL OF HOSPITALITY

L. M. SACASAS

LONG AGO, in the mid-1990s, between stints as governor of California, Jerry Brown hosted a talk-radio show called *We the People.* The show featured an eclectic set of guests including Noam Chomsky, Gore Vidal, and Allen Ginsberg. On March 22, 1996, however, Brown aired a remarkable conversation with two guests one would hardly expect to appear on a politically oriented talk show: the philosopher of technology Carl Mitcham and Ivan Illich, a scholar and social critic best known for his wide-ranging critiques of industrial society in the early 1970s.

We no longer live in the early 1970s, or the mid-90s for that matter. We live in what can seem like a different world altogether, marked chiefly by the rise of digital technologies, which appear to raise very different issues than those raised by the industrial-age tools and institutions that were the target of Illich's critical acumen. Nonetheless, in this interview, and in his larger body of work, Illich offers us both a trenchant and a helpful diagnosis of our social disorders as well as glimpses of a way forward. Illich's diagnosis remains pertinent because he saw better than most the deep-rooted and ultimately theological sources of our disorders. The path forward, he suggested, and that he embodied in his practice, was the path of hospitality. As he put it to Brown, "I do

L. M. SACASAS is associate director of the Christian Study Center of Gainesville, Florida, and author of *The Convivial Society*, a newsletter about technology and society.

think that if I had to choose one word to which hope can be tied, it is hospitality."

—

Although in the seventies Illich had achieved a measure of celebrity – he packed lecture halls; his short but dense, demanding books were best sellers; and he frequently wrote for outlets like the *New York Review of Books* – by the 1980s, his work had fallen out of fashion. This was an unfortunate if not altogether surprising development. Illich was an unsparing critic of industrial society, and he took aim not only at its obvious ills like pollution and the degradation of the environment but even at what most would assume were its most salient successes: education and medicine. In the early seventies, he hoped that people would rediscover "the value of joyful sobriety and liberating austerity" by relearning how to depend on each other. The message was lost on the culture of excess and individualism that came to define the 1980s.

As a young man Illich had not set out to become a social critic. Instead, he pursued a religious and scholarly vocation. By the early 1950s, he had earned a doctorate in history from the University of Salzburg, had studied the work of Thomas Aquinas with Jacques Maritain, and was ordained a priest in the Roman Catholic Church. Illich's brilliance and linguistic skills – he was by most accounts fluent in at least eight languages, both modern and classical – marked him as a uniquely gifted rising star in the hierarchy of the church. But for just this reason Illich, who eschewed power throughout his career, set off for a more reclusive scholarly life in the United States, where he intended to study the writings of the medieval theologian and philosopher Albertus Magnus at Princeton.

As it turned out, another path was marked for him. Beginning with his encounter in the early 1950s with people in the recently arrived Puerto Rican community in New York, Illich stepped out of the proverbial ivory tower and into the life of the poor, the strangers, the outcasts. His service among Puerto Rican immigrants eventually landed him an administrative position at the Pontifical Catholic University of Puerto Rico, where he served until he ran afoul of the church hierarchy with his public comments opposing the church's stance on contraception. In 1961, Illich then set off on the next phase of his career when he founded the Center for Intercultural Documentation (CIDOC) in Cuernavaca, Mexico. CIDOC functioned as a language school and training center for North American priests sent to minister in Latin America. It also served as an intellectual hub for Illich and the often radical writers, scholars, and thinkers he gathered around him.

Illich's best-known books came out of his collaborations at CIDOC: *Deschooling Society*, *Tools for Conviviality*, *Limits to Medicine*, and *Energy and Equity*. Each of these works took critical aim at key elements of modern industrial society. And it is in this work that we can still find a prescient analysis of our current experience of institutional failure. In *Tools for Conviviality* (1973) he wrote of a "world-wide crisis of world-wide institutions." With both industrial technologies and institutions in mind, Illich went on to warn that "if tools are not controlled politically, they will be managed in a belated technocratic response to disaster. Freedom and dignity will continue to dissolve into an unprecedented enslavement of man to his tools."

What is most resonant in Illich's early writing, then, is the understanding that a certain set of modern institutions and the way of life they sustained had played themselves out, and that a deep and thoroughgoing renewal of the social order was needed, beginning with a renewed appreciation for the human person.

It is sometimes assumed that Illich simply disliked institutions of all sorts or that his critique was grounded principally in an anti-institutional ideology. But this is not quite right. Illich was principally concerned with institutions that had passed through what he called a second watershed, which often involved achieving a particular size or scale or level of complexity. Beyond this watershed or threshold, Illich argued, tools and institutions become counterproductive and eventually destructive.

In explaining the purpose of *Tools for Conviviality*, for example, Illich proposed the concept of "a multidimensional balance of human life which can serve as a framework for evaluating man's relation to his tools." "In each of several dimensions of this balance," Illich wrote, "it is possible to identify a natural scale." He goes on to add that "when an enterprise grows beyond a certain point on this scale, it first frustrates the end for which it was originally designed, and then rapidly becomes a threat to society itself."

In discussions of Illich's work, interpreters have occasionally missed the underlying ethic of his critique. Illich was specifically concerned with the manner in which counterproductive institutions deskill human beings. But he was not just concerned with the loss of our vocational skills – the skills that a worker loses when labor is automated, for example; or our inability to make repairs when it is so easy to buy something new. He was also concerned about a great social deskilling: the loss of the capacity to relate to and care for one another.

"Progress should mean growing competence in self-care rather than growing dependence," Illich wrote. He believed, too, that the liberation promised by modern industrial society amounted to a consequent dependence on institutions that increasingly dictated the terms of human worth relative to standards and criteria that had little or nothing to do with the good of the people they claimed to serve. By contrast, the freedom men and women need, according to Illich, is "the freedom to make the things among which they can live, to give shape to them according to their own tastes, and to put them to use in caring for and about others."

In Illich's view, we are increasingly caught in networks designed ostensibly to empower us but that, in fact, make us all the more dependent on their operations. Having outsourced care to institutions (preschools, nursing homes) and the service industry, we are more helpless and more adrift, bereft not only of a measure of dignity but also of the human consolations of giving and receiving help and comfort.

Illich believed that people have "a native capacity for healing, consoling, moving, learning, building their houses, and burying their dead." Unfortunately, we had, in his view, ceded each of these capacities to the professional classes. What is most troubling about this development is not merely the loss of personal satisfactions and the sense of purpose that might arise from being useful to another. Rather, it is that these practices, which we hardly ever now undertake for one another, were also what we might think of as binding agents. Through my care for another I reach out beyond myself and even beyond the confines of my home to the wider community, to my neighbors.

Jesus' story about the good Samaritan was incredibly important to Illich. As Illich always observed, Jesus is not answering the question, How shall I treat my neighbor? He is answering a deeper question: *Who* is my neighbor? Illich recognized that Jesus, "that most upsetting guy," as he put it to Jerry Brown on that show in the nineties, was abolishing "the limitation of hospitality to the in-group." The point of the story, as Illich went on to explain to Brown, is this: "I can choose. I have to choose. I have to make my mind up whom I will take into my arms, to whom I will lose myself, whom I will treat as that vis-a-vis, that face into which I look . . . from whom I accept being who I am as a gift." The intimacy of the encounter was critical for Illich.

An experience of community is not so much a state to be inhabited as it is a condition to be achieved, and it is achieved by constant practice. By caring for my neighbor in a time of need, I forge a communal bond. My neighbor becomes less of an abstraction: he or she takes on flesh and blood. Their history and my history intertwine. We build up a narrative stock over time that further binds us in memory. But when we have outsourced all of our mutual care to institutions and professionals, these ties atrophy. We recede from a common world of mutual interdependence into our own private enclaves of consumption, becoming as Illich put it slaves of envy or slaves of addiction, unable either to care for ourselves or for our neighbors.

—

In 1975, Illich disbanded CIDOC. This marked the beginning of the third phase of his career, during which he assumed the role of itinerant scholar, splitting his time among universities in the United States and abroad, chiefly Penn State and Bremen. It was during this latter phase of his life that Illich's intellectual interests shifted to questions related to media and their effect on human perception, culminating in his last major work, *In the Vineyard of the Text*, an exploration of the emergence of the scholastic culture of the book. He framed it as a commentary on the work of twelfth-century theologian Hugh of St.

Victor. Another theme, always latent in Illich's thought and practice, becomes increasingly prominent as well during this time: hospitality and friendship.

While Illich made his name as a critic of industrial technology, he early on recognized the significance of computer technology and digital communication tools. One prominent theme in Illich's work, which appears at various junctures in his conversation with Brown, is the significance of the body. It is clear that Illich worried about the degree to which the body, and as a result the person, was lost through the use of modern means of communication. In his exchange with Brown, these concerns come across through a poignant reflection on how the gift we receive from the other is our own self, which turns on a discussion of the etymology of the word "pupil."

"I want to just go back to a great rabbinical and also as you see, monastic, Christian development beyond what the Greeks like Plato or Cicero already knew about friendship," Illich tells Brown about midway through their conversation. "There's a little thing there. They called it *pupilla*, puppet, which I can see in your eye. The black thing in your eye."

"Pupil, puppet, person, eye. It is not my mirror," Illich explains:

> It is you making me the gift of that which Ivan is for you. That's the one who says "I" here. I'm purposely not saying, this is my person, this is my individuality, this is my ego. No. I'm saying this is the one who answers you here, whom you have given to him. This is how Hugh [of St. Victor] explains it here. This is how the rabbinical tradition explains it. That I cannot come to be fully human unless I have received myself as a gift and accepted myself as a gift of somebody who has—well, today we say distorted me the way you distorted me by loving me.

This discovery of the gift that is the self we receive from the other occurs uniquely in the context of the face-to-face encounter, when two people are present to themselves in the fullness of their embodied reality, as the Samaritan who encountered the Jew by the side of the road.

This portion of the conversation then evolves into a broader discussion of the renewal of the political order. Illich believed that the ancient relationship among virtue, friendship, and politics had been undone. In the classical view, a good society fostered virtue in its citizens, and friendship was in turn the culmination of the virtuous life. Alluding to Brown's political service, Illich laments, "I do not believe that friendship today can flower out, can come out, of political life." But there was a measure of hope in recognizing that the ancient paradigm could be reversed.

"I do believe that if there is something like a political life to be, to remain for us, in this world of technology, then it begins with friendship," Illich tells Brown. "Therefore my task is to cultivate disciplined, self-denying, careful, tasteful friendships." He goes on to add,

> Mutual friendships always. I and you and I hope a third one, out of which perhaps community can grow. Because perhaps here we can find what the good is. To make it short, while once friendship in our western tradition was the supreme flower of politics I do think that if community life if it exists at all today it is in some way the consequence of friendship cultivated by each one who initiates it.

But Illich recognizes in his prescription an implicit challenge to the way we ordinarily think about our obligations in an individualistic society: "This is of course a challenge to the idea of democracy which goes beyond anything which people usually talk about, saying each one of you is responsible for the friendships he can develop because society will be as good as the political result of these friendships will be."

Nonetheless, it is the only way forward as far as Illich is concerned. There can be no substitute for the work of rediscovering our common humanity in the practice of hospitality, which, insofar as it flowers into friendship, will be the starting point of politics.

Yet, here again, Illich is clearheaded about the obstacles thwarting hospitality. First, his earlier arguments about what I've called our social deskilling are still valid even if they have been unheeded. Illich often referred to these skills in the older formulation of an art we learn to practice. We have lost the art of dying and the art of suffering as well as the art of living. Specifically, we are unpracticed in the art of hospitality.

But there is a further complication. "Hospitality," Illich insists, "requires a threshold over which I can lead you, and TV, internet, newspaper, the idea of communication, abolished the walls and therefore also the friendship, the possibility of leading somebody over the door."

This may seem like an odd thing on which to insist, the necessity of leading someone over a threshold, but it reflects Illich's conviction that we must encounter one another in the fullness of our humanity, which can only happen when we meet face-to-face, when we can behold ourselves in the pupil of the other. So Illich tells Brown, "Hospitality requires a table around which you can sit and if people get tired they can sleep."

Two years later, in a lecture at Bremen, Illich warned in a similar vein that "the quest for truth cannot thrive outside the nourishment of mutual trust flowering into a commitment to friendship." He then spoke of how he set out to identify the "atmosphere" that makes such a flowering possible and that which undermines such a flowering. "Only persons who face one another in trust can allow its emergence," he concludes.

To drive the point home, in that same lecture, titled "The Cultivation of Conspiracy," Illich drew on the ancient Christian practice of *conspiratio*, the holy kiss of the liturgy in which the participants "shared their breath or spirit with one another." It was in this conspiracy, literally, this co-breathing, that the atmosphere conducive to pax, or peace, was established. It was in this practice that Illich found the sources of the practice of community that emerged in Christian Europe. "The shared breath," Illich explained, "the *con-spiratio* is peace, understood as the community that arises from it."

It is striking to observe the contrast between the altogether different kind of conspiracy that has in fact flourished in our midst: a spirit of conspiracy born out of our alienation, our distrust, and the cultivation of bad faith that seems to flourish in the disembodied spaces that now function as our public squares.

Perhaps it seems altogether impractical and inadequate to suggest that the crisis of our moment should be met with a practice so seemingly humble and fragile, whose results can't be readily scaled up or optimized. Perhaps it even seems naive. But I would argue that the naiveté lies with those who fail to recognize that our present crisis is so grave that to meet it adequately requires nothing less than the slow, deliberate work of rebuilding not just our institutions but the recovery of an even more fundamental reality: the experience of a common world and shared humanity.

Near the end of his conversation with Brown, Illich told him that "a practice of hospitality recovering threshold, table, patience, listening" could generate the "seedbeds for virtue and friendship . . . [and] for rebirth of community." We could do far worse than pursuing such hospitality even as we labor in other ways for our world and for our neighbor. ⚜

POLITICS STRIKE BACK

JAKE MEADOR

IN A FEBRUARY 2020 piece for *Scientific American* Zeynep Tufekci tried to make the case for why Americans ought to take appropriate precautions as our nation braced for the arrival of the Covid-19 virus. The short answer: For love of neighbor. Tufekci explained:

> We should prepare, not because we may feel personally at risk, but so that we can help lessen the risk for everyone. We should prepare not because we are facing a doomsday scenario out of our control, but because we can alter every aspect of this risk we face as a society.

> That's right, you should prepare because your neighbors need you to prepare—especially your elderly neighbors, your neighbors who work at hospitals, your neighbors with chronic illnesses, and your neighbors who may not have the means or the time to prepare because of lack of resources or time.

In short, by preparing for the virus ahead of time, Americans could have taken steps to lessen the impact of the virus on everyone. If those who could have prepared had done so, those who could not prepare would not have been so adversely affected.

We know how that went.

JAKE MEADOR is vice president of the Davenant Institute and the editor-in-chief of *Mere Orthodoxy*, a magazine covering the Christian faith in the public sphere.

The journalist Anne Helen Petersen captured something of the tragedy of all this in her *Culture Study* newsletter, pithily summarizing the problem by saying, "I don't know how to make you care about other people." That cuts to the heart of the problem: In a society catechized in the creeds of expressive individualism and personal freedom, we are radically unprepared to respond to disaster with the sort of care that such a disaster calls forth from us. Indeed, so great is our inability to regard our neighbors that even something as simple as "companies providing supplemental support for employees with children" has become an object of controversy, as the *New York Times* reported earlier this year:

> When the coronavirus closed schools and child care centers and turned American parenthood into a multitasking nightmare, many tech companies rushed to help their employees. They used their comfortable profit margins to extend workers new benefits, including extra time off for parents to help them care for their children.
>
> It wasn't long before employees without children started to ask: What about us?

That is the problem before us: Childless employees at some of our nation's largest companies, many of whom are working in highly lucrative jobs, are upset that their coworkers with children are receiving additional help from their employer. Every employee faces challenges in their day-to-day lives, they reasoned, so why should parents be treated differently?

How was the problem resolved? The article concluded with this bit of reasoning from one consultant, intended to help pacify the childless employees:

> A question that we might ask the employees who are feeling some frustration about their co-workers being on leave is what do you think is going to happen if that person quits? . . . You're going to actually be stretched further.

This entire saga, beginning to end, is quintessential pandemic-era capitalism in the United States, in which absolute equality between individual people is regarded as the highest value and appeals to solidarity fall on deaf ears. When relational conflict arises, as at these tech companies, the only grounds to appeal to in pursuit of reconciliation are . . . back to commerce: What will happen to *your* job if this person has to quit theirs? There is no appeal to neighborliness—a shared communal bond that causes me to regard your needs as being as significant as my own—because the underlying assumptions of our era rule out such lines of thought from the beginning.

It does not have to be this way.

In fact, we should say it more strongly: It cannot be this way for long because such a solipsistic regime is radically unnatural, cutting against the grain of human nature and twisting individual people into pitiful (and pitiable!) figures who, beneath their workplace bluster, are often sad and alone.

What is the alternative? There are two ways we might answer that question—and both of our answers actually, contrary to many critics of modernity, do not lead us away from our nation's Protestant roots, but back toward them. Far from needing less Calvinism in our national life, as Petersen suggests in her newsletter, I want to suggest that we need *more* Calvinism—provided we're talking about Calvinism as it actually exists in the sources of Calvinist thought rather than the parodied form that haunts the minds of secular progressives.

The German political theorist and Calvinist Johannes Althusius gives us the first answer. He says that the purpose of all human social life is *symbiosis*—mutually beneficial arrangements in which the flourishing of individuals is premised on relationships of mutual care and fidelity. And, Althusius says, there is actually one such example that is, or ought to be, naturally available to everyone: the family. He calls the family "the most intense society . . . the seedbed of every other association." For Althusius, the naturally fruitful love of family life instructs us in the basic practices of peaceable living. Pope Benedict XVI suggests a similar idea in a World Day of Peace address, saying that "the language of the family is a language of peace; we must always draw from it, lest we lose the 'vocabulary' of peace."

Likewise, the early twentieth-century Dutch Reformed theologian Herman Bavinck notes that in the biblical account, "the history of the human race begins with a wedding." It begins, in other words, with two separate people pledging themselves to one another for each other's mutual flourishing, with symbiosis. And yet this relationship does not end with two, but radiates outward toward children – and in this the family's life resembles the inner life of the Trinity.

> Each child born is the fruit of fellowship, and as such is also the fruit of divine blessing. The two-in-oneness of husband and wife expands with a child into three-in-oneness. Father, mother, and child are one soul and one flesh, expanding and unfolding the one image of God, united within threefold diversity and diverse within harmonic unity. This three-in-oneness of relationships and functions, of qualities and gifts, constitutes the foundation of all of civilized society.

Yet it is important to be clear on what is and isn't unique in the family compared to other human communities. The family naturally reproduces itself. The family is the first society any of us will belong to. And yet the family is not distinctive in many other ways. Rather, it is a template for human society writ large. While my life does depend in quite literal ways on my father and mother when I am an infant, my life also depends in countless other ways on the many other nonfamilial relationships that I develop and enjoy over my life.

We might put it this way: When we say that people are social creatures, political animals, we should point to the family, but we also ought to point to countless other human relationships as well. Contrary to the fever dreams of the libertarians and liberaltarians alike, the natural gregariousness of humanity is seen not merely in the form of a crying infant searching for its mother's breast, in naked necessity, but also in the smiles shared between friends, the long-standing inside joke that always provokes laughter, the easy body language we adopt when with trusted, beloved people, an experience that many of us have so missed during the pandemic.

Unfortunately, under the sort of modernity dominant in America today we have mostly forgotten all of this. The mid-twentieth-century Swiss reformed theologian Emil Brunner makes the point well in his theological ethics when he writes that modernism is, too often, a dreary "Robinson Crusoe affair," in which we attempt to "interpret the individual human being solely in the light of his own personality, and society as the coalescence of individuals." We are, in this view, self-determining bundles of neurons that occasionally collide with other self-determining bundles. The best we can reasonably hope for, in such a world, is to find a way of arranging these collisions to cause the least damage or, if we really did brilliantly, to somehow make the collisions mutually beneficial. This is, says Brunner, not a true account of how human beings actually are. "Human existence, as such," he writes,

> is existence in responsibility. This does not mean that man ought to know that he is a responsible being, as an ethical truth; no, I mean something which lies behind all ethical consciousness and conduct, namely, that the very being of man owes its humanitas to the fact that human life is, in its essence, responsible existence.

He then goes on to suggest that the image of a suspension bridge might be a useful one for considering human identity:

> Just as the tension of a suspension bridge is due to the fact that it hangs between two supporting towers and in so doing unites them, so also the peculiar tension which gives its quality to human life–responsibility–is determined by the fact that the "I" is always confronted with the "Thou." This unity through tension is the human element; apart from this responsibility human existence simply does not exist.

For Brunner, then, it is nonsensical to suggest that an individual person would be self-determining, for in becoming self-determining they cease to be a person; they turn away from the responsible existence that is their nature. To possess personhood is, for Brunner, to possess responsibility toward others. Thus the world we have made these past seventy-five years is seen to be a deeply inhuman world in the most literal possible sense of the term; by eroding our responsibilities to one another, such as the responsibilities we might owe to coworkers who have children, this world has quite literally devoured our own personhood. Ours has become, to borrow from C. S. Lewis, a world of "unmen," because we have rejected the communal responsibilities that come to each of us naturally and attempted to erect a new form of man, stolid, proud, and impregnable.

The horrible sound of sirens blaring that has filled America's cities in 2020 is the sound of that regime toppling to the ground. Like all inhumane things, its fall has been horrible. It has laid low millions, killed hundreds of thousands, and irrevocably torn the fabric of virtually every half-realized community that Crusoe's world had not yet eradicated fully.

And so now we must consider what is to come next. We have sought to deny our natural state of existence in responsibility. That denial has failed us. All that remains, then, is to determine the meaning and shape of what our responsibility to our neighbor will be. Perhaps, in this very limited sense, the coronavirus can serve as a kind of harsh instructor. Tufekci demonstrated as much nearly a year ago, before the virus had swept our nation. For while it is true that the human person always needs bonds of responsibility and affection with other human beings, this need is felt more intensely during a pandemic. And so perhaps it may be the case that Covid-19 not only exposes, unmistakably, the death of our current order, but in its attack on each of us individually it also calls us back toward one another, toward the grammar of peaceable living and mutual love. ⚘

November 25, 2020

GOD HAS HEARD

Grief and Hope in Dialectic

JOSHUA BOMBINO AND CHELSEA LANGSTON BOMBINO

JANUARY 5, 2020. The World Health Organization reports there is a "pneumonia of unknown cause" in Wuhan, China. Most people are blind to what is coming. Covid-19 is not yet a household word.

My husband and I are also blind to what is coming. For us, January 5 marks one year, one month, and one day that Samuel, our infant son, died of SIDS at the age of two months on December 4, 2018. And while this looms large for us, most people are blind to this fact too.

The date of Samuel's death has become the default metric for tracking our personal lives and societal events: the births and deaths, yes, but also the things that can't be so distinctly organized into the one or the other.

Being created human is itself a liminal existence. A now. A not yet. The womb gives us our first container to embody our humanity. Our families, as first society, incubate our capacities to live out what it means to be human. And social institutions, as Joseph Campbell explains in *The Flight of the Wild Gander: Explorations in the Mythological Dimension*, are a kind of "second womb," providing the social and spiritual structures within which we continue the

JOSHUA BOMBINO is a social worker directing a homelessness program for those with psychiatric disabilities.

CHELSEA LANGSTON BOMBINO serves as a program officer with the Fetzer Institute and as a fellow with the Center for Public Justice.

process of human development. Healthy human formation necessarily involves the development of rituals and habits.

In *God's Sabbath with Creation: Vocations Fulfilled, the Glory Unveiled*, James Skillen connects these rituals to the *imago Dei*: "The discernment of the creation's revelatory character emerges in the course of human experiences and is expressed through multiple similes, metaphors, and figures of speech as well as in art, architecture and liturgies of worship and life." These metaphoric sacraments situate us within the rhythms of those communities and ultimately connect us to the unfolding of the human story in relation to Creator God.

In the human life cycle, we move from our mother's womb, to the womb of society, to the womb of our Creator, in whom we hope for eternal communion. But how do we situate ourselves within the experience of loss, personal and communal, when it feels like that loss slouches toward nothing? What do we do when the social architecture – that second womb – that incubates our shared practices of grief is stripped of the metaphorical and spiritual symbols that nourish our individual and collective identities? What happens when we are severed from the incubator?

In our culture, even among Christians, many of us have lost a collective lexicon of rituals that help us relate to ourselves, to each other, and to God. These shared sacred practices are relevant during seasons of transition from one life stage to another, perhaps especially in grief. In the months after Samuel's loss, we read about the sacred mourning practices of different spiritual and cultural communities. We searched for how others made meaning, connected with God and each other, and restored themselves to the rhythms of life that continued around them in the midst of loss.

What follows is an offering for those who mourn. It is a timeline, a gallery of grief and hope in dialectic. Here are remnants of letters, notes, poems, laments, and sacred texts that we turned to surrounding the loss of our son. Samuel's death was the lens through which we saw the series of ambiguous communal losses – pandemic, racial violence, unraveling political community – that we are now experiencing.

July 30, 2018. Letter to Samuel at Twenty-Four Weeks' Gestation
  —Joshua

I worry I cannot be the father you need. This world you are about to enter into is so damn hard and complicated. My uncle told me that all ceremonies are for the promotion and redemption of life. That's why we need them, to help us get through this damn world. My uncle also said he was taught that in life all people must answer four questions:

1. Who am I?
2. Where did I come from?
3. Where am I going?
4. What am I here to do?

No matter where you end up in life or how complicated this world gets, you will have four simple questions to answer. That's your job. In the meantime, know that my job is to promote and redeem your life. When we pray, my uncle told me, we should just ask for two things. Health and help. This is what I want for you. I've never understood that so viscerally, so intuitively, until now.

October 3, 2018. Samuel's Birth —Chelsea

My body was birthing our son too early. His life source, his nourishment, his oxygen—all provided through the placenta—all severed from his being. The medical term is placental abruption. The spiritual term felt like separation from God.

"Complete separation." Those were the last words I heard before I lost consciousness and underwent an emergency cesarean at thirty-three weeks. All because this mysterious organ, that my child and I co-created, was failing us both. The placenta is a physical and spiritually symbolic microcosm of the interconnectedness of all of human life. The placenta is unique in that it is the sole organ made of the tissue of two persons—mother and child—in mutual interdependence. Kristin Marguerite Collier explains that some cells from the child navigate across the placenta to the mother, and vice versa. Even after the child is born into the world, part of the child's very cellular essence remains with the mother, supporting her body through the postpartum period and for years to come.

I lingered in the dreamlike space between image and word, as I regained consciousness. "Samuel," I uttered.

"He is alive, he is okay," my husband Josh murmured. His voice and his body hold me at once, word and flesh. Alive. Okay. God had heard.

1 Samuel 1:20: So in the course of time Hannah became pregnant and gave birth to a son. She named him Samuel, saying, "Because I asked the LORD for him."

November 2, 2018. Samuel, an Idea of God —Joshua

Samuel is almost a month old. I had him for the whole day. It felt manageable. No, empowering. Samuel. Hebrew Scripture tells us your name means "God has heard." Someday, I'll introduce you to your secret namesakes, Beckett and Shepard. They are going to blow your mind. Samuel, a creature that, as Mary Oliver says, is "the beautiful crying forth of [an] idea of God."

Being a father makes me reflect on my childhood. I think I understand something about my parents that I couldn't until now. I grew up during the final rusting-over of Bethlehem Steel. The Bethlehem slouch. An industry, a community, that produced the raw material for so much of the infrastructure of modern American civilization. The Moravians founded Bethlehem on the three pillars of God, community, and industry. What happens when one of those falters?

Bethlehem. House of Bread. Bread of Life. What else could the body of Christ be but bread? Bread that nurtured civilization. Now, the Moravians and Bethlehem Steel host cold and empty industrial buildings along the banks of the Lehigh River and Monocacy Creek. But bread is still warm, yeasty, crusty. Waiting to have its aroma inhaled, its flesh eaten. Waiting to turn itself into nothingness to nourish others.

I try to soothe my baby's cries. I speak the name of God. I pen lines of a bad poem in my journal. I speak the name of God. Author of life. I put beans in the slow cooker. Cornbread in the oven. I say Your name. Nourisher of my soul.

Do what you must for Samuel. Lord make me bread for my son, for his life. For him all things. Ends and beginnings.

December 21, 2018. The Dying of the Light —Chelsea

Samuel passed away in his sleep on December 4. It was quiet. God was quiet. The no-answers kind of quiet. Did God still hear?

I think about the words of a song by Abigail Washburn and Béla Fleck about the death of a loved one. Samuel, a month after I first met your dad, I went to hear bluegrass in a cavern in Tennessee with a man I barely knew. That was the first time I heard this song. They wrote it during the months after the birth of their son. They decided to collaborate on a project so they could keep their family together in the first years of their baby's life. I made your dad listen to it on repeat the whole ten-hour ride home. "Not track 2," he would say. And then he would play it for me. The words resonated in me before your conception, birth and death. Did my soul know?

> I feel you hanging on my frame
> I smell your body, I spell your name. . . .
> Remember my long brown hair
> And the way I loved you everywhere.
> ("Ride to You," Abigail Washburn and Béla Fleck)

The loss of Samuel brought the season of quiet. The season of Advent was already upon us. The season of the dying of the light coupled with hopeful anticipation of its return. We, too, were waiting for our baby to come, yet we knew he would not. We did not work. We read and wept and prayed. We fought. We went to a Winter Solstice concert at the Cathedral of St. John the Divine in New York City. Reliving a yearly ritual from Josh's childhood. Joseph Campbell, in *Thou Art That,* says, "The cathedral is the temple represented as that opening through which transcendence breaks . . . God . . . pours into the field of time." We lit a candle for Samuel there. We held hands in the dark as Paul Winter brought in the promise of the coming of the light. All the time knowing we were lying. In God's sanctuary.

> 1 Samuel 1:27–28: I prayed for this child, and God gave me what I asked for. And now I have dedicated him to God. He's dedicated to God for life.

> 1 Samuel 2:21: The boy Samuel stayed at the sanctuary and grew up with God.

April 9, 2019. To Nurture a Soul —Joshua

Chelsea is pregnant again. She is due two days after Samuel's due date. I am still mourning Samuel. I don't know how to hold both these things together. The worst feeling is whatever you feel when your baby dies. My own spiritual heritage is complex, raised by my mother in the Episcopal Church, by my father in a spiritual community practicing Lakota ceremony. In *The Sacred Pipe: Black Elk's Account of the Seven Rites of the Oglala Sioux*, Joseph Epes Brown documents the Lakota ritual of mourners tending their own grief in the first year of a loved one's passing through a practice called "keeping of the soul." Black Elk's account tells us the origin story of this rite: a family had a beloved child who passed away in infancy. The bereaved father sought out the keeper of the sacred pipe, the spiritual center of the community, for guidance. The holy man gave the grieving father instructions on how to nurture his child's soul every day for a year, and then how to release it. Black Elk gives us a glimpse of why participation in the process of the ritual itself is the key: "You should remember that the habits you establish during this period will be with you always. The keeping of a soul also helps us remember death and Wakan Tanka [Great Spirit], who is above all dying."

Samuel's ashes sit on a shelf. Next to him is his picture. He is wrapped in red cloth, as you wrap all things that are sacred. He is surrounded by the colors of the four directions. There is a star quilt, given to us by a friend who also lost a child. This is an altar where something sacred is revealed.

December 24, 2019. Word Became Flesh —Chelsea

> 1 Samuel 2:20: Eli would bless Elkanah and his wife, saying, "May the LORD give you children by this woman to take the place of the one she prayed for and gave to the LORD." Then they would go home.

I return, again and again to the body. My body has grown and borne a healthy living child, Benjamin. My body that will never again, on this earth, hold Samuel. My body. Samuel's body. The body of Christ. The placenta—the organ that made Samuel and me one—had failed him. Because Samuel lived in my womb and was nourished by our shared placenta, some of Samuel's cells continue to live within me. I read Charlie Camosy's interview with Kristin Marguerite Collier, doctor and mother and believer. She gives me language where, among other losses, my own words are gone.

> The Word became flesh in Mary's uterus. Therefore, the uterus is a sacred space because it held our Lord and Savior. . . . We can assume that some of Jesus' cells transferred across the placenta in Mary's womb. . . . What we could take from this is that even when Jesus physically left his mother, part of him remained in her and remains in her forever. . . . We know that mothers have always thought, in some way, their children, even after death, were still with them. Now we see, through the lens of fetoma-ternal microchimerism, that they still are.

1 Samuel 2:6–10 (The Message):

> God brings death and God brings life, . . .
>   he rekindles burned-out lives with fresh hope,
> Restoring dignity and respect to their lives—
>   a place in the sun!
> For the very structures of earth are God's;
>   he has laid out his operations on a firm foundation.

March 12, 2020. A Bird's Nest. Apparent   —Joshua

Many things are happening very quickly. Yesterday was the first day that we had a caregiver for Benjamin while we were both at work. For a moment, it seemed like we might start having a little more freedom. But that afternoon the WHO announced a global pandemic. Chelsea learned that one of her coworkers may have been exposed to Covid-19. Chelsea's doctor wants her to self-isolate in the house for two weeks. We can't have anyone else here, and I will be providing all the child care for the next two weeks while trying to be an essential worker from home. None of this fits. None of this works. This is a mess. Although I convinced myself that things are better, the specter of Samuel's death is

still over us. I put on a brave face for Chelsea. As a mental-health professional, I know that I have not worked through my grief, but am merely
pretending. It keeps overtaking me. It keeps overtaking Chelsea. I had
put it away in deference to the pregnancy. It has been over a year, and
every time Benjamin takes a nap, I cannot get settled. I am distracted.
If I leave the house, I pray I do not come home to the worst feeling a
second time. Now I have to go it alone for two weeks. Chelsea and I are
about to get very intimate with complicated grief. As the world begins
shutting down, we will have fewer places to hide. What are the rhythms
to sustain me? I turn to the pages of this notebook.

> How does the ordinary person come to the study of the tran-
> scendent? . . . Study poetry . . . [another] significant approach is
> ritual. (Joseph Campbell, *Thou Art That*)

> I am a bird's nest,
> Come into the world piecemeal
> Bit by bit detritus woven
> Intricate and impossible
> Far outpacing the sum of its parts
> A mystery even to me:
> How I should fit into a divine plan,
> Order out of chaos,
> An impossible heap –
> And to host something nascent.
> How was such nobility ever bestowed
> Upon such common twigs, thread, grass?
> And all too soon
> Giving winged flight
> Alight to the future
> Soar to summer sun
> I,
> Left to shrink and wither,
> Brittle, a hoary winter cipher,
> Apparent.
> I am a bird's nest

March 20, 2020. The Emptying Time —Chelsea

Josh says I should write. Write down this experience of isolation and trauma. This is not a time for filling. Filling of pages in a notebook. Filling of my days with the rituals that sustain my life, and my baby's. Filling my baby with milk taken directly from my breast. This is a time of empty pages. Of breast pumps mechanically emptying me every three hours. The emptying of meaning. Empty time. Empty hope. The only things that fill me are memories too painful to recount. The last time my child, suddenly, was gone from me. My head seems to know this is different, temporary isolation. The emptying is temporary. Benjamin is alive. My soul cannot comprehend. My body cannot comprehend. My soul keeps time by the breath of my child and the suckle of his mouth, rooting for milk. Each heaving chest a sacrament. Each feeding a liturgy. Benjamin's living flesh, made in my womb. A few rooms away.

April 26, 2020. The Labor of Grief —Joshua

The Department of Labor is reporting that unemployment is reaching rates not seen since the Great Depression. There is a sign on my uncle's farm that someone hung twenty-five years ago or more: "Work is worship." Labor is not just an act of providing for our needs. Labor is how we create the world. We labor through childbirth, through personal and communal exile, grief, and loss, to rebuild communities of shared purposes. We used to gather for shared purposes to cry, sing, laugh, and listen for God in the silence. Now we gather around a screen. The ever-present chyron ticks off 53,000 US Covid deaths. This too is an altar where something sacred is revealed. "God has heard," but what did he hear? My uncle told me that God answers all our prayers, but sometimes the answer is no. As a parent I can relate. We ask if God heard when we experience loss: personally for children that slip through the veil, collectively when the institutions that sustain us crumble. We mourn during Covid-19 for the loss of our way of life. The death of family and friends. The death of an industry. The long slouch of a pandemic. These things commingle, fluid and messy. The slow, collective grieving for the death of my childhood's landscape and culture. The slow, personal grieving for the death of Samuel. For both, I crave spiritual and cultural communities that invite ways of making meaning out of loss. An emptying.

This is a sacred mystery. Only when we empty ourselves are we filled again. We can do the emptying, but only God can do the filling. I ask God, "Fit me to your singular purpose of life. If you do not mend what is broken, within and without, give me eyes to see its wholeness. Its holiness. For the promotion and redemption of life."

The Bethlehem Slouch

The Bethlehem slouch is that
    No one ever left home
The Bethlehem slouch is
    An industry's barren fruit
The Bethlehem slouch is
    A shuffle that never gets ahead
The Bethlehem slouch is
    Winded from pork roll and perogies
The Bethlehem slouch is
    Bellying up at Windish Hall
The Bethlehem slouch
    Is surrendering community to commercial
The Bethlehem slouch
    Cedes all and seeds nothing.

October 31, 2020. For Which One Do You Grieve
    —Chelsea and Joshua

The long summer is ending. It was too much to take in. Benjamin's fever is breaking, and he is eating again today. Was it something benign, like teething, or something worse? He is a year old now, and we are told SIDS is no longer a concern. Still, fear lingers for all the dangers that may still come. He has so much life yet to live.

We remember a Buddhist parable about a grieving mother. A young woman had a child, whom she named Jiva—*alive*. In infancy, Jiva died. The bereaved mother's daily ritual was to go to grounds where bodies were cremated and cry out for her daughter. One day, the Buddha passed through the region where the grieving mother lived. She listened to his parables and then left to weep for her daughter. The Buddha asked her why she was crying, and she told him her baby had died. He pointed to the ground beneath them, emphasizing the countless who had already returned to it in death. Buddha said,

Eighty-four thousand daughters
All with the name "Jiva"
Have burned in the funeral fire.
For which one do you grieve?

Mourning is a human expression, which germinates in our isolation, but is given full expression through relationship, and is made flesh, through shared sacred practices. The act of speaking Samuel's name acknowledges "God has heard." Grief is a paradox. The lives lost to racial violence – Floyd, Arbery, Taylor, and too many others. The unraveling of our civic institutions. The rising death toll. The rusting-out of rituals that hold our lives together. *For which one do you grieve?*

How do we speak these things and then acknowledge God has heard? We live the season of perpetual Advent. When will we see the return of industry and normalcy? When will we see the end of separation, the end of racism? When will we find the peace that surpasses all understanding? We must labor on and develop the sacred habits to sustain us until that day, which may not come in our lifetime. We are learning how to pray virtually, work remotely, celebrate from a distance. The sacred ritual of voting is upon us now. Now and not yet is the time to raise up those who are cast down, to make this world anew. This is how we make our collective voice heard. What will the answer be? How will we celebrate, grieve, and accept that God has heard?

Book of Common Prayer, *Good Friday*

O God of unchangeable power and eternal light: Look favorably on your whole Church, that wonderful and sacred mystery; by the effectual working of your providence, carry out in tranquillity the plan of salvation; let the whole world see and know that things which were cast down are being raised up, and things which had grown old are being made new, and that all things are being brought to their perfection by him through whom all things were made, your Son Jesus Christ our Lord; who lives and reigns with you, in the unity of the Holy Spirit, one God, for ever and ever.

Amen. ⚘

WINTER

ARYANA PETROSKY ROBERTS

STUART MCALPINE

HEATHER C. OHANESON

OLIVER O'DONOVAN

W. BRADFORD LITTLEJOHN

ANTHONY M. BARR

MICHAEL LAMB

SHADI HAMID

SAMUEL KIMBRIEL

CHRISTINE EMBA

BRANDON MCGINLEY

JOHN CLAIR

KURT ARMSTRONG

PETER WEHNER

JONATHAN HAIDT

December 2, 2020

PRAYING THROUGH THE POLITICAL DIVIDES IN THE FAMILY

ARYANA PETROSKY ROBERTS

THIS SUMMER, I returned to my rural hometown of Gardnerville, Nevada, for rest and retreat, leaving behind the intensity of Washington, DC: the August heat and humidity, the tiresome awareness of Covid-19, the grief of racial injustice, the helicopters circling above my apartment, and the ever-present political fray.

I expected tranquility. Instead, I found a clash.

The day after I came home, an estimated two thousand counter-protesters gathered, overwhelming the forty-ish Black Lives Matter protesters on Main Street. Militiamen dressed in camo, mostly locals, flooded into town. Some citizens slung assault rifles over one shoulder and strapped handguns to their belts; others held signs that ranged from earnestly patriotic to viciously partisan.

As I drove by twice, I felt sad, but mainly confused. No longer a resident of the community, how should I respond to the situation? How, in particular, should I react to my father's participation as a counterprotester against the BLM activists?

It made for a heated debate on the first morning of my vacation.

My hometown is a place of sublime beauty. Home is where desert turns to valley, and valley turns to sheer granite mountain. Twenty minutes over the mountain sits Lake Tahoe. It is a liminal

ARYANA PETROSKY ROBERTS is senior associate of the American Enterprise Institute's Initiative on Faith and Public Life. She holds a bachelor's degree from Azusa Pacific University.

space where God's presence *feels* tangibly closer: much closer than the marble canyons of DC.

I woke up early the morning of my arrival, still on East Coast time, and sipped coffee as I watched the sunrise over the desert mountains on the other side of the valley. I was staying at my grandparents' brick home tucked at the base of the Sierra Nevada mountain range, the setting of some of my most cherished childhood memories. In true rural Nevada fashion, my parents slept outside in an RV, while my husband and I slept in a nearby camping trailer. The acre plot of land is dotted with sagebrush, and the sun starts and ends each day atop the mountain rims on either side of the valley. The two ridges are distinctly different: one is starkly naked and acts as a barrier against desolate desert; the opposite ridge, where my grandparents' home sits, is covered with pine trees and hides alpine lake after alpine lake in the folds of mountain granite bowls. As I've become older, I have grown to be captivated by the easily overlooked beauty of the raw desert mountain landscape. It is an austere but vivid and changing canvas of purples, yellows, and oranges.

I watched as the sun rose higher, eyes prickling with gratitude as I inhaled the sagebrush scent and crisp morning air. With the difficulty of travel in the midst of a pandemic, I had been terrified I would not make it home to the place where time and again the sun, dust, and silent contemplation in the presence of God have restored my soul. But here I was. Home.

The protest, and the counterprotest, happened later that day: this part of the country proved itself no more immune than the rest to the fear and alienation that are overcoming us. Tensions boiled to the surface in my small hometown when, in early August, the director of the Douglas County Library proposed that the library issue an official statement in support of Black Lives Matter. It was unclear whether this statement was meant to support the organization or the movement, and, of course, this came in the middle of a summer when support for Black Lives Matter became synonymous with calls to abolish or defund the police. In response, Douglas County Sheriff Dan Coverley issued a public letter to the library board. "Don't bother calling the police" if you're in trouble, he said–a threat he quickly walked back. Not, however, before it made national headlines.

On Saturday, August 8, about forty people from a nearby Black Lives Matter group arrived to protest the sheriff's comments. In response, the rural community quickly formed a counterprotest, afraid that stores on Main Street would soon be looted, as they had seen happen in cities across the country.

Fresh in my bodily memory that morning was a march organized by Thabiti Anyabwile, pastor of Anacostia River Church, which had taken place in Washington at the beginning of June. I participated with a sign that said Black Lives Matter on one side. I'd written the "Prayer for Social Justice" from the Anglican *Book of Common Prayer* on the other side. We chanted, "Love mercy, do justice." We sang "This Little Light of Mine" as we walked down Pennsylvania Avenue. It was the first protest that I had ever participated in, and it was powerful. We hadn't been meeting. It felt like church.

In Douglas County, 62.5 percent of voters voted for Donald Trump in 2016, which never surprised me; however, I still found myself shocked at the number of flags, signs, posters, and stickers supporting President Trump at what appeared to be almost every single house, farm, and business. It's possible I simply did not accurately remember the lead-up to previous presidential elections, but it seemed as though politics had somehow seeped deeper into the soil of every conversation and public space. The pre-political aspects of life, even in the home, held onto a faint margin.

Strangely, this trip home made me feel like a coastal elite. A cosmopolitan. Even though I work at a conservative public-policy think tank, my language and cultural ties have changed over the years. I grew up as a nondenominational evangelical on the West Coast; I now attend a theologically orthodox, and relatively conservative, Anglican church on the East Coast. On paper, my résumé is filled with politically conservative affiliations. In reality, I am another millennial who finds myself politically homeless. Now when I visit home, this uncomfortable cognitive dissonance between my current ways of thinking and the values of my family and hometown have slowly overshadowed the warm glow of remembering a childhood spent walking lake rims and camping under the stars. Politics has moved into crannies where it should not have reached.

In a time when politics have bled into every sphere of daily life and become closely intertwined with individual identity and even religious affiliation, how we respond and productively engage in the public square with those who hold different political views matters.

But how do I respond to my dad?

The sun, now higher in the sky, starting to bear down with the dry desert heat that I have grown to appreciate after experiencing DC humidity, was beginning to make me sweat. The prayerful posture of gratitude from my quiet time was replaced with the jitteriness of too many cups of coffee and not enough food.

I had prepared for conversation with my father for weeks, and had several questions to pose to him: Is America truly a Christian nation? Should it be? Are we really at "war" with our political opponents? And even if we are, should Christians participate in this political "war"? What is our public witness, and what does it say about our values? Should we think of politics as being ultimate? What is "politics"?

I don't know the answers to all these questions.

Although I grew up in a church that shied away from political conversations, I have spent the last several years of my life reading St. Augustine and Reinhold Niebuhr (among others) and have been knee deep in contemporary debates on liberalism, integralism, nationalism. Complicating conversations with my father, and with others from my rural hometown, is that I am conscious that most people don't typically engage with these texts or debates in daily life. I didn't want to come off as if I had everything figured out. I don't. What I wanted to say was this: "We are already saved."

Before I could roll back my tongue and, with love and respect, enter into a conversation with my father as I had been preparing to in the preceding weeks, things escalated. Both my mother and husband ran for the hills when it started. I never brought out my notes.

Dad and I both started to get upset as we argued about video footage of the death of George Floyd. I knew we were about to enter the point where we both had deaf ears, loud mouths. I knew then, as I know now, that political debate doesn't change minds. I knew that I loved him. I knew that I don't know everything. I knew that I might easily be a fool.

So, on a whim, I asked my dad if he wanted to pray with me.

It was a long prayer.

After we finished, we continued our discussion with significantly less tension and considerably more empathetic listening. We covered what it means to have a physical presence at a protest, how our Christian faith can inform political practice, and the different manifestations of public witness. I didn't change my father's mind, and he didn't change mine. But we left the conversation still as father and daughter, not political rivals.

When we joined the communion of saints in prayer, we entered a narrative larger than our current political moment, larger than the protest about to occur. We declared, together, that Christ is King. That was a political act. We acknowledged together that we are indeed already saved, and as a result, the rules of political combat were changed. In fact, it became evident that combat is maybe not the right method at all.

In this liminal space at the base of the Sierra Nevada Mountains, heaven slightly broke through and defused the worded missiles that my father and I had hurled at each other.

The cultural and language barrier surrounding faith and politics seems to grow ever higher when I talk to my family. Prayer is practical political theology that begins with transcending political differences and has shown me a sliver of hope in this time of extreme polarization. It provided my father and me with a common language. It is an invitation for Christ to enter in to the middle of our political and pre-political messes.

Many of us have just been through a good-and-bad-and-complicated Thanksgiving. We're headed into Christmas.

Pray. ✝

December 4, 2020

GOOD GRIEF

In Search of a Theology of Lament

STUART MCALPINE

They would put upon God their own sorrow, the grief they
  should feel
For their sins and faults . . .
Let us mourn in a private chamber, learning the way of penitence,
And then let us learn the joyful communion of saints.
                       —T. S. Eliot, "Choruses from 'The Rock'"

ORIGINALLY A MILD OATH, "good grief" is like many sanitized
cursings that replace the outright blasphemous use of "God" with
another more acceptable "g" word. It is well and truly vernacular
thanks to its popularization by Charlie Brown, recognized by *Time*
magazine in 1958 as his "characteristic lament." There are few of
us who have not uttered it, whether in a purposefully audible tone
or under our breath. The curious thing is, what is actually "good"
about it?

Christianly speaking, there is a strain of grief that though it is
sourced in deep sadness and pain, can and should be described as

STUART MCALPINE served for forty years in pastoral ministry, thirty-three at Christ
Our Shepherd Church in Washington, DC. He is the international director for ASK
Network, a prayer movement in over thirty nations, and Senior Teaching Fellow for
the C. S. Lewis Institute. His publications include *The Road Best Traveled*; *The Advent
Overture: Meditations and Poems for the Christmas Season*; and *Just Asking: Restoring the
Soul of Prayer*.

good grief. Jesus himself affirmed "those who mourn . . . you who weep now" and the dominical blessing that acknowledged a good grief went on to promise good outcomes: "they will be comforted" and "will laugh" (Matt. 5:4; Luke 6:21). This suggests that there is a journey to forgiveness and healing, to consolation and joy, to restoration and renewal that cannot avoid passing through the vale of tears, the Valley of Baka that the psalmist describes as the necessary passage for all "whose hearts are set on pilgrimage" (Ps. 84:6). In the Psalms of Ascent, it is understood that an answer to the prayer "Restore our fortunes, LORD" will be given to "those who sow in tears" but who will "return with songs of joy, carrying sheaves with them" (Ps. 126:4–6). The "reaping" is not without "weeping". T. S. Eliot more than intimates the same in "Choruses from 'The Rock,'" the private chamber of lament and repentance being the prescribed precursor of the public communion of joy.

Although this matter of lament has been on my heart's radar in the past, it has been brought back up close and personal this year, provoked principally by the desperate state of my nation of domicile, the United States. In particular I have in mind the present state of race relations in our nation and the unresolved reckoning and unfinished repentance of past and present national sins, including the genocide of one people and the enslavement of another. And of course, the more we fill the political hustings with calls for a revival of real Americanism, the more racist we become, and the more we think that we can make America great again, blindly ignoring the same moral appeals of conscience and commandment as our forefathers, the more we condemn our nation to the same founding principality and power of divisive and idolatrous mammon.

This return to lament was reinforced by four books I read earlier this year, all of which appeal to the Scriptures for their authority. *One Blood: Parting Words to the Church on Race and Love* is the latest book from one of America's oldest apostles of reconciliation, the beloved John Perkins, founder of the Christian Community Development Association. He writes, "Lament is God's gift to us, the church. It urges us to come together and be healed." Another, written by one of the most promising Christian historians of the next generation, Jemar Tisby, is titled *The Color of Compromise: The Truth*

About the American Church's Complicity in Racism. Acknowledging that his work "may cause some grief," Tisby writes that "grief can be good" if it becomes a natural response to the suffering of others. "It indicates empathy with the pain that racism has caused black people. The ability to weep with those who weep is necessary for true healing." Later he suggests, "The American church can learn from the black church what it means to lament." Black worship, particularly as expressed in the spiritual, is the expression of lament in which the triumph of hope eventually arises out of the trough of hopelessness and helplessness. Hear an echo of the Psalms, anyone?

The third book was *Prophetic Lament: A Call for Justice in Troubled Times.* Soong-Chan Rah writes, "The loss of lament in the American church reflects a serious theological deficiency." The theology of celebration has out shouted the theology of suffering. The loud praise song has silenced the quiet dirge. This was the indictment of God on the sanctuaries of Israel through the prophet Amos: "You strum away like David . . . but you do not grieve over the ruin of Joseph" (6:5). We "strum away" singing naive and sentimental lullabies to an insomniac culture, self-deceptively desiring all to be always well with the world, to experience "your best life now," as one author heretically puts it in a best-selling book by that title. It is the evasion of any reality that smudges the cosmetics of our "be happy" prosperity and populism.

The fourth book was Esau McCaulley's *Reading While Black: African American Biblical Interpretation as an Exercise in Hope,* in which he compares the rage of Israel against enemies and injustice with the anger of black Americans. He argues for the necessity of lament as the context for both expressing rage and grief, and for seeking healing from trauma. "The fact that Psalm 137 became a part of the biblical canon means that the suffering of the traumatized is part of the permanent record. . . . We need to lament injustice and call for God to right the wrongs." McCaulley laments the justification of slavery through manipulative "white" exegesis of Scripture: "I too am frustrated with the way that Scripture has been used to justify the continual assault on black bodies and souls. . . . We lament its distortion." I recommend all these treatises as essential reading in our present context.

AVOIDING ARROGANCE

There are now two equal and opposite dangers. The first is that lament becomes its own kind of buzzword, a new "in" word. Always a thoroughly biblical expression of spirituality, it plays little role in current worship, whether public liturgy or popular hymnody. Most churches want to be defined by their experience of laudation, not lament; they would rather hire praise bands than invite mourning minstrels. There are not many guitars that know how to "gently weep." (Interestingly, there is a verse that George Harrison wrote that was excised from the final version: "I look at the trouble and hate that is raging / While my guitar gently weeps / As I'm sitting here doing nothing but ageing / While my guitar gently weeps.")

In our lament we cannot be pridefully comforted that we are among the few who "really get it." How can lament that is the handmaid of humility and brokenness be turned into a badge of enlightenment and spiritual pride? It is vital to remember that our responses of lament are not original, not primarily rooted in our experiences or perceptions, but rooted in the character and heart of a reconciling and redeeming God.

The second danger is that we engage in a kind of check-the-box spirituality of the conscientious consumer. Lament here will be treated as a temporary expression that remains unincorporated into our understanding of hallowed ordinariness in our worship, discipleship, and community life. Lament? I read the book, attended a webinar, did a Bible study, skimmed an article, and even wrote a lament psalm in a practicum once. What's next? Lament can only cease if the intimacy of prayer ceases. Lament is not a stand-on-its-own subject, not even a self-conscious practice or a means or a method. It arises unannounced, inarticulately and passionately out of our communion with God about the reality of our lives and times. Lamenting and asking of God are inseparable. If we do not pray much we will not lament much. Of course, it may well be stirred initially by suffering or crisis, either of self or others, but if it is not connected with the nature and character of God, it will just end up as a sad soliloquy and possibly degenerate into complaint and self-pity, eventually petering out.

With dry eyes, we lobby for our bastardized version of evangelical morality and cease to weep over the consequences of the abandonment of God's righteousness in the public square. The parable of the publican and the Pharisee is foundational to Jesus' teaching about prayer. The former beat his breast, lamented his sin, and asked for mercy; and the latter, the defender of public morality, sanctimoniously asked for nothing in his self-centered soliloquy disguised as prayer. Hard-hearted pride knows nothing of soft-hearted weeping. Self-confidence, especially in one's own righteousness, cannot and does not lament. Again, what different outcomes Jesus showed between the one who lamented with a godly sorrow and left "justified before God" and the one who left self-justified and just the same.

Like Israel of old, my nation is deceived by its own sense of exceptionalism, for our "Americanism" expresses our strutting arrogance not just before the watching world but before God. T. S. Eliot described those who "walk proud-necked like thoroughbreds for races . . . Thinking good of themselves." Not surprisingly, this is followed by "Let us mourn." Israel forgot that the experience of God's favor does not make one an above-the-law favorite. Truly, "God shed His grace" on us, but our national hymn's lauding of this favor so that our "alabaster cities gleam / Undimmed by human tears" is not helpful. Our cities do not gleam but groan, and grief increasingly waters the topography. Dimming tears are exactly what are required to blur this deceptive vision of ourselves and our achievements, this disinformation about our purity, our protection of our citizens, our transparency, and our commitment to healing, all qualities traditionally conveyed by the symbolism of alabaster. If we do not learn to lament our fall now, we will, like Israel, be forced to learn it, exiled from what we thought was our positional place in the world, and our folk belief in our deserved protection by divinity. Again, like Israel in Psalm 137:1, we will sit down and lament in captivity the loss of our freedoms. If it is the eventual grief that leads to repentance it will be good grief, but what about good grief now before it is too late?

DISTINGUISHING BETWEEN GODLY
VERSUS WORLDLY SORROW

What could possibly make ultimately good something that feels presently bad? Writing to the Corinthians Paul distinguishes between the kind of grief that is good, "godly sorrow," and a grief that is not, described as "worldly sorrow" (2 Cor. 7:8–13). He acknowledges that an earlier letter he had written to them had caused them sorrow, but that he did "not regret it." Helpfully, he explains why his emotion is so contrary to theirs: "not because you were made sorry, but because your sorrow led you to repentance." This was a godly sorrow that "God intended" for good spiritual consequences because it "brings repentance that leads to salvation" and "leaves no regret." But there is also a "worldly sorrow" that is not good grief because it brings spiritual "death" with all its loss and despair.

Not all laments are equal, and the outcomes of godly and worldly sorrow could not be more different. Unlike godly sorrow, worldly sorrow eschews repentance in favor of regret that some have described as "unconsummated repentance." Like regret, remorse is not necessarily repentant, and may be the response to being found out—not the result of a conviction that asks for forgiveness. Consequently, worldly grief neither seeks nor experiences change, and more often than not simply leaves a trail of unresolved emotional debris in its wake. It is self-centered rather than being God or other-centered; self-pitying rather than merciful. It is more concerned with personal pain than the possible suffering of others. It counters the shame felt by self with the blame of others.

Through the prophet Malachi, God tells the people that though they appear to be lamenting ("You flood the LORD's altar with tears," 2:13) they are actually weeping and wailing because they are not getting what they want on their terms. God is specific here and says that he should not be expected to respond to their lament while evil continues to be pursued. What appears to be a public obedient act of lamentation is actually compromised and corrupted by the unholy motivations and intentions of the heart. It is a worldly sorrow.

For Paul, godly sorrow is always known by its fruits. "See what this godly sorrow has produced in you." He then gives a checklist of outcomes that endorse the goodness of the grief: "what earnestness, what eagerness to clear yourselves, what indignation, what alarm, what longing, what concern, what readiness to see justice done." There is no sorrow for oneself here. There are grievous situations that we bring on ourselves, specifically our sins that engender this good grief when conviction is accepted and not quashed by denial or dishonesty. There is a righteous response to the seriousness of the cause of grief, to what requires not just a clearing of name but a cleansing of conscience. There is no cloying and hopeless condemnation but a resolve to seek justice and resolution with an indignation that goes hand in hand with compassion. The humility of godly affections leads to the obedience of godly actions. The self-focused passivity of worldly sorrow is contrasted with the forward- and outward-looking passion of godly sorrow. Worldly sorrow has the power to imprison us in its imploded emotions and to bind us to thoughts and feelings that subvert our peace, our hope, and our joy. The places and times, the events and relationships where consolation failed and grief was unassuaged can become the coordinates of bitterness and hopelessness. Our retaliation undermines God's restoration. Only our wounds are perceived, and we lose the efficacy of the salvific wounds of Christ. It is spiritual death to Paul, precisely because it refuses resurrection life. Godly sorrow waters hope. Worldly sorrow drowns it.

Frankly, lament does not appear to be good grief to many who are religious because it can run the risk of not sounding theologically kosher. Indeed, lament challenges a comfortable armchair theology that is diffident about bringing reality into the presence of God. Psalm 88 is described as the most helpless of all laments because it does not come out of the downward spiral with a sudden yank of the emotional joystick, with some "I'm thankful really" line or an expression of definitely unrealized but desperately anticipated hope. The last line of this psalm has been immortalized by Simon and Garfunkel in the opening line of *The Sound of Silence:* "Hello darkness my old friend." No one is talking about a future dawn here. Welcome to canonical lament. But it is out of the painful questioning of God that there comes a recovery of prayerful asking of God, and for God, a return of intimate conversation out of the incommunicado brokenness of feeling abandoned or justifiably aggrieved.

But lest we satisfy ourselves only in observing the discomfort of the religious, when it comes to lament, it also does not pass as spiritually mature for those whose understanding of the "charismata" is only about Pentecostal exuberance. We like to characterize Pentecost more by the tongues than the tears, but one of the consequences of the Pentecostal bestowal of the Holy Spirit was that Peter stood up to give an explanation for what had just been experienced, with this recorded response: "When the people heard this they were cut to the heart" (Acts 2:37). The revelation of what their sin had done to "this Jesus . . . by nailing him to a cross" did not result in ecstatic joy and singing in tongues, but in a massive public lament. The presence of God that swirled like a mighty wind did not render unnecessary the responsive outpouring of lament. Indeed, the church's first recorded apostolic sermon (Acts 2:14–30) hammers home the necessary relationship between lamenting and repenting. It is one of the non-negotiable manifestations of any coming of the Holy Spirit that it brings conviction and confession. Lament is charismatic, and serves to help us know, feel, and bear the grief of God.

LAMENT AND THE PROPHETS

The Bible has so much to say about this good grief. Of course, there are many reasons why we do not choose to attend to it, or express it, especially if we suspect strong emotions, or are threatened by them, as was Eli the priest who chose to put Hannah's grief down to pouring too much wine and beer, not to the "pouring out" of her soul before the Lord. The default positions of steeling oneself, suppressing, hiding pain, shutting down, interiorizing, and keeping a stiff upper lip will all render lament discomfiting and disturbing. It does not fit in cultures that condition people to be emotionally constipated. Is it really helpful to say that lament is "not British" or "it's un-American" at the very moment these nations need to lament? Barbarians did it because they were uncouth and uncivilized, but lament has never been the business of the cultured or the wise, the intelligent, or those who were strong in their own eyes.

Nehemiah's story is a powerful illustration of the interrelationship between lament and prayer, between godly sorrow and godly action. Lament is the context out of which the restoration of Jerusalem arises from the rubble. When he heard about the state of his nation "he sat down and wept" (1:4). It was through lament that he both received the burden for change and discharged that burden. Lament baptized him in reality, the necessity to face the facts: "great trouble . . . disgrace . . .walls broken . . . gates burned with fire" (1:3). General observations suddenly became personal confrontations. Like Nehemiah, we have to stop and let it sink in and absorb the shock. Like Kurtz in Joseph Conrad's *Heart of Darkness*, perhaps we need to be hung over the abyss in order to utter the same response: "The horror!" We should take a long look and then first lament our indifference. What affects us? To the extent we are affected we will act. Someone has said that we cannot repair the ruins we have not wept over.

Lament is not an occasional flavor of the month – cultural, national, and personal crises permitting – but an integral part of the DNA of a normal relationship with God. Contrary to many commentators' views on a text like Lamentations – that lament is an aberration not to be distracted by – Old Testament scholar Walter Brueggemann rightly contends that lament is not some minor key in the prophets but a major, resonating, unmissable chord, foundational to both their personal prophetic calling and to their prophetic call to the people. Their anticipation of lament was spiritually logical because they knew that the nation could not be sustained, living as they were living, any more than we can. Not surprisingly, it is the man known as "the weeping prophet," Jeremiah, who has so much to teach us about this.

Following a graphic inventory of national sins, in which Jeremiah describes Israel as an easy lay, the grace of God cries out as God himself laments and cries to the heavens, "Be appalled at this!" Suddenly the focus moves from Israel's appalling guilt back to God's appealing grace. So eager is God's heart for godly sorrow and its fruit of repentance that he even gives them the script to ask for repentance and to confess their sin and disobedience, shame, and disgrace (Jer. 3:25). But this divinely required response is a lament.

"A cry is heard on the barren heights, the weeping and pleading of the people" (3:21). From now on, the asking of the people for the mercy of God for the nation is in the context of lament. This is the same in Lamentations: "The hearts of the people cry out to the Lord . . . let your tears flow like a river day and night; give yourself no relief, your eyes no rest" (2:18–19). When it came to prayer, lament was not an option or elective, an additive or an adjunct.

Lament becomes the key prophetic means by which protest is expressed against falsehood and its effects, insisting that we engage the truth about what God hates as well as what he loves, confronting and denouncing a wrong theology. It could be argued that the loss of lament leaves us uncritical of what is false and deceptive, and encourages us to stay tolerant of things as they are. The language of lament is a weapon of our spiritual warfare in its challenge to principalities and powers, calling into question their rule and despotism. Lament causes you to feel present reality in a way that you have to think and consider, remember and act, protest and advocate, denounce and confront. The entirety of Amos's prophetic word to the places of worship that were packed precisely because they were being fed a false message is chillingly relevant: "I will turn your religious feasts into mourning and all your singing into weeping" (8:10). It is not about full churches but faithful believers. The background music for all that follows is not high-souled worship. It is a requiem Mass.

Lament is learned in a prayer room, not a classroom, especially when we join others and experience it as a community commitment, as a corporate lament. We cannot bear it alone. When you read Lamentations, there is a distinctive change from individual and personal lament to a corporate, collegial, community expression of grieving together. To begin with, it talks about "the man who has seen affliction" (Lam. 3:1). The references are to "me . . . my skin." But before the chapter ends there is a change. The need is for a corporate confession. The prayer is now "Let us examine our ways . . . let us return to the LORD. . . . Let us lift up our hearts and our hands to God in heaven and say we have sinned" (3:40–42). God is no longer referred as "he" but as "you," suggesting a recovery of relationship. Lament recovered relationship through the agency of prayer and recovered these Israelites as agents of God's mercy because they persevered in prayer.

LAMENT IN THE PSALMS

Although the biblical prophets describe the need for lament, most of us first encounter lament in the Psalms. A third of the Bible's prayer manual consists of laments, while it is estimated that not even one percent of present worship or prayer includes lament.

The Psalms contain many different and distinctive genres, but the largest category is the psalmody of lament, "the valley of weeping" (84:6), that makes pain audible, that expresses distress of one kind or another, for one reason or another, and that engages the reality of suffering, ranging from what looks like clinical depression (88) to sharp accusation (89). These psalms are crammed with complexities, perplexities, anxieties, affliction, and dereliction in search of consolation. The psalmists neither hide their hopelessness nor mute the cries for deliverance. They long for presence while feeling absence. Perhaps it is this genre that attracts most readers, because we need companionship in identifying pain and getting help to voice it in a manner that is not piously religious. These laments lift the lid, Psalms 42 and 43 being among the most well-known: "Why are you downcast, O my soul?" They illustrate many of the different reasons for lament: being perturbed by oneself, one's own thoughts and feelings (42:5, 11) and addressing one's own soul; being agitated and frustrated by God himself: "Where is your God? . . . I say to God my Rock, why have you forgotten me?" (42:3); and being angry because of others, who have become enemies of our joy and peace and maybe even our view of ourselves. "Why must I go about mourning oppressed by the enemy . . . my foes taunt me" (42:9–10).

The central statement of the lament is that it is "a prayer to the God of my life" (42:8). Again, the heart of lament is prayer. People see this in different ways, some saying that lament leads to petition and others that petition will lead to lament. It is pointless arguing the progression. They are inseparable and not even two different activities or expressions. Listen to Scripture: "I have heard your prayer and seen your tears. I will heal you" (2 Kings 20:5). "My intercessor is my friend as my eyes pour out tears to God" (Job 16:20). "They mourned, wept, and fasted . . . for the nation" (2 Sam. 1:12). Lament is brave asking, preserving us from the repression and suppression that do such incredible damage to body, soul, and spirit. Lament is good psychology, not just good theology. It does not remove prayer but improves it. There is always a journey at hand, not only within individual psalms but also within the whole collection: from predicament to praise, from woe to worship, from hell to hallelujah, from humiliation to exaltation, from fear to faith, from depths to heights, from grief to gratitude, from darkness to light, from pain to peace, from rage to reconciliation, from sin to salvation, from lament to laughter.

So many things may instigate the psalmist's lament: personal, communal, or national suffering; enemies; fears; experience of loss and death and consequences of sin. These laments have a pattern in their structure, usually beginning with a cry for help, followed by the complaint, and, if it's really bad, a cursing that inveighs against the enemies. Typically, before a total wipeout, there will often be some expression of confidence or recovered hope in God, and if this produces enough encouragement and resurgence of faith, the psalmist may even squeeze out a muted blessing. "Put your hope in God for I will yet praise him!" (42:11; 43:5).

When you analyze the lament psalms, you notice that there are different but repeated prayers: "Arise, O Lord" (3, 7, 9, 10, 17, 74, 94). "Give us help" (60:11–12). "Remember your covenant" (25:6). "Let justice be done" (83:16–18). "Don't remember our sins" (51:1; 79:8–9). "Restore us" (80:3). "Don't be silent" (28:1–2; 86:6). "Teach me" (143:10; 90:12; 86:11). "Vindicate me" (35:23–24). The refrain here is that you cannot engage prayer in the psalms without engaging lament.

LAMENT AND PAUL

Outside Jesus, it is Paul's prayer life that we know more about than anyone else's in the New Testament, and not surprisingly, he knew what it was to lament personally, as well as urge others to lament: "I travail in birth again until Christ be formed in you" (Gal. 4:19). "I am afraid I will be grieved over many who have sinned" (2 Cor. 12:21). "You are proud! Should you not rather have been filled with grief" (1 Cor. 5:2). He talks to the Philippians about the mercy of God that intervened "to spare me sorrow upon sorrow" (2:27). When he thought of the state of the Jewish people not accepting their Messiah he wrote, "I have great sorrow and unceasing anguish in my heart" (Rom. 9:2). It was out of lament that he actually wrote some of his letters like 2 Corinthians: "I wrote this lest I should have sorrow from them of whom I ought to rejoice. . . . Out of much affliction and anguish of heart I wrote to you with many tears" (2:3–4). His summary statement of his own life and ministry is telling: "I served the Lord with great humility and tears" (Acts 20:19); "Remember that for three years I never stopped warning each of you night and day with tears" (20:31). What an epitaph! His prayers for his people, for the church, and for others were melded with deep lament.

However, as exemplary and instructive as David, Jeremiah, and Paul are when it comes to learning about both the experience and expression of lament, we need something even more foundational. A proper theology of lament has to be rooted in a doctrine of God, not a doctrine of man.

LAMENT AND GOD

All good theology begins with the nature of God, not the needs of man. A theology of lament begins with an understanding of the lamenting of the Godhead before it is about my lament, in the same way that a theology of suffering begins with the suffering of God, and specifically his redeeming work in and through Christ on the cross. You can hear the cry in Lamentations: "Is it nothing to you, all you who pass by? Is there any sorrow like unto my sorrow?" (1:12). If it is only about my suffering or our suffering, as defensible and understandable as that might be, it will likely end up in complaint, not lament, and there is a big difference.

Scripture is clear about the relationship between divinity and lament. There is a grief that God appears to allow, even bring, when he ceases to strive with man's self-destructive willfulness, and withdraws his presence and leaves us to our own devices.

Micah talks about God's love that will gather "those he brought to grief" (4:5). For the psalmist, it was God who had "fed them with the bread of tears" (80:5). Lamentable events are used by God to get people to at last turn to him and lament their sin and ask for help and deliverance. However, "Though he brings grief . . . he does not willingly bring grief " (Lam 3:32–33). There is also the grief that God feels. Only nine generations after Adam the book of Genesis tell us, "The LORD saw how great man's wickedness on the earth had become. . . . The LORD said, I am grieved that I have made them" (Gen. 6:5–7). But even after the covenantal rescue with Noah, and with Abraham, the unfolding history of Israel was summed up by the psalmist: "How often . . . they grieved him" (Ps. 78:40). Lament is the response of God's grief to our sin but also our infirmities. The psalmists understood this: "You consider their grief" (Ps. 10:4).

It is Jesus who is the ultimate "man of sorrows and acquainted with grief" (Isa. 53:3); the one who has "borne our griefs and carried our sorrows" (53:4). This is the substitutionary work of Isaiah's servant. We can never forget that the laments of the Savior and Redeemer were sourced in that which we are called to lament: our sin and wickedness, our wrong and guilt. The book of Hebrews tells us that Jesus offered his prayers and petitions "with loud cries and tears" (5:7). This was his modus operandi. In the Gospels he shed tears when he encountered a refusal to accept his revelation (Bethany), his requirements (rich young ruler), and his relationship (Jerusalem). In the Upper Room he did not spare his disciples the impending lamentations. "You shall lament" (John 16:20). His lament in Gethsemane was so overwhelming that he described it as a "sorrow to the point of death" (Matt. 26:38). Lament was the crucible for submitting to the will of the Father. And was it not the harrowing psalm of lament, Psalm 22, that he cried before death? "My God, my God, why have you forsaken me?" (Ps. 22:1; Matt. 27:46). We should not forget that as prophet Jesus gave the signs of his coming in Matthew 24, saying that the litany of disaster and dereliction that was going to come upon the world was only "the beginning of sorrows." Lament, Jesus confirmed, is a subject that we will engage, whether willingly or not, whether now or later.

Long before Paul pleaded with the Ephesians not to "grieve the Holy Spirit" (4:30), Isaiah described the rebellion of God's people that "grieved his Holy Spirit" (63:10). The grief and lament of the Holy Spirit is the response to so many sad failures on our part: failure to recognize his person, to remember his purpose to mature and perfect us, to realize his presence, to respect his purity and thus harden our consciences, to respond to his promptings thus avoiding conviction, to receive his provision of his gifts and graces. Again, lament is trinitarian. Thus a theology of lament must be grounded first in the character of God, not the crises of man. Our lament has to be responsive to more than circumstance, because the fact is that we are not always moved by need. God's response is utterly true and consistent. Reacting to the circumstance my way and for my reasons replaces relating to the character and heart of God and discerning his meanings and responses. If there are legitimate and righteous grounds for lament, then God in three persons is the chief lamenter.

COLLECTING OUR TEARS

Perhaps the first response to the evident lack of spiritual lament over the brokenness of nation and citizen, over our response to the evil and viral injustices and consequent irreconciliations that divide and fragment the people, should be repentance. If lament is divinely commanded, then our refusal to do so, our cultural evasion of it, is quite simply an act of disobedience. God commanded the prophets to call the people to lament "with broken heart and bitter grief" (Ezek. 21:6).

Repentance will sift our motivations as we lament our own sins before we lament the sins of others, and it will invite us to move on with a humbled and chastened heart. Having been forgiven for the disobedience of not lamenting, we will be more sensitive to the need to forgive the very parties that are indicted in our lament. Again and again, whether an Old Testament prophet like Joel commanding us to "return with weeping and mourning" (Joel 2:12), or a New Testament apostle like James commanding us to "grieve, mourn, and wail" (4:9), lament is not a divine elective. It is a normal spiritual response to backsliding, to sin, to unfaithfulness, to spiritual adultery that cannot be faked or fabricated. For the prophet Jeremiah, it was a normal, logical response: "Since my people are crushed, I am crushed. I lament" (8:21). For Paul, writing to the Corinthians, to be filled with grief and lament was the normative response to sin that breaks the fellowship of the community: "Shouldn't you rather have been filled with grief?" (1 Cor. 5:2).

There are no wasted tears. "Put my tears in your bottle," requested the psalmist (Ps. 56:8). The choice for us as we face challenging personal as well as national situations is this: Are we going to chuck our hope in the trashcan, or are we going to put our tears in a bottle? Will we be able to say like Paul, "I served the Lord . . . with tears"? It is distressing and shameful that there is so little lament when there is so much that is lamentable. Lament is the maternity ward of spiritual affections – but in birth there is pain. We would rather have love without labor, and laughter without lament. We want the actions without the affections.

Of course, there is lament right up to the last book of the Bible. In Revelation 5:4 John says that he "wept much." He lamented that there was no one to open the scroll. But hope broke through the grief: "Then I saw a Lamb." Yes, we live in this vale of tears, but we live with the blessed hope, that the day is coming when "he will wipe every tear" from our eyes (Rev. 21:4) and there will be no more lamenting "or crying or pain, for the old order of things has passed away."

Lament has been described by many as prayer in a minor key, as the vocalization of pain. Minor it may be, but its vocals can be majorly loud. We need its volume in our triumphalist culture that is obsessed with success and avoidant of suffering. We need both its tutorage and tutelage as we learn how to be courageous with our perplexities and pains, as we stretch for the right words to help us to grope our way through the brambles of grief. These stifled articulations, despite the sorrow, reach out to grasp a divine grip that assures of redemptive and healing purposes and possibilities. Lament is a grief, but it is also a grace. It is a given, but it is also a giver and a gift. We need lament – good grief. ✝

PREPARING FOR DEATH

HEATHER C. OHANESON

"WHEN I BUY a new book, I always read the last page first, that way in case I die before I finish I know how it ends. That, my friend, is a dark side." Do you remember those lines from *When Harry Met Sally*? The main characters are starting out on their long road trip and, with it, their complicated friendship; as the conversation turns to death, Harry and Sally banter. (Harry, of course, is portrayed by a now insanely young Billy Crystal; Sally, by Meg Ryan, whom film preserves as a bright ingenue.) Crystal's character is cavalier in announcing the importance of his preoccupation with Thanatos; Ryan's is resolutely cheery, bearing a life-affirming disposition, which corresponds to Eros, or at least matches her fluffy golden curls.

> Harry: "Do you ever think about death?"
> Sally: "Yes."
> Harry: "Sure you do, a fleeting thought that goes in and out of the transom of your mind. I spend hours, I spend days."
> Sally: "And you think this makes you a better person?"
> Harry: "Look. When the s— comes down, I'm going to be prepared and you're not. That's all I'm saying."

HEATHER C. OHANESON is a writer and professor. She holds degrees in philosophy and religion from Barnard College and Columbia University. She is at work on a spiritual memoir rooted in church music, *With My Face to the Rising Sun*.

Sally: "In the meantime, you're going to ruin your whole life waiting for it."

Is Harry's claim true? Are meditations on death necessary for dying well? Does thinking about death – regularly, relentlessly – equip a person for the end? How many people meet death unprepared and suffer for it? Or, as Sally suggests, is giving one's mind so thoroughly over to death a way to ruin the precious time one has to live?

Although the overall human mortality rate has not changed (every human being will still, at some point, die), the quandary – train your mind for death or keep your focus on life – has taken on a stinging relevance in 2020. The frightening death tolls in the early months of the pandemic caught many people unaware, forcing some to say early goodbyes to loved ones, beckoning others to (re)write their wills, bringing still others to take stock of their pantries, if not their own lives. Stories of ordinarily healthy people who faced life-threatening complications from the Covid-19 virus came through news broadcasts as screams. Even seemingly minor conditions like asthma took on the weight of "comorbidities." Reports revealed how nurses, doctors, and EMTs occupied a particular point of frontline horror in the national tragedy. Our medical heroes watched patients succumb to respiratory failure or stroke day after day without being able to pause long enough to process the losses themselves. Death – not reflection on it – came in relentless waves.

If the Covid-19 crisis has not put death and its allies front of mind for you, perhaps other catastrophes of 2020 have: round after round of racialized police brutality (George Floyd, Breonna Taylor, Jacob Blake, Walter Wallace Jr.); record-defying natural disasters, including wildfires in Australia and hurricanes so numerous they have exceeded English-alphabet naming conventions; the explosion of 2,750 tons of ammonium nitrate in Beirut that killed hundreds but thrust thousands more into prolonged precarity; ongoing, overlooked famine in Yemen; calamitous warfare in Nagorno Karabakh, replete with festering corpses on the battlefield. Things are grim. Directly or in narrowing degrees of separation, you may have had an unusually close brush with mortality this past year.

As the severities of illness and death bombard us—and here I am making inferences from my life and the lives of family, friends, and acquaintances—we mostly face away. That is, we refuse to allow our attention to be held by fatality or its possibility *for us*. Even in "lockdown," plenty of escape hatches are available: another Zoom meeting to attend, another child's class to oversee, another chore to do, another mouth to feed, another cooking project to try, another batch of supplies to buy, another book to read, another podcast to listen to, another show to watch, another glass of wine to drink. Busy, we keep our minds occupied with fleeting things. We remain distant from ourselves, our inner silence, our natures.

So thorough is our denial of death that we may not even be aware of the lengths we go to avoid contemplating it. While certain events in my young adulthood punctured my own oblivion to "the end," I mostly lived through an ever-extending sequence of this-worldly preoccupations, like a Netflix suggested-programs page that elongates and then elongates again. "Life," as John Lennon said, "is what happens to you when you're busy making other plans." My mind was trained on little things, not the long-term picture. This was the case even though I was a Christian who believed in "the resurrection of the dead" and "the life everlasting." If anything, those creedal phrases, which are essential to orthodox Christianity, served to emphasize what follows death rather than death itself. Central Christian teachings about salvation did not translate to my imagining what my own demise would be like. I was healthy, I have lost few loved ones, I have lived far from war. Looking ahead to the terminus of my existence did not register. It is not as if I felt bad about deferring that work; it simply was not on my radar. Preparing oneself for death is the sort of issue that is not a problem until it is a problem.

Two things have challenged this, finally: philosophy and experience.

In studying Plato and Aristotle, Montaigne and Pascal, Heidegger and Derrida, I have found myself beginning to see philosophy as something that exists in relation to death. Plato portrays Socrates' nobility in the face of execution in the *Apology*. More than that, Plato assures us that Socrates was able to meet his unjust death with a cool dignity because he spent his life valuing the mind over the body. In some sense, Socrates had been giving up his body all along. In the *Nicomachean Ethics*, Plato's student Aristotle teaches that the evaluation of a well-lived human life cannot come until the end of that life, or even from beyond the grave. It is only when you take into account the welfare of your descendants that your own "happiness" (*eudaimonia*) can be measured. The tradition of theorizing about death continued through the twentieth-century Continental philosophers. Heidegger's notion of being-toward-death, found in his magnum opus *Being and Time*, serves to motivate a life of attention and authenticity. Derrida, inspired in large part by Kierkegaard's *Fear and Trembling*, approaches the biblical story of Abraham's willingness to slay his son in terms of paradox, secrecy, and divine alterity in *The Gift of Death*. Of these thinkers, the early modern pair of Montaigne and Pascal affected my orientation to death most of all.

I first encountered their ideas in the spring of 2009, when I was enrolled in Pierre Force's graduate seminar on the French triumvirate of Montaigne, Descartes, and Pascal at Columbia University. In those months as we met around the table in his office in Philosophy Hall, Professor Force's formality and rigor temporarily transported me, in my imagination at least, to the even more illustrious world of the Sorbonne and the *École normale supérieure* (his former institutions). As I muddled through class with my inferior language skills, I became fascinated with the topic of diversion – *divertissement* – and its relation to death, *la mort*, which definitely should not be confused with, or sloppily pronounced as, *l'amour*.

The title of Montaigne's essay "That to Philosophize Is to Learn How to Die" is, quite frankly, more memorable to me than any single aspect within the piece. The title says it all. Not only can one learn how to die – itself a shocking idea, given that a person only dies once – one can learn how to die by doing the work of philosophy, which is ultimately the activity of sustained thinking. Indeed, death is one of the notions that a philosopher can contemplate. And so Montaigne intones, "It is uncertain where death awaits us; let us await it everywhere." To do that, to master death as the Stoics and Epicureans of old attempted, to "rid it of its strangeness, come to know it, get used to it," you think about it. Constantly. Like Harry.

Not one to focus on the mind at the expense of the body, Montaigne relays a physical brush with death that he experienced in a riding accident in "Of Practice" (probably my favorite of the works in the genre-defining, 850-page collection of his *Essays*). He writes vividly of how he took a small horse for a jaunt near his house one day during one of the religious civil wars in France. (This would have been between 1567 and 1570 in the wine-producing hills of Bordeaux.) The famous scene reads,

> This man, in order to show his daring and get ahead of his companions, spurred his horse at full speed up the path behind me, came down like a colossus on the little man and little horse, and hit us like a thunderbolt with all his strength and weight, sending us both head over heels. So that there lay the horse bowled over and stunned, and I ten or twelve paces beyond, dead, stretched on my back, my face all bruised and skinned, my sword, which I had in my hand, more than ten paces away, my belt in pieces, having no more motion or feeling than a log.

Unlike Montaigne's times of deliberate concentration on the idea of death, where he sets out to find through contemplation what death is like, in this moment a taste of death comes to him unbidden. It overtakes him from an unforeseen force (a charging servant rather than warring Protestants and Catholics), which itself seems to be a lesson in what death can be like: from an unexpected source, impenetrable, blindsiding. In the absence of his dear friend and fellow humanist Étienne de La Boétie, to whom he might normally relay such a powerful anecdote, Montaigne tells us, his unknown readers, how the fall renders him inanimate, making him less human, more log. Whereas the horse is only stunned, he is, in his own words, dead.

What does Montaigne find out from within that state? Does he have a *Heaven Is for Real* revelation? True to his "What do I know?" (*Que sais-je?*) project of self-discovery, Montaigne reports the first stirrings of life in his body and soul. Several hours after the accident, he throws up buckets of blood, and tries to make sense of what happened:

The first thought that came to me was that I had gotten a harquebus shot in the head; indeed several were being fired around us at the time of the accident. It seemed to me that my life was hanging only by the tip of my lips; I closed my eyes in order, it seemed to me, to help push it out, and took pleasure in growing languid and letting myself go. It was an idea that was only floating on the surface of my soul, as delicate and feeble as all the rest, but in truth not only free from distress but mingled with that sweet feeling that people have who let themselves slide into sleep.

Montaigne captures the ephemera of his dying thoughts. Convinced by something like firsthand experience – by practice – that he was correct in his earlier theorizing about the ease of death, Montaigne discovers that he can sweetly rest in peace about Resting in Peace. The dead are not to be pitied for their dying, he assures us, which is a relief not only for ourselves ("when our time comes," as we euphemistically say) but also for those who have predeceased us. He tells his readers, whom he treats as intimate friends, that focusing on death frees one from fearing it. After all, who fears slipping into sleep?

What moved me about reading "Of Practice" were not Montaigne's particular claims about the nature of death as much as the vividness of the WHAMMY scene of equestrian danger, which could represent any life-changing, perspective-shifting moment accessed viscerally from a place of deep interiority. It was the fact of his phenomenology that struck me and then stayed with me. Through his writing, Montaigne successfully opened up the first-person reality of his experience for me. In some rather magnificent, loopy way, reading about his being thrown from the horse knocked me off my metaphorical horse. Pinned in my memory, the passage has given way to fundamental questions of identity and reality – Who am I really when I am unconscious? How does my conscious life prepare me for other states? Am I present to myself, even when I am absent? Are near-death experiences truly indicative of what dying will be like?

After having tarried with Montaigne's *essais*, I still suspect that the oncoming of death could be terrifying, akin to collision-with-a-freight-train instead of gently-succumbing-to-the-comforts-of-a-down-pillow-at-the-end-of-a-long-day. Despite its appeal, I am not solely convinced by Montaigne's stance, which implies that being hit by an eighteen-wheeler (or whatever gruesome form of death you wish to imagine: Alzheimer's, a mass school shooting, suffocation) could at the soul level be experienced *without distress.* My instincts run in the opposite direction. What if dying in one's sleep is the soul-equivalent of being violently mowed down? Philosophy, it's time to meet Theology.

Pascal, the Christian apologist, polymath, and inventor of the first calculator, comes along in the 1660s and furthers Montaigne's attack on mindlessness toward death, but he does so with an eye toward salvation. In his incomplete *Pensées,* he uncovers the human lot: "*Man's condition.* Inconstancy, boredom, anxiety." Obsessed with opposites, Pascal insists that human beings partake in the extremes of greatness and wretchedness. We are susceptible to the powers of infinity and nullity. And yet Pascal continually presses for a middle way, whether it comes to a painting (do not look at it from too close up or too far away) or to human nature (we are neither beasts nor angels). In his frank dealings, he skewers people who can be so easily and thoroughly captivated by chasing hares or balls. An equal-opportunity critic, he levels his accusations against ordinary people and kings alike.

The main idea that I learned from Pascal in that class, and that I have carried with me in the intervening years, is that boredom, in its very painfulness, is a helpful step on the way to finding God. We do not have to be led by diversions, lemming-like, off the cliff of life. By sitting with the difficulties of existence, we create the space to seek "a firmer way out" of our despair:

> *Wretchedness.* The only thing that consoles us for our miseries is distraction, yet that is the greatest of our wretchednesses. Because that is what mainly prevents us from thinking about ourselves and leads us imperceptibly to damnation. Without it we should be bored, and boredom would force us to search for a firmer way out, but distraction entertains us and leads us imperceptibly to death.

Very often, when I am waiting for the subway, say, or am headed out on a walk, I pause—because of Pascal—before I decide to take out my phone or put my headphones on. Would it be better to spend that time in noiselessness to see what thoughts arise? Do I owe myself the discomfort of the silence to confront what is wrong with myself or the world, to acknowledge it and not simply stuff it down, down, down? To be available to another person? To learn about myself and what I idolize? To perhaps lift my thoughts to God? Even if I routinely choose the distraction, my behavior has emerged from the realm of habit and risen to the level of consciousness, and I have Pascal and Professor Force to thank for that.

After Pascal reveals and ridicules, he redeems. Pascal does not seem to believe in the sufficiency of the solution that other philosophers have offered. "It is all very well for philosophers to say: 'Withdraw into yourselves, you will find your goodness there'; we do not believe them. Those who do are the most hollow and stupid of all." Instead, he points to divine grace, which moves the heart. He names the inner void, which people try to fill with all manner of things—adultery and stars are on his list, but so are, oddly, cabbages and leeks—and then he suggests that rather than finite things, we look to fill the infinite abyss with the infinite God, who is "alone our true good." I was drawn to Pascal's views because of the Christian sentiment that I found there, one that was paradoxically tough and tender. And I was touched by Pascal's own dying words: *Que Dieu ne m'abandonne jamais!* (May God never abandon me!)

Over and above what I learned from Montaigne and Pascal, I was schooled by death and change.

Later that year, in the fall of 2009, I fell grief-stricken by the sudden passing of my friend and former boss, Karen. A fit fifty-four-year-old civil rights lawyer from Paducah, Kentucky, she died in her sleep of an aortic aneurysm. In addition to the sheer loss of her presence in my life, her death shook me by its very possibility. It was the first time since childhood that I sensed how terrifying the world could be.

When I flew to Tennessee, where Karen had been living, to meet her sister and attend her memorial service, I was floored by the *in medias res* state of her house—all the signs of a life in process that shone a spotlight on the suddenness of her death. Was Karen in any way prepared for her last night on earth? In the remaining second of her life, did she have an emergency "this is it" final thought? Did she even realize she was dying? Is one way of exiting (knowingly, unknowingly) more desirable than the other? By perishing, had she lost the self that could be aware of nonexistence? By the morning, was there no longer a self to be aware that she did not wake up?

Though mundane, the details from that funereal visit were searing for me. There was a single copy of the *New Yorker* neatly laid by Karen's bedside. There were the cashews in her pantry, part of the healthy lunch she would always bring to the office. The odd intimacy of seeing her food without her there and immediately feeling the familiarity of her tastes hit me—WHAMMY—a wave of grief recognizable to the bereaved. ("Bereaved" means "deprived or robbed," which is a hauntingly accurate way of describing the experience of the death of a loved one.)

The overwhelming propriety of Karen's home lodged in me as a kind of accusing memory. Everything was clean and in its place—prepared, as it were, for us, her unexpected guests. Sometimes, today, when I look around at the disarray of my own apartment, including my stacks of unfinished, undiscarded *New Yorkers*—those silent piles of shame and aspiration—I think about what people would find if I were to die like Karen did. But preparing your space for those who find you dead is not the same as preparing for death.

Moving was another experience that inched my consciousness forward. In my mid-thirties, getting ready to relocate across country, I cleaned out or boxed up the contents of my tiny Manhattan apartment—all the things that had accrued from years of living there, the majority of which I had carried into the apartment one at a time. During the weeks leading up to the move I consciously (but unintentionally) experienced the purging and packing as an exercise for death. Why? Handling *stuff* that touched on different parts of my life was emotionally intense. It stirred memories.

Moving day was not Judgment Day: when the moving van rolled up and parked illegally in front of the M7 bus stop by my building, I did not come to know a divine reckoning firsthand. Nevertheless, I was cognizant of the way in which I was taking stock of who I was through what I owned. Even if the things—the books, the notebooks, the mementos, the trinkets, the framed pictures, the clothes, the jewelry, the hangers, the shoes, the Christmas ornaments, the cookware, the silverware, the mugs, the collection of Moroccan bowls, the photos, the CDs (!), the rug, the sheets, the pillows, the bedding, the towels, the toiletries, the luggage, the furniture—were not exactly integral to my being, they told the story of my life in a material way. They added up to the person I had become. Loading those objects onto a truck and watching them roll away for an untold number of days as they made their way to California was a severing. A chance to practice letting go.

That, incidentally, was how I also experienced returning the piles of library books that I would routinely and gleefully acquire as a graduate student. When they were due, I had to give them back. Clearing my shelves was moving in miniature, a concrete reminder that on my last day I will not be able to carry anything over. It all has to be given back. Term up. Renewal denied.

It could be said that, for most of the span of those decades, I practiced for death in an implicit manner—I kept the Sabbath. I would observe a day of rest in an idiosyncratic way, which is to say, I would go to church on Sundays, refraining from work and chores and email but not refraining (as my Orthodox Jewish friends would) from spending money, using electricity, or writing things down. Feeling somewhat rudderless as to what I could or could not do when I first began to keep the Sabbath in college, I focused on literal rest, taking luxurious naps. Like an overrun piece of technology, I powered down. Sleep, it turns out, is 1/60 death, and Sabbath is 1/60 of the world to come, at least according to the Talmud.

Rich theologies of the Sabbath permeate Jewish and Christian traditions. Shabbat (the seventh day) or Sunday (the day of Jesus' resurrection) functions as a boundary, telling work as God told the sea, "thus far shall you come, and no farther" (Job 38:11). The day of rest is a day of freedom (both negative liberty—freedom from work—and positive liberty—freedom to praise). Moreover, rhythms of rest can serve as explicit reminders of our humble dependence on a good and faithful God. We no longer "get to" or "have to" be defined by our labor. Week by week, we see the globe still spinning without our efforts. The cessations in self-importance brought about by the Sabbath are not unlike the relief from self that sleep regularly provides. For some not-insignificant proportion of our lives, we have to be unconscious. The Sabbath is a longer nighttime – peaceful, restorative, mysterious, and a way to prepare oneself existentially for that eternal Sabbath, death, which may be unending, paradisiacal life. But the Sabbath is remarkably unlike sleep too: it is a sacred time of *heightened* consciousness, when one awakens to God. Rabbi Abraham Joshua Heschel (throughout his short book *The Sabbath*) and Augustine (in the final pages of his magisterial *City of God*) are theologians of resting in the eternal, which perhaps adds credence to Montaigne's findings after all.

Purposeful reflection on death is not a widely recognizable cultural practice in much of Anglophone twenty-first-century North America. We lack role models for it as an activity; there is no social pressure to direct our thoughts toward death, no widely shared Day of the Dead–like holiday or ritual. But we can and should take clues from specific Christian practices like Ash Wednesday (when we are told the words of Ecclesiastes 3:20, "All are from the dust, and to dust all return"), the sacrament of baptism (in which we are plunged into Christ's death and raised into his new life), and spirituals ("I wanna be ready, I wanna be ready, I wanna be ready to put on my long white robes").

In some versions of the Catholic and Anglican traditions, sermons on the four Sundays of Advent are preached on the Four Last Things, of which death is the first. In that way, Christians are invited to keep death in view as they approach the miracle of Jesus' birth – a birth that ultimately ushers in the hope of a day beyond death.

And so resources are hidden in the breadth of Christian praxis to complement and supplement the wisdom of the ages. Together, theology and philosophy teach us that we prepare for dying by thinking about death, but we prepare for *death* by living well.

As I was writing this essay, there was a moment where I thought I was dying. I was in the bathroom when a searing pain raced blazingly like a red-hot wire through the anterior right side of my brain. The intense sensation came and went quickly, but its duration was long enough for me to have a series of rapid thoughts. Is this it? Am I going to die in the middle of working on a piece about dying? I don't want to die yet! Was thinking about death helpful?

And then I kept thinking. And then I lived. ☩

January 8, 2021

POLITICS AND POLITICAL SERVICE

OLIVER O'DONOVAN

LET US BEGIN with a commonplace thought: "politics" is the name of a *discussion,* an exchange of speech, and in that discussion we all participate, as of right. There may and must be many privileged, restricted, and technical discussions in the practice of politics, in which most of us should not expect to be involved; yet the political realm "belongs" in some sense to everyone in the political community, and not to any group in particular. That is the legacy of Roman republicanism, which discovered the concept of "the public," and identified the political community as the "public possession" (*res publica*).

But what kind of "possession" is it that we all have a part in? It is from the Christianization of the Roman tradition that we have come to think of it as a discursive, rather than a material, possession. Western civilization learned from the Christian gospel of community in the Word, a common life held together by a common truth, out of the infinite resources of which every member could speak. It learned to think of its secular institutions, as well as its sacred, in that light.

Of course, there are public lands, public buildings, public roads, public institutions, and public revenue, but they depend on

OLIVER O'DONOVAN held chairs in Oxford and Edinburgh, and is now an Honorary Professor at St Andrews. An Anglican priest, he is a Fellow of the British Academy and of the Royal Society of Edinburgh. His books include *Resurrection and Moral Order* (1986), *The Desire of the Nations* (1996), *The Ways of Judgment* (2005), *Self, World and Time* (2013), and *Finding and Seeking* (2014).

something more fundamental, a public *society* created by a public *discussion*. Someone who has no part in our discussion is not a member of our political society; someone who has no part in *any* such discussion has no membership in any political society, and lacks one dimension of human freedom, the freedom to participate actively in a society.

But the political is a practical discussion, a deliberation on how we shall act and on the conditions that determine the possibilities of our acting. It seeks to answer the universal practical question, What is to be done? But it seeks to answer it in a distinctive form, different from the way we answer it in natural communities or in the deliberations of our own heads: it asks, What is to be done by us *together*? For in politics we conceive of an action as "ours." To act together, of course, we must act through dedicated institutional structures and agencies, through representative officials and leaders. But the logic of what they can do will always trace back, even if circuitously, to the deliberations of the political society as a whole. That is the source of all *public* authority and defines its scope.

Something similar, of course, is true of all organizations, of cities, corporations, universities, business enterprises; indeed, of any association of those who do not form a natural community in some common project. Institutions and offices are created and filled by publicly accepted processes; they are governed by laws arising from public deliberation. But political society, not associated by any particular project other than that of living together, is especially dependent on its offices and institutions. They make it visible, and give concrete form to the indeterminate "We" that composes it. They form a bulwark against having to begin the political discussion again from scratch, reinventing it every moment; they are what allow it to extend across time and develop a persisting identity. Only with their help can common deliberation acquire a recognizable self-coherence over time.

For the fabric of common speech that binds us together is vulnerable. It is vulnerable to the here-and-now immediacy of its object, which exposes it to the dangers of acting in ignorance or forgetfulness, and to consequent passions and recriminations. It is vulnerable to distrust, especially in the larger and more complex institutions that give structure to deliberations and produce the leaders and officeholders to frame and enact the policies that emerge. It is vulnerable to the sheer complexity of the private interests within a political society and the differing views of public need that they encourage. It is vulnerable to losing sight of major factors that affect the well-being of participants.

The reason that any sector or interest in a society may come to think itself as systematically neglected or ignored is that in the course of discussion so much *is* constantly neglected and ignored. And the frustration generated by a failure to be heard or understood, a failure to gather the necessary insights or to have agreed concerns effectively acted on, can undermine the will to participate in the political discourse, and therefore undermine the political community as such.

What recourse do we have when we face a breakdown in political discussion, when everyone speaks to themselves and nobody listens? Faith in God has something distinctive and important to say to this: we speak to one another *because we have first been spoken to*. We make laws and regulations because a law has first been given us. We form institutions to enact decisions because we have been entrusted with a task, that of judging the right from the wrong within our common affairs. Behind the political discourse and the public forms it generates there stands the command of God. And this is what distinguishes political society in the strict sense from the many quasi-political social organizations we may construct to serve various ends. It is on this that it founds its claim to "eminent domain," its right to override, for public necessity's sake, the decisions of all other associations.

Mere size or scale could not confer such a right, but only the specific tasks of justice. Subordinate societies pursue utilities and interests of various kinds, and they may very well serve the common good by doing so. But political society, which pursues no particular interest and no particular utility, has the burden of judging among all utilities and interests. Political discourse, in the fullest sense, then, is not simply a discourse about "What are we to do together?" It is a discourse about "What should we do, in order to practice justice in our life together?"

With the failure of political discourse comes violence, which is the breakdown of common discourse par excellence. But here we must be very careful of the language we use, and jealous for the traditional distinction between "force" and "violence," a distinction that it became fashionable to ignore in religious circles in the last generation. Why should we favor the "force" of the police over the "violence" of the gangland bosses? The distinction hangs on one point alone, but it is of supreme importance. "Force" is institutionally bound into the structure of political discourse by a responsibility to law and to representative government. "Take away justice," Augustine wrote famously, "and what are kingdoms but large criminal syndicates?" That remark points in two directions. On the one hand, the state apparatus may perhaps come to be distinguished from the criminal syndicate only by its size, which is not a sufficient ground for any moral distinction between the two. On the other hand, the two become indistinguishable only when we "take away justice." It is the structural ordering of the state to enact the judgments that God has commanded that makes us view its conduct, even when it may be materially indistinguishable from that of its adversaries, in a different moral light from that of a criminal group.

Force exercised by institutions of government may sometimes be exercised deplorably. When it is, we know that it still belongs to the authoritative structure of government precisely when political discussion takes the matter up, seeks to redress its wrongs and to improve the standard of public practices. Concealing the wrongs of governmental institutions is, in the plainest sense, to treat them like criminal syndicates. We have to preserve the distinction between wrong committed *in the inadequate pursuit* of practices of lawful judgment and wrong committed *in defiance of* practices of lawful judgment. The latter includes, of course, wrong committed by public officials who consciously ignore the law they are given to administer.

The distinction may often be difficult to make in a given case: did the police behave badly because they forgot what they were commissioned to do, or because they were ill-trained, ill-equipped, and ill-supported? We may not know, but we must know that we *need* to know, because the difference is all-important. If the problem is one of "bad apples," it needs criminal prosecution. If it is one of political and organizational structure, it needs political and organizational reforms. We had better seek some clarity about which of these we really need.

Political societies are plural, and each of us is a member of only one among many. All political societies are called by God to the practice of justice, but all start from different places and operate in different conditions in responding to that call. One of the most curious results of the communications that now govern our news and our imaginations is that we very easily forget those differing places and conditions. We imagine ourselves as belonging to a single world society in which certain central places count for much more in our thinking. An ugly piece of police abuse in Minneapolis created a worldwide reaction that still goes on. A much larger and more cold-blooded police massacre of civilians in Lagos, Nigeria, will certainly not arouse anything like the same notice. We ought to ask why that is the case, and what is wrong with our imaginations of the world that encourage it to be the case. Those of us who live outside the United States but feel ourselves part of the same wider economic and civilizational world sometimes give the impression of having forgotten where we live. Growing up as a British Christian I was taught to pray each Sunday for Queen Elizabeth and the government under her. Today, I notice, British clergy commonly fail to pray for the government of Britain, and like to pray in tones of benevolent impartiality for "all governments everywhere," which fosters the illusion that we are all citizens of the world with no need to be citizens of any place in particular. But we have a responsibility to the justice of our place, the place, whose institutions make our daily existence possible. We have a responsibility for political neighbors sitting at our gate, who have first call on our engaged attention.

And this sense of focused, located responsibility is what is properly meant by "patriotism," perennially an unpopular virtue. It is the virtue of recognizing our special duty to the health and justice of the discourse that constitutes our own political identity. It is not patriotic to think of our political community as somehow "better" than others – that is just stupid. True patriotism is the virtue of those who know where in particular their time on earth is spent, and are conscious of what they owe to the discourse of that place. It is a virtue of concreteness. Politics becomes the more fantastic the more it is divorced from the ordinary contexts of our lives. The political neighbors at our gate may ask a great deal that we do not feel able to give, but there is one thing that we must be able to give them, which is attention and discourse, a hearing and an answer. We may not confuse them with other people a thousand miles away, nor make them disappear from our imaginations and arguments because they do not fit in with ideal projects of reform or construction that are dear to our heart, but not to theirs. ✝

January 13, 2021

JUSTICE IN A TIME OUT OF JOINT

W. BRADFORD LITTLEJOHN

LAST FRIDAY, as I drove into Arlington, Virginia, for a lunch meeting, I rounded the curve of the Potomac and saw the Washington Monument and then the Capitol slide into view. Many times before I'd enjoyed that sight, my heart stirring with pride at the symbols of American greatness – and the vague thrill of proximity to the world's greatest center of power. This time, though, I felt a wholly different sensation – a tight knot in the pit of my stomach, a sense of grief and dread – the sense, it struck me, that one has in driving to the funeral of a friend. A fitting feeling, I thought, as I drove past the Iwo Jima Memorial, with its six sculpted Marines striving to plant an American flag beneath an iron-gray sky; after all, something had died within me last Wednesday, and in the hearts of every American patriot.

On that day, a crowd of "freedom fighters" had gathered before the White House, to cheer their defeated chief to one last act of resistance, to turn back, if they might, the inexorable tide of his defeat then being certified in the United States Congress. Exhorting his followers to "take back our country," President Trump stoked their rage to the boiling point and dispatched them to the US Capitol.

W. BRADFORD LITTLEJOHN is a senior fellow of the Edmund Burke Foundation and president of the Davenant Institute. He is the author of *The Peril and Promise of Christian Liberty* and numerous other writings in the areas of Christian ethics, political theology, and Reformation history. He lives in Leesburg, Virginia, with his wife, Rachel, and four children.

By one in the afternoon, the crowd, now an angry mob, was surging against the outer walls and staircases of the Capitol, waving American flags and Confederate flags, Trump banners, crosses, and crucifixes. In between singing snatches of the national anthem, some shouted curses at police, denouncing them as traitors, while others stood nervously by or snapped pictures for friends and family back home.

Within two hours, the underprepared and overwhelmed police, their thin blue line protecting the sanctuary of the republic, had been routed, and the more violent members of the mob had poured into the Capitol building via unlocked doors and shattered windows. The lawmakers within, interrupted in the midst of their own solemn sham of debating the election results that had already been affirmed in court, were forced to unceremoniously flee for cover, crawling on the floor and donning gas masks. Angry rioters rampaged through the hallways, beating policemen and vandalizing offices. In one corner of the vast building, shots from the Capitol Hill police rang out and a woman crumpled to the ground, bleeding to death; while in another corner, protesters in outlandish costumes posed for selfies in Senate offices. By the end of the day, five were dead or dying, including one policeman, with many dozens more injured, and millions in a state of shock.

In the face of such chaos, the breaking of our 230-year tradition of peaceful transfers of power, we reach for words strong enough to express our own fear and anger: last Wednesday's events have been called "an insurrection," "a coup," "domestic terrorism." They are the expression, we are told, of hate, of racism, of white fragility, of a desperate attempt to hold on to power, of mass delusion. Some of these descriptions may be accurate enough, but if we remain at that level, we minimize the depth of the great aching wound in our body politic; we sidestep, I believe, the most illuminating moral description of what happened: vigilantism.

NO JUSTICE? NO PEACE

Those who stormed the Capitol last Wednesday were seeking justice. If they had dared to repeat it, their motto might have been "No justice, no peace." In their minds, a fraud had been committed, an election had been stolen, the will of the people was being systematically trampled on, and what other remedy did they have? After all, why should there be peace? Why should we quietly roll over, resign ourselves to oppression, and let the powerful enjoy their spoils?

Many readers will immediately object that the only fraud was that which the protesters themselves propagated, that the only oppression was in their febrile imaginations. Reality matters. Truth matters. But this misses a crucial point, just as right-wing commentators who have questioned the pervasiveness of race-motivated police murders missed the point. Unless we grapple with this point, we cannot begin to restore our nation's faith in the possibility of politics. For the protesters storming the Capitol, as for the angry activists in Minneapolis or Portland, the time was out of joint, the task of public judgment had failed, a gap had opened up between truth and appearance, and cursed spite though it might be, only they could set it right.

The reference to *Hamlet* is no mere rhetorical flourish. Shakespeare's masterpiece is a profound meditation on the lure of vigilantism, the sense that if falsehood has been enthroned in the seat of justice, then those who have been permitted an awful glimpse at the truths that lurk on the dark underside of power must take justice into their own hands. Vigilantism and revolution (which is, after all, only vigilantism writ large) are always waiting in the wings of every political system, waiting for the moment when the fragile truce that society makes with the imperfectability of human judgment breaks down. Trapped within his own private reality, the vigilante can no longer be sure whether he is acting to vindicate the corrupted order of public justice or merely to achieve some private catharsis. Even when the vigilante achieves his end, however, as the irresolute Hamlet finally does, it turns out more often than not to be the end of the body politic that he had sought to renew. The play ends to the tramping boots of an occupying army.

The modern-day masterworks of filmmaker Christopher Nolan wrestle with the same paradox: in a world of corrupt institutions and systemic deception, only private agents seem able to enact judgment; and yet the result of such vengeance never seem to be justice after all. From Leonard Shelby in *Memento* to Robert Angier in

The Prestige to a whole string of heroes and villains in the Dark Knight trilogy, Nolan's characters work in the shadows to uncover and avenge the wrongs that society can't be bothered to make right, but they never seem to be able to find their way back to the light. Shelby discovers that his supposed quest for justice was an elaborate fiction, a saga of self-deception serving to convince himself that his actions had meaning in a world that no longer had any of its own. Angier apparently succeeds in bringing his nemesis to justice, only for a cataclysmic reveal at the end to expose that he has helped hang an innocent man, and is in fact his own murderer. Harvey Dent of the Dark Knight films, despairing of the inexpungible corruption of the justice system he himself had idealistically led, embarks on a nihilistic quest to enact a justice so unbiased that it hangs on the flip of a coin. Dent's own death then becomes the foundation for a faux restoration of the shattered political order, ironically by making a scapegoat of another vigilante, Batman, and promising a "law and order" crackdown in response. In the final act of the trilogy, these unstable foundations are then demolished by the villain Bane, who reveals the rot at the heart of Gotham, storming the city's public buildings and promising to bring long-deserved judgment on its corrupt institutions.

THE THORNS OF UNCERTAINTY

The plots of these stories, like the plot of the slow-motion unraveling of America that we have watched the past year, each revolve around a crisis of judgment—in both senses of the word. We use the word "judgment" not merely for the act of public justice but also for the epistemic act of determining what is true. Indeed, this is no coincidence, for the enforcement of justice depends on a determination of truth; otherwise it is mere violence.

But therein lies the problem, for we feel ourselves compelled to form our own judgments about the adequacy of public justice. As soon as we attempt to do so, however, we are brought face-to-face with the limits of our knowledge, with the sheer opacity of human affairs. Why was Breonna Taylor killed? How and why did George Floyd die? Are lockdowns necessary? Do masks work? Why did the vote count change? Is there evidence of widespread election fraud? The only thing these questions have in common is the fact that, as individuals, most of us are totally unfit to answer them with any degree of certainty. Whatever certainty we do possess on such questions is likely to derive from networks of trust, from belonging to an epistemic community in which certain authorities command respect and assent. The successful practice of politics relies, as much as possible, on a shared public discourse, within which we can at least broadly agree on what has happened, even if we may always debate what is to be done next. Once doubt creeps in, once some Ghost whispers to us that this imposing façade of consensus may all be a lie, we are thrown back on our own resources.

In such a crisis, we are apt to take one of two courses. Either we may, like Hamlet, dither in a paralysis of indecision, or else we may, like Leonard Shelby of *Memento*, seek to wring certainty out of the veil of ignorance by sheer act of will, even if it means making up our own truth. The former would seem to be the malady of many of our intelligentsia and political elites, while the latter has become the strategy of our citizenry. Most versions of such self-certification are not so solipsistic as Leonard Shelby's. Most, rather, take the form of what Eric Voegelin called "gnosticism": a community of shared grievance discovers (or creates) some source of hidden knowledge, an insight into the real nature of the evil that lies under the thin veneer of polite society, and the radical solutions needed to overcome it. They have, they believe, cracked the code: discovered the universal pattern to be all wrong, and how to fix it. Having "woke" up (or been "red-pilled") to what's really going on, the community latches on to its narrative with a fierce hunger for certainty, and, lest anything should disturb the comfort of this newfound confidence, learns to shut its ears against the satanic siren song of contrary evidence.

As Richard Hooker, one of the keenest diagnosticians of this condition, wrote in 1593,

> After the common people are thoroughly convinced that the Spirit has persuaded them of these things, then they learn that believing in this . . . is a sign of being born of God and that earnest love for this discipline is the surest way to distinguish

God's people from all others. This has caused them to use terms that sharply distinguish between themselves and the rest of the world: they call themselves "the brethren," "the godly," and so forth, while the rest are termed "worldlings," "time-servers," "pleasers of men, not of God," and so forth. Because of this, such people are led to believe that they must do everything they can to strengthen one another and make themselves manifest to the world, lest they quench the Spirit.

Once this condition is adopted, it becomes very difficult to escape, and there is no telling where it may lead. Writes Hooker, "This is the very point for which I write: my purpose is to show that when the minds of men are once erroneously persuaded that it is the will of God for them to do those things they fancy, their opinions are as thorns in their sides, not allowing them to rest until they have put their speculations into practice. Their restless desire to remove anything in their way leads them by the hand into increasingly dangerous opinions, sometimes quite contrary to their original intentions." Those who began by crying, "Honor the Stars and Stripes" and "Back the Blue" may find themselves denouncing policemen as "traitors" and bludgeoning them to death with flagpoles.

Those who have ridden this train of private judgment to its dark and lonely end deserve our pity more than our anger; there are few more terrible fates that can befall a person than to become trapped within his own self-justifying reality. That is why we must counter this cancer at its source.

IMPERFECTIBILITY AND THE HUNGER FOR ESCHATOLOGICAL JUSTICE

Doubt in our shared reality begins in disappointment, disappointment with the stubborn imperfectibility of human judgment. Even the best and most zealous human judge, after all, is woefully imperfect in the pursuit of justice because he is human, because his knowledge extends to such a narrow slice of reality, and his reasoning so often falls short. In *City of God* book 19, Augustine wrenchingly chronicles the fallibility of the judge, his knowledge that he sometimes allows the innocent to suffer and the guilty to escape, as one of the greatest evils of life under the sun. But of course, it is worse than that, because every judge is also tainted with bias, corruption, ambition. Every judge and political leader is in some measure part of the problem with society, rather than part of the solution. We are thus tempted to conclude that judgment must start at the top, that there can be no peace until we have purged the halls of power, drained the swamp.

Nolan's Dark Knight trilogy offers a relentless critique of this temptation. In the first film, Bruce Wayne, embittered by the corruption that allowed his parents' murderer to go free, encounters the League of Shadows, which invites him to live by a code of ultimate justice rather than corrupt human justice. First he must execute a murderer whom "corrupt bureaucrats" have failed to punish, and then lead a force to destroy Gotham, dealing out summary justice on a city that is corrupt "beyond saving." Wayne refuses, and dedicates himself to trying to prove that an imperfect order is still worth saving, until the antihero Bane comes as the agent of the League of Shadows to expose the city's corruption and destroy it utterly, and Gotham is saved by learning to reconcile itself to its imperfection.

There burns within each one of us a hunger for eschatological judgment. And rightly so; it is this hunger that drives us to fight corruption and seek reform rather than throwing up our hands in complacency or despair. We must fight racism, tyranny, and fraud wherever they rear their heads. But we must do so as a public, not as vigilantes, and that means we must enact justice with sometimes maddening imperfection. The cry "No justice, no peace" is truer than we know, for justice cannot be truly served until the reign of the Prince of Peace. In the meantime, though, we should be grateful that justice has *not* been served, else we should be like Sodom; we should be left like Gomorrah. This is the point of Jesus' famous encounter with the adulteress: "Let him who is without sin cast the first stone." Before the Lord of Justice, all of us deserve to be stoned. And when we try to set ourselves up in his stead and demand perfect justice here in this life, we are apt to begin stoning one another.

It is to protect against such a judgment day that we accept the rule of law, that we agree to submit ourselves to judgments we know to be imperfect. As Richard Hooker writes in defense of this principle, "We are so prone to willfulness and self-liking that strife will never end, unless we abide by some sort of definitive sentence, which once given, must stand, and a necessity of silence be imposed on both parties." Indeed, the Lord himself teaches us to submit, "even if the decision seems to be utterly at odds with what is right in [our] private opinion." The rioters who looted Louisville the night a grand jury exonerated Breonna Taylor's killers, the anti-masking protesters who cursed policemen attempting to enforce Covid-19 restrictions, the angry mobs at the Capitol last Wednesday were each in their own ways resisting judgments utterly at odds with what was right in their private opinions. Of course, imperfect human judgments are revisable; laws may be repealed, and court rulings appealed. But not indefinitely so; a judgment that is infinitely revisable is not a judgment, but simply a negotiation, and one apt to degenerate into violence. Life under the rule of law requires learning to "abide by some definitive sentence," and a willingness to await vindication ultimately from God, rather than man, in order that the fragile bands of life together in this age may persist even in the midst of irreconcilable disagreement.

WAITING FOR A KING

Although imperfection is a perpetual feature of earthly politics, there are times when it looms so large as to almost swallow our whole field of vision. The year 2020 has been such a time. I would be willing to wager our political leadership today is worse on the whole – more hypocritical, less unbiased, less grounded in reality – than it was ten years ago, or twenty. But I would also be willing to wager that the difference is incremental, not categorical. Our laws and our leaders had problems aplenty in the year 2000. So why have we lost such faith?

I would suggest at least two reasons, and with these I shall conclude this meditation.

First, history shows that societies can long tolerate the ambiguities, uncertainties, and imperfections of political order so long as they see the judgments it enacts as *their* judgments, so long as political authority is seen as representative – and thereby becomes representative. In *The Dark Knight Rises*, Gotham does not become a true polis until it sees itself represented in its deliverer. And as this story suggests, such representation is far more aesthetic than it is procedural. We forget this lesson – as we have largely forgotten it in the late modern West – at our peril. Countless political orders flourished *before* the advent of liberal democracy because they successfully embodied a people who saw themselves pictured in their leaders, and countless liberal democracies have crumbled because they failed to move the imaginations of their people (most memorably and warningly, Weimar Germany). Donald Trump's success is owed in large part to his cunning recovery of this aesthetic dimension of politics, his willingness to offer himself to his followers as the imaginative projection of all their hopes and fears. Many of those yearning for a politics after Trumpism think that the genie can be put back into the bottle by a healthy dose of procedural liberalism. They will be sadly disappointed.

Second, we have lost faith in politics because we have lost faith in the judgment that lies beyond politics. The US Capitol was stormed on January 6, the Feast of the Epiphany. "Epiphany" means an "unveiling" or "manifestation," and certainly much that we would rather have remained hidden was unveiled last Wednesday. But this is the feast on which the church has long commemorated the unveiling of the infant Jesus as the King of all kings, the desire of all nations. It is, with Ascension Day, one of the two great political holidays of the Christian calendar.

It has been centuries since we lived in Christendom, but even living in Christendom's long shadow has been enough to remind us that the justice we enact itself lies under judgment; that we can afford to see through a glass darkly, and to behold the oppressions under the sun, because they do not have the final say. We can bear the torture of uncertainty knowing that he who has suffered in our place will not leave us there forever. We can repress our rage in the face of miscarried justice knowing that the judge unjustly judged in our place will in his own time render a just verdict. We can wait patiently in this vale of tears knowing that a day is coming when he will wipe every tear from every eye. As we mourn the death of the America we once knew, let our patient prayer this Epiphany season be "Come, Lord Jesus." ⸙

WHAT IS POLICING FOR, AND HOW DO WE REFORM IT?

ANTHONY M. BARR

A FEW YEARS AGO I visited dear friends in Louisiana during a spring break that happened to coincide with Mardi Gras. At around ten in the morning, we pulled out a pack of red Solo cups and joined the multitude to watch the parade. My memory of the day is admittedly pretty hazy, though I do distinctly remember eating lots of king cake, adorning myself with as many beads as I could get my hands on, and accepting Jell-O shots from strangers hosting front-lawn house parties.

We almost definitely broke the law. New Orleans ordinances allow for public drinking, so long as it is not open-container, but we were in Spanish Town outside of Baton Rouge – and after spending five minutes googling this, I'm still not clear whether public drinking is allowed there by ordinance or merely tolerated for Mardi Gras. Regardless, that was not the main offense. Louisiana allows eighteen-year-olds to drink, but it does so only when those eighteen-year-olds are accompanied by a legal guardian, which the underage member of our party was not.

The other thing I remember distinctly about that day was seeing random drunk twentysomethings offering red Solo cups to police officers (who politely declined) and taking selfies with them.

ANTHONY M. BARR is a first year master of public policy candidate at Pepperdine University. He has done research on political theory, education policy, and civic and moral virtue for various nonprofits, businesses, and independent publishers.

Thinking back, there were a lot of uniformed police on site, but none of us felt remotely threatened, even though, and I stress this again, we were *actively breaking the law.*

There are two main ways of thinking about the appropriate goal of policing. The first mindset is that the police are there to enforce every law on the books by identifying and punishing any infraction (no matter how small). If that's the goal we have in mind, then the police failed miserably during that Mardi Gras celebration; my group of friends and I *broke the law* (I would like to clarify). So did a ton of other people. Broke the law. And we were not subtle! They could have caught us! We were right there! They could've just asked to see IDs!

But there is another way of thinking about the purpose of policing. We might have as our goal for our police that they help to maintain community standards of public safety and order. If this is our evaluative framework, then the police were highly successful that day; their presence helped to deter purse-snatching, vandalism, and most fistfights – all things that weaken public safety and order and undermine the ability of a community to celebrate together.

There are two parts to my argument in this article. In the first part, I want to convince you that the "community-standards" model of policing is a more theoretically sound and practically effective approach. And in the second part, I want to explore concrete policy for meaningful reform based on that community-standards model.

PART 1: WHAT IS POLICING FOR?

In 1829, Sir Robert Peel created the Metropolitan Police Force to deal with rising crime in England. This was the first police force in the modern sense, the alternative to the night watch, to the hue-and-cry system of community self-policing (which in practice came close to mob justice), and to private security, and it proved extremely successful. It would later serve as a model for the nation as a whole, and indeed for the police forces of several other nations including Canada and New Zealand.

What were the police? It is crucial to understand what they were not: they were not the military. Peel emphasized the civilian nature of the police force, often observing that the "police" are just members of the public "who are paid to give full-time attention to duties which are incumbent on every citizen in the interests of community welfare and existence." A formulated list of principles for law enforcement is often ascribed to Peel, based on the ethos that he cultivated. Among these principles are the following four:

- The basic mission for which police exist is to prevent crime and disorder as an alternative to the repression of crime and disorder by military force and severity of legal punishment.
- The ability of the police to perform their duties is dependent on public approval of police existence, actions, behavior, and the ability of the police to secure and maintain public respect.
- The police must secure the willing cooperation of the public in voluntary observance of the law to be able to secure and maintain public respect.
- The degree of cooperation of the public that can be secured diminishes proportionately to the necessity for the use of physical force and compulsion in achieving police objectives.

Comparing this list to various recent moments in the United States, we can see the dramatic failure of our various police forces as measured against each of these four principles. When cities across the nation mobilize militarized police to respond to peaceful crowds by using chemical weapons to disperse groups of citizens practicing their constitutional rights to free assembly, speech, and political expression, it is clear that the principle of crime prevention has given way to that of authoritarian repression of public protest. Likewise, these same principles are violated when stop-and-frisk policy leads to racial targeting and overt systemic bullying in New York; when the practice of so-called rough rides leads to unlawful deaths of citizens in police custody in Maryland; when a city's own officials are giving the directive to use aggressive civil-forfeiture-based policing as tax revenue as was the case in Ferguson. And this isn't even digging into the only slightly less recent history of policing in America, such as the decades of systematic torture of over one hundred black men by police forces in Chicago.

But let us set aside the obvious cases of malpractice and even malevolence. Even in relatively good times, it is entirely unclear to me that Peel's views are in any way normative in policing across the States. And I don't think the blame for this can be placed solely on the police as an institution. Instead, we need to talk about the "public" more broadly.

"In politics," wrote Oliver O'Donovan for this publication, "we conceive of an action as 'ours.' To act together, of course, we must act through dedicated institutional structures and agencies, through representative officials and leaders, but the logic of what they do will always trace back, even if circuitously, to the deliberations of the political society as a whole. For that is the source of all public authority, and defines its scope."

This insight is important because while many of us can feel alienated from policing as an American institution, that feeling does not actually remove us from the political society we are situated in as citizens. This model of policing has been called "policing by consent," but the kind of consent is subtly different from that envisioned by literalist understandings of social contract theory. In 2012, the UK government Home Office explained that under the model of policing by consent, "the power of the police come[s] from the common consent of the public, as opposed to the power of the state. It does not mean the consent of the individual," noting that "no individual can choose to withdraw his or her consent from the police, or from a law." This seemingly paradoxical vision is at the heart of O'Donovan's conception of political society, and thus of what might be called an O'Donovanian approach to policing. As O'Donovan writes, "There are public lands, public buildings, public roads, public institutions, and public revenue; but they depend on something more fundamental, a public *society* created by a public *discussion*. Someone who has no part in our discussion is not a member of our political society." Thus to the extent that we are members of this society, we all, collectively, bear a certain responsibility for those political structures, processes, and outcomes that are produced by the society we together constitute. We have the responsibility and obligation to obey the laws; we have the responsibility and obligation to help shape them, and to shape as well the form of civility, of public life that exists at a more subtle level than that which law can touch.

What we owe each other, says O'Donovan, is "candid speech." That means we bear responsibility for the conversation as well: Conversations have consequences. When we listen in on the public conversations around policing in America in the 1980s, for example, we hear widespread and understandable fear concerning high rates of violent crime in America cities. We also hear the language of "superpredators" applied to black men as a demographic; we hear other racist tropes about "black criminality" deployed in ways that tend to make the "black criminal" a special category of person. When the time came for policy to be made, for these conversations to make their way into practices and laws, the pathologies in our public discourse translated directly into harmful (and often nefarious) principles of policing and sentencing in direct contradiction to the insights that Peel and those in his camp had articulated.

I don't mean to suggest that the problem with American policing began in the 1980s, with the top-down initiatives from Presidents Reagan and Clinton, or with the bottom-up practices like heavily racialized and antagonistic stop-and-frisk policies adopted by local police departments. I don't mean to imply that its failures are as neatly categorized as what I've briefly outlined here. For one thing, policing in the States has never fully adopted Peelite principles; it has a mixed origin. Early nineteenth-century municipal police departments were similar to those adopted in England – but the context was different: unlike in England, the history of American police-like activities before the nineteenth century included slave-catching, and the "public order" that post–Civil War police were in many places required to keep included enforcement of Jim Crow laws. Far more can be said. But all of those things that can be said don't invalidate the positive vision of Peel's principles. Those who are currently waking up to the need for police reform, for "community policing," for the abolition of militarized police, are waking up to what the original vision for municipal policing actually was. The wrong they are noticing is precisely the distance between Peel's principles and what policing often looks like in the United States.

All of this leads us back to our starting question: What is policing for? Are the police in Spanish Town there to catch underage drinkers (more or less) safely celebrating with close friends and family members? Or is there a more fundamental purpose, something more directly and tangibly tied to the well-being of a community and its members, a kind of celebratory order in which the officer is a participant, albeit one with a particular role?

Broken-windows theory, the idea that visible signs of civil disorder create an environment that encourages further disorder including violent crime, gets a bad rap these days, almost exclusively because of its connection to stop-and-frisk. And indeed you can draw a straight line between interpretations of the theory and the murder of Eric Garner, who was strangled by an officer (using an illegal chokehold technique), and whose crime (such as it was) involved the selling of cigarettes on a street corner. But stop-and-frisk is a bastardization of broken-windows theory. Consider the original piece written by George L. Kelling and James Q. Wilson and published in *The Atlantic* in 1982.

The authors begin by describing the results of New Jersey's 1972 "Safe and Clean Neighborhoods" program, which, among other things, increased foot patrols for local police. The authors note that police departments were initially resistant because foot patrol is more decentralized, more physically taxing, and not necessarily likely to actually lead to lower crime rates. After documenting these reasons why the program seemed doomed to fail, the authors report what actually happened:

> Five years after the program started, the Police Foundation, in Washington, D.C., published an evaluation of the foot-patrol project. Based on its analysis of a carefully controlled experiment carried out chiefly in Newark, the foundation concluded, to the surprise of hardly anyone, that foot patrol had not reduced crime rates. But residents of the foot patrolled neighborhoods seemed to feel more secure than persons in other areas, tended to believe that crime had been reduced, and seemed to take fewer steps to protect themselves from crime (staying at home with the doors locked, for example). Moreover, citizens in the foot-patrol areas had a more favorable opinion of the police than did those living elsewhere. And officers walking beats had higher morale, greater

job satisfaction, and a more favorable attitude toward citizens in their neighborhoods than did officers assigned to patrol cars.

Did you catch that one little detail, that the foot patrol did not actually reduce crime rates? If your Mardi Gras policing model is about "number of underage drinkers cited," you'd look at the New Jersey program as an utter failure. But in the context of broken-windows theory, which is to say in the context of community standards of public safety and order-based policing, this 1972 reform is cited by the authors as a great success and one worth emulating. Many folks may "get away with" some kinds of minor wrongdoing, but it will be non-pathological wrongdoing. Rigid enforcement of rules will give way to a kind of personalized shaping of the overall flavor of a community. Crime is reduced where it needs to be reduced in order to prevent a neighborhood from falling into decay, and to protect the vulnerable.

Here's how the authors describe the daily interactions of an officer and his community:

> The officer – call him Kelly – knew who the regulars were, and they knew him. As he saw his job, he was to keep an eye on strangers, and make certain that the disreputable regulars observed some informal but widely understood rules. Drunks and addicts could sit on the stoops, but could not lie down. People could drink on side streets, but not at the main intersection. Bottles had to be in paper bags.

The point to underscore here is not the specifics of the informal rules, but rather that these rules were not imposed top-down from a militarized force disconnected from the relational dimensions of communal life. As the authors note, "These rules were defined and enforced in collaboration with the 'regulars' on the street. Another neighborhood might have different rules, but these, everybody understood, were the rules for *this* neighborhood." In other words, the particulars of policing were directly tied to the particulars of the kind of public deliberations (though informal, and a matter more of culture than of parliamentary speeches) that O'Donovan argues helps to constitute public society. In this model, there is public ownership of policing outcomes. In other words, when Mardi Gras policing is about upholding the standards a community has set for itself, then members of that community will not be alienated by policing, but instead will trust and respect it as a vital piece of communal infrastructure.

The failure in translation of broken-windows theory should disabuse us of the notion that simply advocating for "community policing" will mean that no miscarriages of justice ever occur. But even in those instances, this model of policing is worth our attention precisely because it allows for public discussions by the community to hold officers and officials accountable. As O'Donovan writes, "Force exercised by institutions of government may sometimes be exercised deplorably. When it is, we know that it still belongs to the authoritative structure of government precisely when political discussion takes the matter up, seeks to redress its wrongs and to improve the standard of public practices." And so long as there is actual recourse and redress—not at all a given in many places in the United States—then individual instances or even prolonged patterns of bad behavior can be addressed without the awful rending of that fragile trust between a community and its guardians.

And on that last point, it's time to get into the weeds about the specific concrete policy reforms that we should advocate for in order to reform our policing institutions such that they align with the model I've argued for here.

PART 2: HOW DO WE REFORM POLICING?

I want to be clear right away that this section is meant to be illustrative, not fully comprehensive. If you want the long version of this, you can start with the Department of Justice's 2015 report on twenty-first-century policing. But I think what follows provides some starting points to inform our public discussion about police reform.

Let me start with what I consider to be the low-hanging fruit. These reforms are simple and should easily garner bipartisan support. And because they can be implemented at the federal level, these reforms are also easily standardized and applicable for everyone as soon as the bill is signed into law:

- **Just say no to free military supplies.** We should abolish or reform the 1033 provision. One main reason that law enforcement has become more militarized is because of this provision in the National Defense Authorization Act that allows federal, state, and local law-enforcement agencies to access obsolete or unneeded military supplies (with certain limitations, e.g., no tanks) for no cost aside from the price of shipping.

This has allowed hundreds and hundreds of local law-enforcement agencies to equip their police force in ways that run directly contrary to Peel's principles. And I'm not just talking about guns. I'm also talking about uniforms that look more like paramilitary gear than anything associated with civilian-based community policing.

Major metropolitan areas need a bomb squad, but the argument that every department in America needs military gear is suspect. The point of police is that they are not the army. One practical tweak might be that departments have free access to noncombat supplies (computers, medical supplies, etc.) but must pay at competitive rates for everything else. If 1033 combat gear came at a cost (even at below-market rates), we could expect to see this gear only going to the departments that actually need it, with the vast majority of departments choosing to allocate their resources elsewhere.

- **Mandate clearly accessible use-of-force policy.** I want to be able to visit any local government website and see their internal use-of-force policy, as a form of communal accountability. This is something Congress could enact as federal law, binding on every law-enforcement agency in the United States. More transparency here would also allow law-enforcement agencies and the communities they serve to survey best practices and implement changes on that basis. Along these same lines, it is worth pursuing federal legislation that would require all law-enforcement agencies to report any use-of-force incidents to the Justice Department to allow for a more comprehensive database. This could also be another form of implicit accountability, as agencies quickly realize that required reporting means the Justice Department is keeping tabs.

- **Treat civilians you're policing at least as well as you treat enemies during wartime.** This means outlawing the use of tear gas. The Geneva Convention outlaws the use of chemical agents like tear gas as weapons during wartime, so why on earth should we tolerate its use domestically against civilians? We shouldn't. It's really that simple. I include this in my list of low-hanging fruit not because I think it would be easy for Congress to pass a law on this on their own accord, but rather because it *should* be easy to create a broad populist movement in America that demands Congress pass such a law.

- **Ban use of carotid neck restraints (chokeholds).** As expertly reported by the *Los Angeles Times*, carotid neck restraints have been touted by law-enforcement agencies as effective and safe despite the troubling racial history of the technique and despite its consistent record of leading to serious injury and death. It's time to say "no more." And while we're at it, I think we need serious scholarship that can provide an empirical basis for what kinds of force should be tolerated as normative practices; anecdotal evidence is not good enough.

- **Abolish no-knock warrants.** Frankly it's hard to conceive of a more fundamental violation of civil liberties than law enforcement breaking into a home in the middle of the night, with no announcement of identity or purpose, in order to serve a warrant. And Senators Rand Paul (R) and Tulsi Gabbard (D) agree, which is why they are proposing the Justice for Breonna Taylor Act, which would prohibit such no-knock warrants.

In addition to these, there are also some harder sells that are worth mobilizing around and seeking to initiate, though these reforms will likely need to be implemented on the state and local level. For example:

- establishing residency benchmarks for police officers to ensure that the people who are policing a community are actually members of that community, while being sure not to compromise recruitment standards;

- decriminalizing various offenses including jumping the turnstile, possession of small amounts of controlled substances, street peddling, nonobstructive loitering, and so on;

- ending the reliance on civil forfeiture to meet budget deficits and fund pensions;

- decoupling departments from overly powerful and democratically unaccountable police unions that provide cover for misconduct;

- shifting to community-policing models but without the surveillance-state apparatus that often accompanies this model;

- implementing civilian oversight boards that automatically review all use-of-force incidents and that avoid common constraints and mistakes;

- increasing funding for foot patrols in communities that could benefit from more face-time with officers, based on the latest empirical research; and

- implementing carrot-and-stick incentives for de-escalation training and other such initiatives.

These reforms only begin to scratch the surface for what is needed. But they are also actionable in a way that "abolish the police" slogans on protest signs are not. They do not throw the baby of civilian policing out with the bathwater. We are in desperate need of reasoned public conversation about policing in America, complete with concrete proposals and the political will to ensure that those proposals are implemented. This is in reach. It's real. And it is based on a set of historical policing principles which many US police officers themselves recognize as an ideal.

—

"What do we need to do together to practice justice in our common life?" This is, as O'Donovan writes, the fundamental question of political discourse. I think that is an important question to carry with us as we think about policing and a whole host of related policy challenges.

And ultimately, I think this is a question we need to have the courage to raise in the most immediate circles that constitute our local community: in our own cities, in our own circles. For, as O'Donovan notes, "we have a responsibility to the justice of our place, the place whose institutions make our daily existence possible.

We have a responsibility for political neighbors sitting at our gate, who have first call on our engaged attention."

The prophet Micah entreats us to do justice, love mercy, and walk humbly with our God. As we set out to tackle the challenges that lie before us in 2021, this massive task of rebuilding trust and justice in the post-Trump era, these simple commands should be the guiding light for all our public discourse in service to our shared pursuit of justice and the common good. ☩

BIDEN'S AUGUSTINIAN CALL FOR CONCORD

MICHAEL LAMB

ON THE STEPS of the US Capitol, the site of a violent attack two weeks earlier, President Joseph R. Biden tried to unite a divided nation.

In an inaugural address focused on unity, Biden cited a passage from St. Augustine, quoting his vision of a "people" as "a multitude defined by the common objects of their love." Biden invited citizens to consider "the common objects we as Americans love": "Opportunity, security, liberty, dignity, respect, honor and yes, truth."

President Biden's Augustinian invocation was a powerful appeal to unity in a moment of deep division. It takes on even more meaning when we examine what Augustine meant in his own context.

A Catholic bishop from North Africa during the decline of the Roman Empire, Augustine is known as the great theologian of love. For Augustine, love is the animating force of human life, the spring of all emotion and action. Whether we are virtuous or vicious, he argues, depends on how we "order" our loves. To understand the character of a person or a people, "we have only to examine what it loves."

MICHAEL LAMB is the executive director of the Program for Leadership and Character and assistant professor of Politics, Ethics, and Interdisciplinary Humanities at Wake Forest University. He is the author of *A Commonwealth of Hope: Augustine's Political Thought*, forthcoming from Princeton University Press.

According to Augustine, Rome loved glory, which fueled a "lust for domination" that led them to conquer enemies to prove their power. Their violence reflected disordered love. Swollen with pride, they were more concerned with increasing their glory through domination than loving their neighbors through justice and sacrifice.

Augustine's answer is to encourage human beings to order their loves ultimately to God, not to self. Some critics have suggested that Biden's speech neglected this aspect of Augustine's vision. On their view, Augustine believes God is the only common good that can unite a "true commonwealth."

Yet while Augustine affirms that the "City of God" transcends any earthly kingdom and sets the standard of "true justice," he does not dismiss the importance of earthly commonwealths or the goods they secure in this life. And he rejects the idea that politics necessarily requires theological consensus. Instead, he encourages citizens – of different religions, cultures, and creeds – to unite around common objects of love in the commonwealth. Members of both the "earthly" and "heavenly" cities, he argues, can "make common use of those things which are necessary to this mortal life," even as they direct them to different ultimate ends.

For Augustine, the most important of these temporal goods is peace: "For peace is so great a good that, even in the sphere of earthly and mortal affairs, we hear no word more thankfully, and nothing is desired with greater longing: in short, it is not possible to find anything better."

In emphasizing peace, Augustine does not ask citizens simply to hold hands and get along. His vision of the "good things appropriate to this life" is more rigorous and robust. It includes "temporal peace . . . consisting in bodily health and soundness, and the society of one's own kind; and all things necessary for the preservation and recovery of this peace," such as "breathable air, drinkable water, and whatever the body requires to feed, clothe, shelter, heal or adorn it." In the midst of a global pandemic, when social division, climate change, and economic insecurity threaten the lives and livelihoods of Americans, Augustine's focus on tangible goods—food, housing, health care, and clean air and water – highlights what is needed to sustain a healthy body politic.

Augustine also recognizes that laws, norms, and institutions are necessary to secure civic peace, but he does not see peace as the mere absence of conflict or violence. Rather, he affirms what another Augustinian, Martin Luther King Jr., calls a "positive peace," the peace of civic friendship born of justice and mutual affection. "The order of this concord," Augustine writes, "is, first, that a man should harm no one, and, second, that he should do good to all, so far as he can."

Yet Augustine is not naive or sentimental. He knows that civic peace is fragile and that friendship cannot guarantee complete agreement on every moral or political matter. Even when we can unite around common objects in theory, we may disagree about how best to realize them in practice. Conflict and contestation are part of the political condition and often necessary to challenge injustice and hold power accountable. Politics, therefore, should not seek a totalizing uniformity that dominates those who are different, but a humble harmony that gives justice to all, welcomes others into community, and forges unity in plurality.

Here, Augustine's analogy of "concord" is apt. He cites Cicero's comparison of civic peace to musical harmony, made possible by the union of diverse voices: "What musicians call harmony in singing is concord in the city, which is the most artful and best bond of security in the commonwealth, and which, without justice, cannot be secured at all."

This vision of concord is as relevant in contemporary America as it was in ancient Rome. Augustine's questions are ours: What objects of love will bring us into harmony? Will we, like Rome, lust for glory and domination, or will we embody the love that does justice and secures unity amid plurality? Will we sustain civic peace in the midst of deep difference, or will we allow our disagreements, real as they are, to finally sever our bonds of affection?

How we answer may determine whether we can sustain a commonwealth at all. ✟

January 26, 2021

WHAT IS UNITY?

Is it possible? Is it good?

CHRISTINE EMBA, SHADI HAMID, AND SAMUEL KIMBRIEL
IN CONVERSATION WITH ANNE SNYDER

After 11 months of Covid-19, a historic explosion in social and racial reckoning, a hotly contested presidential election and a siege on the U.S. Capitol on January 6, 2021, Breaking Ground *hosted a webinar six days after President Biden was sworn in to discuss the themes of unity and the common good laid out in his inaugural address. How realistic is unity? Exactly what is it? How we might strive toward it in ways top-down and bottom-up, and what precisely is the good inherent within it, if any? Here is an edited transcript from that event.*

ANNE SNYDER: These are wild times. I want to ask: How do each of you define unity? It's a word that has been in the air this last week, and in some ways from the beginning of this nation. What is it? And maybe just as important, what *isn't* it?

CHRISTINE EMBA is a columnist for the *Washington Post* writing about ideas and society. She was previously the Hilton Kramer Fellow in Criticism at *The New Criterion* and a deputy editor at the Economist Intelligence Unit, focusing on technology and innovation.

SHADI HAMID is an American author and a senior fellow at the Brookings Institution. He is also a contributing writer at *The Atlantic*. He has been called a "prominent thinker on religion and politics" in the *New York Times* and was named as one of "The world's top 50 thinkers" in 2019 by *Prospect Magazine*.

SAMUEL KIMBRIEL is a teaching fellow in philosophical theology at the University of Nottingham. He is the author of *Friendship as Sacred Knowing: Overcoming Isolation* (2014).

CHRISTINE EMBA: I know that this is a very "high school essay" thing to do, but I thought that I would actually define unity using the dictionary. Merriam-Webster would tell us that there are three main options to define unity.

One is "the state of not being multiple" – so, oneness, which is not my favorite definition. The second is "a condition of harmony or accord," which I think is somewhat better. And the third is "a combination or ordering of parts that promotes an undivided total effect." That's actually the literary or artistic definition, which is also my favorite. It points not to sameness, as the first definition would say, but simply to being ordered toward something together. Contributing in our own different ways toward a commonly-held understanding of the good, or at least a goal.

That's actually what I think unity is, properly defined. It doesn't necessitate a flattening or an indivisibility, but simply having the same aim in mind.

ANNE: Shadi, what do you think of that?

SHADI HAMID: At the most basic level, I see unity as the state of not being divided. Somewhat similar to the first definition that Christine mentioned. I personally am not the biggest fan of unity, and we'll unpack why that might be.

I was reminded a couple of hours ago just how hegemonic the word unity is. A friend of mine saw that I'd posted this event on Instagram, and he texted me like, "Shadi, what are you thinking, man? How could unity possibly not be a good thing? Are you some sort of monster?" He didn't say that I was a monster, but that was the implication.

I think that's how most Americans, the NPR listener type, think. They just assume that unity is a good thing, and the very idea of questioning it is odd.

The musical analogy is a good one here, because when I think about the idea of harmony, it makes me nervous. If we want to avoid certain definitions, maybe that's one we don't want to aspire to. That may be because I like music that has a kind of dissonance, that has an edge to it.

The basic issue is what Christine said about trying to be ordered to a common aim or to a common approach as citizens. That would be nice in theory. I'm just very skeptical that it's possible in practice, because we as Americans – and throughout the world, a lot of societies – are growing more diverse. We don't share as much as we might have done before. One or two hundred years ago, many societies, especially in the West, were more homogenous on religious, ethnic, and ideological grounds. Now we're less so.

So in that sense, how can we be ordered to a common aim when we have foundational differences and divides as Americans? We don't share the same premises. We don't share the same first principles.

But I would add, I don't think we *should* necessarily share the same premises. Because if our differences come from a place of conviction – whether that's religious or ideological conviction – I worry that when we talk about unity, we're basically asking people to put aside their deepest convictions in the name of the greater good.

ANNE: Sam, do you think of unity as a uniquely American ambition in the history of nations? Or is it always necessary for any kind of group survival?

SAMUEL KIMBRIEL: I'd actually like to start pre-political. It seems to me that the question of unity, in a lot of respects, is the primary question that started philosophy going. It was the question of whether things are first of all disharmonious—in basic, fundamental conflict, in a war against one another—or whether they have a primary way that they do actually coordinate and come together in a basic sense.

This question ends up being a prompt for reflection on reality generally, and then that flows into how we think about societies. I share a lot of Shadi's worries about prematurely thinking that society is united. It seems to me that the question of how you might bind together as a population is actually one of the fundamental and hardest questions of political philosophy as a whole. But we have gotten off on the wrong track in terms of how we think of unity.

There are two different models. There's the model of thinking about a society as a machine, a whole bunch of different parts that have to be designed and organized in the right way so that they have a coherence with one another. That tends to be our primary model.

The other common model is to think about society more like an organism, specifically like a tree. There are diverse parts, and they don't obviously fit together. But somehow the basic coherence of the organism—something that is not created within society, but precedes it—can then flow into how the society works.

That's the point where our crisis sits. We don't actually understand how anything that's pre-political, or deeper than politics, can flow into our society any longer. And as long as that question can't be answered, you're going to end up with the view that we're simply a machine with all the pieces falling apart.

It does seem to me that a theory of unity is implicit in every successful society. Societies think about how to hold themselves together, and most notable works of political philosophy or political theory actually begin with that. They say, "Hey, why are we not all just a bunch of people who are at war with one another?" And the way that they try to work out their specific answer to that question seems to be the way that societies branch out in different directions.

ANNE: Pulling on this nervousness around a mis-sequenced understanding of unity, when we think about a nation or a society bounded by a set of ideals, could you name a little more explicitly the dangers that you see? Not just theoretically, but what is going on that is making you uncomfortable today?

SHADI: When we talk about unity, we have to ask a second question: on whose terms? Who decides what constitutes this unity? This is where power relations become relevant. It's those who are culturally hegemonic who decide what this unifying source is and what values all Americans should buy into. We even saw a bit of this in Joe Biden's inaugural speech.

In some ways I don't fault him for talking a lot about unity. If I was president, that's what I would do. But at one point he alluded to a major divide in American history between the forces of progress and the forces of bigotry. And that gets at the problematic aspect here: if I was a Trump supporter, one of the 74 million – for better or worse there are a lot of them in this country – and I was listening to Joe Biden talking about unity, I would take him to mean implicitly that the loyalty of the many Trump supporters to the unifying values is in doubt. Because they're the ones who are tied to a racist ex-president.

That's one problematic implication. And we're seeing a move toward a new kind of conformity. We see this with tech companies adopting rules that constrict speech in some ways. I think that sometimes they're justified – I personally supported the ban on Trump on Twitter. But if this keeps on going, and now that we have cultural power and political power on the center-left or the left, there are temptations to go too far. That's what I get concerned about.

I should also clarify that at a very basic level, there obviously have to be some things that Americans agree on. Where I differ from a lot of people is that I want those to be as minimal as possible. I want a low common denominator. So for me, the major thing that I expect all Americans to sign onto, regardless of anything else, is respect for democratic outcomes, and certain democratic ideals that are implicit or explicit in the American story. That's fundamental. Because if you don't respect democratic outcomes, there's no way to regulate or manage conflict. And we saw how dangerous that was with the Capitol insurrection. If you have a chunk of the country that isn't willing to respect the legitimate results of an election, then you have no way of regulating who rules and who has the right to power.

CHRISTINE: I want to push back on Shadi's qualm about the idea that unity assumes people are coming from the same premises or have the same background. That's what I was trying to say that I'm not particularly interested in – the idea that everybody must have the same background, the same religious beliefs, the same favorite color, the same presidential favorite. There is a distinction to be made between premises and aims. We can all have different premises, but I do think that most people, and most Americans, can in fact aim for the same things.

I actually think Joe Biden made a pretty useful and safe statement at his inauguration. I'm not sure what part you were thinking of, but I'm looking at a quote here where he says, "Our history has been a constant struggle between the American ideal that we're all created equal" and the harsh reality that that's not the case. So on some level I would actually say that the definition of unity that I have might even be on a lower – or some might say even higher – level than your qualification, which is a belief in democratic norms.

The most important component of the unity in a political state – certainly in America today, where we are not a homogenous state and do disagree on many things, including religion, including political beliefs – is just the basic belief in equality. In human dignity. In, as you say, treating people with respect. That is a far more important ground-level definition that would allow people to unify, if not in personality, background, or religion, then at least in some understanding of how we treat each other and what we should ideally want for ourselves – and for other people who we assume to have the same value as ourselves.

We ask for government to provide a lot these days. But if we think about what governments are for, they're actually meant to provide for very basic needs – or not even necessarily provide them, but at least try and ensure them for all members of the state or nation. Many of these needs are pretty low on our hierarchy of needs, and they are things that most people could agree with, whether they come from different religions or different places: People want to be able to have families, people want to be able to feed their children, people want to be able to live unmolested. What is unifying, I think, would be to assume that everybody is allowed to have these things. And that's where unity has most often fallen apart in the United States. Certain groups have been denied those very basic opportunities.

SHADI: Christine, could I add a very quick follow-up? In theory, if you polled the vast majority of Americans they'd say, "Yeah, equality is great. Who could argue with that?" The problem is, we as

Americans don't agree on what equality actually means, or what justice actually means, or on definitions for any of these words that seem self-evidently good. From the very moment that Trump won, there was a move in some quarters to say that anyone who voted for Trump was by definition a bigot or someone who was empowering racism. By that kind of approach, tens of millions of our fellow citizens would be considered outside the fold – people who don't believe in equality. Even though if you'd ask them personally, they'd probably say they *did* believe in equality.

So I don't think that we would even come to the same agreed-upon definition of equality or progress or racial justice. And racial justice has become a lightning rod between left and right, where even reasonable never-Trumpers or people who don't like Trump a lot on the center-right are very much opposed to the "woke" move that we see on the center-left and left.

SAMUEL: I'm interested in how we develop or go about the process of moving forward in our ideals. It does seem like there may be a basic set of assumptions that people now, at this very thin slice of history, can agree on. But when you read enough history you realize both how parochial that agreement is and how tenuous. How many people don't agree with, to take what you were saying, even what a family is or how it might have come about.

Now, as the parameters of debate around one of those minimal ideals stretch out and we find ourselves disagreeing in certain respects, one of the things that strikes me is that we have very, very limited resources for having any kind of debate once those things start to be questioned.

So I'm curious what the implicit assumption is in terms of how we arrive at ideals, and then how we might go about adjudicating or developing them if we do find ourselves in conflict.

CHRISTINE: We've moved to the meta part of the conversation extremely quickly. How do we adjudicate these basic ideals? I think that's actually the hardest part of this fight for, or discussion of, unity. Perhaps the most flawed and somewhat damaging assumption – and I think Shadi was getting at this earlier too – is the idea that unity means a place of stasis, where we've all agreed on one thing, and now we are all of one mind and all the same. We have the same premises; we have the same beliefs.

The best calls to national unity – and I'm quoting Richard Hughes here via David Brooks's column – are in fact arguments. Arguments about what these ideals are. Arguments about how we can best reach them. Arguments about what they might look like in practice. When I talk about equality and participation, part of what I'm thinking is simply that every person should be allowed to take part in these arguments. Every person's vision of the good and understanding of who they are as a human and what they want to be valued can be in some way taken into account. They may have to press for it. They may have to – hopefully civilly – argue their case. But the fact that they are respected as a person and a part of the community means that they are allowed to take part.

I can see where these worries are coming from—that Trump supporters, say, are being seen as almost not people, not fit to take part in the conversation. The people with a differing view of family might not be fit to take care of children or fit to adopt, et cetera, et cetera. That is actually what we want to push back against. We want to push back against spurious definitions of unity that in fact close the boundaries of our state and country and leave citizens outside. Does that make sense?

ANNE: Is unity a collective state of being or a collective mode of action? In other words, do we need to do a better job of agreeing or a better job of disagreeing? And, depending on how you answer that, what do you see as the institutional containers and vehicles to allow either one of those to be trained and to occur peacefully?

SHADI: Part of the problem is that increasingly, at least in my lifetime, I feel like Americans have become more uncomfortable with the idea of difference. We see difference, and our instinct is to paper over it, dismiss it, transcend it, or resolve it. I don't think any of those things are appropriate. I don't think differences should be resolved. I think they can be managed, but in a way where we respect deep differences. We take them as a given, they're there in society, and they come from a place of conviction.

Then the question is what we do with that. And my answer would be that we say, "Hey, I'm not trying to convince you that you're wrong and I'm right on these deeply-held first principles." I'm going to listen to them, and I'm going to say, "Hey, I think that's bad, but I'm going to try to understand where it comes from through your standpoint." And if we speak frankly and openly about those differences, then it's possible to actually live together.

But the problem is, that's a very hard thing to do in our current context for a lot of complex reasons. One of them is technology and social media, but also the fact that more and more Americans are – at least relative to decades ago – well-educated and politically inclined. We have more people who see politics as a hobby. And unfortunately with lower levels of religious observance – specifically Christian observance as the largest religion in the country – be careful what you wish for, because as Christianity declines, we have an ideological vacuum. Something's got to take its place, and what's taking its place, in my view, isn't necessarily better. People are basically attributing theological intensity to political debate.

I don't think politics should be theological. I think the more important things in life are family, friends, religion, faith, whatever spiritual practices – it could differ from person to person. It doesn't have to always be about God. But we've especially seen this during Covid, that people can't really just take a step back, chill, and focus on what I consider to be the more important things.

That means politics becomes a space of endless combat, and I don't think that's the initial aim of politics. Politics should be, at least in theory, not about things that are final – not about things that have a permanent effect. I think the things that have permanent effect are religion, heaven, hell – or, if you don't believe in them, then perhaps nothingness.

So how we conceive of difference, how we deal with deep difference, is the fundamental question. Is difference a problem to be solved? Or is it a reality to be accommodated in a guise of respect, in a spirit of respect and mutual accommodation?

ANNE: Are we back to tolerance, like the early 2000s, when it comes to fierce moral disagreement?

SHADI: No, no.

ANNE: I was just thinking back to a buzzword of a lot of our youth. I want to just get a little more pointed here, to get clear on the very real fault lines I think we all feel at different degrees depending on where we are socially, geographically, et cetera. Over the last few years, quite a few people have come into contact with a deep dread. Sometimes it's a low, vague, tiring ache that you don't quite know how to put your finger on, and sometimes it's drawn more acutely into this really sharp fear of the abyss of our divides in our country, when you experience them.

Because of what I do for a living, I've been a part of lots of gatherings to talk about our divisions. There are moments when I've felt what many people have felt, which is: could we actually descend into a second Civil War? And whenever I think this and say this out loud, people older and smarter than me will remind me that it's almost impossible to think that through, because weapons are so different and geographic realities are so different than the 1860s. And it's also hard to envision anything that would involve just two sides.

But I think in the heat of the last few weeks in the U.S. since January 6th, we've all felt some intensifying, pressurizing force that squashed complexity and nuance where a "but" or a "both, and" is just not allowed. I was feeling this almost at a level I couldn't quite articulate a few weeks ago when the insurrection on the Capitol occurred. I just thought, "Look, I don't know if logistically a war is actually possible." And I hope it isn't.

But if there were one, and if it were binary, you do have to make a choice. And nuance goes away, and you have to choose what you see as the moral good. As I was thinking about this, I was wondering, "What would actually be the fundamental fault lines between sides?" I thought initially that it would be between those who believe in and want to fight for the dignity of all – this is related to Christine's point about dignity – and those who feel like they can't because to do so would somehow be to shut down their own dignity in the process. But then I thought, "No, that just takes us back to liberalism versus illiberalism, somehow."

I lay all of that runway out in order to ask, what are the most foundational divides as you see them? Divides that must be overcome if we're ever to maintain something smacking of a peaceful commons? (And we haven't even talked about the difference between commons and unity.) Which foundational divides could be left alone, or at the very least tolerated? Unbridged, and yet we would still hang together? Could you name the things that allow us to snap as a society?

CHRISTINE: I think that you hit on the question really well, or perhaps the answer. I was thinking of the reasons why people might be afraid of the question of what is unity, or what is the common good. Why it is in some ways frightening to talk about that. The United States in particular does have a history of leaving people out of the common good. Outside of any conception of unity. Outside of any conception of equality.

I don't necessarily mean equality in a metaphysical way, although I sort of do – I mean the very basic equality of being able to walk on the same sidewalk, or drink from the same water fountain, or be seen as 100% of a person instead of three-fifths of one.

I think when people ask about who is deciding here, they fear either being left out on the one end, because there is remarkable precedent for that here, or – and we talk about America having an original sin very frequently but I think it's an extremely true analogy – they have an underlying fear of things being done to them that they, or their ancestors, or people in parts of American history that they relate to more closely, did to others.

I'm thinking, for example, of the reflective fear of voter fraud, or voter disenfranchisement. Or this fear that if we give some people welfare, it will be taken from us. That if we acknowledge that black lives matter, then white lives are going to start mattering less.

When we think of unity as a zero-sum game, and when we think of goodwill and the commons as in fact not a common space but something that is taken from one person and given to another, something that's not shared, that is where a lot of fear can erupt and has erupted in our society.

One of the things that is anathema to any real discussion of unity is falsehood. Untruth. Politicians and leaders continue to claim that somebody will be taking something from you, that you are losing something, when in fact that's not happening. That is not what America must do in the future. There are other possibilities.

To have any possibility of unity, you have to be engaging in good faith. That also means that you have to assume that other people are also engaging in good faith, that they are not necessarily out to get you. That they are doing the best that they can for generally plausible – or at least good to them – reasons. There's a difference between argument or conflict that is productive – that is moving toward something – and argument or conflict for no reason, for the sake of a lie, a falsehood, an untruth. Or, in Shadi's description, people who are just a little bit too obsessed with politics and have nothing else to do, so they cause trouble on Twitter for fun. That pointless activity, that activity based on falsehoods and false premises, is what actually tears unity apart. Because there's just nothing behind it. There's nothing that anyone could come together on.

ANNE: That's beautifully said, Christine. Thank you.

SHADI: I think Christine gets at something really important, which is the zero-sum nature of American politics today. I don't know how you undo that, and it might be too late to undo it. Once things really set in and become entrenched in the body politic, you're stuck with it to a large extent, unless you have very powerful forces that are able to reverse it. So if we have the zero-sum vibe for the foreseeable future, I think one way of addressing it is to try to lower the stakes of politics by de-emphasizing national politics.

This is why I think federalism and localism and other terms that people use – subsidiarity, communitarianism, just thinking more about how to devolve power and redistribute power away from the center – will have to be a focus. Because I think we're going to have a problem that whichever party wins, the other party is going to see the party in power as an existential threat to their dignity. As Christine alluded to, there is this reciprocal thing.

Not to draw a moral equivalence – I'm on the left side of the spectrum so I think one side is more right than the other, but I can't necessarily prove that to my fellow Americans on the right side of the spectrum, or Trump supporters, because they don't share my premises, so we're stuck in that way – but I do worry about the centralization of power. Not just when we think about government, but when we think about the fact that a few very large, dominant companies are able to structure and shape the way we have national conversations – not to go back to the tech monopoly issue. That's another kind of centralization that I think is something to be worried about.

SAMUEL: One of the principal things that worries me, that I think sits behind the potential civil conflict, is a basic kind of fragility that seems to be present in most people, and in most communities, as they kick out into public and national life. That goes to Shadi's point about the question of how you might distribute good parts of life at levels that are not just a zero-sum game at the national.

But I also think there is a question of why we see conflict at the national level in the lens that we do. It seems to me that we've moved from a society – or that there has always been a feature of American society that has preferred to see itself through the terms of will rather than through the terms of intellect. So the will society is that different groups are just necessarily incommensurable with each other. That might be because they have different interests, it might be because they have different origins, it may be because they simply have different visions of human life. But in some basic sense, there's an incompatibility. It seems to me that we're at this point where that is the background assumption of most things that happen at the political level.

And it's also why people feel really fragile. There is a question of where you go, if you're outside of everything else. There's a basic state of alienation in that sense. And that does feel impossible to resolve in a pretty basic way.

To Christine's point, that fragility has always been there. Our mechanisms for groups that are excluded to come in and say,

"Hey, this isn't working for me. There are things that are not present in our society that are absolutely essential to who I am, to our community" – there has always been a tone-deafness there. But as that model of incommensurable interests has risen to the surface, we find ourselves in a really difficult spot.

The real question that I've been trying to work through is, what's happened to the set of resources that have given us the possibility of working through all this in certain ways? Just after the Capitol thing happened, Shadi and I were texting about the decline of the secularization thesis. The initial sense of the secularization thesis was that society will just get more and more rational, like a machine. It will work better and better, and then all of these superstitious things like religion will just shuffle away.

One of the first moments at the national level where that really began to diminish was after 9/11. Religion is just present, and a very significant feature of public life. So people are like, "Well, this might be different." I think we see it in a different way now, which is that the resources that we've assumed to hold us together are somehow not mechanical resources. They're not about how you design the system. There's something else. There's something about how we trust one another, what holds communities together, what the aspirations of human life are. And it seems to me that the apparatus that we have fixing the machine part of society just cannot fix that much more fundamental, organic part.

Whether we can find those resources is an extremely hard question, but it does seem to me that that's the place to start looking. If there is a way out of this zero-sum, triumph of will over will thing, it's going to have to be in trying to figure out what those background resources are that don't have to do only with control.

ANNE: I'm going to be chewing on that for a while, Sam. Thanks.

I'm going to turn to the audience questions now: "Cancel culture is a very frightening reality at the moment. How can people feel safe to have productive dialogue and build unity when people are afraid to engage in discussions that have conflicting ideas on opposing sides? Having safe spaces to discuss issues, no matter how opposing, is important to move the hearts of people to change their thinking and misconceptions."

I'm going to put a sub-question under that from someone else, namely, "Is it ever appropriate to say that a voice, a participant, should be shut out of the conversation? Why and how?"

SHADI: It's telling that the person who asked about cancel culture identified as anonymous. I think that gets the point across.

That's a really good question, because I've been struggling with this as of late. People generally think of me as having pretty thick skin. I get attacked a lot for a variety of reasons that we don't have to get into right now. But I've even found that for myself, the last few months have been even more difficult than usual. I feel like it's taken a personal toll on me. I'm becoming more careful about what I say online in a way that I feel goes against my sense of self, which is a bit sad. But also, this is the real world, and we decide what battles we want to fight and how we want to spend our time.

Actually, just earlier today, I tweeted something which wasn't even controversial, but some people didn't like it. I'm just like – do I really want to be getting into this kind of conversation when I have other things that I have to focus on? So I deleted my tweet. I don't know what you want to call that. But I think that there's always this pressure to read the room. People kept on telling me over the past six months, "Shadi, we see the point you're making. We kind of agree with you, but is this the right time? Read the room, man." And I'm like, "Okay, fine, but which room am I supposed to read? Where do I find the room? How do I know how to read it?" And so on and so forth.

I'm someone who likes intellectual combat. I worry about people who aren't used to it. They're going on Twitter and they're seeing how vociferous the nature of debate is, and how personal and ad hominem people get, and they say, "Listen, I don't want to share what I really think." I think a lot of us get DMs or messages on private group chats where people say, "Hey, I'm not comfortable saying this in public." And there's been a lot of interesting survey research over the past year about how large numbers of Americans say they're not comfortable saying what they think on big issues. That's pretty frightening.

CHRISTINE: Two thoughts here, more responding to Shadi, perhaps, than directly to the question. But one thing I've been thinking about a lot is American precarity and how afraid so many Americans are – rightly, frankly – of losing their jobs and then losing their house, losing everything, and having nothing. There's no safety net and no support, and our welfare system is nearly nonexistent. I come at this somewhat from the left, as you can probably tell. And this overwhelming fear of cancel culture is a symptom of this, and for good reason. If you think that by speaking your mind you might lose everything and be left with nothing, that's pretty scary. I can understand why you wouldn't want to speak your mind, and I find it hard to blame people who do actually fear that that is the case.

I think that it's more the case for everyday Americans than many of the professional speakers who complain about cancel culture in public. Josh Hawley says that he's being muzzled from the front page of the fourth largest newspaper in the United States. I think he's fine. But for everyday, normal people that's a verifiable fear, and I can understand that.

About what Shadi said – about reading the room and being advised to read the room by other people – I think the inability to read the room, or in fact gain an understanding of the room, is an interesting and unfortunate casualty of social media, actually, and of the way that we constantly thrust ourselves into interactions, not with people we know, not the people who we can assume are interacting with us in good faith, not people whose opinions, in fact, we may even be interested in. There's this feeling that we must be shouting our opinions into the void. That we should be sharing things not just with our family or friends but with however many millions of followers we have, with however many Facebook friends we have that we may not have even met.

It's impossible to read the room if the room is the size of the world and you have no idea who's in it. And that is, I think, not necessarily the fault of any individual, but it's the way the medium that we now participate in has shaped things.

Shadi also mentioned this idea of subsidiarity, of smaller places and smaller communities. This is one of the places where you can make a really strong argument, actually, for thinking closely about subsidiarity and building your own smaller communities. As I've said multiple times, I do really believe that one of the conditions for unity – one of the conditions for discussion that moves forward – is being able to assume that the people who you are in conversation with have some understanding of who you are. Also that they have some inclination toward good faith and that you're engaging on premises that are real. That you are talking to each other for a purpose, not just to make noise.

So I think we will have to continue to look and look harder for places where we can make this assumption of good faith. And unfortunately, even though social media has taken over many of our lives, that is not a place where good faith can be assumed. Unfortunately, perhaps, even the workplace in this moment is not necessarily the place where good faith can be assumed. And unfortunately, this larger failing – and it's also just a failing of everyday people who are not perfect – can lead not just to an unpleasant argument with a friend but to losing a job or a position. That is frightening. That is a fault of the larger political structure that we have, but it is something that we have to be aware of. And I'm not sure we have a way to fix that particular issue yet.

ANNE: In some ways that relates to the very first segment of this: the flattening in terms of the word "unity." This flattening of all the spheres. We haven't really gotten into this tonight, but there are certain spheres within each of our lives and our civil society that are much more accommodating of deep difference naturally by their very telos, how they're oriented, to what they're oriented: a family versus a synagogue versus a workplace versus the norms inherent therein. So anyway, something to talk about vis-à-vis differentiation, localism, and differentiation of spheres.

I just want to end on this note. *Breaking Ground* is a platform that was explicitly created in this last year of crisis in collaboration to embody unity and plurality. But we really call ourselves a web commons. So we use all these different words, but we bring what we've called two thousand years of Christian social thought and specifically Christian wisdom to the problems of the day. Both to accompany them and to act as a lens to see. To equip people of faith in particular to navigate these times and all that's being revealed. And perhaps, to reimagine and create something new.

So I bring that up to say that when I think about the word "unity"–the three of you at the beginning of this conversation articulated for me my own discomfort. Perhaps, Shadi, you most of all. Or not discomfort, but some hesitancy. I'm much more comfortable with this notion of the commons vis-à-vis our society. But when I think of the word "unity"–and I know we're an interreligious group here, but I will speak as a Christian–I think of it as a supernaturally graced reality. And there's a famous prayer that our founder prayed in the Gospel of John: "that they may be one as you are one."

So I think of it very much in terms of the church. And obviously those of us in the States are feeling extraordinarily fractured in that regard as we look at Christian nationalism et cetera. For those of us who are people of faith–and in this case I'm thinking of our three monotheistic religions, where there is maybe a deeper sense of unity that can't be perfectly established in the temporal sense, but is nonetheless real–what is the unique invitation in this hour in the United States, when it comes to contributing to our nationally creedal "more perfect union"? What is the nature of the invitation, if anything? Do we carry gifts for this moment, or do we also bring risks with us that are not good? I'm curious if you could reflect on that. Any one of you.

CHRISTINE: Shadi touched on this beforehand, and actually he has a great piece on this in *Comment* magazine. He's in some ways an excellent Christian apologist–as someone who's not a Christian! But I think one of the important things for unity and for an understanding of the commons, and that people of faith can bring to the table, is this understanding that success lies elsewhere. We will never be fully unified here. Which, on a good day, can bring you something of an immunity to disappointment, or at least make disappointment in certain goals or aims feel less like a death blow.

A risk here for Christians and people of faith is that this immunity can disappear – as we've seen over the past four years – when faith becomes too aligned to a specific person, a specific regime, or a specific form of politics that we've merged too closely with our faith, which should be something else, something separate, something not of this world. So I think there is some experience in holding a shared good, in holding an ideal, in holding out hope for a form of unity, knowing that it may not come in our lifetimes. Knowing that we may not be successful in bringing it, and yet that the world persists and that our faith can persist, despite certain disappointments.

SHADI: I'm sure Sam will have something to say about this. I mean, he wrote a book about friendship as sacred knowing, and I think that's relevant here. But from my standpoint I'll say—and thanks, Christine, for mentioning my piece where I do go into this in more detail. If you're interested, you can just search for "One Nation Sinful Under God, *Comment* magazine," which Anne is the editor of, so highly recommend the whole issue. But I'm a Muslim who has a deep respect for Christianity and Christian thinkers. And in this piece, I talk about a Dutch theologian who's really influenced me, Abraham Kuyper. And one major takeaway, to generalize, that we can all take in our own lives, is that we're all broken. And specifically from a Christian standpoint, one might talk about being broken by sin, being fallen in this temporal world.

I think there's something important there, this idea that we acknowledge this world, and politics in this world, as a site of uncertainty. There are no final victories in this world, because there's something very small and modest about this life that we live. If we think about history, the universe, and the power of God, we're humbled by how small these debates sometimes feel. We're getting in debates about things that I think a lot of us will realize ten years from now, or decades from now, that we were spending all this time freaking out and getting into fights with people.

And I think at some level there has to be a generosity of spirit where we say, "Hey, we don't have all the answers." In Islam, when scholars or clerics issue edicts known as fatwas, they historically have ended their fatwas with the Arabic phrase for "And

God only knows." The idea there is that although you're a cleric, and you know a lot about God's word and the corpus of law, at the very end you acknowledge your modesty and the fact that despite all your knowledge, you might still not know the truth. And that in the end, God is the only one who is the true repository of the good and of ultimate truth.

ANNE: Thanks, Shadi. Wow, this is leading to a lovely benediction. A trinitarian benediction I wasn't even expecting. Sam, do you want to bring us home?

SAMUEL: I'll say a couple things. I think one of the tragic things that strikes me about how faith has played into all of this is that it very much has drawn out a sense of ultimacy – that there is something real or true, and that thing is worth dying for, or potentially worth killing for. We see a civic severing, which is intensifying that ultimacy without having the religious convictions that have traditionally gone alongside that, which do have to do exactly with the kinds of things that both Shadi and Christine are talking about.

Despite the losses, despite the potential for profound sorrows, reality is not fragile in the end. There is a resilience and coherence that can endure past a given moment of tragedy, or difficulty, or loss, which I think is the relevant category here. You may well lose political battles, but that's in fact good.

Just to reference a philosophical source at the end, there's a refrain that goes throughout Plato's corpus about Socrates, where he keeps saying that it's better to suffer from injustice than to do injustice yourself. And the basic sense is that that's true for you. It's worse for you to end up being someone who is doing injustice than someone who is suffering injustice. Finding the way to be gentle and sensitive to the kind of fragility that people feel – that the desire for ultimacy is coming out but not the sense that reality is coherent – seems to me to be absolutely essential. And in a certain way, that can only be done in the confidence that we do actually have enough internal solidity and strength to be gentle and forbearing with the people we disagree with.

It's interesting the degree to which all three of us are thinking through the same issue in different ways. How can you cope with very basic fundamental disagreement in a way that has a certain level of dignity to it? And that does mean not being hasty, not foreclosing the level of difference very quickly, but having a certain degree of mercy.

ANNE: On that note—mercy—well, thank you, all three of you, so much. Shadi, Sam, Christine. You've been such friends to me, and intellectual exemplars. And it's been a real gift to our listeners. With every hope for all of you watching, with hope for your health, for the wisdom of your steps and perhaps most poignantly right now, just the navigation of your relationships, we at *Breaking Ground* wish you goodnight. ⚕

January 29, 2021

RELATIVISM IS OUT.
TRUTH IS IN.

BRANDON MCGINLEY

THIS HAS BEEN noticeable for some time now. Five years ago, "speaking your truth" in politics still sounded reasonable; now, while the habit of speaking in terms of skepticism and subjectivity has not been broken completely, a cursory scan of our politics demonstrates that certainty and objectivity are the new norm. In public health, racial justice, climatology, and innumerable other intersections of science and sociology and politics, our discourse emphasizes and enforces a winner-take-all struggle between truth and falsehood, good and evil. The sight of a mob of Trump supporters, convinced at least that he was the rightful victor and at most that he was about to bring down an international cabal of adrenochrome-eating pedophiles, was if nothing else a wakeup call. We need to stop indulging in make-believe. Maybe in that way, we can meet each other on the common ground of the reality that, willing or not, we all inhabit.

And the new president's inaugural address echoed this. In what will be remembered as one of the sharpest uses of theology in modern American rhetoric, Joe Biden invoked St. Augustine's formula that "a people is a multitude defined by the common objects of their love." And what loves unite Americans? "Opportunity. Security. Liberty. Dignity. Respect. Honor. And, yes, the truth."

BRANDON MCGINLEY, a *Plough* contributing editor, is a writer and speaker whose most recent book is *The Prodigal Church: Restoring Catholic Tradition in an Age of Deception*. He lives in Pittsburgh with his wife and four children.

In another day, with a president of a different party, the reaction in our country's organs of respectable opinion would have been swift and brutal. Each of these concepts offered as "common objects of love" would have been picked apart as insufficient and insincere, none more so than the last: truth. The old habits of relativism would have returned: Founding a people on truth would be exclusive, benighted, dangerous. Truth as a common object of love? There would have been shudders: There is, we would have been reminded, only my truth and your truth. Only tolerance of different perceptions of the true and the good, they would say, can keep this people together.

But that's all gone now. Truth is in. But, we are justified in asking alongside one of history's most infamous cynics, what is truth?

Pontius Pilate's intention in making this inquiry of Christ is ambiguous. It has been called "jesting," or one of the greatest philosophical queries of all time. What I see in the Roman governor, though, is resignation – not despair of the reality of truth, but of whether it matters either way.

Consider Pilate's next move: He knows the truth, and he tells it. "I find no crime in him," he announces to the braying crowd (John 18:38). Pilate is not a skeptic. But in the face of the riotous reality of the mob, the abstract truth doesn't matter, and so he deploys that damned contrasting conjunction: "But you have a custom that I should release one man for you at the Passover; will you have me release for you the King of the Jews?" (John 18:39). Of course they decline and demand Barabbas; thus he has washed his hands (as he does literally in Matthew's account) not only of the injustice of Christ's conviction, but of his responsibility to the truth.

Truth and justice are intrinsically related: Justice involves, fundamentally, the duties we owe in virtue of the truth—the truth of the human person, the truth of virtue and vice, the truth of equity, the truth of God.

And so Augustine would have endorsed the president's identification of truth as the essential foundation of the commonwealth. We should, we must, be a people formed by our common love of the truth, or we cannot be a people at all.

But Joe Biden was not speaking outside of place and time: He was speaking here and now. And so I think of the commentary of

Theophylact of Ohrid, whose notes on Scripture were relied on by St. Thomas Aquinas, on Pilate's question: "For [truth] had almost vanished from the world, and become unknown in consequence of the general unbelief."

What is truth? Was the election illegitimate? Was Mexico ever going to pay for the wall? Was George Floyd murdered? Is Donald Trump a Russian intelligence asset? Did Joe Biden sexually assault a staffer? Did Donald Trump sexually assault several women? Is Hunter Biden under federal investigation? Do cloth masks suppress respiratory viruses? Did antifa incite the Capitol siege?

These are all questions with answers, most of them known or easily knowable. But do those answers, to return to Pilate's cynicism, really matter? Of course they do morally, with regard to the acts themselves and to justice. It matters whether George Floyd was murdered, so that his murderer might be punished. (He was.) It matters whether masks work, so that we might calibrate our epidemiological regulations properly. (They do, generally.) But do these answers matter to the way our society is *actually run*? Do they inform our choices in leaders, and do they matter to those leaders?

In response to this question, we should make two observations: Donald Trump was particularly brash in his indifference to the truth, but Joe Biden promises nothing more compelling than a return to the more carefully stage-managed deceit of American politics, in which he has participated his entire adult life.

Trump's frontal attack on truth *as such* exploded a public relationship with truth in politics that was, in the wake of decades of lies about scandals and wars and policies and the very nature and dignity of human persons, already a shambles. Truth had already almost vanished from the world; Trump made that fact undeniable; Biden promises to return us to a state of plausible deniability. This may be an improvement, but it is not a healing.

Healing would take a much higher dose of the love of truth than we seem able to bear. We love the *idea* of truth, and of truth-tellers, but what the polarization of our politics—more accurately, the calcification of a politics of anti-solidarity—means is that we love the selected truths that flatter the assumptions and prejudices, and advance the interests, of our side. But if we really love truth, then we can't pick a side, at least in the uncritical way usually demanded. Is abortion morally acceptable health care, a locus of irreproachable liberty like choosing a house or a college? If an elementary school student finds that she does not identify as the sex her anatomy presents, has she found out that she is in fact not that sex, such that her parents and doctors would be failing her if they did not put her on puberty blockers? Are endless wars punctuated by drone strikes that fail to discriminate between soldier and civilian a legitimate foreign policy? Joe Biden would answer the first and, in agreement with Trump, the third in the affirmative; it remains to be seen how this administration will answer the second.

But the answer to all of these questions is in fact no. The apparent fact that Biden believes them to be true does not change this. Because they are false, to enshrine them in law and policy would be unjust. Acquiescing or assenting to falsehoods that are given the slick veneer of truth – or are whitewashed to obscure the claims they make – will not bring unity, but tyranny.

It seems that we are, again, stuck with Pilate. Truth exists, and peoples and commonwealths must be founded on it. Justice requires it, and without justice, civilizations tear themselves to bits. But – there's that damned conjunction again—in the face of mobs and tyrants and corporate behemoths, does it matter? Do we just have to go along?

But remember the man – the God-man – to whom Pilate was speaking. The words of Christ that elicited Pilate's query were these: "For this I was born, and for this I have come into the world, to bear witness to the truth. Every one who is of the truth hears my voice" (John 18:37). And of course four chapters earlier in John, he said, "I am the way, and the truth, and the life" (John 14:6). Christ could have answered the governor's question, had he been given the chance, with two words: "I am."

When truth is so unclear, and when facsimiles are wielded recklessly to excite passions, then the Christian's first response to the question, What is truth? is to reword it: *Who is truth?* There we have a definitive answer. We don't have to retreat into relativism or to embrace convenient lies; we can stand our ground and point to the cross. We can affirm with the president that society needs truth, and then show him the Truth, bloodied and triumphant.

Truth is in, and that's good. It's much better for Christians, and for everyone, for the terms of discourse to be made clear, rather than obscured behind the false neutrality of skepticism and relativism and tolerance. But if we try to contain truth within American political categories, just as when we try to tame Christ and his teachings, we will continue to do violence to it, and to him.

A commitment to truth means an openness to others and a willingness to listen and to learn, not in skepticism of truth but the mutual and cooperative pursuit of truth that is an aspect of the love of neighbor. We can practice and demonstrate this among ourselves as Christians, showing that the truth–the real Truth–does form and sustain communities, does make living together not just possible but joyful, does bind us together while making us servants of all.

We can and should celebrate truth when we see it in American politics, but with that innocent wisdom (Matt. 10:16) that allows us to distinguish posturing from probity. We can affirm the abstract correctness of Joe Biden's "shared loves" remark while wisely recognizing that in our context it simply does not reflect the real state of things: Americans do not all love the real truth, and the truth the president offers us is in places adequate, in places incomplete, in others perverse. It would be a lie to say anything else.

This is an uncomfortable, even painful posture to adopt, but the Christian is a pilgrim, an exile, a sojourner: We were never promised, nor should we expect, to exist comfortably or guilelessly with the powers of this world. And so if we take the president's words to heart–and we should–they should inspire us to regard critically precisely the man himself, and all those who invoke the idea of truth while mistaking, or misusing, the genuine article. ✝

February 10, 2021

TAKING IT OUTSIDE

Political Violence and the Future of the United States:
A Police Chief's Perspective

JOHN CLAIR

ON JANUARY SIXTH, I was working in my office at the station in downtown Marion, Virginia, on some long-term legislative issues we expect to confront at the next session here in the Commonwealth, when I received a text from a friend: "The Capitol has been overrun." I turned on the news in my office just in time to see something I'd never imagined – the House Chamber door barricaded with furniture, several plainclothes agents with their service weapons drawn, anticipating a breach.

I think what I said was, "Holy shit."

After being honorably discharged from the US Army as a military police officer, and before entering service as a municipal police officer, I'd worked a few years as a physical security contractor for the Department of Justice Protective Service and the Department of State Bureau of Diplomatic Security. Although those missions were certainly quite different from the security mission at the Capitol, I know enough to know that this was bad. Really bad. As the news began to spread around the DC-area law-enforcement community that I'm a part of, the commentary quickly shifted from "Wow. . . this protest went a bit too far" to "They better get this under control before someone gets shot."

JOHN CLAIR is the chief of police of Marion, Virginia, and a board member of the Virginia Association of Chiefs of Police. He has served in law enforcement for over twenty years, and resides in southwest Virginia with his wife and four children.

Then it happened. A protester – should we call her an insurgent? a patriot? what is it that was going on? what did she think she was doing, and what was she actually doing? – who was attempting to breach a door was shot with a single well-placed round and died almost immediately. I know many of those there said that nothing would stop them from preventing what they saw as an election theft in process, but I can't imagine they had any intention of confronting a 115-grain jacketed hollow-point. I know that the Capitol police officer who shot her never dreamed of having to confront what he confronted that day.

That was when I called my wife and told her to turn on the news, to make sure our four children were watching what I am convinced was the most *significant political event of their lifetimes* so far. Everything will be different from this point forward. It had finally happened.

But what was it that had happened?

THE POLITICAL FLAT EARTH

Up until this year I was pretty active on Facebook, and enjoyed keeping up with old friends and making new acquaintances online. Then, after the murder of George Floyd, and the riots that followed, there was what seemed like a sudden shift in the conservative and loosely Reformed Christian circles I was in. Police, in those circles, had tended to be seen as the "good guys." But this summer and fall, without any buildup, some of my closest ideological allies started talking about how they wanted to purchase guns to protect themselves *from the police*. It was as if their entire view of the world had suddenly changed, and now it was the police who were their personal enemies. These interactions alone caused me concern: What was it that they thought was going to happen? But what really worried me was the sudden eschatological tone of much of the political discussion among Christians, even those Christians who typically weren't prone to reading such things as signs of the times. It wasn't just the Pentecostals: politically inflected millenarianism was affecting people across denominations and traditions.

Over the next few months I saw many people I knew well become what I can only describe as political flat-earthers, falling deeper and deeper into thinly evidenced conspiracies about everything from the pandemic to the election. In response, a rock-solid "official narrative" grew up about how normal people should regard these things. "No," said the talking heads on MSNBC, "there was no election fraud at all, and also BLM protests are not superspreader events while anti-lockdown protests are. No, there is no hypocrisy to see here." There was no room to question that narrative without being labeled a conspiracy theorist and a right-wing extremist. In what seemed to be a kind of reaction, some of those who did question it seemed to step outside the realm of normal debate altogether, entering into some kind of widespread psychosis amounting to a literal break with reality. And the fact of the bizarre beliefs and behavior of some on the right allowed some on the left to be confirmed in their regard of all of those on the right as contemptible, dangerous, and insane.

I don't understand fully what has happened. But one thing that is clear is that the power of social media to shape reality is part of that picture: in the attack on the Capitol, the memes materialized. Written words and images unleashed a universe of tactile forms. All of the rhetoric had finally found its final form. Blood.

SUMMER OF FIRE

The summer had prepared us for this. Whatever one thinks about the both-sidesing of some post-January 6 rhetoric, from a law enforcement professional's perspective, what is happening is related in its sheer material reality: mobs on the left, and then on the right, have, over the past ten months or so, made political violence normal in the United States.

Just as we saw the violence at the Capitol, and in response prepared for potential further violence on January 20 – violence that, thank God, did not materialize, in part because of our preparations – over the summer we saw the riots and destruction spread from city to city across the country, and prepared, uneasily, for potential violence in our own town.

Over the summer, we had two protest events: one small, one regionally large. In these events, we saw people motivated by the entire spectrum of expression, from average citizens on both sides of the political aisle merely concerned with exercising their rights of freedom of speech and assembly, to advocates for anarchism and of white supremacy. We literally had it all. During the first event, a fiery exchange of words occurred at the site of a Confederate war memorial on the courthouse grounds. That was followed up by a crossburning in the local BLM organizer's yard. Suddenly our event went from somewhat run of the mill to making national and even international news. The vitriolic local exchanges, both in person and online, went up in intensity accordingly. And of course everyone who was planning to protest, and counterprotest, locally had been watching the way protests were going elsewhere in the country: watching *their own* media, with their own stories about who the bad guys were and who the good guys were in each protest, and preparing themselves with their own scripts of action and rhetoric.

This intensity resulted in the largest law enforcement deployment in southwest Virginia history, with over two hundred police officers in Marion (population five thousand) on the day of the second event. Even with so many officers on the ground, we still were at a significant disadvantage with five hundred to a thousand protesters and counterprotesters, just about evenly split, packed into an area less than an eighth of a mile square, all ultimately converging on a three-block radius in downtown Marion. In preparation for what we knew would be head-on collision, we developed a system of barricades and "gates" that I informally thought of as "the Thermopylae Plan"—we used tall buildings and narrow streets to create more manageable geography, making several contingency plans if the situation got out of hand.

Bear in mind, participants on both sides of the debate were heavily armed, open-carrying rifles. This is, after all, Virginia: it's all completely legal. And my officers were in the middle. The most intense moment was at the conclusion of the march, when both groups met, separated by barricades about thirty feet apart, at the main intersection in town. A twenty-minute verbal exchange ensued. I hear myself describing it like that, with the police officer's passive voice: let me try again. People in the crowds were talking to each other. They were screaming at each other. Slogans, chants, accusations. Also ideas, jokes, heated conversations. It seemed to be on the edge of catastrophe. I spent half my time encouraging my guys on the radio to assess properly what they were dealing with: yes, that BLM protester has a gun, but look, it doesn't have a magazine in it, he's not a threat. Yes, that counterprotester is getting in your face: let him. I allowed it to go on, because I was convinced that *it needed to happen.*

Politics is a public conversation. And this was freedom of assembly, freedom of speech. For better or worse those words needed to be exchanged, and as a police officer it's my job to protect those rights, and physically protect those exercising them, to enable them to continue to do so. In the end, there were no arrests, no injuries, and no incidents of property damage.

I didn't just try to protect those conversations; over the summer: I had them too. During one of the summer's conversations about defunding the police, I spoke with one protester who insisted that "we don't need the police in our communities."

I'm sympathetic to the ideal of community policing. But there is a core job here that I do not think is one that most community members are able to do by themselves. "How do you determine who the offender is, and what happens to him?" I asked. He did not answer.

JUST THE FACTS

I believe this brief exchange highlights one of the most serious problems facing our nation today: *a lack of confidence in processes and institutions.* A whole lot of processes, and a whole lot of institutions. Let's face it, adherents to both parties believe national elections are a sham, either through Russian interference or absentee voting—we may as well just have a revolution. Most everyone, it seems, feels the same way about the criminal justice system, because either it fails to dispense "true" justice—it's part of the "deep state"—or because it's merely an arm of oppression. This despair is not a partisan issue. It's an infection raging in the social body of our nation, and it seems almost no one has any intellectual immunity against it.

Suddenly it seems everyone would rather simply *take it outside.* We saw these images in almost every city and town in America.

Images of violence in exchange or action, splattered across the national news in waves not seen in decades.

A key job of the police, and one that other citizens are less well-equipped to do, is to do what people don't have the time or temperament or training to do when they are in a mood to take it outside. That is to find out what actually happened: to investigate.

In the judicial system, we require evidence beyond a reasonable doubt – *it's not about what you know*, I was told again and again, *it's about what we can prove*. As a young officer I can't count the number of times I "knew" someone had "done" the proverbial "it" but found that I was unable to prove what I thought I knew. As a more mature officer, I think about how many times I would have gone wrong if I had acted on what I "knew." I can tell you from thousands of firsthand experiences that eyewitness testimony isn't all it's cracked up to be, and rumor, unless it is substantiated, is worth nothing at all: as my father would say, "Don't believe anything you hear, and only half of what you see."

The reason for this is simple: your brain has a habit of trying to help you out. When traumatic events occur, or when events occur at speeds you have trouble processing, your brain will help you process them by filling in gaps with predictive information or historical data. This is also why we see police officers accidentally shoot suspects who pull out cellphones, swearing they saw a weapon—because they most likely did "see" one, or at least their brain led them to that conclusion. Yet in police work we fight these phenomena with every available investigative and evidentiary tool. We know the problem exists and we strive to counteract it. This is what vigilantism lacks; it lacks it by design *because the act of vigilantism is intensely personal.* If your goal is to get what you want politically, your brain will give you the reasons to justify your actions. And your Twitter feed, curated to give you stories of a certain pattern, will be doing its helpful best to beef up those reasons as well.

Police training is absolutely vital to help officers develop good judgment as well as possible. Civilians have no such training, and those who are passionately committed to their political cause are not likely to be effective at sifting evidence and getting at the reality behind each incident, and each apparent pattern.

This is frustrating. Vigilantism boils down to a desire for relevance, for individual agency against injustice. The mob-violence version of vigilantism is designed to scratch the itch of making political action, political enmity and comradeship, personal in a very satisfying way. But it is not well-calculated to give justice to a community.

Objective processes, by design, have a tendency to minimize individual relevance – in many ways that's the entire point. The problem of course is that the balm of vigilantism applied to wounded individual relevance doesn't actually soothe anything, but rather results in a deeper alienation from the very populace it seeks approval from, creating an unending chain of violence. We have to find ways for members of the public on both sides to actually have political agency, relevance that do not come at the barrel of a gun, the invasion of a public building, or a swung crowbar. That is why a crackdown on political speech and the freedom of assembly would be counterproductive: we can't attempt to emasculate citizens and then act surprised when, on both left and right, they lash out.

I'm the kind of law enforcement professional who continually prepares for the worst outcome, so my team does well when the reality is anything better than that, and if we do face the worst, we can at least handle it adequately. We prepared for violence on Inauguration Day that did not come. It may be that the new administration will see a general calming of the national temper. But that may not be the case. What we are doing is preparing for intense and public political discourse, with bad actors and violence sprinkled in, as we saw this summer. What we must not do is prepare to shut down that discourse. It is our job to protect it.

THE TROUBLES

It's natural, and helpful, to try to find analogues in current political violence in the past. I'll be spending this year consuming any and all written after-action reports from critical events in an effort to identify weak points in our own command and control and event preparation. Almost by chance I had done significant study into events like the Charlottesville tragedy just before we experienced large-scale protest events in our region, and the lessons I learned from those events were invaluable to peaceful conclusions here. Our main focus will be contingency planning, threat identification, and command training in the hope we can make good initial decisions before events unfold. One obvious, but little considered, aspect of the police response to critical incidents is that law enforcement is always outnumbered. This requires us to use a lot of passive barriers, and to always make sure we use structures and geography to our advantage, all of which require intense sand-table planning.

But Charlottesville is not the only parallel. I come from a police family; my father was a police officer in Sugarcreek, Ohio, and my grandfather was the first chief of police of that department at its formation in the 1970s. I remember well the atmosphere of the 1990s in regard to law enforcement. Although during that time none of us were active-duty police, I suppose we always still felt as if we had some stake in the discussions. We all watched and read about a sudden series of what seemed like enormous law enforcement missteps: first at Ruby Ridge, and then at Waco. Then came the Federal Assault Weapons Ban in response, and then – boom. A bomb went off at the FBI building in Oklahoma City.

As I think back on those events, I can't help but feel like we are on a trajectory toward a similar outcome: A large portion of the population feels disenfranchised politically. A few troubled souls are seeking relevance. We have seen a year of law enforcement missteps that have alienated large portions of the population from across the political spectrum. The accelerants of rhetoric and violence have been pushing the velocity of events higher and higher.

I am extremely concerned that it won't be long before the next boom: the propaganda of the deed, politics by other means. And I am extremely concerned that law enforcement may make similar errors, as a wave of popular fear of "domestic insurgents" encourages harsh crackdowns.

A major difference this time is that radicals on *both* sides seem to regard themselves as at war with their enemies, as oppressed minorities for whom violence is a legitimate choice. One could look at Germany in the 1930s or Kansas in 1861, but in my opinion the most accurate parallel is Northern Ireland, during the Troubles of the 1970s and 1980s. As in that case, both "sides" are nongovernmental actors, and police have an ambiguous relationship to them; a sense of political grievance and injustice has sparked off what seems to be a potential spiral of political violence. The Belfast-esque Christmas Day car bomb in downtown Nashville only confirmed what I had begun to see.

If this is what we are facing, then it seems to me that we must learn our lessons from the missteps not just of the FBI in Waco and at Ruby Ridge but also from those of the police in Northern Ireland. What we must do is police in such a way as to protect the public realm, not to shut it down to any one group, and in that way cut short our transformation into a society of vigilantes.

ROUGH JUSTICE

What's wrong with political vigilante justice? At the very basic level, it is not justice, because the vigilante is by his nature passionately and partisanly engaged in the political issue at hand. The ideal that we absolutely must fight to make a reality is that of a police force that acts for the true common good, apart from personal and political influence. This is not easy: it is the reason for the professionalization of policing in the first place.

D. H. Lawrence told us that "the essential American soul is hard, stoic, isolate, and a killer." I don't know of a nation on earth that doesn't have some literary advocate who ascribes to it a unique strain of truculence. Yet the mystique of vigilante violence does seem to captivate the most in the American context. After all, isn't that How the West Was Won? Imagine the scene. A hardscrabble family winding its way through the Ohio Territory confronts a murderous and bushwhacking band of thieves. The resolution comes through frontier justice, delivered by a man willing to take on the burden of sovereignty where there is no state – all aided by the majesty of Technicolor.

If no one has told you up to this point, let me be the first: The realities of the frontier were far less captivating. Fast-draw rigs didn't exist in the Old West, most gunfighters were shot in the back, virtue went unrewarded, and more importantly – justice wasn't always done.

The same goes for justice generally, vengeance always, and violence particularly. It's not as magical as it seems. In my twenty years of law enforcement service, I have fired my service weapon only once, and that time only after having been on the receiving end of gunfire. It was neither beautiful nor glorious, neither adventurous nor particularly fulfilling, neither heroic nor noteworthy. I responded to a call for a domestic situation that turned violent, and when I arrived I found the suspect fleeing in a vehicle and along with other officers confronted the suspect. He exited his vehicle, leveled a Sig Sauer 9mm in my direction, and pulled the trigger. I saw the muzzle flash, and had one thought – my youngest daughter, Gwendolyn, would never know me. In the end, we all lived because we all missed (the suspect included), we didn't feel particularly brave, and after countless hours of forensic and investigative work, along with days of courtroom testimony, the suspect was convicted in a court of law of four counts of attempted capital murder.

JUSTICE IN PUBLIC

I suppose this brings me to the point: the satisfaction in justice is found in the glory of the law, and the process by which it is brought to bear on those who transgress it, not in lust for blood, for action. The navigable stream of evidence, investigation, and deliberation is what takes us from the transgression to absolution or conviction. This process may not deliver justice perfectly, but to abandon it is to abandon the attempt. We may not know much about how to solve racism in America, for example, but we can know that it is unjust to destroy an innocent man's business, and therefore we know that that injustice will not serve the cause of justice. We may not know how to clean up political corruption or create a political culture where all Americans feel adequately represented, but we know that breaking into the Capitol building and attempting to murder the Speaker of the House will not do that job.

There are no shortcuts here, because how it all feels, seems, or looks to those passionately watching the news can't be allowed to determine what is decided in court. The only relevant metric is *how it actually was*, as best we can tell, based on evidence that can be publicly produced and evaluated. I admit that at times this process can be difficult and, when weighed in the balance with immediate satisfaction, often found wanting. The slow and tedious work of investigation, interviews, and analysis is the work that every police officer in this nation dedicates their professional life to. The work of the justice system to determine the facts of the deed, and the intent behind it, is a work of public moral and legal evaluation. It is hard. It is imperfect.

Finding at least some of the truth is not impossible. But it does not come from social-media mobs who decide on the guilt or innocence of people based on cellphone video clips, and it does not come from those who create mental conspiracy charts based on Reddit rumors.

The art of public life, it seems to me, lies in balancing the need for protecting space for the public conversation that is the heart of politics – conversation that we ought to strive to conduct rationally and in friendship, even in the face of profound disagreement, but in which there must also be room for the antagonistic and the down-right loony – with the need for protecting space for the careful and dispassionate sifting of evidence, the slow and annoying work of police and lawyers and juries.

Both sides of this public work need each other. If police, or elections, become corrupt – if police departments are racist, or politicians are self-serving – the public must hold them to account. But what the public must not do is to despair, to give up, to decide that the work of conversation and politics and marginal improvement is useless.

It is my hope that as the new administration contemplates the action that it will take in response to both the events of the summer and of January 6, they are guided by this same conviction. It is our job to protect the public realm, and that means protecting the space for exchange – even heated exchange, even stupid exchange, even ill-informed exchange, even exchange based on premises with which we disagree or in terms that we do not understand. This exchange must take place in a public realm that is physically safe: people must be protected in their rights to speak and to assemble. But they must not be protected from the conversation. That conversation simply is politics. ✢

WORDS AND FLESH

Pastoring in a Post-truth World

KURT ARMSTRONG

IN HIS BOOK *The Emperor of All Maladies: A Biography of Cancer*, cancer physician Siddhartha Mukherjee recounts the history of a disease that has haunted humans for millennia. Paleopathologists, he says, have discovered evidence of cancer in a human jawbone dating to 4000 BC, and descriptions of a disease sounding very much like cancer appear in an Egyptian papyrus from 2500 BC. *Karkinos*, Greek for "crab," first appears as a medical term in about 400 BC, around the time of Hippocrates. "Crab" vividly describes the mysterious illness: a firm, subcutaneous mass, like a shell, which seems able to crawl through the body and create pain "like being caught in the grip of a crab's pincers," says Mukherjee.

Claudius Galen, a second-century Greek doctor, classified illnesses according to the four humors, the wide range of human diseases caused by an imbalance of blood, mucus, yellow bile, or black bile; and cancer's hard carapace, he said, was the result of an excess of black bile. Galen's taxonomy prevailed in Western medicine for well over a thousand years, spawning an exotic range of cancer treatments designed to restore the body's balance of fluids, including ointments and salves made from crab's eyes, goat's dung,

KURT ARMSTRONG is a handyman and writer in Winnipeg, Canada, and a part-time lay minister at Saint Margaret's Anglican. He has written for *Plough, Image, Paste, Sojourners, The Globe and Mail, CBC Radio, Mockingbird, Faith Today,* and *Geez,* among others, and is the author of *Why Love Will Always Be A Poor Investment.*

tortoise liver, boar's tooth, fox lungs, and extracts containing arsenic and lead.

But with the development of the modern medical autopsy, physicians' understanding of cancer began to shift from speculation to observation, marking the beginning of modern cancer treatment. Upon examining the bodies of men and women killed by the disease, doctors could find no evidence of "black bile," discovering, instead, a wide range of tumors throughout the different bodies they were dissecting. At this time the language of cancer – the description of its location within the body, properties of various tumors, observations of their growth and spread – became much more useful. Doctors discovered that, unlike the ominous "black bile," which could be anywhere and everywhere in the body and generate random outcroppings, cancerous tumors were local and could sometimes be removed. The cure was often worse than the disease: until the development of antisepsis in the mid-nineteenth century, surgery usually led to massive infection, often fatal. But antisepsis, along with the discovery of reliable, safe anesthetic, combined with the empirical discoveries of the modern autopsy, marked the beginning of a revolution in cancer treatment.

"To name an illness is to describe a certain condition of suffering – a literary act before it becomes a medical one," writes Mukherjee. "A patient, long before he becomes the subject of medical scrutiny, is, at first, simply a storyteller. To relieve an illness, one must begin, then, by unburdening its story."

—

I have always trusted that medicine is precise, objective, and empirical, so storytelling is the last thing on my mind when the radiologist takes an x-ray of my knee or the lab tech draws my blood to check my cholesterol. But like every other cultural activity, medicine is entwined with narrative and metaphor, those great, ancient, world-making gifts. God made Adam creation's first gardener, but before any of the digging, planting, or grafting, the first task for the human was literary: give names to the creatures, from the aardvark to the zorilla and everything in between. All of our ongoing acts of naming, including those of the cancer researchers, are a continuation of that same primordial language-arts assignment. It's the story: the story's the thing, and Mukherjee's incredible book is saturated with narrative and metaphor.

Storytelling and mythmaking are ancient and global practices, and as with all things cultural, story and myth evolve, adapt, and are renewed in the rich, drawn-out process of cultural transmission. But something new has emerged in Western culture, not an evolution but a drastic break with the process itself. The grand cultural narratives we have long been telling to one another and to ourselves in order to shape our minds and lives and communities have been undermined and discredited because those primary literary and spiritual creative acts of naming and storytelling have become suspect. Language, we are lately told, is nothing but a social construct and therefore arbitrary, making meaning amorphous and indeterminate. All of the grand metaphors, under the guise of theology, politics, society, and human nature, are fundamentally ideological, tools of power and domination and violence. No longer confident that our word- and world-makings are in any way sacred callings, language and meaning are largely up for grabs. Meaning is secondary at best, fundamentally subject to the overarching demands and machinations of power.

And this in a time when a near-infinity of writing is available via the internet. When a medieval monk copied a manuscript, not only did he write with such care and attention as to not make even a single spelling or transcription error, he illuminated texts to highlight the sacredness of words. Writing was an act of worship, elevation. Today, by comparison, we are so entirely saturated in words they seem disposable. At a superficial level, the glut of throwaway words seems like an innocuous sign of the times. Twitter hashtags, an updated Facebook mood status, dozens of "likes" for your Instagram post of today's expensive brunch are as forgettable as they are trivial, and the catchy, provocative, punchy slogans that clog up browser sidebars to get us to shell out cash are a seemingly harmless hybrid of the seductive and the fatuous, hardly a matter of life and death. But even supposedly disposable words can be potent and dangerous. Tossed-off tweets can inflame real hatred – can suggest that a president would support an insurrection, can suggest that a public figure would support the burning of a downtown – and once you begin excavating the painful truths beneath the glamorous sheen of advertising slogans you wind up having to think about labor conditions, the ecological impact of production and consumption, and toxic-waste disposal; then on to the great perennial, existential questions about well-being and health, rights and community, justice and violence, life and death, all of which center, in one way or another, on questions about the "person."

We have some real evidence that language and words still seem to have serious power and meaning, but our *shared* common sense of that power and meaning is wobbly at best. Even that general sense of the "person" is anything but general; we no longer share anything like a basic response to Wendell Berry's question: What are people for? The Christian narrative tells us the human being is made in the image of the divine, formed from dirt and breathed into by God the Creator, and that story has been absolutely essential to our politics and culture. But those teachings have been disputed, discredited, and discarded, leaving us, at least for the time being, in a grand, haunting metaphor void.

In Mukherjee's "biography" of cancer, research and treatment of the disease move forward as the language and narrative of the illness move closer to the actual flesh and blood of the patients. It is *the truth*, not abstract thought, that heals: the more precise the narrative, the more effective the treatment. By contrast, our disparate and disputed metaphors for what a human being is seem to be carrying us ever further away from meaningful, effective treatments for our cultural and psychic maladies. It becomes ever more difficult to diagnose, let alone treat, our human condition when we are entirely unclear about what it actually means to be human. Absent any kind of shared, basic anthropology, the ethical problems pile up quickly: How is it possible to discern a compelling moral *oughtness* to our behavior if we believe that the human is nothing more than stardust plus time plus chance? What if the evolutionary biologists are correct, having us pegged as the most highly advanced primates? Does that then imply significant, detailed moral obligations? If so, how, exactly? And which ones? Are the modern ethicists and anarcho-primitivists right, that a human is just another animal, no more or less meaningful than Fluffy or Fido, mongoose or mouse? Or does a self-described reductionist like E. O. Wilson have us properly pegged as blind carriers of genes, slaves to our DNA? What if we are economic beings, *Homo economicus*, the value of each person measured by his or her contribution to the GDP? The Industrial Revolution gave us a powerful image of the human as complex, fleshy machine, now taken up and digitized by the priests and apostles of Silicon Valley, but we don't hold machines accountable for their "actions." What moral impetus then for us, mere meaty hardware? Maybe the most pervasive image of the human, at least in North America, is hard to see precisely because it's right under our noses: the human as consumer, in which case George Bush's "go shopping" response to 9/11 was exactly right. Maybe that's the closest thing we have to a shared anthropology: our most cherished understanding of what it is to be human is that we are free to choose. It is choice itself, not the substance of the choice, that we insist on. *Homo eligens*: the deciding being. Absent any general agreement as to what we really are, it's you pick your meaning and I'll pick mine.

—

I don't mean to be nostalgic for some imaginary, sentimental golden age when folks said what they meant and meant what they said because they all believed in a capital-g God, but I recognize my need to be cautious. I am at the age when I've got increasing symptoms of GOMS (Grumpy Old Man Syndrome), the first sign of which was when I caught myself saying, "Well, now, when *I* was a kid . . ." Warning us against exactly this sort of thing, Annie Dillard writes, "The good times, and the heroic people, are all gone. Everyone knows this. Everyone always has. The mournings of the wise recur as a comic refrain down the vaults of recorded time." Duly noted: even a small dose of historical relativism can help keep in check the latest crest of anxious fretting over cultural decline and whatever it is the kids are up to nowadays.

That said, a polite, nonjudgmental nod at the erosion of long-standing cultural traditions is the quintessential posture of our postmodern, hypercapitalist, postcolonial, constructivist, tolerant, connected, mediated, tribalized, technologized, globalized, individualized, post-truth times. Kindly accept whatever comes and goes and you'll find some place that you can fit in just fine. Stand firm for something, claim to actually believe something significant and true, and, bolder yet, suggest that it's not just true for you but for others as well, and you'll find yourself in a hard swim against a very, very powerful tide.

—

I'm trying to make sense of language and metaphor that maybe seems like a trifling exercise alongside a global pandemic, the background threat of extremist politics and responses to them, civil unrest in Ethiopia and Uganda, carbon in the air, and powermongering politicos. After all, everyone seems to be getting along fine with language as it is. We still send birthday greetings; still send flowers on Valentine's Day; still type caustic, witty replies in the comments section; still look for language, awkwardly, when we hear of another death. There's no shortage of words floating around. But there remains some fundamental connection between words and flesh, the mysterious braid of thought, word, and deed, and when that relationship is wound with suspicion, doubt, and cynicism rather than love, we pretty quickly wind up slogging around in vertigo-inducing arbitrariness. With meaning in flux, our greater collective moral ambitions are eroded by our inability to even speak clearly to one another. The center is missing; "The glue is gone," says Edward Hoagland. Freed from the supposed tyranny of our grand narratives, free to choose, we have cut the thread to history and to the transcendent, and genuine communion is the first casualty.

It is nothing new that men and women tell lies, break promises, and deceive others, or that ideologues use propaganda to hijack meaning in the service of unholy ends, but our collective suspicion and distrust of language seems like something different. So while the partisan camps scream back and forth at one another, the rumbling remnants of deconstructionist rhetoric make it impossible to know where to begin to establish anything like common ground. It has become very, very hard to argue compellingly why any of this really matters because we supposedly now inhabit a "post-truth" era, a phantasmagoric mix of critical theory, raw power, populism, and serious cultural wobbliness. Faith in words erodes, language becomes unusably soft, and any claim to genuine meaning sets the supposedly respectable intellectuals hollering "Fascism!" I find cut-up, dislocated abbreviations and slogans that make up texts, tweets, and posts annoying, but that grand disintegration of meaning, the supposed arbitrariness of truth, the fundamental, seismic separation of words from flesh keep me up at night. Pilate's "What is truth?" unwittingly presages our postmodern, post-truth world. Can words actually carry meaning, or are they nothing more than blunt instruments of ideology and power? Can words convey truth, or is that an idea well past its best-before date?

—

I'm way out of my league here, I know. I am not a philosopher, theologian, or linguist. These are some seriously big issues I'm trying to work with here, and by this point you and I can both see I'm in way over my head. I'm trying to braid together a cord of language, meaning, and life itself, and if you tease out any one thread, the cord weakens or breaks. My attempt to articulate a philosophy of language in a few thousand words is reckless, but my quest is fairly urgent because what I'm trying to do mostly is persuade myself that we can still use language meaningfully, still say *something* real about our deepest longings and loves.

I'm a part-time lay minister at an Anglican church, and, until pandemic restrictions made it impossible, I would spend a lot of time over breakfasts at the local diner, pastoring people in my congregation, mostly young men, all of whom are struggling to discern some kind of genuinely meaningful calling amid the various roles they enact: the well-paid worker or the unemployed, single or married, father to some or childless. Over more than a decade I've had hundreds of conversations with a man I know who's been paying for sex for years, trying to break the habit he knows won't get him what he really wants. I've spent a lot less time but still a helluvalot of emotional energy with the middle-aged father of two who came to me to say he wanted to be a good father; meanwhile he was wandering further and further from home, searching for elusive happiness way outside the edge of domestic orbit until he finally drifted beyond the gravitational pull of his vows and left his wife for another woman, hoping for satisfaction in an ad hoc midlife Plan B. I've spent dozens of hours with a sensitive young man with a drinking problem who recently started the twelve steps. I remember conversations with the husband who told me he was going to leave his wife because he wanted to "play the field." For more than five years I've been having occasional breakfasts with the father with two young boys who stays with his wife not out of a speck of affection but simply because he gave his word; last month they decided to get a divorce. I have had countless cups of coffee with the husband trying to hold on to his marital vows as his wife's existence is decimated by mental illness, and many long, weighty talks with a young dad who recently tried to kill himself. And on and on and on it goes.

I sit there, dumbstruck by the gravity of their situations; dumbstruck, too, by the ubiquitous, underlying skepticism about language and meaning. I dig through my familiar religious vocabulary for words like "vows," "covenant," "faithfulness," "forgiveness," and "grace," and I'm not afraid to use the "s" word – "sin." But every one of those words feels tinny and malleable as soon it comes out of my mouth. "I have tried to learn the language of Christianity . . . and I feel the falseness," writes the poet Christian Wiman, "or no, not even that, a certain inaccuracy and slippage, as if the equipment were worn and inadequate – at every step." I'm not even confident using the word "love," which, it seems to me, is what *everything* hinges on. That great suspicion of language is in my head too, not just "out there" where story and meaning are so thoroughly distrusted. So I sit, listen, eat my breakfast, try to find ways to encourage, call them back to hard-to-picture promises of love and fidelity, what they could do, who they could be. I offer them my presence and promise to meet them when they need. I carry their trust, as much as they feel they can hand to me, and I offer communion, even as I struggle to find the words. And as they speak, I circle with them around the miracle of being, trying to see through the poisonous vapors of betrayal, disappointment, suffering, trying to find something real and solid to hold on to. I cannot take on the disintegrated meaning in any other way. I am here, I am for you, even if I am not on your side. I am recalled to the trust and care, meaning sustained with words over bottomless cups of coffee and the breakfast special at the corner diner.

Mukherjee shows that the truer the metaphors, the better the treatment; as in medicine, so in the rest of life. Critical theory and its more diffuse and far-reaching descendants, skepticism and cynicism, want to persuade me there is no truth, that our world is now *post*-truth so just get on with it, yet here we are, going on using words anyway, *as if* they truly do mean something. And when my pastoral charge tells his wife, "I don't love you; I haven't loved you for years. And today I am leaving you," some very real, tangible things take place. It's a kind of black-mass incantation of de-creation, calling into being a very real, weighty cluster of feelings, responses, actions, and consequences that carry on and on.

—

So that cultural slurry of philosophy and self-help sentiment that foists the burden of self-actualization on us, that we really can be true to ourselves, means people go around saying and doing all kinds of things that are simply untrue. And while I imagine a young, clever, critical-theory professor reading over my shoulder pointing out the gaping philosophical holes in my argument, it's the fumbling, mumbling young father across the table from me, coolly trying to justify his infidelity, or the weeping young man with his face in his hands trying to find the courage to stay with his wife, or the middle-aged man recounting his lifelong self-hatred and suicidal ideation that I need to attend to. There is weight and meaning in the words I hear them use. What do I say? What should I tell them? I can see how words can be used to manipulate, mislead, wound, deceive, and abuse, but I trust that words can also tell the truth. I suppose that's the elusive, mysterious thing I'm reaching at here: truth.

I like Mukherjee's book for all kinds of reasons, but what has stuck with me most is how the truthfulness of words is serious business. The metaphors we use and the words we choose have actual consequences. Mukherjee describes the metaphors and shows how the image we use tells us what to do because it helps us see what we're actually looking at. Metaphor is not simply poetic or decorative: it points to reality. Metaphor is a way to understand, and the better the metaphor, the better our understanding. "We may know that we are forming a conclusion on the basis of provisional or insufficient knowledge," writes Wendell Berry, "but we must act, nevertheless, on the basis of *final* conclusions." Life requires action and response, and some responses are better than others.

If to be human is to be a choosing being there's not much real point in carefully trying to weigh the value of words and images because the choices are preferences. Of course this is empirically false: most of who and what we are is bestowed, not chosen. Life is gratuitous, meaning is a gift, and neither is a sheer act of will. I didn't make myself, and neither did you. My parents made me the old-fashioned way, just like yours made you. I owe my capacity for language to others. I am a passable cook (I'd give myself a solid B+), but I grow and raise very little of my own ingredients. My backyard is too small for cattle; urban chickens aren't yet legal. I can't grow decent corn, and don't have the acreage for wheat. I don't make my own clothes or cars, and I didn't build the computer I'm using to type this, but even if I could, I would need the history of technology and electronics plus the industries of resource extraction, trade and transportation, processing and manufacturing.

You get the idea; it's the same for all of us. We depend on others; we need others. Our lives are not our own. We are connected, inextricably, to one another, not in touchy-feely imaginary ways but *actually*. Society is not a fluke, and it is not a blight. It is a gift. And ontology implies telos – what we *are* points to what we are *for*. If the human is anything anyone wants it to be, then do as you please. If life is a miracle, and we humans bearers of the image of God, we ought to care for one another. We are made for love, for binding together, for self-giving.

—

There's an authentic back-and-forth relationship between language and those who use it. Meaning is a product of a loving, mutual exchange. When we use words like "love" and "truth" and "life" with care, language can do extraordinary work, and do it well, even if it's impossible to figure out precisely how it all works. "You can't spend your whole life questioning whether language can represent reality," writes Wiman. "At some point you have to believe that the inadequacies of the words you use will be transcended by the faith with which you use them. You have to believe . . . or you have to go silent." In the opening pages of his masterpiece *Real Presences*, literary critic George Steiner writes, "Any coherent account of the capacity of human speech to communicate meaning and feeling is, in the final analysis, underwritten by the assumption of God's presence. . . . The conjecture is that 'God' is, not because our grammar is outworn; but that grammar lives and generates worlds because there is a wager on God." Meaning is possible because of the actual presence of God: an outrageous claim in our age of science and progress, skepticism, and cynicism. If meaning is arbitrary and the human is whatever we choose, care is optional. But, if a human being truly is a bearer of God's image, we really are our brother and sister's keeper.

I don't see how it is possible to practice that trust, as Wiman says we must, without God somehow being part of the equation. The stakes are way too high for me to simply shrug it off and say, "Truth is illusory; meaning is arbitrary," because the consequences of our speaking and living are very real: just ask the ex-wife of the man who has gone and changed his mind on "forsaking all others / till death do us part." Words matter, and meaning matters, because *life* matters, but that depends entirely on the presence of God and truth. Absent the Almighty, the whole enterprise is so weak because it is strung together in such arbitrary ways. I don't know about you, but I need something stronger than eeny-meeny-miny-moe to make sense of meaning. Go ahead and recount for me, in as much detail as you think necessary, all the historical blemishes, missteps, and failures of Christianity, but I bind myself to that broken tale anyway. I throw my lot in with the transcendent, with the tale of a Creator hard at work, brooding over all that has been made like a mother hen with her chicks. I bind my words and flesh to the Word made flesh, and I believe in order to understand because that polite, feeble consolation of pick-a-path meaning, you've-got-yours-and-I've-got-mine tears like a sheet of wet paper in the brutality or paralyzing, numbing boredom of life. I need something stronger than skepticism and doubt.

The Christian account of human origins, that we bear the image of an all-powerful God, and that our being is a miracle of Christ, the Word made flesh, are all completely strange ideas, unlikely, and difficult to believe, I know, but I find the rendering far more compelling, generous, rich, kind, and *beautiful* than the alternative immediately at hand. Like Puddleglum says to the Witch in C. S. Lewis's *The Silver Chair*, "Suppose we have only dreamed, or made up, all those things. . . . Suppose we have. Then all I can say is that, in that case, the made-up things seem a good deal more important than the real ones." Drawing together word and flesh – and Word and flesh – is poetic and metaphorically rich, but so much more as well. Because sometimes our words can be a matter of life – and death. ✝

February 19, 2021

ARGUMENTS FOR THE SAKE OF HEAVEN

JONATHAN HAIDT AND PETER WEHNER
IN CONVERSATION WITH CHERIE HARDER

On February 19, social psychologist Jonathan Haidt and New York Times columnist Peter Wehner sat down – remotely – with Cherie Harder of the Trinity Forum, for an extended conversation on healing our fragmented society. The Trinity Forum seeks to provide a space to engage the big questions of life in the context of faith, to offer programs like this online conversation to do so, and to come to better know the Author of the answers. What follows is an edited transcript of that conversation.

CHERIE HARDER: One of the questions it seems that we all have to wrestle with is how to understand and respond to the deep divisions that have, especially over the last year, so poisoned relationships, split families, fractured our society, and even undermined the practices of our democracy such that the secretary of state

JONATHAN HAIDT is a social psychologist at New York University's Stern School of Business, where his research focuses on the intuitive foundations of morality, and how morality varies across cultures. He is the author of *The Happiness Hypothesis: Finding Modern Truth in Ancient Wisdom*; *The Righteous Mind: Why Good People Are Divided by Politics and Religion*; and *The Coddling of the American Mind: How Good Intentions and Bad Ideas Are Setting Up a Generation for Failure.*

PETER WEHNER is vice president and senior fellow at the Ethics and Public Policy Center, a contributing opinion writer for the *New York Times,* and a contributing editor for *The Atlantic.* His books include *The Death of Politics* and *City of Man.*

recently called domestic division our greatest national-security vulnerability. How do we contend with the fear and the anger that we encounter both in our personal relationships and in the public square? And how do we envision and encourage means of bringing hope and healing to a hurting culture? Obviously, these are thorny issues, and there are no easy answers to them, but it's hard to imagine two people who have wrestled with those questions with more intellectual rigor, insight, or grace than our guests today.

Both of our guests are public intellectuals who hold very different religious and political convictions. They've both written prolifically, and sometimes provocatively, on controversial issues, and they've also developed a friendship over a shared commitment to the topic before us.

DEEP DIVISIONS AND SOCIAL MEDIA

CHERIE: We'll just dive right in. Jon, as you know, there have always been divisions in the country. But you have argued that there is something different going on now: that the cleavages are not only deep but different in nature—more ideologically extreme but less coherent, and perhaps arising less out of a loyalty to a group or idea than simply an aversion to the other side. What's going on?

JONATHAN HAIDT: I've been concerned about political polarization and how nasty things were getting, and my original research was on how morality varies across cultures or nations. Around 2004, I switched over to looking at the Left and the Right, which were becoming like different nations that lived in different worlds. And things have gotten a lot worse since then. There are many reasons, but I think the number-one reason why things just got so weird in the 2010s is changes in the media ecosystem.

The mid- to late twentieth century, the era of broadcasting, was the anomaly: for a brief time, there were only a few places—three major networks—where most Americans got most of their news; the centrism that that encouraged bled over into the "neutral" and centrist approach of newspapers in that era. Before then, newspapers were partisan and nasty. And after that brief respite, you get narrowcasting: cable TV, with Fox News in particular having a big impact on Republicans. And then you get the internet. And now we have a situation where anybody can find "evidence" for any conspiracy they want to confirm.

Then came social media, and the key thing that I've been focusing on is the way that social media changed between 2009 and 2011. Before then, it wasn't very polarizing. It was just, "Here are my friends, and here are the bands that I like." But then Facebook adds the Like button; Twitter adds the Retweet button. Now, suddenly, both platforms are really engaging their users, and they use algorithms based on that engagement to optimize the news feeds for engagement. Engagement is driven by passion—and, most typically, anger. Social media connects us, which you'd think would be good. Historically, it's good to be connected. But it connects us in a bizarre way: whatever we say is being rated by strangers. Now we are not just talking to each other, we're also talking to strangers who are having opinions about us. This is changing the gravitational force of the social universe. Everything got weird after 2012.

THE EPISTEMIC CRISIS

CHERIE: It seems like now, along with our polarization, we're not only divided over what is right or wrong, but increasingly over what is true or false. Why are we having such a hard time sorting out what has actually happened? And what happens when we the people can't figure out reality?

PETER WEHNER: A lot of bad stuff happens. If you have an epistemic crisis, if you can't agree on what's true and false, if you don't have a common set of facts, a common understanding of reality, then self-government gets very, very difficult because persuasion becomes impossible.

Social media added a kind of jet fuel to all of these issues, but the soil was, in a sense, prepared for some of this bad stuff to happen. The trend of polarization has been in motion for many decades. We've had geographic sorting. We've had two-party sorting. When I was growing up in the 1980s, you had liberal Republicans like Chuck Percy, Bob Packwood, and Mark

Hatfield, and you had conservative Democrats like Joe Lieberman and Daniel Patrick Moynihan. You don't have that anymore. So the two parties began to polarize, and that was a problem. And then you have alienation, a loss of authority, isolation.

The social soil was ready for some of these more pernicious seeds to take root. The political conversations I have with people today are just profoundly different than they were fifteen or twenty years ago. Some of it is located in what Jon mentioned: conspiracy theories have always existed, but now people can create a community online that lives in a different epistemic universe. Links that people send each other: well, seeing things online makes it feel as though those things have the force of authority. There is also a phenomenon called affective polarization: what now binds people to their political tribe or religious tribe is not primarily a feeling of affirmation for their side as much as a distrust, alienation, and hatred for the other side. We demonize each other; we dehumanize each other. In the past, there would be a sense of, "look, we disagree on issues," but it wasn't an indictment of a person in terms of their character. Now it is, and our modes of discourse fortify those impressions we have of each other.

AFFECTIVE POLARIZATION

JONATHAN: The interesting thing is that Americans are not getting more polarized in terms of their beliefs about issues. We're not really further apart. The polarization is affective – that is, it's emotional. We don't disagree more about policy matters or ideas, we just hate each other more. And that's really important to keep your eye on, because when you really hate someone, you will believe anything that casts them in a bad light; you're less likely to check sources. You could say that this made us uniquely vulnerable to Russian manipulation, but it turns out, the Russians, you know, they put some fake stuff in, but they didn't actually need to put fake stuff in. They didn't need the bots. We were doing this to ourselves more effectively than they could. A big study at MIT showed that basically Americans hated each other so much by 2016 that they used whatever ammunition they had.

The other new thing is the power of massively distributed video production. Watching a video about a conspiracy theory, with someone explaining it, tends to create a greater affective response than, say, reading a mimeographed sheet about that conspiracy. So the affective polarization, the hatred, is way up, and that drives everything else.

There are a couple of additional reasons for this increase in hatred. There are actually so many of them that it's a really fun time to be a social scientist, and a really scary time to be an American. The media change that we were talking about is the first thing. The second major factor is the loss of a common enemy. The best way to unify people is to have Pearl Harbor be attacked, or to have a 9/11; throughout the twentieth century we had very clear enemies, and after 1989, thank God, that ended. And without a common enemy, things kind of come apart. Third, rising education levels are a risk factor for polarization: people with a college degree are much more involved in symbolic issues, while working-class people are more concerned about bread-and-butter issues. They're less likely to get all involved in the nuclear freeze, or in things that don't directly concern their interests. Fourth, there's rising diversity. We had very low diversity and very low immigration for much of the twentieth century. And while diversity is great in many ways for the economy and for the creativity of industry, it does reduce social capital and trust unless managed very, very well. And we have not often managed it very, very well.

So we have a more educated public on a more outrage-inducing media platform, without any common enemy, and with eroded levels of social capital and social trust. And now we are each others' enemies. We're always going to do the good-evil game, but we do it against each other rather than aiming it externally. And all this has come to a head.

FOUNDATIONS OF IDENTITY

CHERIE: So our politics are growing much more extreme, but our identities are also growing more linked to our politics. I think it was a colleague of Jonathan's who did a study recently which found that what used to be the foundations of our identity, the "unmoved movers," were our religion, ethnicity, and gender identity: these shaped our politics. Now, the force is frequently in the other direction: political identity is primary, and politics can change those other identities. What has thinned out our nonpolitical identities such that they are now increasingly subsumed by the political?

PETER: There has been an attenuation of what might be called identity-forming institutions in people's lives. Church is one of them, although it's not the only one. Part of that is a broader trend of mistrust toward institutions and a movement toward radical, extreme individualism. And that's a philosophical current that's been in motion for a long time, but picked up a lot of momentum, particularly in the mid and late sixties. It wasn't a trend that was without benefits. Some tremendous injustices were corrected by this movement. But I think it went too far. People became isolated, and institutions don't have the shaping influence that they used to have. And then a lot of the people who run institutions, whether they're political, religious, or educational, view them, as our friend Yuval Levin has talked about, as performative rather than formative. We have people leading institutions who don't see their task as soul-shaping; instead, these institutions are platforms for their own performance.

So the institutions began to fail in their tasks of identity formation, and at the same time, political movements and parties began to take over those tasks. I'm sure you've both had this experience: when you have conversations about differences on political issues today, frequently you get a sense with a lot of people that they feel their identity is under attack by your disagreeing with them. That's very tricky: if you as an individual feel like your core identity is being attacked by somebody, the armor goes up. The swords are drawn. And it's not going to end well unless one of the people involved in that conversation has the capacity to steer it in a more constructive way.

A GOD-SHAPED HOLE

JONATHAN: Political scientists called attention in the 2010s to an increase in the degree to which politics is identity and performance.

This is the theme of Ezra Klein's *Why We're Polarized.* Politics has become identity. What we haven't talked about so far is the psychology of religion. The subtitle of my book is *Why Good People Are Divided by Politics and Religion,* because I trace both back to our original human nature and the evolutionary processes that made us good at being in groups and at competing with other groups. And we see that play out in the arenas of both politics and religion. Even though I'm a Jewish atheist, and I say so in the book, I've been invited to speak at a lot of Christian colleges and organizations, and it was in preparing to speak at the Council of Christian Colleges and Universities that I finally looked up that quote I'd heard from Pascal, "There is a God-shaped hole in the heart of each man." It's a commonly cited quote, but it's not complete, and the translation is off. Here's what Pascal actually wrote, which is even more helpful. He said, "There was once in man a true happiness, of which all that now remains is the empty print and trace. This he tries in vain to fill with everything around him, though none can help since this infinite abyss can be filled only with an infinite and immutable object, in other words, by God himself."

That quote gives you a much richer sense of that hunger; people are trying to pull something in. They have an emptiness, and I think that's what we're seeing as Christianity has receded from not just public life but individual people's lives. Churchgoing is down. The numbers for participation in religious congregations in America are down. By far the fastest-rising category is "spiritual but not religious." Well, if you're spiritual but not religious, you're probably seeking out that ultimate meaning somewhere, and it's going to be hard for you to see the political campaigns to fight injustice as anything other than ultimate. As traditional religion has receded from the lives of people who still experience themselves as spiritual—well, they're hungry. As I see it, politics has taken that place. We can see that in the cultish nature of some of today's Right. Donald Trump was a cult of personality. In my world, in universities and on the left, wokeness is playing a similar role, though without the personality-cult aspect. John McWhorter and many others have been writing about how this new political movement on the left has all the signs not just of religion but of Christianity specifically: of original sin, and the quest for absolution.

SLIVERS OF TRUTH

CHERIE: Let's talk about truth-telling. One of the things you have both written about is something you've called epistemological modesty. It sounds a little bit like squishiness or relativism, like: who's to say what is true? And yet both of you are well known for at times rather fiercely articulating a point of view you believe to be true. So what is epistemological modesty? Pete, how in your mind does it relate to faithful ways of knowing?

PETER: Steve Hayner was a key figure in my life, a very close friend. He was a minister at University Presbyterian Church as I was beginning my Christian journey. Steve was there for me at every key moment in my life, and through periods of hardship and grief too. Steve died in 2014 of pancreatic cancer, and in our last conversation, Steve said that he believed in objective truth, but he held lightly to his ability to perceive truth; that one way to be able to get at truth more closely is to make room for other perspectives, to make room for others at the table. Cindy, my wife, said that she had grown up in a period in which there was a sense that being right was what mattered most, but that in order to find reality, we have to be open to being wrong.

So the way I understand this is that there is an objective truth, but there's a subjective means to that pursuit of truth. And none of us has it completely right. This is a biblical concept, by the way. Paul writes in 1 Corinthians that we see through a glass darkly, but then, after death, we will see God face-to-face. Until then, our understanding is provisional. Indeed, Christian theology notes that our ability to perceive reality has been touched by some degree of corruption, as every part of us has, and in any case we are limited creatures: none of us can see truth as it fully is. The best we can do is to see slivers of truth or part of truth.

But what's essential is to have people in your life who can help you to see what you would otherwise not see. We all have blind spots, and we all have a certain life experience, family of origin, countries that we come from, race, gender, and all of those things shape us, and they shape the way we perceive things. I think our problem is the notion that the way I perceive things is the way they are and the way other people perceive them is not. Taken to its extreme this can become relativism; the idea that there's no objective truth or that it's utterly inaccessible. Everything depends on perspective; we create our own realities. I'm certainly not there. But—and this too is a biblical idea—it's important to have people in your life, and they have to be people who have standing in your life that you trust, who can help you to see things you wouldn't otherwise see.

Part of this is the question of how you view the enterprise of truth-seeking itself, right? Take C. S. Lewis and Owen Barfield. Lewis writes in *Surprised by Joy* about the idea of "first" and "second" friends. For him, Arthur Greeves was the first friend. That's your alter ego: You start the sentence and your friend can complete it. Owen Barfield was a very different person, a second friend, and Lewis described this kind of friendship as one where you read all the same books, but your friend draws what you see as all the wrong conclusions from the books. These are the kinds of friendships we have with people of very different habits of mind. Lewis and Barfield had a deep, forty-year friendship. Lewis describes the conversations they had: they would "go at it hammer and tongs" late into the night. You could feel the weight of the power of the blows of the other person. But over time, they developed this mutual admiration and affection, and Barfield said that Lewis and he, through all of those debates, never debated for victory. They debated for truth.

That's a huge difference. We debate most of the time for victory. We think, "I've got to defend my position, and I'm going to go at anybody who's against it," rather than thinking, what does that person see that maybe I need to hear? Maybe they won't fundamentally change my view, but maybe I'll understand them differently. Maybe their hierarchy of values is different from mine, and that's why they end up at a different position. But Jon knows more about this stuff than I do.

ARGUMENTS FOR THE SAKE OF HEAVEN

JONATHAN: The Jewish tradition is based very much on argumentation; the Talmudic tradition is scholars arguing. And they have a phrase, I forget what it is in Hebrew, but it translates to "arguments for the sake of heaven." So they recognize that through argumentation—in the right circumstances and by religious scholars who are bound together, with their daughters probably married into each other's families, all of that stuff—if you have the right relationships, then arguments get you closer to divine truth. But they're certainly cognizant that most arguments are not like that.

I think that the key concept here is confirmation bias, motivated reasoning. Once you recognize that we all do it, that we all do it automatically and passionately, then you think, okay, what's the cure for that? And nobody has ever found a kind of training that makes people stop doing that. The only cure for it is other people who have a different confirmation bias. And if you're in the right relationship with them, and Pete was describing those relationships, then you make progress toward heaven, as it were.

Thinking this way has really helped me understand what it means to be a centrist. I consider myself a centrist, a centrist Democrat, I would say. You know, people think, oh, centrist, so we're going to, you know, half-condemn Nazis or we're going to be in the middle on everything? No, it's a realization that when you are a member of a team that's passionate, you're almost guaranteed to not find truth. Those epistemic correction mechanisms are not working in your passionate team. This is a modern restatement of John Stuart Mill's case for free speech in *On Liberty*: you have to have that competition of perspectives. It doesn't mean you always come out in the middle, but you've got to consider multiple perspectives.

HOPE AND HEALING

CHERIE: We've talked a lot about some of the centrifugal forces pulling us apart. There are a lot of people hurting, a lot of people who have experienced eroded or broken relationships as a result of conflict and difference. How can we individually, and also within the institutions and communities that we are in, be agents of hope and healing?

JONATHAN: One of the insights that I got from reading conservative writers is their emphasis on low- and mid-level institutions. People on the left tend to focus on the federal government, and then there are individual activists. This is the vision of the French Revolution, where they tried to wipe out everything in between: guilds, religious institutions, and so on. But those are the things that make for a good civil society.

With this culture war that we have now, the politics that had so invaded college campuses – they've been there all along, but they really blew up in 2015, and I wrote an essay, "The Coddling of the American Mind" with Greg Lukianoff in 2015 about these things – have now flooded into companies, into high schools, even middle schools.

These institutions used to be places where people have a job to do; and it is okay to do your job alongside people with different political opinions. But when we make everything about political identity, as is now happening in a lot of companies and schools, things go sour. High schools and middle schools commit to "anti-racism." This sounds good, and it is of course great to be against racism, but what is meant in this context is "anti-racism" as it is understood in the particular ideology of, for example, Ibram X. Kendi, in which the whole of reality is understood as conflict between groups, which is an ideology with which it's perfectly legitimate to disagree: not to agree with Kendi's particular analysis does not mean that you're a racist or that you are not against racism.

We need to find ways to address racism that don't polarize people. We need to find ways in which employees can have a voice in their companies, but yet they don't bring in all of their personal political agendas and demand that the leadership acknowledge their values. We are in danger of really blowing apart here. And we need to take action to avoid that, in our places of work or our schools, in our churches or synagogues.

There are so many cases where there's a conflict with someone, but part of us wants to make up, or will readily accept an overture. So the best piece of advice I can give is to be the first one to make that overture. In every argument, the other person is right about something. They might not be right about the thing that you're centrally focused on, but that's kind of the point: we're always centrally focused on slightly different things. So if you can acknowledge, you know, "I was pretty harsh with you, and I think when you said 'X' you're actually right about that." It's amazing what happens when you acknowledge that the person is partially right. By the power of reciprocity, they will often come right back and say, "Yeah, you know, I overreacted. I was angry and I'm sorry; you were right about Y." Humans are tribal. We are easily provoked into conflict, but part of being tribal is also being really good at reconciliation. Be the first one to make the first move.

PETER: One thing we can do is simply to ask questions; try and understand where the other person is coming from. Don't assume you know what they think or what their motivations are, and when they tell you, don't assume bad faith.

RELATIONSHIPS THAT SURVIVE DIFFERENCE

CHERIE: We're going to turn to questions from our viewers. Michael Murray asks, "What's involved in building relationships that are strong enough to deal with intense differences?"

PETER: Sometimes you find out in intense political times just how deep those relationships go. If you're in a relationship that is only about political agreement, that can be shifting sand. Another story about Steve Hayner. At one point, Steve and I had what I thought was going to be a difference on a political matter. And I wrote Steve because I was worried about it, and he wrote me back and he said, "Pete, I can't imagine there's any issue I would ever not love you over." If you have a relationship like that, it'll survive political differences.

PERFORMANCE-BASED DEBATES

CHERIE: From Randall Paul and Deborah Christiansen: How do we debate the most important issues of the day, especially issues on which there are irreconcilable ideals that can't honestly be compromised involved? How do we do it with civility in the midst of such a highly polarized and hyperbolic environment?

JONATHAN: The older ideal of "let's all get together and talk," an all-company meeting where everyone's encouraged to speak up, that kind of thing, is no longer really possible or advisable. People come to every public conversation knowing that what they say might be tweeted out of context; the cost can be very high. That line between what we're doing here in our company or our school, and my life on social media, well, there's no longer a lot of a wall between them. I think Pete used the phrase "performative politics." Especially for young people who grew up with social media, everything is performance, and so there's really no point in having a debate or discussion with a lot of people because it's going to turn into a performance and people can't be honest. So you have to have very small groups and a commitment that nobody's going to record this or nobody's going to report it out. It's very hard. The more we are tied together, the harder it is to talk, unfortunately.

PETER: One very good exercise in discussion is that before a debate, each person debating has to express the view of the other person in a way that the other person will say, yes, you understand what I believe and why. The second exercise is simply to be able to identify what the differences are and name them, not necessarily to reconcile them, but to say: this is where our points of departure are. The third is more of an understanding: the understanding that disagreement is okay: you can hold a different view and still be a good person.

A QUESTION FROM MIDDLEBURY

CHERIE: Maggie Connelly writes from Middlebury College that she's in the middle of your book, Jonathan, *The Coddling of The American Mind*, the section in which you discuss an incident that took place at Middlebury. "I find your book to be extremely insightful to my current environment," she says. "What is your best advice for a student like me, in the heat of it, who seeks to find truth and fight against extremism, but also fears social alienation?"

JONATHAN: The background to this is that Middlebury had one of the major widely reported blow ups; the mood is very similar at a lot of America's top liberal arts colleges. What I would say is, if you are not part of the dominant political group, or even if you are, but you see that there are issues or difficulties, don't just keep your head down and say nothing. I met one student who said her motto is "silence is safer"; just don't say anything. Don't let that be your motto. But be careful about speaking up in a public setting where everyone else is performing, or you could be strung up as a witch. If you speak to people privately, you'll find that people are actually much more open and nuanced in their thinking one-on-one than they are when they're performing. Be very wary of that. If you're on the right, you can't avoid talking to lots of people on the left. But if you're on the left, you're going to have to seek out those smaller groups: seek out the people on the right because they're the ones who are going to help you grow. It's those differences that help you grow.

CHRISTIANS IN THE PUBLIC SQUARE

CHERIE: Brad Edwards writes that it's very popular to beat up on social media as the cause of polarization. Is it a cause, or is it only amplifying what's already there? And can you talk about how the church, how Christians, can mitigate those effects in the public square?

PETER: So many of these problems predate this moment, or the last five years. Geographic sorting, the political parties becoming more polarized, and the fracturing of information, as we discussed. What can Christians do about it? I think the first thing I would say is, I would be grateful if Christians first stop making things worse, stop being accelerants to these worse tendencies. What can be done to actually heal the breach? Paul uses the phrase "ministry of reconciliation," and Christ is referred to as breaking down the dividing walls between peoples: this is part of what we need to do.

Then, of course, there's this concept of grace. As far as I know, grace in the technical theological sense is an idea that's specific to Christianity. We have received grace, in that sense, and in the more ordinary sense, that should allow us to demonstrate grace in how we conduct ourselves. Philip Yancey is a friend of mine; we were exchanging notes the other day, and he referred to a phrase from Martin Luther King Jr.: We need to be "weapons of grace." When a watching world sees people of Christian faith manifest grace, it is the thing that most breaks through. Even if they themselves aren't Christians or don't become Christians, they see it, and they will say there's something to that that's important. That involves having one's affections and hearts won over to Christ.

JONATHAN: Well, if everybody on social media were to radiate grace, I do agree that it would be a lot better. But short of that, I think that major structural reforms are probably what we need. I think the questioner is right that people love to beat up on social media, and I'm one of those people. I always note that social media does a lot of good things. It creates a lot of value for others. So I'm not saying, oh, it's terrible, we've got to go back to the 1990s. But I think that we are wired up now in a way that is radically different from how we were even in 2007 or 2008. It really changed between 2009 and 2012. The optimistic view is that this is like when they invented the printing press and we had a couple hundred years of religious war, but ultimately we learned to deal with information flowing all around, including propaganda. So odds are that in ten or twenty years, things will be better in most ways, as Steven Pinker has argued has been the trend in general. And odds are social media, I think, will be more constructive. But we have been on a rough ride these last five to eight years, and I think that could go for the rest of the 2020s. It remains to be seen. So for now, I will continue beating up on, while also praising, social media.

THE AMERICAN ELITE AND THE POPULACE

CHERIE: Patrick Wilson asks, and I paraphrase: The great historian Gertrude Himmelfarb made much of the Victorian elite's desire to reform themselves and remoralize themselves. She argued that this effort, much maligned today, was actually a healthy revulsion by learned Christian people, by what we might call elites, against decadence and coarseness, and was oriented toward the idea that the poor had a claim on us, and were even in some ways moral superiors. Does this apply to your understanding of our current moment?

JONATHAN: Just in the last month or two, I've realized that I have left out the role of corrupt and incompetent elites in my list of reasons why we're getting more polarized. The reason I've seen this is due to the work of three great thinkers who have really been pointing to elites as part of the problem.

Peter Turchin, with his mathematical analysis of history, says that a repeated historical pattern is that you get these periods of dislocation and conflict with three conditions, one of which is a surplus of elites. Too many college grads and not enough places of prestige for them. So they try to get followers, try to make a name for themselves. Michael Lind, a really brilliant political commentator, is savage on the current elites and how they've left working people behind. And the third is Martin Gurri; his book *The Revolt of the Public and the Crisis of Authority in the New Millennium* is extremely good on this.

The elites in the Victorian times, you can say well, they were aristocrats; or at least inherited bourgeois: they were elite because of their heritage and who their father was, and isn't that undemocratic. But in America and the UK and other countries since the 1980s or 1990s, the elite are the people who did really well on exams. We sort people on this basis beginning in high school. By the time you get to the top, you think you earned it, that you deserved it, that you are smarter and worked harder and are better. Today's elites aren't aristocrats: they're meritocrats. They really have a sense that they earned it. And that means that they have no sense of obligation or of being given something: they can go off to their gated communities or their islands to wait out Covid with a clear conscience. So, yes, I think it would be great to look back to previous periods where the elites took responsibility and took some blame upon themselves and stopped having so much contempt for the masses.

PETER: Elites have gotten a lot wrong. Some of the social divisions we've been talking about during this conversation are due to the failures of elites, including in the political class, which created a major counterreaction. There is an attitude of the elites toward the populace—and particularly conservatives and often people of faith—that can be patronizing and contemptuous.

There were so many projects after Trump: people trying to understand Trump voters. I was at an event in November 2016 with Arlie Hochschild, a sociologist who had gone to the bayou country in Louisiana and then wrote a book called *Strangers in Their Own Land*. She was struck by how kind they were to her personally, but they feel dishonored and disrespected. And she said that Donald Trump for them is an antidote to that kind of dishonor that they feel. So there is undoubtedly an attitude of elites toward others that has contributed to this.

There's a tendency to pick sides. It's the elites or it's the masses who are to blame. And, you know, the masses have a lot to answer for too. I'm a conservative, not a populist. And if you go back from Burke to the founding, to Madison, Burke, and then to Lincoln's Lyceum speech in 1838, all of them warned about the danger of mob mentality and the masses. The reason we're a republic and not a democracy is so that we "filter, enlarge, and refine," in the words of Madison, the public view. I think there's a tendency sometimes on the right to excuse some inexcusable behavior among the masses and say, well, they're angry, they have grievances. Well, yes and no. In the end, people are responsible for their actions, grievances or no, and I think some of this has just gotten out of control. Everybody is a part of the problem, everybody has a piece of the action, which means everybody has to be a part of the solution.

CHERIE: I'd like to give each of you a last word to close out our conversation. Jonathan, the floor is yours.

JONATHAN: So, given that what you are trying to do here is to bring forward the best of Christian thought, I could certainly end with the quote that I've used throughout my career studying moral psychology, which is, "Why do you see the speck in your neighbor's eye you did not notice the log in your own?" And that is such a deep piece of wisdom. But I think it's important to note that this is a great truth that we get from many of the world's religions: we are too judgmental, too quick to attack each other. We need to slow down and be more forgiving. So I'll end with this wonderful quote from a Chinese Zen master, Sengcan, in the sixth century. He wrote, "The perfect way is only difficult for those who pick and choose. Do not like, do not dislike. All will then be clear. Make a hairbreadth difference and heaven and earth are set apart. If you want the truth to stand clear before you, never be for or against. The struggle between for and against is the mind's worst disease."

PETER: Cherie, thanks for hosting this. In an era in which institutions are failing, the Trinity Forum is a beacon. I really appreciate what you're doing, and it's been a real honor to be with you and with Jon. My quote is from a poet, Christian Wiman, who wrote a book called *My Bright Abyss*. Wiman says:

> The spiritual efficacy of all encounters is determined by the amount of personal ego that is in play. If two people meet and disagree fiercely about theological matters, but agree, silently or otherwise, that God's love creates and sustains human love and whatever else may be said of God is subsidiary to this truth, then even out of what seems great friction, there may emerge a peace that though it may not end the dispute, though neither party may be convinced of the other's position, nevertheless enters and nourishes one's notion of a relationship with God. With this radical openness, all arguments about God are not simply pointless, but pernicious, for each person is in thrall to some lesser conception of ultimate truth, and asserts not love, but less, and not God, but himself. ✝

SPRING

Dhananjay Jagannathan

Phil Christman

Gregory Thompson

Duke Kwon

Carlo Lancellotti

Tara Isabella Burton

Charles C. Camosy

Joseph M. Keegin

Luke Bretherton

Tobias Cremer

Elayne Allen

Anne Snyder

Susannah Black

March 10, 2021

COURAGE, CITIZENSHIP, AND THE LIMITS OF AUTONOMY

DHANANJAY JAGANNATHAN

OVER THE PAST few weeks I have been volunteering at one of the largest vaccination sites in Manhattan, run by New York Presbyterian Hospital and located at the Washington Heights Armory, which in more ordinary times is a track-and-field complex. The site's administrators knew they could not staff the effort alone, so in January they recruited volunteers from Columbia University, whose medical center operates in tandem with the hospital. I signed up right away.

Most of my fellow volunteers seem to have a background in medicine or at least medical research, but others, like me, do not. I decided to plunge into the abyss of electronic medical records and volunteer as a patient-intake registrar. My task is to help patients complete a medical questionnaire and ensure their demographic and insurance information is recorded in the hospital's systems. My favorite part of the job is handing each person their vaccination card at the end of the process, a fragile piece of card stock that represents, perhaps, a ticket to relative freedom or at least tangible proof of the whirlwind, lifesaving experience of receiving the vaccine.

The Armory is one of the few indoor spaces I have been during the pandemic where I feel safe, with the cavernous roof rising high

DHANANJAY JAGANNATHAN teaches philosophy and classical studies at Columbia University. His academic interests include ancient Greek and Roman philosophy, ethics, political philosophy, and the philosophy of literature. He has written for *Plough Quarterly* and *Earth & Altar*.

above the track and strict protocols everywhere in effect. Still, before my first shift, I was nervous to be interacting with so many people: we've had a year to be trained to be afraid of each other, physically.

What I discovered was a deep well of solidarity, springing up here in my own community to nourish me. I did not know I had been in the desert. The eagerness of our mostly elderly patients, the compassion of the medical and support staff, and the dedication of my fellow volunteers—all these blend into an atmosphere of hope and the renewal of life.

The truth that we need one another, practically and existentially, has become steadily more vivid during this pandemic. First, we needed one another to stay home, except for those of us who keep our community alive. Then and even now, we have needed one another to be prudent—to follow public health guidelines, to be watchful of our breath lest it endanger others.

Now especially, we need one another to be brave.

—

Courage is a dazzlingly complicated quality of character. A tempting thought, explored in many of Plato's dialogues, is that courage might be a sort of endurance. The reason that courage resembles endurance is that, in order to be courageous, you must be willing to resist the ongoing temptation to flee danger. But, as Socrates points out, some who are capable of enduring danger are not necessarily courageous, most notably professionals with special training in managing predictable risks. The somewhat mysterious Platonic example is well-divers; we might think instead of electricians, who dare to do what we would not because they know how to do the job safely.

In our present circumstances, endurance and courage look very far apart indeed. All of us have endured an ever-present and invisible danger for a year or more. Yet, especially for the most privileged among us, the virus has become a manageable risk, one we are "living with," as the saying goes, not avoiding altogether.

What, then, is courage?

The conversation in Plato's *Laches* suggests that for someone to have genuine courage they need not only endurance but also a wise appreciation of "what is worth fearing and what is worth daring."

The dialogue leaves it unsettled whether courage is endurance transformed by the presence of wisdom or simply is this wisdom alone. But in either case, it will turn out that the courageous person has a discerning eye for what is precious in human life and the times when even this must be given up.

In the context of a largely stable liberal political order where conflict is minimal and warfare is outsourced, our imaginative conception of courage tends to be rather narrow. Courage is reserved as a term of praise for extraordinary people in extraordinary moments, especially professionals like firefighters or nurses who have defined social duties and, for that reason, have the chance to exceed these duties, at least on occasion.

It is less well appreciated that we *all* have social duties, that courage is demanded of us as human beings living together, who must face risks not only for our own sake but also for the sake of the common good. This fact tends to be occluded because wisdom is not generally demanded of the liberal political subject, except the occasional wisdom to elect leaders wiser than we are. Accordingly, the kind of courage infused with wisdom is also not generally demanded of us. But the current state of the pandemic offers an especially important context for its exercise.

—

The vaccines that are our best and perhaps only hope for a return to more normal social life, an end to death and disease but also an end to an isolation that has taken a grievous toll we have scarcely begun to measure, are a wholly novel medical treatment for this novel virus. The Pfizer and Moderna vaccines, in particular, are based on an mRNA delivery system that is itself new. The clinical studies that proved their safety and efficacy were undertaken with almost miraculous speed. There is no question, to my mind, that these vaccines are safe despite the emergency authorization of their use, but neither has there been long-term study of their effects.

At the same time, our medical culture prizes patient autonomy. To some extent, the turn to autonomy has been salubrious, preventing doctors from dictating treatment to patients without adequate consultation. This shift has been especially important given the biases that mar modern medicine, which is characterized by scientific expertise and specialization and so also by the arrogance that accompanies these features everywhere in life.

The distribution of the vaccine has been seen, in part, as an aggregate of decisions by individuals to opt in as an exercise of such autonomy. This framing of the solution to our public health crisis introduces a perplexity: it is quite possible that vaccination will fail to achieve its core aims unless enough of the population opts in. Even those already vaccinated are waiting for so-called herd immunity, perhaps more aptly described as communal protection, the phenomenon whereby any given interaction is vastly safer because virtually all chains of transmission are interrupted.

It would be better, therefore, to think of vaccination for this virus as a social duty, rather than as a merely personal choice. There are some who cannot receive the vaccine or will not be able to for some time yet, not least younger children for whom approval awaits further clinical trials.

The doctrine of patient autonomy holds that every person has the right to refuse medical treatment. But we must be able to say also that people who are, for one reason or another, afraid to be vaccinated and thereby refuse when their turn comes are doing a harm to the rest of us. That is why we need courage to survive this pandemic, not just the sort of courage that has been shown by nurses and grocery-store workers, but the courage demanded of each one of us.

—

My claim about vaccination fears may seem acceptable in abstract form, but it poses serious problems when introduced to our cultural and political context. In the United States, there are two groups of people in particular whose vaccine hesitancy has been well-documented.

The first group is black people, many of whom are skeptical of vaccination because of the long history of both malign treatment and harmful neglect by the medical profession, the horror of the Tuskegee experiments serving as an example of the former and the appallingly high rate of maternal mortality indicating the latter. The fears of black people to go first in the queue to be vaccinated—as nursing-home workers, for instance, have been asked to do—are not outrageous. The profound and uncorrected failures of the medical professions are primarily to blame for this lack of trust.

Still, once evidence emerges that the vaccines are safe, not just in clinical trials, but in widescale distribution, vaccine hesitancy grounded in such a generic fear will become increasingly unreasonable. It is incumbent on both the medical and political establishments and community leaders to make this evidence manifest.

As vaccination rates for black Americans continue to lag, it is also incumbent on politicians not to treat vaccine hesitancy as the sole reason, given the inequities that have marred the early phase of distribution. At the Armory, I have witnessed firsthand the excitement of black residents of Washington Heights and Harlem to receive the vaccine, one of whom recently showed me a video he was posting on social media to encourage others to follow in his footsteps when they could.

The second group of those with high rates of vaccine hesitancy are white Republicans, especially Trump supporters. This is to be expected when nearly every aspect of the public health response, from mask guidance to lockdowns to the very reporting of hospitalizations and deaths, has become subject to extreme partisan polarization in the United States. Moreover, this group is generally skeptical of institutions, even more so than other Americans. It is no surprise, then, that the Trump movement has absorbed anti-vaccine sentiment into the miasma of conspiracy theories that maintain it.

An underappreciated aspect of partisan polarization is the way that the qualities of character prized by different groups have come apart. For years, it was conservatives on the right who insisted that people did not have the untrammeled right to do whatever they wanted because of negative social consequences. The Trump movement is not conservative in this way, and many of its most extreme members, to the extent they have any ideology at all, are right-libertarians.

Right-libertarians do, of course, have a conception of courage, which in the American context is particularly associated with the need to resist the incipient tyranny of government. Resisting tyranny is certainly an occasion for courage, but the misapprehension of tyranny in the bureaucratic state or the vicissitudes of democratic politics has instead become an occasion for delusive heroism, as the political violence at the Capitol on January 6 so vividly illustrated.

More broadly, the common good shrinks, in the libertarian worldview, to the private sphere, to one's family and friends. The possibility that courage, rightly ordered, serves others thereby vanishes. Even leaving aside the fantasy that we can opt out of our interdependence, we should reject the libertarian vision of courage, not only for its theoretical shortcomings but also for the damage it does to our hope for an escape from this pandemic.

As I noted earlier, however, liberals – whether on the center-right or the center-left – tend not to emphasize the need for courage in our common life. While liberals, unlike libertarians, generally recognize that autonomy and freedom have their limits, the articulation of these limits requires a positive and robust conception of the common good (and, to a degree, of human nature) that liberalism eschews. Worse yet, the prevailing liberal political order asks only some to sacrifice for others, as it has with essential workers during this pandemic, a position that amounts to "virtues for thee and not for me."

What's more, the urban professional avatars of this order, especially of a left-liberal stripe, have sometimes tended to revel in a sanctimony that sees their own privileged position as a universal experience. This sanctimony minimizes the depth of the loss that we all have experienced in staying apart this year, treating as a mere annoyance our grief over the absence of the ordinary goods of physical communion: seeing our families, sharing our meals, hugging our friends.

Neither the libertarian position, that courage is preservative of the self, nor the liberal position, that only some people in our society need courage, can make sense of the qualities of character the present crisis demands.

As the ancient philosophers continually emphasize, the virtues only get their meaning from their social use. Nevertheless, these qualities, including courage, do not demand self-abnegation. As Aristotle argues, it is the courageous who are most keenly aware of the value of their own lives.

I am not saying, then, that we simply need people to behave more altruistically in the face of the pandemic, to give up their autonomy and get vaccinated for the sake of others. Rather, what we need is collective and individual wisdom, or in other words, the imagination to see ourselves as creatures who are vulnerable and called on to act in the face of this shared vulnerability.

———

An important consequence of the pandemic is that moral and political reflection have been forced to become concrete, not least because the differences in the worldviews held by our political leaders can be measured in death and devastation. But especially for those of us who have been largely stuck at home for a year, a space has opened up to think about what we want our individual and collective lives to be like when this is all over.

Talk of our path out of the pandemic has focused on the revival of economic life, not unreasonably given how many are out of work or otherwise suffering in material terms. Also important is the question of how we will learn again to be with one another, to occupy the same space, the same air, without unreasonable fear. Everyday life will require us to navigate a path between reckless risk-taking and timorous retreat. Ordinary acts of intimacy and sociality will demand a proper appreciation of their value.

For my own part, in spending time with the elderly and others of those most at risk in my community at the vaccination site, I have come to see better the preciousness of life in its essential vulnerability. To live without this awareness is to deaden oneself to the sense of what is worth fearing and what is worth daring. If endurance transformed by wisdom is something like courage, then fear transformed by wisdom is, perhaps, reverence.

April 9, 2021

HOW TO BE WHITE

PHIL CHRISTMAN

IT SEEMS THAT we are called to do something about whiteness. What that something we are called to do is, and what that whiteness is that we are called to do it to, or about, are some of the questions that it is difficult to ask. To speak in this way feels like treading in some way on ground that is cursed. Is there a way to avoid invoking this curse?

It is not enough to be against racism – we must *abolish* whiteness itself. As we figure out how to do that, we can, in the meantime, *abandon, unlearn, undo, undermine, divest* from, or *dismantle* it. If we do not, at the moment, feel up to those projects, we might consider *interrupting, interrogating,* or *dreaming of a self beyond* it. This all sounds like it would involve paying whiteness a great deal of attention. But hold on – we must also *decenter* it, while not forgetting to *see* it, *address* it, *own* it, and *watch it work.* (The author who asks us to decenter it remarks, perhaps helpfully, that decentering it will require focusing on it.) If all that effort leaves us winded, we might turn ourselves to the more modest projects of *defining* and *reinventing* it – this time in a nice way, presumably. Having done this, we could then be pardoned if we wished to *embrace* and *steward* it. In any case, we must talk about it. We might wish to form a study group.

It is always easy to be snarky about activist language, especially when, as today, that language is so deeply influenced by a style of

---

PHIL CHRISTMAN teaches first-year writing at the University of Michigan and is the editor of the *Michigan Review of Prisoner Creative Writing.* His work has appeared in *The Christian Century, Paste, Books & Culture, The Hedgehog Review,* and other publications.

portentous inexactitude indebted to the postwar French academic Left. And I am at least somewhat sympathetic to the basic project of nearly every author I just cited. I am sympathetic, too, to the way that any discussion of social processes, as carried forward by even the smartest and most word-careful people in the world, can still find itself chasing its tail. A thing in motion is hard to draw. The constant injunctions, in recent left-of-center discourse, to *verb* whiteness make me smile sometimes, but it's not usually a smile of contempt.

Sometimes it is a smile of puzzlement. Ending racism, a vast set of institutionalized practices, is hard enough, but "Destroy whiteness" hits my ears as though it were a koan or aporia, a thing you say because you want, for some spiritual or other purpose, to make thinking itself grind its gears. What even is "whiteness," and how would you destroy it? How do you kill an ill wind?

We're all familiar enough with the common distinction between *ethnicity* (what we can't help having, insofar as we come from somewhere and were born to somebody) and *race* (a larger category that subsumes various ethnicities into a supra-historical, quasi-mystical unity). Some of America's finest minds – W.E.B. Du Bois, Theodore Allen, Edmund S. Morgan, Nell Irvin Painter, Ta-Nehisi Coates, Toni Morrison – have devoted whole careers to examining, or documenting, or dramatizing, how the fiction known as "race" came to be inscribed overtop the far more particular realities of ethnicity or nationality. Once upon a time, when human beings wanted to make smart or stupid generalizations about other, further-away human beings, they did so based on ethnicity, religion, place, or language. Thus Strabo thought that Ethiopians cursed every day the sun that had so blackened their bodies, and Sir Thomas Browne, that humane man, explained at great, learned length, to countrymen confused on the point, that Jews did not invariably stink. Under these systems of classification, world-historical depredations took place – various slave trades, things that looked like what would later be colonialism, pogroms, the entirety of recorded and unrecorded history before the origin of race. When we speak of the invention of race, we are talking about the origins of a new way to justify evil, not evil itself.

(The theft of America from the peoples native to it might strike you as a bit of a lacuna in this story, as it struck me. From my limited research, it appears that the plunder of Native Americans was initially justified early on in terms more redolent of ethnicity – tribes, lineages, kingdoms – than of what people came to call "race," though there are reports of Natives initially taking Europeans to be strange and monstrous animals because of their white skin. King James I, according to one story, didn't want John Smith to marry Pocahontas because he was afraid that Smith would then claim royal blood – she was, after all, a princess. It's as though he thought of this people, to whom Europeans collectively constituted a great curse, as though they were just another rival power. Obviously, as the idea of "race" came together, Indians, too, became "raced.")

During the Enlightenment and Industrial Revolution, as local habits of production and livelihood were melted down and recast as global capitalism, so were these quaint methods of generalization liquefied and remade into the new scientific discourse of "race." In this way of thinking, scientists scrutinized body pigmentation and skull shapes – not place or family – for evidence of transhistorical, translocal group memberships. The anthropologist and skull collector Johann Friedrich Blumenbach was, for example, particularly taken by one of the items in his collection, which had formerly belonged to a sex slave of Georgian origin. He thought it the prettiest skull he'd ever seen. It so happens that the Caucasus Mountains stretch through Georgia. On this extremely solid foundation, we call people "Caucasian" to this day. For a long time, this Caucasian race was also thought to consist of various subtypes, some of which – the Celt, the Jew, the people so permeated by the miasma of the Great Dismal Swamp that it turned them sallow – faced race hatred of their own. After World War II, an embarrassed world reshuffled its categories, reducing them to whites, blacks, and Asians.

This is the story that Nell Irvin Painter tells in *The History of White People*. To it, we could add the story that Theodore Allen told over the course of his lifework, which Painter herself draws on. Allen points us to the startling fact that colonial law made no racial distinction between black slaves and white indentured servants in the early seventeenth century; the legal categories "black" and "white" take most of those hundred years to emerge. (Indentured servitude was not necessarily a better deal, in the early years, than chattel slavery: many workers weren't expected to survive the seven years of their term, and didn't. On this point, Eric Williams, early in his classic *Capitalism and Slavery,* devotes a revealing passage to the similarities between the seventeenth-century slave ship and the conditions in which Irish servants traveled.) For Allen, the history of "whiteness" pivots on Bacon's Rebellion in 1676, when indentured servants, free blacks, and enslaved blacks fought alongside each other.

The colonial upper classes saw a threat here. They thwarted it in the same way that, today, a cop might force a wedge between two men falsely arrested, to induce the one to testify against the other: Admit the one to certain privileges and confidences, while threatening him with terrifying punishments. Treat the other guy worse, and be theatrical about it. Whip him, pour vinegar on the wounds, whip him again. Thus the eeriness, the sense of a limitless horror lurking under everything, that reading about the history of American slavery often induces: this strategy requires the elaboration of endless new refinements of suffering. If hell is a misery that has no limits, men truly built hell here. Indeed, even during Bacon's Rebellion, this dynamic was already partially in place – the battle was part of a power struggle between two colonial lordlings, one that involved, among other issues, the euphemism known as "Indian policy."

This stratagem is also not new – perhaps it is as old as tyranny itself. But it soon found scientific justification in the work of all those European skull-fanciers. It lost, at least for its perpetrators, the stench of sheer opportunism, and became an "objective" fact about the world. With modifications, and – thanks to technological development – far more lavish inducements, in both directions, this strategy continues to work today.

There is your whiteness: a vast, flimsy thing. With a few dozen reading hours, a smart teenager could debunk it. Millions have seen through it without being able to read at all. And yet how much of American democracy – which truly is a great and unique historical achievement, the destruction of intra-European class and race distinctions that must have been seen as immovable in their time as white supremacy does now – rests on it? Perhaps Europeans, stepping off their different boats, could have learned to see each other as human beings even without positing a second category of person onto which they could project their hatreds and fears. We can't know; that is another, sweeter history. This is ours.

Our literature contains little memories of how contingent it all is: a dream is only convincing while you're in it. In George Schuyler's novel *Black No More* (1931), a crank scientist invents a process by which black people can be turned white. This trope, which also appears in Stephen Wright's *The Amalgamation Polka* (2006), both literalizes and reverses the actual history, in which pseudoscience and opportunism worked together to whiten billions, many of them after the fact. (Was Homer "white"? Was Augustine?) Processes can be reversed and are dynamic. During the Trump era, Latino people lost several degrees of whiteness more or less overnight. Among committed white supremacists, the danger is always that the old intra-European ethnic divisions will resurface, and a great deal of energy is put into stamping out national and ethnic feeling in favor of a unified whiteness; American white supremacists in particular find themselves frequently stymied as they attempt to recruit European nationalists into whiteness.

Whitening is a process without an obvious endpoint. "Whiteness" is always somewhere out a bit ahead of you. The concept is impossible to define in terms of traits, because describing anything was never its function.

And yet everybody tries. Sometimes this means taking the white supremacist's definition of whiteness – rational, brave, scientific, humanity's future – and simply asserting that these things are bad: anti-racist museum exhibits that list "rugged individualism" and "emphasis on scientific method" among the sins of whiteness. (The museum in question later apologized.) It takes boldness to position whitened people as particular valuers of rationality and individualism, in a historical period when millions of them are turning their minds over to an emerging cult based, literally, on internet-forum posts, or flinging themselves and their families at the Covid-19 virus as though it will be cowed by their bravery and walk off. This behavior was not transmitted genetically; it's the product of the specifically toxic individualism of the suburbs. Few people who aren't whitened would be allowed the level of privilege where they could learn to think like this; this doesn't make it a "white trait." Millions of people who would be designated as white, again, can't identify with it at all. In other cases, one attempts to describe "white people" by fastening onto characteristics that have to do with class, or region, or ethnicity, or with the necessary blandness of mass-culture products. When people talk about "white people food," they talk about what Norwegians eat, or what the Irish (were forced to) eat, or what McDonald's produces, not what Italians or Spaniards eat.

On the fringes of black radical thought, one finds the clearest and closest-to-coherent articulations of the white man's special qualities. These stories, at their falsest, retain a certain crude power – the power of the sharp and specific pain behind them. I find, for example, the theory that I am the product of an ancient scientist's breeding experiments deeply insulting, as I am surely intended to, but after spending enough time observing the impersonal cruelty and stupidity of the bureaucracies that maintain, among other things, the illusion that whiteness exists, even I have appreciated the explanatory value of old Dr. Yakub. I can see how a person whose most frequent encounters with whitened people involve cops, prison officials, or other contemptuous functionaries might find an intuitive plausibility in the idea that lack of melanin makes people weak, cruel, and resentful. (*Something* sure as hell did.) One afternoon, as I left a courtroom where I had watched a black friend get railroaded, I found myself thinking the words, *I hate white people.*

It's revealing as well how often these theories both dovetail with and resemble anti-Semitic mythology. Theologian J. Kameron Carter argues that Western Christianity's rift with Judaism, and the anti-Semitism that resulted, was an intellectual and spiritual precondition for modern racism. In a deep historical irony, however, one of the most consequential uses of anti-Semitism was as a scapegoat onto which the European perpetrators of capitalism could deflect the blame for their own depredations. The story of the rise of international banking owes much to the Fuggers and Medicis, but you rarely hear of the former, and we mostly know the latter as a family of titillatingly debauched art enjoyers. When it comes to financial speculation, its invisible powers and corrupting effects, the name everyone knows is "Rothschild." When you need a racial explanation for the specific horrors of international capitalism, you tell a story of secretive, powerful, cunning, and, in some essential way, soulless men. You call them the white man, or you call them the Jew. Sometimes you do both.

In more mainstream forms, such attempts to define whiteness as pathology often focus on the character traits that accrue to "unearned" privilege. (As soon as we say "unearned," we have baked in the idea of meritocracy – which is some white bullshit.) The white person, especially the white man, is inescapably mediocre, as if by hereditary taint. She or he or they are entitled, neurotic, fragile, narcissistic, vain. He is named Bryce or Heath or Connor and wears shorts in the winter – so severed is he, at a basic level, from the truth of things. (Perhaps he just doesn't care if his knees are cold.) She is named Karen, unless her hair is good.

This approach, too, has a crude descriptive power. Stereotypes often do. In an extension of this process, "white" becomes a name for certain varieties of bad politics: the conservative, the nationalist, the NIMBY progressive, the can't-we-talk-about-this-later socialist, the you-looked-at-me-funny-so-I'm-calling-the-cops feminist. In all these cases, "white" functions as a name for a kind of secular American freedom: freedom-from, or freedom-over. It's the freedom of the minor aristocrat – this being the type of person who gave us far too much of the Enlightenment political thought that permeates our institutions – or the freedom of the children of the Southern rich, the group that, disproportionately, has given us that bizarre and misnamed American political tendency known as "libertarianism." (The word has a far nobler meaning in European contexts.) The libertarian is, spiritually speaking, a plantation owner's son. He wants his taxes lowered, his employees free to work for free, and – with an eye toward those employees' daughters – his age of consent abolished. His freedom requires that no one else be free. But all of these are positions, not traits. Many whitened people reject them, and many people of color buy into one or another of them. Given that the forms and shapes of exploitation are likely to shift in a world that America no longer dominates, this is important to keep in mind.

There are two other intellectual problems with this approach. One is the term "privilege," as it is often used in these sorts of conversations. As we've seen – and as has been endlessly pointed out, to no avail – the "privileges" that whiten a person's life may simply be created by conjuring new forms of suffering and applying them only to some people. As a result, "privilege" as used in this conversation "conflates 'everyone should have this' with 'no one should have this,'" as David Kaib has said. It can mean on the one hand that the cops did not shoot you in the back and plant a gun on your still-warm body – or that, if they did, it was for some other reason than blackness. It is clearly true, tautologically, that whatever hardship a whitened person experiences in life, he will not experience the hardship of anti-black racism. But that is not necessarily to say very much about the totality of a man's experience, either white or black.

Or "white privilege," added to the advantages of wealth, may mean the easy freedom and contented stupidity of the plantation heir. (A powerful portrait of this sort of privilege asserting its power to warp character can be seen in the character of Rufus in Octavia Butler's *Kindred*.) Even in these cases, the effects on character, on the real question of the development of the self, are unpredictable: a well-off white boy might become Eric Trump, or he might become Mr. Rogers, and whatever "white privilege" is, it certainly formed both men.

This means that the psychological effects of "privilege" are hard to generalize about. We can say that a millionaire's son will in most cases move through the world with an assumption of invulnerability and an air of command, such that he will be morally lucky if he can grow up merely into an amiable dunce in the Bertie Wooster mold. But it may be the case that millionaires' sons are bad per-force. A black millionaire's son might talk more about "uplifting the community" than a white man's does, but he will be tempted to do it while making many of the same exploitative decisions; such language may reveal a virtuous intent, or it may provide rhetorical cover, or (as is more likely) the truth may be mixed. The psycholog-ical effects of privilege here are mostly those of wealth.

To ask, on the other hand, what psychological deformities or bad habits may result from someone's mere failure to get murdered by the police is ghoulish and, in its effects, reactionary. (In a country where the police think of themselves as an occupying army, it doesn't make the situation better when millions of people lament the ham-burger that was served to Dylann Roof.) And many of the effects of "privilege," in the sense "no one should have this," are as likely to accrue to elite black people as to whitened ones, and do not accrue to millions of the people we call "white." People often point this out because they wish to derail discussions of racism *tout court*; this is not because it is false but because true statements make good derailers.

The third most common response, among the people designated "white," to the radical critique of whiteness – the most common is to dismiss the whole issue, or to fly to the defense of the assailed white man – is a wholesale adoption of this way of defining it: as a kind of shared sin. Because the concept of whiteness has both excused and inspired some of the worst and longest-running crimes in human history, every person we call "white" has a terrible, Faulknerian secret, which they must publicly acknowledge, describe, and lament, in classes, trainings, book clubs, personal essays, and inappropriately anguished conversations with the nearest black acquaintance. It's as though we developed an excellent structural account of society just so that we could turn that, too, to the task of self-development, enumerating personal flaws, while the boss takes notes.

Whitened people who resist these rituals, in which structural injustice and personal guilt are shuffled with the dazzling speed of the three-card monte dealer, are called "fragile." When they partic015ipate in these rituals, when they respond to these often moralizing and personalizing claims, in exactly the way a person is supposed to respond to such claims – with some combination of personal guilt, apology, embarrassment, shame, or special pleading – they are called narcissists. "There you go again, making it about you. White people always center themselves," they are told, by the (often white) facilitator. A metaphorical or actual microphone is dropped.

The most obvious fact about the ritual is its uselessness. It may fix hearts (although this is doubtful). It doesn't fix houses, lives, or waterpipes. It doesn't redraw school districts or reallocate police funding. At its conclusion, nobody gets forty acres and a mule. And nobody feels more human, more at ease, more powerful in solidarity. The ritual's uselessness in addressing root issues probably helps explain its ubiquity; it is acceptable to enough powerful people that it can be widely adopted. (Robin DiAngelo, currently the most successful proponent of this approach, more or less concedes as much.)

But if social stasis is the *outcome* of the ritual, I am not so sure that that is its sole purpose. I think many white people submit to the ritual *because* it feels bad – and because many Americans have been trained to believe that feeling is a form of labor, perhaps the most meaningful, while practical help only fixes symptoms. When a child feels the natural impulse to give a panhandler money, we tell them, if we're stupid, that he only wants it for drugs, or if we're slightly less stupid, we recite a certain platitude about men and fish. (It's hard to pay attention to a fishing lesson if you're starving, just as it's hard to ace the ACT if you haven't eaten or slept.) Our pundits talk of money as a "Band-Aid"; they talk of "throwing money at a problem" as though money were not, very often, precisely the thing that needs to be thrown. All this acculturation certainly helps somebody. But it does the least for the people who believe in it most. (The rich don't believe it; they leave their money to their children.)

The form of Christianity most widely practiced on these shores stresses faith over works, to the point where good works are some-times treated as suspect. It then talks about faith as a set of feelings. It's obvious – and many people have pointed out as much – that the ritual resembles this type of Christianity, where, classically speaking, the subject must be brought to an exquisite pitch of self-recrimination before they can be said to be saved. The newly converted frontier evangelical, however, had the love of Jesus to look forward to, while the white person who has Done The Work can only anticipate the rigorously impersonal, loveless worlds of civics, activism, or – if we're thinking of DiAngelo's anti-racism specifi-cally – the vague approval of the HR department. (DiAngelo's main function, I suspect, is to protect corporations from liability in the case of a discrimination lawsuit and to reduce solidarity between white and black workers. In the latter case, it will often enough be true that she is widening a gulf that already exists.)

Activism is a utopian pursuit with generally dystopian interper-sonal dynamics. As for civics, the whole promise of the endeavor (at least under Enlightenment liberalism, the impersonal rationality of which resembles the worst of what "whiteness" is held to be, which may give us a clue as to its real identity) is that it *doesn't* require love. Part of what a secular anti-racism necessarily aims at is a world where black people could, if they wanted to, ignore white people safely, as millions of white people lead reasonably contented lives without reading, dating, or seriously befriending any black people. Anti-racism must also secure for black people the right to be, without punishment, as irritating, mediocre, or dysfunctional as, say, a reasonably prosperous suburban white man may be. These are legitimate goals that, as far as they go, any fair-minded white person must try to help bring about. My point is only that such a world – in one way radically transformed, and in another way depressingly the same as ours – makes for an odd conclusion to a ritual so dependent on personal conviction. The critique we imply by pointing out the religious character of the ritual is simply that of a mismatch between ends and means. But white people who respond like newly evangelized subjects to an evangelical ritual are not "centering themselves"; they are following the instructions buried in the situation.

The people who will inflict this kind of psychological self-harm on themselves fall, in my experience, into two camps, which sometimes overlap. On the one hand, there are kindhearted people with pathologically low self-esteem, often, and not accidentally, women. They are used to taking the blame; DiAngelo's voice sounds like the voice in their own heads. On the other, there are people so prosperous that they can afford, in effect, that daily three-minute self-hate, as a kind of legal/social inoculation against feeling the moral necessity of looking at, for example, the conditions of those they employ. The great mass of white people, whose "wages of whiteness" still leave them unable to afford their rent, will look at these exemplary flagellants and say more or less what working-class city whites used to say about school integration: if we're going to do this, you rich guys should go first. It is the kind of task that people who can afford to do it are far too prone to accepting on behalf of others who cannot. But no one can really afford to hate themselves, or to see themselves as inherently deviant, or ontologically inferior to other people. Black people have written a number of classic novels on this theme, which one might read with profit and enjoyment.

I have taken to using the term "shit-eating allyism" to describe these sorts of emotional displays. Shit-eating allyism has two main manifestations. On one hand, it consists of simpering declarations of deference, testaments to the oppressed groups' superior and hith-erto-historically-unexampled virtue, or laments about one's own privileges, even when these have barely been enough to keep one alive. In its other form, shit-eating allyism names those occasions when a person of privilege suspends, at least rhetorically – most of the time it is only rhetorical – their own, or their family's and communi-ty's, claim to basic self-respect or human rights. Shit-eating allyism is often but not always associated with the more extreme forms of what Matt Bruenig calls "identitarian deference," and Olúfémi O. Táíwò calls "epistemic deference": the idea that whiteness, maleness, or some other form of privilege has so corroded one's ability to assess reality that any judgment marked as coming from the oppressed community in question, however outlandish, unsupported, or unrepresentative, would automatically be better than whatever judgment this person reaches after research and careful consideration.

When a white professor named Jessica Krug, who had spent decades pretending to be a black woman, was at last caught doing so, she wrote, in (inevitably) a long Medium post, the following hilarious sentence: "You should absolutely cancel me, and I abso-lutely cancel myself." Many onlookers were quick to point out that Krug failed to specify the nature of the punishment she was asking for – "cancellation" means a lot of things, none of them fun, many of them survivable. Yet Krug was also practicing the sort of defer-ence that belongs to this political world. It is not for her to say what her punishment is, because it is not for her to say what anything is. White people are epistemological children, in this way of thinking. This person could not conceive of a righteous version of herself except in blackface. She had canceled herself a long time ago.

In light of this dilemma of whiteness – the way it "toggles," as Nell Irvin Painter puts it, between monstrosity and banality – some of our era's most thoughtful critics, including Painter herself, have proposed the construction of a non-racist white identity. Jessica Krug needs a safe place to locate herself, where she is a danger neither to herself nor to others; anti-racists must build her one.

The attempts at this that I've seen are notable most of all for the way they try to ennoble blandness. The best a white person can do is to serve as a sort of human tofu. Take, for instance, Ta-Nehisi Coates during his five-year run writing Captain America. These comics have attracted little commentary in the literary-critical precincts that received his earlier work with such ecstatic warmth, which is odd, because Coates has been open about the way these comics, as well as his (somewhat better-known) work on Black Panther, function as extensions of the arguments he made in *Between the World and Me*. Captain America, he has said, represents "the Dream" of whiteness, and Coates's treatment of the character is his attempt to imagine what a good man living the Dream might look like. In one early issue, Cap observes to T'Challa, the Black Panther, that he "shouldn't be shocked" by some new depredation that their shared fascist enemy has performed. T'Challa very kindly rebukes him: Innocence is part of Captain America's greatness. What strikes one about Captain America, both in general and in Coates's telling, is that he's barely there. The arc of Coates's story largely involves Cap, defeated by various plot machinations, learning to trust a group of women superheroes, to whom he makes himself humbly useful, but not particularly important. He is a mascot, seemingly without motives.

Another fascinating instance is Young Jean Lee's play *Straight White Men* (2014). She has described the work's genesis as follows:

> When I was at Brown doing the first workshop, there was a room full of students, people of color and queer people, a very diverse room. And they started talking very harshly about straight white men. I said, "Okay. Now I know all the things you don't like about straight white men. Why don't you give me a list of the things you wished straight white men would do that would make you hate them less?"
>
> So they told me all these things, and I wrote down the whole list, and then I wrote that character. And they all hated him. They hated him. . . . They hated him because he was a loser.

Lee expresses this conflict by creating a white man who is the perfect ally: he sabotages his own career prospects and downplays his own skills in order to help others. His family members, whom Lee is careful not to depict as mere villains, take it that he is enacting a kind of masochistic penance. (We might call him a shit-eating ally.) Lee leaves open the possibility that he is self-actualizing and healthy: he wants this life. Admire him or hate him, he is not a dynamic character.

Painter, in an essay published immediately after the exposure of Rachel Dolezal (another white woman who pretended to be black), suggested that white people construct a new identity by looking to the white abolitionists of the nineteenth century and to white allies of the civil rights movement. I am not being even a little ironic when I say that I recognize a great kindness in Painter's intentions. She wants something better for me than to be either Rachel Dolezal or Dylann Roof. I recognize, too, a weary pragmatism in her gesture: the lie of race isn't going away just because I show you, in great, scholarly detail, using my many decades of research, that it is a lie. (Before she turned to writing about white people, Painter first devoted many years to understanding how black people came to be as a people—how they were, as the title of one of her earlier books insists, created. She has the right to be weary and pragmatic.) We could say that blackness is an oppressive fiction, and yet black people rarely wish to have the designation lifted off them. It gives them a sense of commonality with other people, which is a useful thing to have in this world. The sense of *surviving together the designation of blackness* makes a people where there was none before. Theologically, we could even say of blackness—and the theological is an appropriate register in which to speak of it, given both the disproportionate religiosity of that community and the metaphysical weight of the crimes against it—what Joseph said of his brothers' crime against him: What you meant for evil, God meant for good.

All of that may be true. And it might be that "blackness" would go on being a useful, living concept—not just a sort of anthropological phlogiston—even in a world where it has ceased to convoke a people by oppressing them. There is a very real sense in which that question is none of my business. But the well-known incongruity that sometimes arises when one tries to compare the "white" situation to the "black" one imposes itself here as much as anywhere. To consciously "choose" and "build" an identity, in this case, is already to confess to an older, more recalcitrant one: White people, more than any other, have been the people who get to live in the illusion that they build themselves. So right at the outset, you're perpetuating the pattern you want to end.

The theologian Willie James Jennings writes eloquently of the "convening power" of the concept of whiteness. It is revealing that the white group accomplishments he then goes on to describe – imperialism, colonialism, conquest – are simply the operations of capitalism. To make that an effect of whiteness is to put the cart before the horse. "Convening power" is precisely what "whiteness," as compared to "blackness," *lacks*. The concept "black" has called people together to be exploited, stolen from, and abused, but by that same token, it has called them together to survive. "Whiteness" has not called a people together except to do crimes and bury the evidence; it does not name a people who share a common good or common experiences. And it can easily function by calling together a minority even of that people. (The percentage of the American population that genuinely loves Donald Trump is a rump. Out of a hundred white people, it only takes ten Klansmen and seventy bystanders to keep the entire system going.) Whiteness has not laid a common burden on people's shoulders. ("White trash" as a concept has done so, but it's the "trash" part that does that, not the "white" part.) The myth of whiteness is simply that one is human, and that this fact is more interesting than any particulars. But this myth is also a truth, made untrue only when I fail to acknowledge that it's also true about everybody else. "Whiteness" designates only a common absence of oppression. Into that absence, every human thing, everything that makes me both a member of a species and a particular being, falls. It's too much to make a people.

The one universally binding experience of whiteness might be this: that racism exists as a possibility for you, even if it's one you work not to express. It's like a Chomskyan Language Acquisition Device for evil. I'll give an example, although it is a humiliating one. I grew up in an extremely small, mostly white town – I explained the near-absence of black people, when I thought about it, by the theory that I wouldn't live there if I could help it either. Because my consumption of pop culture was somewhat limited by my circumstances as a fundamentalist, and because my homosocial bonding was limited by my late-developing social skills, I never learned that I am supposed to feel threatened by sexual competition from black men, nor that I am supposed to take it as axiomatic that I am sexually ill-equipped compared to them. I learned that I am supposed to feel this way – I swear before God that this is true – from reading, as a college student, in *The Nation*, a review of a book that debunked this and other harmful myths. Of course, the minute that I learned that this was a way that I should somehow both feel (as an American) and not feel (because it's a myth), suddenly the paranoia was there, fully fledged. I had been absorbing various other mythemes about black people – good at athletics, good at fighting, therefore highly physical, et cetera – from the culture, and this detail slid in among them; my mind didn't have to stretch much to fit it. I'm an American; I'm a sucker for a new insecurity. From then on, this dumb idea existed in my mind the way an optical illusion does after you've seen through it: it's still there to be ignored.

This is not to say that white people are not responsible for our opinions. I take it that every person's mind is a sort of junk shop full of beautiful and terrible ideas and images and possibilities and phantasms, and all of their opposites, which we have absorbed from our world. (Psychologists can speak of "upsetting" or "invasive" or "unwanted" thoughts precisely because we don't like or want everything we find in our brains.) You have to make the best thing you can from your junk shop. Equally, it's the responsibility of political movements and organizers, as of moral and spiritual leaders, to magnetize people via the best ideas they have, to bring particular ideas so to the forefront of people's minds that their less noble thoughts acquire dust and are forgotten. Most white people probably have the makings of an anti-black bigot stashed in their head somewhere – even black people struggle with internalized anti-blackness. The parts of the bigotry machine sit in their heads too. In the same way, any heterosexual man can probably become a tyrannical sadist, if he isn't careful. And so on, down even to those people so marked out for oppression that there is no rung of the ladder beneath them. They kick, as the old joke goes, their dogs.

But even racism can't be the unifying trait that makes "whiteness" a useful concept. Racism in the sense of anti-blackness is, as I've said earlier, a thing even black people must struggle against.

Racism in the sense of "a belief that races are real, and hierarchi-cally arranged" is also, as we've seen, a trait found in many groups, including black people. Racism against other groups, and other sorts of prejudice, can also be found in every community, including black communities. (There is a long-running argument over whether we should call this sort of racism "prejudice" instead of racism. This strikes me as an attempt to legitimize such beliefs, however slightly, but it's also true that there is no history of black people turning such beliefs into laws. So here I leave readers to their own judgment.) But it is morally obtuse to make much of specifically black bigotry when black people writ large are still so clearly frequently at the bottom of every pile. (This is why discussions of black homophobia, for example, are distasteful. We can acknowledge its existence, but separating it out as an issue distinct from homophobia in general is like talking of "black-on-black crime": it implies that it's somehow worse when those people do it.)

—

The scholar Noel Ignatiev's solution to the problem of whiteness was straightforward: White workers must simply refuse to accept deals that advantage them against black workers, even when this means, for example, that a union must turn down the sorts of informal pro-white racial preferences, the deals with management, that were popular at the time Ignatiev began to write. What they lost at the time, they would make up when the black, white, and (presumably) other work-ing classes, undivided, grew strong enough to conquer. In the world that resulted from this overturning, racial categories would dissolve, and ethnic differences would assume their true proportions, or at least different proportions.

Microaggressions, since they would no longer carry the reminder of a vast interlocking system that can "kill you and say that you enjoyed it," would become, at worst, the routine human pain of being misunderstood. (Where would writers be without that?) Residential segregation would lose on one side its sting (who cares, if my house is worth just as much as yours) and on the other its point (the myth that black people lower property values). We would not all see each other truly, but we would see each other with one world-historical falsehood removed. To this, Ignatiev added: White people must respond to any attack on a black person as they would to an attack on themselves. (This is harder to do if you are continually reminding yourself, as white allies are supposed to do, that you could never, ever understand the *uniquely horrible* pain that is being a black person.)

I would still say, personally, that uncompromising cross-racial humanist solidarity is the only road to a truly decent country. Or, believing as I do in original sin, I would reformulate the statement: the degree to which any future America is good is determined by the degree to which this happens.

Still, I can see hindrances to the wide adoption of the plan. The organizer who adopts it wholeheartedly becomes, let us say, an insurance risk. Some white man would have murdered King sooner or later, but it's at least worth noticing that when he died, he was advocating this very strategy. Fred Hampton, who undertook the dangerous and surely often thankless task of opening dialogue with white workers, got an FBI hit squad for his trouble. One could even argue that authorities fear leaders like Hampton more than they do advocates of indiscriminate anti-white violence (Eldridge Cleaver) or outright black supremacy (Frances Cress Welsing, Leonard Jeffries). Or consider the racially integrated West Virginia coal-miner unions of the 1910s and '20s, who could often be recognized by the red handkerchiefs around their necks. These brave and resourceful people we memorialize with the word "redneck." They spent a lot of time getting shot.

There are subtler ways than bullets to deal with whitened workers who, en masse, refuse to be fobbed off with a place near the bottom of a ladder that doesn't have to exist. Capital adapts. As recently as the mid-to-late 2000s, the Democratic Party regularly sought to reassert its dominance among whitened working-class voters by downplaying issues seen as "black," as well as those of gay people. Hillary Clinton's 2008 campaign against Barack Obama, for example, was all but openly racist. By 2016, the party, including Clinton, shifted its rhetorical strategy, though not their legislative one, which arguably doesn't exist. Broad anti-poverty programs fell under fire. "Breaking up the banks won't end racism," said Hillary Clinton, who intended to do nothing about either banks or racism.

Progressive pundits raced to agree with her. They echoed–though rather faintly–the work of historians such as David Roediger and Ira Katznelson, who had traced the way black people had been partly or totally excluded from earlier broad anti-poverty programs.

Defending any aspect of the New Deal, seen at the time of its passage as a breakthrough for black people even with its racist exclusions of them, became a thing you'd only do if you were blinded by privilege. I have had actual conversations in which the claim that the working class often "gets coded" white meant that any discussion of said class secretly "centered" that group–when the interlocutors pointedly did not modify the phrase "working class" with "white." (I sometimes feel that if the CIA did not invent such maddeningly vague phrases as "centering" and "coding" as a way to keep activists uselessly busy, that is only further evidence of American imperial decline.) People can use "working class" in a cynical or racist way, but it's simple enough to point out that this is happening, in a way that doesn't effectively forbid all discussions of workers.

And so now the Left is riven by a pointless debate between a supposed "class-only" Left and an "identity" Left. There are valid criticisms to make of "identity politics," the most obvious being that it tends to toggle between being a theory of everything and being a simple, commonsense set of observations. But no sensible person should seek to altogether do away with identity politics in a society as riddled with invented divisions as this one; it would be like asking every country to disarm except the biggest one. And while it's true that accusation of "class-only" leftism befalls anyone who talks about class, that is no reason to lean in to the stereotype. The anti-identity Left points out that identity politics is often used by "capital" to keep the working class apart; when a group of leftists becomes hostile to the mere discussion of black-specific experiences, though, they are playing out the other side of capital's little plan.

Most people who are not simply saying indefensible things to build their brand will agree that racism originated in class exploitation, but operates somewhat independently. The question is how much, and as this is not a question that can be answered in the abstract–it can only usefully be assessed about particular situations–the general "class versus identity" question should be given a wide berth. Suffice to say that if you are truly worried about workers, you will always try to notice who they are, and which of them is worst off. You will, if you do this, find yourself fighting racism, and also sexism, transphobia, homophobia, ableism – every systematized cruelty.

To me, the useful idea is not "whiteness." It's not race at all, but – and here I am drawing on, or simply parroting, Karen and Barbara Fields's *Racecraft* – racism. Thinking about "racism" helps me to reach all the useful conclusions; it only spares me the useless ones. I can reach, for example, the conclusion "I should be willing to pay reparation taxes" simply by acknowledging that racism is an ongoing crime, whose victims deserve, and more to the point *need*, compensation to help them live well in the aftermath of that crime – just as would a raped woman, or an Asian man hit by a car, or a white man hit by a car. "Whiteness" adds nothing to my ability to reach this conclusion, nor to the way I live it out. All it gives me is a guilty look and a heightened self-consciousness around black people. This struck me as an elegant solution when I first read *Racecraft* several years ago, and it still does, though the Fields sisters have unfortunately been taken up by some prominent thinkers who wish to discuss neither race nor racism. (Again, good ideas make the best pretexts.)

The *Racecraft* move simplifies our thinking. And we need it to do so precisely because racism is such a vast, powerful, complex system. It can even turn good deeds into bad ones, can make what a whitened person intended for good into a source of evil. I mentioned earlier that I had watched and tried to prevent the railroading of a black friend. After that friend's brief time in jail, my wife and I agreed that we would allow him to stay in our guestroom for free, if he wanted, while he tried to resume life. (He ultimately insisted on paying rent, so we set it at the lowest amount he'd agree to, and then never asked him for it.)

The problem was, we lived in a whitened neighborhood. We had not set out to do so. But we were both making grown-up money for the first time, and so we chose a few amenities – walkability and a decent kitchen. History, housing covenants, and employment discrimination did the rest.

We were not naive. We made a point of telling our neighbors who our friend was, what he looked like, that he had a right to be on "our" territory, so that if they saw him coming and going at odd hours they would not harm him, or call the police. We did not assume that any of our neighbors *in particular* were racists; we just knew that it only took one. We must have forgotten to tell one neighbor, in particular – a nice man, with good politics, himself multiracial. If we apply the one-drop rule or the paper-bag test, this neighbor was a black man. He called the cops on our friend one night, when neither of us were home, when our friend was simply sitting in his car.

Our friend was able to de-escalate the situation, and nothing catastrophic ensued. But we worried – not for the first time – that in trying to help our friend, we might have set him up for other risks. We could insulate him from the particular risks of being a black man in a mostly white neighborhood only by kicking him out, which hardly seemed the right choice. That is the power of racism: it can make even the truest friendship between people a kind of trap. It can make even kindness, even the chastened and sober attempt to use one's privileges to help those who don't have them, into a bad deed. As the privileged person draws nearer the unprivileged one, some of the ethically impossible quality of life under oppression, the sense of choosing between bad options, begins to assert itself. Were we smart enough or good enough to make those choices well? Our friend moved out a few years ago. Thanks to his hard work and all of our good luck, he is doing well.

So I am not downplaying the fiendishness or the embeddedness of racism, the necessity of anti-racist struggle, the need for whitened people to lose sleep and comfort, when I say that I don't think whiteness as a concept is only useful as a name for a powerful and ubiquitous misdescription. Racism is a labyrinth. Some of the sections of the labyrinth have skylights and granite countertops. Some of them have leg irons. The minotaur has his habits, his favorite hunting grounds, but ultimately he reserves the right to eat you in any of them. What we must realize is that, whatever our different names, we are all in the labyrinth. And we are all responsible for ensuring that every single person gets out.

April 9, 2021

THE CALL TO OWN

GREGORY THOMPSON AND DUKE KWON

WHOSE RESPONSIBILITY is it to address white supremacy's centuries-long theft from African Americans? Ask anyone this question
today and the most likely response will be that this responsibility,
if it belongs to anyone at all, belongs chiefly to the US government.
This popular focus on the government is understandable. White
supremacy could not have been birthed or sustained in American
culture apart from the plundering policies, interests, and practices
of the state. Any honest account of our nation's racial history will
lead to the conclusion that the government bears tremendous moral
liability for its perpetration of mass cultural theft.

Notwithstanding the public's broad resistance to the notion
of reparations, the government has already proven its willingness
and capacity to enact reparations programs. For example, in 1946,
Congress created the Indian Claims Commission, which awarded
approximately $1.3 billion to 176 tribes and bands for land taken
by force or deception. The Alaska Native Claims Settlement Act of
1971 provided Alaskan native tribes with nearly $1 billion along

GREGORY THOMPSON is a pastor, scholar, artist, and producer whose work focuses on race and equity in the United States. He serves as executive director of Voices
Underground, research fellow in African American heritage at Lincoln University
(HBCU), and visiting theologian for mission at Grace Mosaic Church in Washington, DC. He is also the cocreator of *Union: The Musical*.

DUKE L. KWON is the lead pastor at Grace Meridian Hill in Washington, DC. He is
active in public conversations around race, equity, and racial repair in the American
church, and he lectures on these topics around the country. His work has appeared
in the *Washington Post*, *Christianity Today*, and *The Witness*.

with the return of 44 million acres of land. The Civil Liberties Act of 1988 provided $1.65 billion in compensation to Japanese Americans who were unjustly incarcerated in concentration camps during World War II. And what about reparations for the enslavement of African Americans? Eight months before the signing of the Emancipation Proclamation, the Compensated Emancipation Act of 1862 freed enslaved people in the District of Columbia and, in a troubling twist of irony, compensated *slave owners* who had been loyal to the Union up to $300 for each freed slave. The question is not whether it is legally or economically feasible for the government to enact reparations; history clearly demonstrates that it is. The question is, and always has been, whether the government and the citizens it represents can muster the moral and political will to own our collective past and to devote ourselves to its repair.

Even so, the work of repairing the ravages of white supremacy is not the burden of the government alone. We believe that the Christian church in America bears a singular responsibility to address the historical thefts of white supremacy, for three primary reasons. First, the church's fundamental *mission* should compel God's people to become agents of repair in a world ravaged by theft. Second, the church's complicated *history*, which tells of both its faithfulness and its failure in the face of white supremacy, demands an honest reckoning and furnishes the church with both hope and humiliation before the call to repair. Third, the church's *moral tradition*, particularly its ethics of restitution and restoration, equips it with the spiritual resources with which to address this history and to begin the work of repair. Indeed, we believe that if the church were to wholeheartedly embrace this responsibility, it could serve as a servant, catalyst, and forerunner to other institutions, including the government, that may endeavor to enact reparations. The church, after all, is called in all things to be a "sign, instrument and foretaste of God's redeeming grace for the whole life of society."

BLINDED WITH THE LOVE OF GAIN

In 1684, John Hepburn departed Great Britain and settled down in East Jersey, where he made a quiet living as a tailor. He arrived in

America as an indentured servant and a Quaker. Both of these attributes, each in its own way, would arouse within him a moral disquietude over the enslavement of Africans—the former by fostering personal empathy for those laboring under lifelong bondage, the latter by embedding him in a religious community on the front lines of the abolition movement. Initially, however, Hepburn's convictions, not to mention his pen, lay dormant.

But year after year Hepburn's disdain for slavery deepened as he studied abolitionist writings from both sides of the Atlantic and witnessed an alarming number of his neighbors purchasing slaves. He also gained firsthand knowledge of the cruelties of the slave trade during frequent visits to Perth Amboy, the port city that became the center of the slave trade in New Jersey. As slavery was increasingly woven into the colony's political economy, and as local slave codes created increasingly unbearable conditions for enslaved Africans, Hepburn grew more troubled in conscience. Finally, after thirty years of waiting silently—mistakenly, he would later confess—he could bear it no longer. Hepburn decided to publicly contend for the truth.

The result was a strongly worded pamphlet, *The American Defence of the Christian Golden Rule*, published in 1715. Writing out of a sense of "Christian duty," Hepburn condemns slavery as "an abominable Anti-Christian practice" and "an Affront upon the ever blessed *Messiah*, and his glorious Gospel." He enumerates the cruelties of slavery, critiques the greed of slave merchants, bemoans the hypocrisy of Christians, and calls slave owners to repentance. But the most remarkable feature of *American Defence* is its argument that the Bible requires a *particular expression* of repentance for the "inriching sin" of slavery—namely, restitution. Not only does slavery "rob men of their *Liberty* and *Labour*"; slavery also, by forcing and compelling God's creatures against their will, entails the "Manifest Robbery" of human agency itself. "Blinded with the love of Gain," enslavers continue this inhumane practice of robbery only in order to "highly inrich themselves by the Bargain." Thus, Hepburn concludes, slave owners not only must repent of these sins but also must return to their enslaved image-bearers all that they had stolen from them:

I am of Opinion, that such Sins cannot be repented of without *Restitution* made to them that they have wronged; for until the *Cause be removed*, I know not how the *Effect should* cease. But they that live and dye without making Restitution to them that they have wronged, how they can expect the Forgiveness of God, I leave this to the Reader to judge, and then they cannot blame the Writer for a false Construction. . . . It cannot stand with the Justice of God that the Negroes or the wronged shall have no Restitution at all; and seeing then that they must be restored of the Wrongs that they have suffered, it must be restored out of the Property of him that hath wronged them; and this Property is his Interest of Eternal Life; and such a proportion of this as will be equivalent to the Wrongs done unto the Negroes or any others, must go to make up this Restitution; for they will have it.

With these words, Hepburn issued an extraordinary call. Many of his predecessors in print had urged Christian slave owners to treat their slaves kindly and to ensure that they had been evangelized. Some had begun to condemn the evils of slavery and call for the manumission of slaves. But none had publicly argued, as Hepburn did, that the Bible requires not only the emancipation of slaves but also their compensation through restitution. And yet Hepburn explained that the basic argument wasn't original to him. He enthusiastically credits his firm belief in the necessity of restitution to two widely published sermons by John Tillotson, the Anglican archbishop of Canterbury from 1691 to 1694. Entitled "The Nature and Necessity of Restitution," Tillotson's exposition of Luke 19:8–9 defines *restitution* as "making Reparation or Satisfaction to another, for the Injuries we have done him," and restoring "a Man to the good Condition, from which, contrary to Right and to our Duty, we have removed from him." Although Tillotson's study was without specific reference to slavery, Hepburn maintains that the archbishop's teaching could be soundly "applied to the wrongs done to Negroes." He declares confidently, "I have Bishop Tillotson on my side"—by which he meant, of course, he had the bishop's Bible on his side. Hepburn passionately urged Christians who had been "blinded with the love of Gain" not simply to see but to own—to own their self-enriching sin and to own their Scriptures. For it is in those Scriptures that they will—and we will—discover, perhaps for the first time, the call to restitution.

OWNING OUR ETHICAL HERITAGE

Today, over three hundred years since John Hepburn declared that enslaved Africans were owed recompense for their manifold injuries, many Americans mistakenly believe that reparations is a relatively new idea—one that originated perhaps during the height of the Black Power movement in the 1960s. Some have attempted to improve upon this historical error by demonstrating that, while it is true that many white Americans were first introduced to reparations during the civil rights era, the movement dates back to the days immediately after the Civil War when Americans sought to hold the nation to its promise of furnishing every freedperson with land and self-determination. During the Reconstruction era, organized efforts to secure compensation from the federal government soared, even as they gradually evolved into an exclusively black endeavor. However, as Hepburn's trailblazing tract demonstrates, the belief that slaves were owed restitution was publicized fully 150 years before General William T. Sherman's promise of "forty acres and a mule," and 250 years before James Forman demanded recompense from the American church. Restitution for the thefts of white supremacy is an *old* idea. Indeed, it is older than America itself.

What is more, *American Defence* also demonstrates that the early call for restitution in America, like abolitionism as a whole, was originally a distinctly *Christian* endeavor. That endeavor remained, for the most part, in the realm of pamphlet and pen; only a small number of Christians subsequently compensated their manumitted slaves. Alas, it is also true that Christians would later be among the most vociferous opponents of reparations. Even so, we must recognize that the earliest public cases for reparations in America were made on the basis of the Bible, and thus reparations have a distinct, if forgotten, place in the history of American Christian thought and practice. Over three hundred years ago, our Christian forebears, both black and white, began to identify a theological kernel that never fully sprouted into mature, collective conviction or action among non-black (and non-Native) American Christians. For Christians today, an engagement with reparations begins with a call to return to that kernel, acknowledge its arrested development, and cultivate the Christian idea that restitution is owed to those despoiled by the scourge of white supremacy.

We believe that to construct a Christian account of reparations, it is crucial that we own not only the church's fundamental mission in a world ravaged by theft, and its complicated history in regard to white supremacist theft, but also its scriptural and theological heritage in regard to the ethics of theft. That heritage raises a fundamental question: *What is morally required of those who are guilty of stealing?* And it offers an unequivocal answer: not repentance alone but restitution. Indeed, the two are inseparable.

RESTITUTION AND ZACCHAEUS

Zacchaeus was a thief in plain sight. All tax collectors were, at least that's what everyone in Jericho would have told you. But as a *"chief* tax collector," someone who had advanced in prominence and supervised other rank-and-file collectors, Zacchaeus was one of the best at what he did. He was an expert at plundering his neighbors for personal enrichment. Such ignominious success was achieved by skillfully exploiting the tax collection system, which operated in the Roman province of Judea in the following way: Tax collectors would offer to prepay the government the duties and tolls to be collected in a district for the coming year, and contracts were awarded to the highest bidders. While they were obligated to deliver no less than the agreed upon amount, the collectors were also afforded the liberty to collect a "surcharge" from the people—whomever they could prey upon and pillage—in order to turn a much larger profit.

As one can imagine, opportunities for abuse and corruption abounded. Stationed throughout well-traveled cities like Jericho, tax collectors would regularly overcharge passersby, pocket the surplus, and, if fraud was suspected, confiscate their goods with force and harassment. Statutes that regulated these practices did exist, and taxation rates were made public and penalties for corruption were threatened. But these laws were rarely or unevenly enforced, and tax collectors themselves were "often the only ones with precise knowledge of the relevant statutes." Thus, not unlike oppressive systems in every time and place, the despoiling practices of tax collectors in Judea, while technically illegal, were permitted by uncodified social norms and facilitated by the control of knowledge. Theirs was a dirty job – synonymous with extortion and greed, and suited, according to one ancient observer, only for "the most ruthless of men, brimful of inhumanity."

At this point, one might notice how little our portrait of Zacchaeus harmonizes with the image of the bumbling, even mildly endearing, character that popularly lives in the minds of modern readers – minds all too informed, perhaps, by children's song and storybook depictions of this "wee little man." We tend to imagine Zacchaeus to be something like Joe Pesci's character in the holiday classic *Home Alone*. In reality, he was more like Joe Pesci's character in the mobster classic *Goodfellas*. The ancient tax collection system promoted nothing less than "institutionalized robbery," and Zacchaeus was one of its very best robbers.

This brief sketch of Zacchaeus's life of theft prepares us for two important surprises that are promptly introduced in the narrative. The first is the surprise of Jesus' *radical kindness*. He is expected simply to pass by, but instead he stops, looks up at the "sinner" perched in a tree, and addresses him personally. This is, of course, what divine love does. Love sees, stops, and calls us by name. What is more, Jesus, in a jaw-dropping, countercultural moment, invites himself over to the tax collector's home: "I must stay at your house today" (Luke 19:5). In the ancient world, the giving and receiving of hospitality was a sign of intimacy and solidarity, a wholehearted exchange of friendship. Any self-respecting Jew, therefore, would have been far more circumspect with his social commitments than Jesus apparently was. After all, tax collectors were widely regarded "almost as the moral equivalent of lepers" – condemned for their habitual stealing, shunned as ritually unclean because of their regular contact with Gentiles, and loathed for their collusion with Rome. In light of these strongly held social perceptions, it is utterly scandalous for Jesus to associate with so despised a figure with such intimacy and generosity. No wonder the crowd grumbles with sharp disapproval.

And no wonder Zacchaeus's life is so dramatically changed. This brings us to the second surprise, the tax collector's *radical transformation*. Both of these surprises are closely related. As Romans 2:4 and Titus 2:11–12 clearly testify, God's kindness leads us to repentance, and his grace teaches us to renounce ungodliness. Surely it is the kindness and grace of Jesus that leads Zacchaeus to renounce his former way of life and pledge to redress his wrongs. He stands as if to make a public vow and boldly declares, "Behold, Lord, the half of my goods I give to the poor. And if I have defrauded anyone of anything, I restore it fourfold" (19:8). With these remarkable and life-altering words, Zacchaeus makes two astonishing commitments. Acknowledging that he, as a tax collector, stood at the center of an extractive system designed to plunder the most vulnerable members of society, Zacchaeus offers half of his possessions to the poor. What is more, he commits to the monumental task of returning all that he had personally stolen from his neighbors. Once a despised thief, now a beloved son, Zacchaeus promises to make restitution. ⨍

Adapted excerpt taken from Reparations *by Duke L. Kwon and Gregory Thompson,* © *2021. Used by permission of Brazos Press. Visit ReparationsProject.com.*

April 16, 2021

THE TURNING POINT

CARLO LANCELLOTTI

IN THE LAST few years, a number of books have grappled with the perception that we are experiencing a period of social and cultural decline. We can count in this category Rod Dreher's *The Benedict Option*, Patrick Deneen's *Why Liberalism Failed*, and Ross Douthat's recent *The Decadent Society*. A new addition to this genre–which however is also about the "rise" that preceded the "decline," and the lessons we can draw from it in order to move forward–is *The Upswing* by Robert D. Putnam and Shaylyn Romney Garrett. In an impressive tour de force of sociological research, the authors analyze a vast array of statistical data concerning four areas of American life between 1895 and 2020 (economics, politics, society, and culture), and detect a common "macro-historical" pattern. Across all four areas, during the first half of the period American society moved from "I" (which is used as a shorthand for economic inequality, political polarization, social isolation, and cultural individualism) to "We" (meaning a more equitable economic system, a significant degree of political comity, more social solidarity, and a more communitarian culture). But then, around 1960 "something happened," and the pendulum started swinging in the opposite direction. By suitably organizing the data, Putnam and Garrett are able to trace

CARLO LANCELLOTTI is a professor of mathematics at the College of Staten Island and City University of New York. His field of interest is mathematical physics, with special emphasis on non-equilibrium statistical mechanics. He has translated three of the Italian philosopher Augusto Del Noce's works into English and has led various seminars on the thought of Del Noce.

a general graph (shaped like an inverted U) that summarizes this "I-We-I" trajectory. The ascending leg of the graph starts from the Gilded Age, goes through the progressive era and the New Deal, and culminates in the cultural and political consensus of the 1950s. Deeply imperfect, shortchanging black Americans and women, this settlement was still one of broader social solidarity and less inequality than had been the case in the Gilded Age. The descending leg comprises the turbulent 1960s and 1970s, the Reagan revolution, and the last few decades, leading to the current situation of decreased solidarity and comity, and increased isolation and inequality.

Besides being an interesting book in its own right, *The Upswing* got my attention in my capacity as the English translator of the works of Italian political philosopher Augusto Del Noce (1910–89). Del Noce was an insightful social critic and historian of culture, and already in the sixties he was arguing that the years immediately before and after 1960 had marked a major epochal change, what Putnam and Garrett appropriately call a "turning point." Del Noce's perspective was strictly philosophical and cultural, but I think it complements the analysis in *The Upswing* in two respects.

First, Del Noce writes from a European perspective, and looks at the evolution of Western culture as a whole, whereas Putnam and Garrett focus strictly on the United States. While this is quite justified as far as economics and politics are concerned, it is less so when we must try to understand culture and society: many of the cultural and social transformations they describe (e.g., the sexual revolution, consumerism, the expansion of higher education) took place almost simultaneously across many different countries, and probably are better understood from a more international point of view.

Second, Del Noce, as a philosopher, can focus on the internal logic of cultural and intellectual life to an extent that is not possible in a sociological study. One of Putnam and Garrett's most interesting findings is that in the postwar period economic and social changes appear to have slightly lagged cultural changes: the culture changed first; economic and broader social changes followed. As they explain, this does not allow us to conclude that cultural dynamics alone drove the "turning point," because material and political interests certainly also exercised causality, in a complex network of feedback loops. Nonetheless, ideas certainly played a significant role. Putnam and Garrett illustrate this interlocking causality by quoting a striking passage from Max Weber: "Not ideas, but material and ideal interests directly govern men's conduct. Yet very frequently the 'world-images' [*Weltanschauungen*, worldviews] that have been created by 'ideas' have, like switchmen, determined the tracks along which action has been pushed by the dynamic of interest."

Weber here makes the distinction between "ideas" and "ideal interests": what he means is that groups of people may have an interest in preserving a set of ideas, or promoting a new one, that goes well beyond whether or not those ideas are true. For example, academic sociologists have an interest in preserving the idea that academic sociology is a coherent but difficult-to-understand field, which ought to be a high-status endeavor with great job security. Advertisers have an ideal interest in promoting the concept that purchasing decisions can be shaped by advertising. Feminist activists have an ideal interest in promoting the concept that the patriarchy is powerful and sinister and that feminist activists have a great deal of important work to do. Those who want to have a great deal of sex without commitment have an ideal interest in promoting the postulate that monogamy and marriage are oppressive institutions, and that, by extension, acting on sexual desire is a kind of healthy self-expression. It is ideas like these that get built up into "worldviews." One may well find oneself with a worldview that is remarkably consistent with one's self-interest.

Del Noce was a specialist in the study of such "worldviews" as they are found in the works of philosophers, artists, and intellectuals, but also in the media and in popular culture, and of their logical interconnections and developments. In particular, he was convinced that twentieth-century history was to an unusual extent "philosophical history" because of how much it was influenced by ideas and ideologies inherited from the previous century. Thus, I think his insights contribute to the discussion of "culture" in chapter 5 of *The Upswing*.

In very broad terms, Del Noce observed that mid-century Western culture responded to the tragedies of the previous decades (two world wars, Soviet and Nazi totalitarianism, the Holocaust, the atomic bomb) by rediscovering the mindset of the Enlightenment. This mindset had first surfaced in the eighteenth century, but then had been countered and partially neutralized by the so-called Romantic reaction, which characterized the nineteenth century and the first part of the twentieth. Whereas Romanticism emphasized a sense of historical continuity, even a love of the past, the attitude of the Enlightenment was marked by the decision to make a break with the past and "start from scratch." And indeed after 1945 scholars, journalists, and artists gradually rediscovered the Enlightenment "as a disposition to declare a break with traditional structures and criticize them inexorably from an ethical, political, and social standpoint." Whereas at the time of Voltaire the past was the "dark ages" of religious superstition, in the 1950s it was "fascism." But the "fascism" that was imagined by the men and women of the 1950s was viewed, for the most part, not as a contingent (and modern!) political phenomenon, but as the expression of "old Europe," which was a culture imagined to be as indelibly dark as Voltaire had imagined the Catholic Church, marred by nationalism, irrationalism, tribalism, racism, sexism, and so on. The perception was that fascism marked the failure of the European tradition, and was in a sense its true face. That was why, according to Del Noce, the thinkers and writers of the 1950s rediscovered the Enlightenment in its most anti-traditional version, and why their recovery of it took a distinctly anti-authoritarian ("anti-fascist") flavor. This antiauthoritarianism expressed itself as an emphasis on personal autonomy and independence from social restraints, and in the language of "self-realization," which became ubiquitous in popular culture. To oppose this was by necessity, they thought, to be in favor of the old Europe that, they fancied, had given us the Holocaust.

This neo-Enlightenment disposition manifested itself also in a different key, one that was in tension with the first: a commitment to the good of the self-expression of the unique individual went along with an emphasis on universal human values over national or local values. These values, however, were not particularly the universal ethical truths claimed by, for example, Christianity.

Chief among the universal values that the bien-pensant of the 1950s looked to was that of scientific rationality, which supposedly provides the only possible way forward away from the horrors of the past, and enables humanity to enter "adulthood." Accordingly, an attitude that became common in the years leading up to 1960 was *scientism*, by which Del Noce means not science per se, but rather the philosophical view that science is the only real rationality, and the only sound organizational principle of society. The political counterpart of scientism is technocracy, the idea that society should be directed by "experts": scientists, technicians, managers, businessmen. This idea had famously been advanced at the end of the "old" Enlightenment by the Count of Saint-Simon, and it punctually resurfaced in the 1950s, the age of the "managerial revolution." Not by chance, this was also the golden age of the social sciences – sociology, anthropology, psychology, sexology, pedagogy – which came to great prominence not only in academia but also in public policy and even popular culture. At that same time philosophy lost much of its previous cultural prestige, as many practitioners turned away from its traditional fields of inquiry (metaphysics, moral philosophy) in favor of fields that made it a sort of *ancilla scientiae* (analytic philosophy, philosophy of science). Natural science, after all, was the real source of knowledge. Everything else was speculation.

For some interesting American illustrations of what Del Noce describes, I would like to refer the reader to chapters 3 and 4 of *The Twilight of the American Enlightenment* by George Marsden, the distinguished evangelical historian. What Marsden calls the "American" Enlightenment is actually the difficult "marriage" that had marked so much of US history: the marriage between the Enlightenment and Protestantism. Thus Del Noce's claim must be adjusted to fit the American context by saying that while in Europe the mindset of the Enlightenment was rediscovered, in the United States (where it was already strong) it felt itself strong enough to walk away from its long-standing, uneasy alliance with Protestant Christianity. With that qualification, Marsden agrees with Del Noce on the essential point: "At all these levels of mainstream American life, from the highest intellectual forums to the most practical everyday advice columns, two such authorities were almost universally celebrated: the authority of the scientific method and the authority of the autonomous individual."

According to Del Noce, another rediscovery contributed to the major cultural turning point at the end of the 1950s: that of Marxism. In European culture Marxism had already made a comeback after World War II, becoming hegemonic, for example, among French and Italian intellectuals. In the United States, of course, during the Cold War, mainstream culture was adamantly anti-Communist. However, in Del Noce's view Marxist ideas had a much broader reach than Communism as a political movement. If one recognizes as the core of Marxism the affirmation of the causal priority of material-economic factors, the tendency to "explain what is higher through what is lower," and the theory of "false consciousness" (which claims that appeals to universal ethical and religious values are generally disguises for selfish economic interests), then one must admit that Marxism had a great influence, for example, on the social sciences. While secular intellectuals generally rejected Marx's philosophy of history (the expectation of the revolution, the messianic role of the proletariat, and so on), many of them broadly subscribed to the scientistic and materialistic aspects of Marxism. Taken in isolation, these tend to persuade adherents to adopt a "total relativism": all values are reflections of material historical circumstances, group, or self interest, and have no permanent validity. It was in this sense, Del Noce wrote, that "the rebirth of the mindset of the Enlightenment and the rediscovery of Marxism have met and compenetrated each other."

As early as 1963 Del Noce diagnosed that this confluence of Enlightenment themes and Marxist ideas characterized a "new" culture, which he variously described as the "technological" or "affluent" society, or as "progressivism." He also predicted that as this mindset percolated from the intellectual elites into broader society (through the "culture industry," mass media, public education, etc.) it would produce precisely some of the effects described in *The Upswing*: growing individualism, social fragmentation, decreased religiosity, growing economic inequality. He based his prediction on the fact that the new culture was radically positivistic, and thus destined to "demythologize" and ultimately destroy the symbolic and religious narratives that glued society together.

To better explain this crucial point, let me refer to the classic cliché "God, family, and country." This slogan has been exploited by many unscrupulous politicians, and ridiculed by just as many sophisticated intellectuals, but it does point to an important truth. People feel united to other people if they share in what Del Noce called an "ideal dimension," which inevitably refers to what he called "the invisible" or "the sacred." In order to be bound together people need to recognize each other as participants in universal experiences and values that transcend immediate individual utility. Religion, family, and nationality are three such fundamental sources of "sacredness." Now, in Del Noce's view the affluent society tends to "desecrate" them, and as a result it slowly becomes a "non-society" formed by "atomized" individuals.

As far as "God" is concerned, Del Noce argues that the postwar period saw the rise of a new form of "irreligion" quite different from traditional atheism. Rather than directly denying the existence of God, neo-Enlightenment thinkers professed a form of scientistic agnosticism. This purported to be religiously "neutral" but in actuality undermined religion at a deeper level, by denying the intellectual and practical value of religious *questions*. From a scientistic perspective "such unsolvable questions are also those that *do not interest us*; meaning that they do not interest those who want to act in the world in order to improve it in any sense." Religious questions are irrelevant to social, economic, and cultural life, except as a potential source of civil strife, which must be avoided by accepting that "democratic politics can only be de-mythologized politics." This attitude relegates religiosity to a strictly private sphere and ultimately leads to radical secularization, "because it erodes the religious dimension until it erases from consciousness all traces of the question of God."

Moving on to "family," Del Noce sees a tight link between scientism and the sexual revolution – whose conceptual framework was provided by the renaissance of scientific sexology and psychoanalysis in the 1950s and 1960s. The experience of sexuality has in nearly all cultures been one that is an avenue of transcendence, one so powerful that it must be carefully ordered. Conversely, "science" knows no transcendence. Scientific sexology and psycho-analysis regard human sexuality as a purely natural phenomenon, devoid not only of transcendent meaning, but even of intrinsic finality (e.g., procreation). From a scientistic perspective sexual urges are simply natural phenomena to be studied by biological or psychological methods, but serve no higher purpose and have no objective symbolic (let alone sacramental) value. Accordingly, the men and women of the affluent society are taught not to find in sex anything that points beyond themselves.

In this sense, the philosophy of the sexual revolution is "posi-tivism for the masses." It views even the most intimate human rela-tionships as essentially "meaningless" except for the meaning "we give them." Sex becomes a romantic (at best) transaction between autonomous and fundamentally isolated individuals, and marriage becomes very similar to what in the nineteenth century was called "free love"–namely, a free association that lasts as long as long as "love" does, and can be dissolved almost at will. Clearly, this "cou-ple-centered" conception of marriage implies a sort of "de-sacraliza-tion" of the idea of "family."

A similar kind of desacralization applies to the idea of "nation." I already mentioned the universalist and cosmopolitan character of the neo-Enlightenment culture that emerged around the time of the "turning point." I will add that also in this case Del Noce thinks that there is a philosophical necessity. Nations were traditionally based on religious or cultural identities, articulated in founding histories, in national "myths" and "heroes," which embodied a col-lective purpose. None of these makes sense from a scientistic-posi-tivistic perspective. A nation is just a form of political and economic organization, completely replaceable by more efficient forms. Love of country is at best a romantic relic, at worst a form of bigotry and source of dangerous passion. If anything, a denizen of the affluent society will feel a greater allegiance to the global community of enlightened managers, technologists, philanthropists, and busi-nessmen than to his or her home nation.

Clearly, in the long run this is bound to create a political frac-ture (within developed countries) between the technocratic elite (typically concentrated around a few great "world cities") and those who share in the older nation-based sense of identity (typically living in peripheral areas). This is just one aspect of a general phenomenon that Del Noce describes as follows: in societies deprived of an "ideal" (religious, philosophical) common ground "the separation between the ruling class and the masses becomes extreme because the members of the former know that every argument in terms of values is merely ideology as an instrument of power." Everything, for them, is already debunked, and those for whom it is not debunked are . . . well, they are unenlightened.

To sum up, Del Noce argued that in a radically scientistic-positivistic culture like the one that became dominant in the West around 1960 all forms of "belonging" grow weaker because of the scarcity of ideal common ground. This crude summary, of course, does not do justice to his analysis. For example, I cannot discuss here his views of the internal critics of the affluent society, in particular the protest movements of the sixties and seventies. I will just mention that in his opinion those movements (which can in a way be seen as the parallels of the Romantic reaction to the first Enlightenment) mostly failed to address the philosophical foundations of the new society, and actually often ended up playing into its hands, by criticizing the "traditional" institutions that in reality stood in the way of the "We-to-I" process (the church, the family, liberal education, etc.).

But enough with the analysis of "decline." Does Del Noce have anything to tell us about the question raised in *The Upswing*? Namely, what will it take to get through another turning point and start moving the pendulum in the opposite direction: moving back toward solidarity?

Clearly, since he believed that culture played a major role in the turning point, Del Noce was inclined to give priority to some sort of "cultural revision" in order to invert the trend. This implies, among other things, that politics can only play a supporting role, while education needs to be a major focus of attention. Not by chance, education is one of the fields that has suffered the most in the affluent-technological society. Deprived of narratives and ideals, education has been impoverished by utilitarianism, which manifests itself as an emphasis on technology in the sciences. Politicization in the humanities seems to be an attempt to retrieve some sense of narrative or ideal, but at the expense of humane and open debate, rigorous curiosity, and a connection to earlier and perhaps richer ideas of justice and human nature. (Or, of course, it may simply be the case that as humanities faculties lose their belief that artistic beauty and philosophic truth are intrinsically worthwhile objects of study and contemplation, they must justify their existence by claiming that their subjects have political, and thus practical, salience.)

Countless attempts at "fixing" K–12 education as if it were a "technical" problem have failed, because there cannot be education without an organic image of what it means to be human, and modern secular culture does not have one, or the one it has is inadequate to the task. So, the real question we should ask is, What cultural resources need to be brought to the educational system, and to the culture at large, to make a new upswing possible?

A simple approach is to look at the ideas that drove the previous turning point (around 1960), and call them into question. Instead of living in a perennially antagonistic relationship with our collective past, we need to make peace with it, which requires being able both to reject its mistakes and to value what was valuable. Instead of rebelling against the constraints of religion, family, and country, we need to recognize what Simone Weil called "the need for roots." We need to understand that universal values can only be realized in local and contingent forms. We need to learn to accept limits, and come to terms with the fact that human beings cannot have a healthy relationship with the *visible* (as Del Noce would say) without somehow coming to terms with the *invisible*. This last observation brings us to the sticking point: a new upswing will be impossible without adequate religious resources. Goodwill, or better policies, or more advanced technical instruments simply will not address the cultural aspects of the crisis. But real religion cannot be manufactured at will. A conversion is necessary. As Del Noce puts it:

> A religious reawakening is needed, because religion, country, and family are supreme ideals and not practical instruments.

And it is certainly a valid point that the formula *corruptio optimi pessima* applies to the deterioration that befalls these ideals when they are viewed, at least primarily, as pragmatic instruments of social welfare. In order to be socially useful they must be thought within the categories of the true and the good; the opposite is impossible. Certainly, such a reawakening cannot be a merely human work. But nevertheless it requires, in order to be realized, that the hearts of men be attentive.

Let us, then, attend.

April 20, 2021

ON GOOD PARTIES

TARA ISABELLA BURTON

A FEW YEARS ago, in the middle of a surprisingly sedate breakup conversation, I tried to explain what it was I wanted out of a relationship, out of marriage, out of life. It wasn't simply that we weren't right for each other, I tried to say; it was that our relationship didn't lend itself to a certain kind of openness, to love of the world. What I wanted out of a partnership, I said – though clumsily – was to be standing together, around an enormous table, with piles of food heaped high, with prosecco free-flowing, with all manner of ragtag people, in all their particular strangeness, in silly costumes and vintage furs, showing up, unbidden and welcome, at the door.

"You're breaking up with me," he said, astounded, "because I won't cohost parties with you?"

He wasn't wrong, not exactly. Nor was he right.

—

I am susceptible to frivolity. I know this about myself. I love beauty; I am weak to surfaces; I am apt to mistake eccentricity for character. I drink more than I should. I love overdressing; I love staying up past midnight; I love breakfasts at all-night diners, and the Irish coffees you order when you can't decide whether it's night or morning.

And I love parties.

TARA ISABELLA BURTON is the author of the novel *Social Creature* (Doubleday, 2018) and the nonfiction book *Strange Rites: New Religions for a Godless World* (Public Affairs, 2020). She is a contributing editor at *American Purpose* and a columnist for *Religion News Service*.

I love going to parties; even more, I love hosting them. I love madcap dress codes; I love taking people's coats and making piles of them on the bed. I love the lightness of meddling in people's evenings, in sitting them next to strangers, in reminding them what they have in common. I love refilling people's drinks. I love convincing them to put back down their coats, to stay another hour, to take a few more biscuits for the road.

—

At various times, and for various reasons, I have been suspicious of this tendency. I have wrestled with the ease with which my love of a good time can curdle into a kind of aesthetic puppeteering, under which my guests become not people but social acquisitions: their introductions bylines. But over the past year and a half, as our parties have taken place – if at all – over Zoom, I have come to appreciate the raucous lightness of in-person gathering in a new way.

Far from being frivolous (and, in many ways, *because* of its seeming frivolousness), the party – at least what I want to call a Good Party – offers us a vision of an affective polity, rather than an ideological or disengaged one. It is a practice for living.

A Good Party is a place where bonds of friendship, fostered in a spirit of both charity and joy, serve as the building blocks for communal life overall. The wedding feast, that abundant banquet of Christian life, is always prefigured in the convivial symposium of friendship.

The kingdom of heaven, when it comes, will be a very Good Party.

—

Good Parties don't merely offer us the opportunity to gather *with* those we love. Rather, more importantly, they teach us *how* to love. Good Parties foster the virtue of loving well. Good Parties improve, too, our moral vision. They teach us to see ourselves, and one another, differently. We learn to see ourselves as part of a community: one defined not by hierarchy or even shared affinity, in the capitalist-consumer sense, but simply by our love for one another. Our *presence* – rather than any of our accidental qualities, our jobs or our family status or even our hobbies – renders us a unified body. Before there is procedural politics, there is the truth of the social life: the fact that we cocreate, through our bonds of love, our sense of us, what formal politics institute.

The Good Party understands that what it means to live in common, in the abstracts elucidated by political theology, can never be divorced from our embodied experience of being with, and loving, other people. It understands that friendship – the family of love, rather than blood or birth – is at the heart of the Christian political life.

The *polis* is not something *out there*, a problem for other people to solve, but rather something we learn to do here and now, together. The work of being with one another, of loving one another, of making one another at ease, of gently correcting one another when we err – all this might differ in degree, but not in kind.

———

Parties, after all, are different from other social gatherings in two major respects.

First, because they are by nature special: the time carved out for a party is always orthogonal to the rhythms of everyday life. For all that parties often *commemorate* certain events in "real life," the space of a party itself is always a little bit liminal; all parties, however sedate, have a touch of the carnival about them, a sense that certain forms of social etiquette (and, vitally, hierarchy) need not apply.

Second, and perhaps more importantly, parties (at least good parties) are different because they are useless. Or, more precisely, the usefulness of a party doesn't consist of a purpose outside itself. It is not a coworking day in a café, a choir rehearsal, or even a church service. Rather, a Good Party's concern is always exclusively with itself, with gathering qua gathering, with the fostering of social bonds. We become closer to those with whom we are already close; we foster, in turn, the relationships of people whom we, the hosts, may know well, but who may not know each other; we invite, too, newer acquaintances into a wider community.

It is for this reason that parties are, properly considered, a *practice*: in the sense of the word Alasdair MacIntyre offers us in *After Virtue*: a "coherent and complex form of socially established cooperative human activity through which goods internal to that form of activity are realized in the course of trying to achieve those standards of excellence which are appropriate to, and partially definitive of, that form of activity, with the result that human powers to achieve excellence and human conceptions of the ends and goods involved, are systematically extended." Tic-tac-toe is not a practice, MacIntyre tells us, but chess is. As is football.

As are parties.

—

Not all parties, of course, are Good Parties. There are parties that exist primarily to offer us what MacIntyre might call *external* goods (fine booze, promising career or social-climbing opportunities, a set of flattering Instagram photos). These kinds of gatherings – networking events, snobbish would-be "salons," and drunken bacchanals alike – I consider Bad Parties. A party that has as its end some temporal goal, the individual social or economic success of its host or its guests, cannot be a Good Party. Neither can a purely decadent rager – a party that exists to provide its individual guests with immediate sensual or erotic pleasure, but never engages its members as anything but an aggregation of individual consumers.

Neither can a party that is designed for those who have come to "see and be seen" – offline or online. Nor a party whose guest list is carefully curated to include only people of a particular cultural stratum, or who possess necessary social capital. Good Parties, after all, are never snobbish.

—

A Good Party, by contrast, whether silly (funny dress code!) or serious (discussing late modernity in the corner), exists primarily for itself. (At Good Parties, Instagram photos are banned.) Its virtues are what MacIntyre would call *internal*: it fosters in its attendees the same qualities of charity, of kindness, of appreciation for one another, of openness and vulnerability and effervescence, that are themselves the party's aims. The guests of a Good Party will, by nature of invitations, have *something* in common (friendship with the host, say, or at least with someone present), yet no quality is required in us but our willingness to show up, our openness to *being at a party* in the first place, and to learning from those around us how to participate in joy.

—

These two elements together render Good Parties inherently democratic.

The very premise of a Good Party – that all who are here are welcome, and thus already in some sense trusted – makes redundant the grasping and pernicious questions ("what do you *do*? Where are you *from*? How are you *important*?") of the good party's wickedest counterpart: the networking event.

The Good Party never undermines its guest list. It is never snobbish in crafting that list in the first place. Everybody who is present is important. They are important because they are here. It is the first principle from which all other aspects of the Good Party must proceed.

The Good Party understands, too, that what we might call *worldly* social hierarchies – of class, of race, of birth, of fashionable types of power – result from our own sinfully warped categories of cognition; a Good Party demands that we rather remake our social bonds, to expand our sense of family, of "in-group," of *us*, to include all those who would participate in a spirit of love.

A Good Party challenges us to know people anew, to *come to know them* within a setting where friendship, rather than formal status, is paramount. It makes strangers into friends, to be sure, but it is also – in the best sense – makes friends into strangers; encourages us to look at them with newer, clearer vision. A silly dress code, a game of snapdragon, a drunken singalong to show tunes, all these provide the opportunity for those we love to show us new sides of themselves. I once developed a whole new affection for a friend of many years' standing upon seeing him show up to a "fruits"-themed party dressed as a lemon peel in a Martini glass.

—

This sense of the carnival, in turn, helps us know one another more deeply.

This is not because, as Erving Goffman might have it, we are *always* playing roles – that we are different people in the boardroom and at the bar, and that there is no inherent self. Nor is it because there is some primordial or authentic self that is somehow stymied by the ordinary course of social relations—that we can only be, or see, our "true" selves outside of more formalized social contexts. Rather, it is because, at a gathering of *friends*, a miniature polis of people united by no fact *other* than friendship, be it of personal affection or shared affinity toward some good (and it is in practice all but impossible to separate the two), we are able to most carefully turn our faculties of attention to those we love. Because a party has no telos other than itself, no productive goal or clear outcome, it allows us to pay closer attention to those we love, as they are; it allows us, in turn, to be vulnerable to those who love us. When we celebrate joyfully with one another, in this liminal space, we are also seeing those we love *as they really are.*

In this, the Good Party is transgressive. I do not mean transgressive in the sense that a merely raucous debauch is transgressive (which is to say: aesthetically only, and fundamentally not at all). The transgression of a Good Party is not defined by anonymous sex or wanton drunkenness or rampant drug use, nor by any other kind of onanistic hedonism, but rather by the reimagining of *how* we know another, outside worldly categories. The carnival aspect of a Good Party allows us to consider the world anew: to question from a loving distance what parts of "real life" are actually real, and which only convention.

Which parts of the world, in other words, could stand to be more like parties.

—

My husband and I are now vaccinated. We will resume, as soon as is prudent, the hosting of parties. But in their absence, as I have reckoned with missing them, I have come to think with more reservations about the difference between Good Parties and Bad ones, about the ones that point to the promise of the new Jerusalem and the ones that simply reproduce the worst of what the world already is, about the ones we go to to be photographed at, and the ones we go to so that other people might transform us; the ones I miss and the ones life is better without. In the post-Covid order, I hope parties will be many and plentiful. But I hope, with more clarity than I once did, that they will also be Good. ⚘

April 27, 2021

THE HORROR OF NURSING HOMES

CHARLES C. CAMOSY

BASED ON MY discussions with other authors, most of us wish we had our book manuscripts back almost immediately after publication. There was almost always at least one significant thing that we missed, or something we could have done better, that just continues to *gnaw* at us.

In my own case, with my last book, *Resisting Throwaway Culture*, it eats away at me that I failed to address nursing homes. And the fact that I failed to address them—in a book that was tailor-made to do so—actually highlights just how good throwaway culture is at keeping the vulnerable populations it discards hidden from public scrutiny.

To be sure, I did talk about the elderly as a throwaway population, and quoted Pope Francis in so doing:

> When the elderly are tossed aside, when the elderly are isolated and sometimes fade away due to a lack of care, it is an awful sign! . . . We throw away the elderly, behind which are attitudes of hidden euthanasia. They aren't needed and what isn't needed gets thrown away. What doesn't produce is discarded.

Writing about this issue in *Amoris Laetitia*, Francis began by invoking Psalm 71, "Do not cast me off in the time of old age; forsake me not

---

CHARLES C. CAMOSY is an associate professor of theological and social ethics at Fordham University. He has written multiple books on ethics, including *Resisting Throwaway Culture*.

when my strength is spent," and then went on to identify this with the plea of today's elderly "who fear being forgotten and rejected." He insists that, just "as God asks us to be his means of hearing the cry of the poor, so too he wants us to hear the cry of the elderly."

This was in the context of a discussion about euthanasia – focused as it is on the sick, the elderly, the disabled, and others who do not fit into our consumerist model of who matters in the culture – a classic example of throwaway culture. I argued that unless we resist it with a counterculture of encounter, the killings of these populations will continue to grow in number and acceptance.

This has certainly been the case in the Netherlands, a country in which more than one in twenty people die via physician-assisted suicide or euthanasia and which sees powerful political movements to legalize these practices for those who declare that they are old and "tired of life." This is a country that saw a physician euthanize a woman with dementia despite the patient telling her doctor three different times that she didn't want to be killed. Ignoring these requests, the doctor stealthily put a deadly drug in her patient's coffee – and was then cleared of murder by the Dutch high court.

This killing of a disabled person occurred where most people with dementia live out their final days in the developed West: a nursing home. Indeed, 50 percent of all patients in US nursing homes have some kind of dementia. In *Resisting Throwaway Culture*, I even suggest that as part of a counterculture of encounter we "consider careers and intense service projects at the service of the elderly, mentally ill (especially with dementia), disabled, and terminally ill. Given levels of depopulation in the developed West we are on the verge of having way more people in need of this care than family members and others capable of caring for them." Yet I never mention nursing homes or other long-term-care facilities. How could that be?

Nursing homes – again, like many institutions doing the bidding of throwaway culture – hide in plain sight. We kind of all know they exist, and that many, many people live out their final years and months in these institutions, but they aren't talked about very much. We would prefer not to be reminded of them. And given how desperately lonely many residents of these institutions are, it appears that even their family members would prefer them out of sight and out of mind.

As I wrote in a piece on nursing homes for the *New York Times* early in the pandemic, one of the few silver linings of Covid has been that it has forced us to look at how we treat the elderly and disabled in nursing homes. Our plausible deniability of how we treat this throwaway population is gone. It took between 40 and 50 percent of all Covid-related deaths being residents of nursing homes and other long-term-care facilities, but our cultural practices in this regard (practices that often perplex immigrants from outside of the developed West) finally got the critical spotlight they deserved.

First, and most obvious, is the clear fact that (despite our knowing that their populations were by the far the most at risk) we simply didn't care about nursing homes during the pandemic. Limited personal protective equipment, staffing, and training went to hospitals, and nursing homes—already at a disadvantage in these areas—were ignored.

Well, that's not exactly true; nursing homes weren't ignored. In states like New York, New Jersey, Michigan, Minnesota, and California, decision-makers (including, most notoriously, New York State's Andrew Cuomo) intentionally dumped Covid-19-positive patients back into nursing homes in order to—you guessed it—make more space for the rest of us in hospitals. You know, the ones who count. Rationing medical resources away from the elderly and disabled is bad enough in a more typical context, but doing it this way sparked uncontrolled wildfires of infection and death.

In Belgium (another European country with an established tradition of assisted suicide), their response to the pandemic included paramedics and hospitals flatly denying care to nursing home residents, even as many hospital beds sat unused. At the beginning of their outbreak nearly two-thirds of nursing home residents who died of Covid-19 did so in hospitals. But at the peak of the Belgian pandemic, 86 percent died in the nursing home itself, never getting a chance at being saved. As a result, Belgium developed, for a time, the highest Covid-19 death rate in the world.

Sweden, famous for not locking down during the pandemic, also had terrible practices when it came to nursing homes. Health authorities there received numerous complaints from people whose elderly relatives who, once suspected of having Covid-19, were given morphine and denied supplementary oxygen, fluids, and nutrition. One nurse said that she felt like she had to lie to patients who asked her what she was giving them. "People suffocated, it was horrible to watch," she said. "Many died before their time. It was very, very difficult."

Something similar happened in Australia. Nursing home residents there suspected of having Covid-19 were also refused hospital admission, and those they thought were at risk of wandering were simply sedated, using morphine or midazolam. When nursing homes and the primary care physicians of these residents called the local hospital they were told that there were no beds for "those type of people at this time."

And this is not just a problem overseas. In reporting for this piece I spoke with a certified nursing assistant who started work in a nursing home during the pandemic here in the United States, and she (let's call her "Annella") had very similar stories to tell. "No one I've seen here gets palliative care or hospice," Annella said. "They all simply get dehydrated to death. We're told in our training that it is a good thing."

In her experience, most doctors stay away from her facility and let an understaffed, underpaid nursing and nursing assistant crew (often without the necessary personal protective equipment) care for patients with incredible needs. Desperately in need of the care of a podiatrist, many of the patients under her facility's care have mangled, misshapen feet and toes due to lack of proper care. They develop deadly pressure injuries due to lack of turning. They sit with soiled clothes for hours. Sometimes they don't even get fed.

And they are desperately, mortally lonely.

Nursing home facilities were already terrible places of isolation before the pandemic; after it, deaths of despair have gone into hyperdrive as these homes locked down and residents were strictly isolated. Annella has been a crusader on behalf of her patients and their fundamental human need for social interaction, particularly on the dementia floor where she worked.

She's fighting a difficult battle. Both systemic and explicit ableism loom in the medical field in dramatic ways, with physicians consistently rating the quality of life of their disabled patients worse than the patients do themselves.

This kind of ableism was on full display in the case of Michael Hickson, a middle-aged, disabled African American man who got Covid-19 while in a nursing home and later died in a hospital in Austin, Texas. Except he didn't die of Covid-19 alone; he also died of neglect. He died of something his wife Melissa described as a murder.

His medical team decided not to treat or feed him for six days until he was dead. Happily, at least for those of us who want this kind of ableism exposed, Melissa (legally) recorded the conversation she had with the doctor who explained the reason for the killing.

While both of them agreed that Michael should not be intubated, the recording begins with Melissa clearly explaining that she still wants Michael to be treated aggressively. His doctor, however, claims that aggressive treatment wouldn't "help him improve" and says, "Right now, his quality of life . . . he doesn't have much of one."

Melissa then says, "What do you mean? Because he's paralyzed with a brain injury, he doesn't have quality of life?"

Michael's doctor, the one who is charged with his most intimate and important physical care, simply says, "Correct."

Somehow Melissa doesn't lose control of her emotions at this point—and she does get the doctor to admit that three of his patients in Michael's situation had survived before. But he notes ominously that her husband's case "doesn't fit those three" cases.

Her husband's "quality of life is different from theirs," Michael's doctor explains. The three patients he had who survived in this kind of situation "were walking and talking people."

Melissa tries to make the case that her husband has value despite his disability, but the doctor had had enough and says, "I don't mean to be frank or abrasive, but at this point, we are going to do what we feel is best for him along with the state, and this is what we decided."

What the medical communities decide about people with disabilities, and particularly dementia, is riddled with rank bigotry, an inability to see the disabled as persons with value. We only have correlation and not causation—at least at this point—but it is worth pointing out that more than half of those who have died in nursing homes are likely to have dementia. One factor that may confound this kind of analysis is that dementia seems to make one more at risk of serious complications and death from Covid-19. Indeed, the CDC has added dementia to the list of conditions that put one at more risk.

But it would be strange indeed if treatment of Covid-19 somehow avoided the effects of the ableism in the medical field. The *New York Times*, for instance, told the story of patients with dementia being "dumped like trash" from nursing homes into unregulated boarding houses. The reason? They make more money off taking patients with Covid-19 and wanted to use the space for that. One result of this policy was that a patient with dementia who was dumped was found later wandering the streets of Los Angeles.

Not every nursing home, of course, is run with the values high-lighted above. Many nursing homes are, in fact, run very well. But many are not, particularly when they don't have resources. And how long will it be before those facing an unspeakably lonely death of despair in an underfunded and understaffed nursing home ask for assisted suicide instead? There is already growing national pressure to legalize the practice widely across the country. If we don't do something to fundamentally change how to do elder care in this country, widespread legalization of euthanasia for those who are "tired of life" is simply inevitable.

But there is an alternative to this logical terminus of throwaway culture. A counterculture of encounter—that is, one that promotes and supports genuine human interaction—could and should be at the heart of the ways we fundamentally treat the elderly.

It should start with the kinds of people we hire in nursing homes. We must change a health-care culture in which this kind of care is seen as "the bottom of the barrel" in terms of prestige for those who provide it. We must be willing to pay to hire profes-sionals like Annella who are willing to treat this population like human beings.

Consider the beautiful humanity she acknowledged and fostered in this story she sent me via email:

> I think "Rebecca" was one of my favorites. The first time I met
> her, she was on the fourth, rehab, just had come back from the
> hospital, and the fourth floor was packed. Everyone was coming

in from the hospital, and everyone was on droplet precautions so that meant we had to gown and mask up before even entering their rooms—only there weren't enough gowns and we only had one mask for a week. Lights were going off constantly and there was only one other CNA with me. We did nothing but run all night.

The Rehab floor isn't for residents. There's nothing homey about it, it's more like a hotel, except with ports for tubes coming out of the walls, and hospital beds and bathrooms. It's one, long hallway, and "Rebecca" was in the second to last room.

She had been a local photographer, a professional, and she was beautiful. You could tell that she used to carry herself gracefully. But when I met her, she was in a hospital gown with an IV attached to her and she had soaked through the diaper, her pressure injury wound pad was saturated along with the bed, and she was crying.

I don't know how long she'd been left there by herself, but it had been a long time. The look on her face was of lost hope.

I think that was the first time I got really angry at the injustice of all of it.

Changing patients is like a choreographed dance. You gather your supplies, you put the bed up high, and you do everything in halves—you strip half of the bed, roll them away from you, tuck everything tight under them, roll them back to you, and the same with the diapers. Roll, roll, roll. It takes so much out of them, when they have so little energy to spare that it's exhausting. But I got her cleaned up, dry, we washed her face, put cream on her arms and legs, got fresh sheets on, and I got her covered up with fresh sheets and a blanket. Pretty soon Rebecca was as snug as a bug in a rug, fast asleep with a very different look on her face.

I nearly cried after reading this, but Annella rightly insisted that we shouldn't consider this to be a big deal. We shouldn't be moved by just treating our elders like they are full human beings. But we often are. Because we often don't.

What else can we do to foster a culture of encounter in these spaces?

Well, I argued in a series of articles early in the pandemic that we ought to make firm commitments—as individuals, families, communities, and as a country – to care for our beloved elderly loved ones at home. We should offer adult day cares with communal activities (along with nursing help and various therapies) during the day, but we should establish a culture where they can come home to home-cooked meals and time with their children and grandchildren as well. For families without the resources to do this, we must provide help – help from networks of local institutions and churches, as well as state and federal programs.

Attempts to resist our throwaway culture by creating a culture of encounter this way have support across very different constituencies. Pro-lifers are for it. Social justice activists are for it. The families themselves are for it. Even small-government conservatives are for it (if they take the time to learn about it) because it is actually far less expensive to pay for in-home and community-based care than it is for even bad institutional care.

Despite this, there are entrenched interests – including the shareholders of the handful of large corporations that now dominate elder care in the United States – who will fight off change in favor of the status quo.

But we must push back that much harder.

Perhaps we can take our cue from Annella, who, while working the overnight shift on the dementia floor, was confronted by a veteran charge nurse who bullied, yelled, and scared the elderly patients on her floor so thoroughly that they cowered in their rooms overnight, afraid to ask for a drink, for help to the bathroom, or to be changed from their urine-soaked briefs. As she watched the charge nurse grab a patient's wheelchair and jerk it around to force the woman to bed, she told her to stop. The patient was entitled to go to bed when she wanted, how she wanted; to be treated like an honored elder, like a person.

This charge nurse had been around a long time. She had the power she had, in part, because no one else would step up and do the job. But there are others – and Annella is one of them – who oppose this abuse, and who are willing to do this work of care and encounter well.

Do we have the courage (and will) to do the same?

May 5, 2021

BE NOT AFRAID

JOSEPH M. KEEGIN

THE MACHINES WHIRRED in my father's hospital room, the monitors beeped, the drips dripped. Through the window the Sandia Mountains shone crimson as the Albuquerque sun made its evening trip earthward, filling the room with warm, golden light. It was January, and a dusting of white snow lay gently atop the peaks, softening the desert's crimson intensity and serving as a reminder of water and of seasons. And in the cardiac wing of Lovelace Hospital, in a dull stretch of city set between the mountains and the Rio Grande, my father lay dying in a hospital bed.

I got the call just days before from his girlfriend of nearly two decades. "Your dad's back in the hospital," she quavered over the phone, "probably for the last time." She'd spent at least fifteen years hating me, so her willingness to make contact itself demonstrated a sense of urgency. My dad's congestive heart failure had made him a regular visitor to the cardiac ward for as long as I can remember, and he'd undergone countless surgeries and procedures to try and bring life back to a withering organ determined to quit. It was a long, ugly fight, and he was finally losing.

My dad was a difficult guy, and our relationship was strained. My parents had separated when I was six, my mom taking me and my sister with her to Florida while my brother stayed with my dad in Marion, Arkansas. A mutual silence held throughout most of my

---

JOSEPH M. KEEGIN is a writer and editor at *Athwart* and *The Point* currently living in Chicago. He blogs at www.fxxfy.net.

teens, broken only by my reaching out to him through email in my early twenties, in a spirit of curiosity and clemency. It was a strange reencounter, an adult son getting to know his dad for the first time as a person rather than simply a parent. We wrote each other about our lives and dreams; he shared insights on music, gleaned from a lifetime of being a virtuoso tenor saxophonist. But I was soon surprised to find that one of every three emails he sent had to do with politics: the Libertarian Party newsletter, Ron Paul articles, conjectures about Obama's birth certificate. (In March of 2011, he sent a wave of articles excitedly weighing the possibility of Donald Trump running for president.)

As the years passed and we grew closer, my dad's obsession with outrage media intensified. Most of our discussions would include a tirade about Obama, a wingnut book recommendation, an anguished plea for people to "wake up." I watched how this obsession gradually alienated him from nearly everyone he knew; friends and family fell by the wayside as he crawled deeper into a cave of conspiratorial logic and monomania. His mind had become a receptacle for slogans and buzzwords that circulated within con- servative-branded political media. And while I sat holding his hand in his hospital room, stumbling through the last few opportunities for conversation we'd ever have, his attention regularly drifted to the television overlooking his bed that played Fox News and OAN on a constant loop. Even in the active unfolding of his death, with the certainty of his end staring him right in the face, his conscious- ness remained absorbed in the engrossing frivolity of the TV screen.

After he died, I learned that my dad—who, at the end of his life, had hardly any income and no savings, and who lived off the generosity and naiveté of his partner—had been sending most of his meager Social Security checks to the NRA, Project Veritas, the Donald J. Trump Foundation, and Hillsdale College. My dad had neither a firearm to his name, nor a college degree. What he did have, however, was a deep, foundation-rattling anxiety about the world ubiquitous among boomers that made him—and countless others like him—easily exploitable by media conglomerates whose business model relies on sowing hysteria and reaping the reward of advertising revenue.

Media's dominion over the public imagination is, of course, not new: many of the great humane minds of the twentieth century devoted some portion of their career to decrying the hegemony of the television and its power to reshape persons and communities. Robert Putnam's *Bowling Alone* blamed the television for the collapse of American social capital in postwar America and the widespread social alienation that followed; Marshall McLuhan predicted the televisual age would bring an end to modern individualism and return us to superstitious primitive collectivity in the "global village," a re-creation of the primordial mythic world shot through with "panic terrors" and "tribal drums." The critiques have already been made; their predictions have largely come to pass.

But for Christians, such critique should carry a different emphasis. Christianity can never be mere theory – it must inform how we live, both individually and collectively. Our theorizing must be understood as part of our long, arduous journey toward mutual edification. We are our brothers' keepers, and we must concern ourselves with the good of those we love and work to aid in their flourishing. And when we find our brothers – or our fathers, mothers, grandparents, aunts and uncles – worshiping at the altar of outrage media, offering up their anger in ritual devotion to false gods, it is incumbent upon us to free them.

Matthew Walther made a beautiful attempt at this in *The Lamp*, rebuking his fellow Catholics' obsession with Vatican inside-baseball and their inclination toward culture-war squabbles:

> I believe that you have become addicts. The drug to which you have become addicted is (like so many of the vices of our degenerate age) one of which your fathers and grandfathers could not have had any conception. I am speaking of the drug of online outrage, the soma of self-aggrandizement that you have become, I say not only accustomed to, but dependent upon, and which, not so incidentally, lines the pockets of those who have become experts in manufacturing it.

His harshness is, in fact, mercy. Tough love has a place in moral life. It is no act of love to stand by "nonjudgmentally" while someone's compulsive behavior drives him to destroy himself. Humans are adaptable creatures, and we can become habituated to—and even derive comfort from—conditions that immiserate us. Baudelaire, more keenly than most, recognized the ways we become slowly habituated to vice:

> The Devil pulls the strings by which we're worked:
> By all revolting objects lured, we slink
> Hellwards; each day down one more step we're jerked
> Feeling no horror, through the shades that stink.

And Plato knew that when someone tries to shake us out of our self-made prisons, we more often than not rebel against them. In his allegory of the cave, the philosopher who returns underground to free his peers from their shackles—and from their addiction to watching the play of shadows—finds himself in danger when those he assists turn on him angrily out of confusion and skepticism. Thus it is, I suspect, with any attempt to free others from their enslavement to addiction. (My dad, for one, always responded very poorly.) But the possibility of danger should not dissuade us from the attempt: instead, it should remind us of the need to wed courage with strategy, and to act always out of love for the ones we wish to shepherd out of bondage.

My father's drug of choice was Fox News. Others' parents may have spent the last four years shooting up on MSNBC, the conviction that a fascist coup was in process paired with an implicit belief that only their attention and fear could act as katechons to this great fall. Trump was deranged. But Trump derangement syndrome was real.

When loved ones begin to fall into the outrage-media abyss, mercy demands that we help pull them out. The consequences of such falls are, on the level of the individual, moral emergencies; at the scale of the whole of society, with huge portions of the populace getting swallowed up, they constitute a political crisis.

The median age of the typical cable-news viewer is around sixty, and more than 80 percent of Americans age sixty-five and over still receive most of their news via cable TV. Whereas younger generations are increasingly turning to a diversity of internet sources for information on current events—which is, of course, its own can of worms—the boomer imagination is still very much shaped by a set of increasingly desperate and increasingly ideological televisual media brands, represented by their respective casts of talking heads, who breathlessly interpret the events of the world in a manner harmonious with the desires and anxieties of their zealous audiences. This is, I suspect, the secret behind much of the "polarization" we decry: less differences in policies than differences in allegiance. Given that all understanding of the world beyond the home and workplace is squeezed through the homogenizing filter of corporate mass-media franchises, it should be no surprise that Fox News/OAN/Breitbart America and CNN/NYT/MSNBC America can find absolutely no common ground to stand on. If they did, it would be bad for business. What those companies sell is their viewers' attention, and they use the viewers' own neurochemical reward systems to harness that attention to hour after hour of commentary. The addictive pleasure of fear and rage is matched only by the addictive thrill of self-righteousness, and the sense that in some way by watching more (and more) you are doing your civic duty: you are part of the #resistance that will overcome the fascist threat, or part of the Real America that will take back the country from the elites. If you stick to your outlets of choice, you will never be surprised: you can count on never being exposed to facts that challenge the purity of the product that MNSBC and Fox supply. They're reliable hookups, and they won't let you down.

Readers will surely have their own stories of chasms opening up between people they love, of holiday gatherings becoming occasions for either open conflict or passive-aggressive eggshell-walking, of long tense silences settling in between friends and kin. For me, my dad serves as an especially representative example among many others. Scarcely a day has passed when I haven't overheard a story of ties being cut over media narratives of current events. Earlier this year, for instance, a retired friend in her sixties ended a decades-old romance over differing reactions to the Capitol hubbub, each party wed to their favored media outlet's interpretation of events. The commitment to their respective narratives proved more compelling than their commitment to one another.

And, if we are honest, this is not just a boomer problem. The pandemic, the election, and the string of protests and riots following the death of George Floyd have countless people glued to their news feeds, desperate for one more piece of information that will grant clarity to the maddening complexity of the world.

We are sick with fear. And often the flood of information that washes over us from the screen of every computer, television, and phone brings only disorientation, and inspires us to seek refuge on whatever isle of understanding we can find, however inaccurate. "Believing that everything will be better if only we gather more information," blogger Michael Sacasas recently wrote, "commits us to endless searching and casting about, to one more swipe of the screen in the hope that the elusive bit of data, which will make everything clear, will suddenly present itself." Finding our way out of this dilemma, Sacasas writes, requires "courage, patience, practical wisdom, and, perhaps most importantly, friendship." But these are hard, and picking narratives to build up your current picture of the world is easy. Unlike virtue, which grants a person freedom from the narrowness of his circumstances, outrage media – like any other addiction – demands more and more consumption. It sows the seeds of confusion and fear to reap its harvest of anger and resentment.

Recognizing fear as the source of the addiction helps us see a way out. When God appears to Abram in a dream to establish his covenant, his first words are: "Be not afraid." And to Abraham's son Isaac at Beersheba: "I am the God of Abraham, your father; be not afraid." An angel to Joseph, and in the Annunciation to Mary, and to the women at Christ's tomb: "Be not afraid." And Christ himself, over and over again to his disciples: "Keep watch; but be not afraid." For the rulers of this world, enlisting our bodily support in their power struggles is never enough: they want the full assent of our souls. And though we must render unto Caesar that which is Caesar's, our souls and bodies, too, belong in the last analysis only to God. The politicians will squabble, but our victory has already been won for us on Calvary. To the extent that we forget this, we open ourselves up to fear.

So what, exactly, do we do? First, dear reader, free yourself from the snares of outrage media. Engage with it as little as possible. There is nothing of real import happening in the world for which Tucker Carlson or Rachel Maddow is the best source of information. Second, try to find small ways to redirect conversation away from outrage matters. In conversation, keep focused on what is proximate and concrete, avoiding the distant and abstract: talk about hobbies and pastimes, people you actually see and talk to, the minutiae of day-to-day experience. It's okay to tell someone "I think you're watching too much of that stuff" or "I'm not really interested in talking about that." Third, it's easier with friends. "It is easier by far," Sacasas counsels, "to take a step into the unknown with another walking alongside of us than it is to do so alone." And it is the constant uncertainty of modernity, this ever-present sense of stepping into the unknown, that drives us to seek comfort in the simple narratives provided by outrage media. If we can find a way to form communities built on a mutual concern for the good of one another—or (perhaps more importantly) to bring this concern into the communities of which we are already a part—we will find ourselves less susceptible to the fear that makes us seek the false comforts of outrage narratives.

My father died mostly alone, alienated from nearly all of his children and loved ones. I managed to make some kind of peace with him, but even in our last few days and hours together, in the hospital room, our conversations were drenched in the blue light of the television. When I told him my plan to propose to my then-girl-friend, he turned toward me briefly, said, "Oh, that's great," and turned his attention back to the news.

But after he died, I learned that his older sister, my aunt, had been in regular contact with him throughout all of his chaotic adult life. Christmas cards, birthday phone calls, the occasional email or handwritten letter. She spoke with him often during the last week of his life, sharing memories, giving consolation, and encouraging him to request the last rites accessible to him as a confirmed—however lapsed—Catholic. He obliged. I think often about my aunt's patient, dutiful care for her younger brother, the love she extended to him despite his many sins and shortcomings, as well as the general drift of life that leaves siblings worlds apart. None of this fazed her. I like to think that the moments they shared near the end broke—if only briefly—the spell of the television, and that her selfless care allowed my dad to glimpse the abundant, self-giving love awaiting all of us in the arms of our Creator. I like to think that in his final moments, she helped him face his death with courage—as the angels counsel, to not be afraid.

May the means by which she gave my father a good death be our means for helping one another to find good lives, free of addiction and fear, and rooted in the rich reality of each other, of the physical world outside our screens, and of God. ⚕

May 7, 2021

RECOVERING
DEMOCRATIC POLITICS

LUKE BRETHERTON

HOW SHALL WE live together? Alongside "What is going on?" and "What is to be done?" this is one of the most basic questions of moral philosophy. The real answer is always the same. We must do politics.

Politics? Surely not. But underneath the polarization, dyspeptic rallies, backroom deals, and rage tweets is the reality that politics is the description of something good, and the stark alternative to three other options that are decidedly less so.

When I meet someone with whom I disagree, whom I dislike, or whom I find threatening, I can do one of four things. I can kill them, I can create a structure of coercion so I can control them, or I can make life so difficult that they run away. Or I can do politics. That is to say, I can form, norm, and sustain some kind of common life amid asymmetries of power, competing visions of the good, and my own feelings of aversion or fear without killing, coercing, or causing them to flee.

Today in America, across the political spectrum, it seems many are on the verge of giving up on politics as the answer to the problem of how to live together and are intent on pursuing one of the other options. This lack of faith in politics is particularly acute

---

LUKE BRETHERTON is Robert E. Cushman Distinguished Professor of Moral and Political Theology at Duke Divinity School. His most recent book is *Christ and the Common Life: Political Theology and the Case for Democracy*.

in the churches. A recent report by Lifeways Research notes that 49 percent of Protestant pastors report having to address conspiratorial beliefs in their congregations – conspiracies that foster exclusionary nationalism, an authoritarian politics, and violent responses to societal problems. These are conspiracies that demonize and vilify those with whom their subscribers disagree, those whom they dislike.

Beyond conspiracy theories is a general paranoid politics that assumes the bad faith of those disagreed with or who have a different set of beliefs and practices. This paranoid, conspiracy-laden politics was most obviously on full display on January 6, 2021, when Christianity was woven into the rhetoric, symbols, and actions of those who took part in the violent attack on the Capitol. Yet an assumption of bad faith and a deep suspicion of those who have a different set of beliefs and practices can be found across all points of the ideological spectrum.

In fact, the problem goes beyond the assumption of bad faith: according to a recent study by the group More in Common, Americans prove largely unable to accurately describe the beliefs of those in an "enemy" political camp. The study found something that will surprise no one who works in a university: the best-educated and most "politically involved" people tend to have the *most* distorted views of what the "other side" believes.

Despite the sociology, the answer to the question of how Christians should live with others not like them and with whom they disagree is still politics. Why? Because loving our neighbors cannot and should not entail killing, coercing, or causing them to flee. But if politics is the answer, we must still ask what this means in practice. Amid a highly volatile and dangerously polarized political culture in which Christianity is a key factor generating division, how can Christians find ways of healing divisions, rebuilding social trust, and undertaking the slow and respectful work of building a common life with others?

This generation is not the first to face these questions. Christian philosophers and theologians faced a parallel set of challenges in the early decades of the twentieth century. Confronted with the rise of totalitarian and authoritarian regimes and a highly polarized and paranoid politics in the 1930s and 1940s, Archbishop of Canterbury

William Temple, Jacques Maritain, and Reinhold Niebuhr all made powerful, timely cases for why Christians should invest in democracy as the answer to these problems. The archbishop, the Roman Catholic philosopher, and the American Protestant theologian found themselves arguing in parallel: they claimed that while Christians do not need democracy to practice their faith, democracy enshrines central Christian commitments, and so democracy should be an aspirational feature of political order for Christians.

But what is meant by democracy? And how can democracy be the answer when it seems to be part of the problem? Temple, Maritain, and Niebuhr gave one set of answers to these questions. However, their answers tended to conflate democracy with the institutions and structures of the liberal democratic state. In what follows I give my own set of answers, ones that develop a more bottom-up understanding of the relationship between Christianity and democracy and that are more relevant to the contemporary moment.

Democracy is not reducible to voting and party politics. It is not first and foremost a system of government, or set of laws, or an ideology. Rather, it is rooted in three things, and it is these things that form the point of connection with central Christian confessions.

The first is a commitment to listen. We must listen to others who differ from us in background and belief because their experiences, their stories, who they are as people matter.

Listening should be the most basic act for Christians. God's address – the Word – is heard before it is read or seen or smelled or touched. The opening of John's Gospel – "In the beginning was the Word" – alerts us that creation is born out of an act of communication: we must hear first so as to be able to respond. St. John is of course deliberately echoing the opening of Genesis, when God creates the world through his Word. Through hearing and responding, the Word becomes our flesh: we are baptized into Christ and become his body, to do his work in the world. We become Christians through faith, which, St. Paul says, "comes by hearing, and hearing through the word of Christ." (Rom. 10:17). The fourth-century theologian and bishop Ambrose of Milan echoes this primacy of hearing in relation to the formation of the people of God. Quoting the Shema (Deut. 6:4–6), which is the fundamental prayer of Israel, Ambrose exhorts: "The law says: Hear, O Israel, the Lord thy God.' It said not: 'Speak,' but 'Hear.'. . . Be silent therefore first of all, and hearken, that thou fail not in thy tongue."

Christians are to echo this in their response to others. As the German theologian and martyr Dietrich Bonhoeffer puts it in his book *Life Together*, "The first service one owes to others in the community involves listening to them. . . . God's love for us is shown by the fact that God not only gives us God's Word, but also lends us God's ear. We do God's work for our brothers and sisters when we learn to listen to them." For Bonhoeffer, listening with the "ears of God" is the necessary precursor to being able to proclaim the Word of God because those who do not listen to others, or who presume to already know what the other person has to say, will soon no longer listen to God.

Small-"d" democratic politics begins with listening. Listening honors fundamental premises of democracy: it marks a way of respecting the dignity of each individual, the importance of dialogue (as against killing and coercion) as means of resolving conflicts, and the principle that people should have a say in decisions that affect them and the opportunity to shape the world around them.

To really listen to others, however, entails ensuring that they can speak freely so that they may speak truthfully. Free speech, in the sense of the freedom to speak candidly, is therefore the complement to the need to listen. Such speech can take the form of passionate cries, stirring lament, and angry polemic, all of which are on occasion vital forms of democratic communication. This is true particularly when speaking against those who hold concentrated power or who are acting oppressively but who refuse to listen. Voicing and enacting (in marches, sit-ins, etc.) what we grieve for or what we are angry about is crucial for generating change. From the Hebrew prophets and Psalms onward, personal lament, anger, and grief birth public speech and action that contest an unjust status quo.

However, while prophetic jeremiads can be powerful, they suffer from the law of diminishing returns, especially if they are the only form of public speech deployed. Moreover, to be sustained, both listening and free speech require anchoring in a shared commitment to the formation of a common life in which the thriving of *all* is the aim. So while we have a responsibility to listen to dissenters, and thereby not merely tolerate but honor dissent as a part of democratic politics, dissent itself has responsibilities. One of these is the duty is to communicate in a way that can be heard. Yelling denunciations at those with whom we disagree provides invigorating emotional compensation to the ones shouting, but screaming rarely produces understanding, let alone change. And no one is under any obligation to listen to vitriolic, contemptuous, ad hominem, libelous slurs, a contemporary example of which is online trolling.

If the first point of connection between Christianity and the practice of democratic politics is listening, the second is assembly. We must gather together as a people, in order to form a polity with each other. We see this organizing dynamic at work throughout the Old and New Testaments. The people of God are founded through covenants, agreements between God and his people, and the first step toward a covenant is organizing an assembly. The people must be brought together to hear God give the law (Deut. 4:10; 9:10; 18:16). This assembly is gathered again before entering the promised land (Deut. 31:30), and again on entering the promised land (Josh. 8:30–35). After the first assembly, all the people (including women, children, and resident aliens) were supposed to assemble every seven years (Deut. 31:10–13). At crucial points in the story of Israel, it is a congregation or assembly of the people that is the basis of the reconstitution of the people of God as holy: Israel assembles to rededicate itself to God, to renounce idolatry, and to recommit to walking in justice and mercy. For example, in Nehemiah 5, an assembly of the people is organized that places limits on the power of aristocratic elites. The completion of the city walls (depicted in chapters 8–9) needed the approval of the assembled people to go ahead.

If democracy is about more than voting, and primarily identified with the negotiation of a common life through shared speech and action by a broad cross-section of an entire polity, then all the instances cited thus far reflect how democratic assembly is a necessary part of political and judicial arrangements in the constitution of Israel as a covenantal people. The church, too, is the *ekklesia* — the word itself is a Greek term for a political assembly. And ultimately the fulfillment of the people of God and the fulfillment of all creation is marked by an assembly of all nations before God at the eschaton (e.g., Matt. 25:31–46). Organizing assemblies is the first step toward constituting the people as those who stand in covenantal relation to God, to each other, and to the rest of creation.

When they assemble, the people are not passive recipients of the commands of God. They are instead active recipients, and the fullest expression and paradigmatic form of God's rule are the assemblies where God and the people speak to and hear each other, often mediated by Spirit-anointed leaders such as Moses, David, Nehemiah, John the Baptist, or Peter. These public assemblies include various kinds of Spirit-anointed speech, including reasoned deliberation, prophetic indictment, legal proclamation, exhortation, cries of repentance, and shouts of acclamation, all of which help constitute the people of God. In Christianity the importance of assembly is marked by the commitment to seeking the collective wisdom generated through an assembly's reflective deliberation (e.g., in a synod or parish council; the great ecumenical councils, beginning with the Council of Jerusalem, are the paradigmatic examples here).

Assembly, whether as a congregation or a demos, does not just happen: it needs organizing. And if the people gathered in this place, at this time, are to be democratic, those people need to organize among themselves to determine their living and working conditions. If ordinary people don't get organized then they are subject to others acting on them, the conditions of their lives being determined by systems and structures controlled by others who either won't listen to them, don't have their interests at heart, or are actively hostile.

And finally, alongside listening and organizing, both Christianity and democratic politics entail shared action. Listening and organizing are the means of coming together, but at a certain point people must act together to move the world as it is toward becoming a more just and generous one in which all may flourish. In acting together, rather than simply being acted on or responding to the decisions others make on their behalf, individuals discover their agency, forge a common world of meaning and action, and in doing so reweave the fabric of social trust and solidarity that makes society among strangers possible.

Shared action that generates democratic politics entails being both salt and light. Salt is a preservative: Being salt means identifying and conserving what is good in our society that we receive from those who came before us, tending and cultivating it so that it can be handed on to the next generation. Light, meanwhile, exposes the deeds of darkness and brings understanding: Being light means identifying what needs changing if we are to move from the world as it is to a more just and generous one. Such movement entails shared action that symbolically and physically contests oppressive or corrupt structures, groups, and practices. This contestation aims at delegitimizing existing arrangements through various kinds of direct action: marches, demonstrations, occupations, boycotts, and the like. But being light also means nurturing and forming new practices and institutional arrangements that prefiguratively embody and exemplify the kingdom of God: "we" become the change we seek, and in the process, we can learn to take delight in one another.

In general, democratic politics builds on the contention that the best way to build up a common life, sustain mutually responsible social relationships, and pursue human flourishing is not first and foremost through law or some technocratic procedure but through associating for common action. To build and sustain the quality and character of relationships that make democratic association possible takes discipline and loyalty. Loyalty or faithfulness is vital both to receiving, passing on, and developing any kind of common life, and to the shared action necessary for countering injustice or corruption, whether systemic or not. Faithfulness denotes reliability, commitment, and trustworthiness. Without it, promises are broken, relations of trust dissolve, and so the ability to deliberate and act together and the long-term reciprocal relations needed to organize and assemble over time atrophy. In this sense, both Christianity and democracy are acts of faith.

In the American and British contexts, forms of popular, local self-organization and common action emerged within the abolitionist, Chartist, labor, temperance, and civil rights movements. These were aligned and had a symbiotic relationship with popular religion. The nineteenth-century Populists provide a good example.

Their critique of monopolistic forms of power combined with the language of the Methodist camp meetings and Baptist revivals generated a powerful rhetoric with which to challenge the status quo. What these movements represent, and what they offer democratic politics, is the assertion of the priority of covenantal forms of social relationships – and the loyalty and solidarity such relations generate. By prioritizing society over state or market, covenantal forms of association are vital to upholding common values and a common life over and against their instrumentalization, commodification, or destruction through state-driven and economic processes.

One concrete approach to doing small-"d" democratic politics of the kind described here is community organizing. This is a practice that begins with listening and has particular ways of assembling people together and generating shared action toward common ends. Community organizing is an approach that transcends political camps and is committed to doing concrete good that addresses what communities actually need. It thereby promises a means by which we may be able to work together across partisan divides at the local level. It provides a concrete model of democratic politics that is nonpartisan and directly addresses, in real ways, urgent social issues such as the need for affordable housing, police reform, quality education, and economic agency. It is a form of politics that provides a meaningful, on-the-ground alternative to forms of authoritarian politics on the rise around the world (in which many Christians are involved) as well as to the highly polarized party politics that dominates the headlines.

As a form of small-"d" democratic politics, community organizing is one in which churches have been the key institutions since its inception in the 1940s. Recent research by Richard Wood and Brad Fulton shows that there are now over five thousand community-based institutions involved in this work in the United States, and of them around thirty-five hundred are religious congregations. These are spread across all denominations. The numbers of individuals directly involved is hard to calculate but is in the tens of thousands. Yet despite being one of the most significant and innovative forms of democratic politics to emerge over the past fifty years, community organizing is little understood either within or outside of the church.

Having researched community organizing extensively and out of a concern that church leaders and many others were struggling to know how to address issues of polarization and political conflict in a meaningful way, I started a podcast that tells the stories and outlines the practices of community organizing. Appropriately enough it's called *Listen, Organize, Act!* In each episode, I talk to organizers and leaders around the United States working in marginalized communities to effect real change for the better through bottom-up, grassroots efforts. I highlight also the places where the church plays a key role in that work. My guests and I discuss theology and Scripture, as well as political philosophy – but we focus on the practical. Each episode is a stand-alone discussion, but when listened to together, the episodes build on each other, with the series as a whole being a foundational course in the meaning, purpose, and mechanics of community organizing. The discussions focus as well on how organizing can connect congregations with local communities to help foster meaningful and transformational change for the better, in both the communities and in the congregations.

What these conversations confirm is that community organizing can help connect democracy and Christianity in meaningful and significant ways, particularly at a local, congregational level. They also bear witness to how organizing embodies a distinctive vision and practice of democratic politics, one that it is vital to foreground in our contemporary moment. Today, many see democracy itself either as an implausible way of solving shared problems ranging from climate change to structural racism, as impossible due to polarization, or as dangerous due to its potential for co-option by authoritarian forms of rule. The initiative for the podcast is born of a sense of urgency that unless churches find ways of practicing democratic politics, the alternatives to politics – namely killing, coercion, and causing others to flee – will become the norm. And none of these represent any kind of way to love God – let alone our neighbors.

May 19, 2021

DEMOCRACY AFTER GOD

TOBIAS CREMER

IN 1964 the prominent German constitutional lawyer Ernst-Wolfgang Böckenförde defended Germany's pro-religious constitutional settlement of church-state relations by stressing that "the liberal, secularized state lives by prerequisites which it cannot guarantee itself." The state needed, he argued, to rely on religion as a unifying ethos and source of social capital.

Today we are once again confronted with the question of what faith can contribute to the functioning of liberal democracy in contemporary multicultural societies. Yet, if one reads recent editorial pages on both sides of the Atlantic, one might be tempted to think that today the answer is: Not much.

In the United States, cross-carrying supporters of Donald Trump stormed the Capitol on January 6 to forcibly halt the confirmation of the democratically elected president. Many observers diagnosed this as "white Christian nationalism," an ideology incompatible, as they saw it, with liberal democracy.

Right-wing populists parading oversized crosses and referencing the West's Judeo-Christian identity in order to advance illiberal policies are also a common sight in Europe, as David Elcott, Colt Anderson, Volker Haarmann, and I discuss in our new book. However, on the old continent things are complicated by concern

---

TOBIAS CREMER is a junior research fellow in politics and religion at Pembroke College, University of Oxford. His most recent book is the co-authored volume *Faith, Nationalism, and the Future of Liberal Democracy.*

over the "threat" of Islam, which in some ways parallels concerns over the threat of some forms of Christianity, with even moderate voices questioning whether "backward" Islamic ideas of public worship, politics, and gender roles are at all compatible with contemporary liberal society.

Fifty-seven years after Böckenförde's statement, and after centuries in which religious movements like the Protestant Reformation have been credited with triggering the rise of the Enlightenment, the Protestant work ethic with laying the foundations of modern capitalism, and Catholic social doctrine with inspiring the rise of welfare states, more and more observers seem to wonder: Has religion exhausted its positive potential, and wouldn't liberal democracy be better served through a complete absence of religion from the public sphere? The voices answering this question with a resounding yes are becoming louder. And they are no longer restricted to the media, academia, and other secular progressive circles. Instead, survey data suggests that the majority of French and Britons now favor further restrictions of religious expression in the public sphere. And even notoriously-religion-friendly Americans are becoming more skeptical of religion. For instance, the share of Americans who think that churches or other religious institutions have little or nothing at all to contribute to solving social problems has almost doubled from 21 percent in 2001 to 39 percent in 2016. In fact, 63 percent of Americans would now prefer that religious figures stay out of political matters altogether (up from 49 percent in 2016).

Yet while the view that a more secular politics would be a desirable antidote to populism, nationalism, extremism, and religious bigotry is gaining sway, and while cross-carrying Capitol rioters and Islamic terrorists seem to be making the progressives' case for them, as a political scientist who spends most of his time researching the relationship between religion, populism, and nationalism, I am less optimistic about the alleged virtues of secularization for political culture.

For one, although we have seen unprecedented and accelerating levels of secularization in Europe and the United States over the last few decades, this has not produced any less virulent, aggressive, or polarized political cultures. On the contrary, in Britain the number of people identifying as Christian has fallen from 66 percent in

1983 to 33 percent in 2018, and today just 2 percent of those eighteen to twenty-four years old still identify with the nation's official
Church of England. Yet, in the same time frame, studies show that
the country has become increasingly polarized, and that the Brexit
vote has given voice to a powerful illiberal sentiment in the population, which has led to repeated constitutional and democratic crises,
and produced abiding social divisions and stereotyping.

Similarly, in France an unparalleled drop in the share of Catholics
in the population, from 80 percent of the population in 1980 to 48
percent in 2019, has coincided with the rise of Jean-Marie and Marine
Le Pen's right-wing populist and anti-immigrationist Rassemblement
National (RN, formerly FN) party from the margins of French society
to the top of the polls. Marine Le Pen has, as a result, a decent chance
of winning this year's presidential election.

In Germany, the eastern provinces of the former GDR are perhaps
the most secularized region in the world, with over three-quarters of
the population identifying as irreligious or atheist. Yet this region
of Germany is also the heartland of the radical Right Alternative
für Deutschland (AfD) party. And even in the United States, trends
of burgeoning social polarization and hyperpartisanship, which
culminated in Donald Trump's presidency and his supporters' riot
at the Capitol, did not coincide with another religious reawakening.
Instead, it ran in parallel with an unprecedented decline of religious
affiliation and practice among Americans (including within the
Republican electorate) as the share of Christians dropped from 80
percent of the population in 2008 to less than 65 percent in 2019.
In contradiction to what secular progressives had hoped for, rapid
secularization has not correlated with more stable and harmonious
politics, but rather with the rise of populism, identity politics, social
polarization, and hyperpartisanship.

Now, correlation need of course not imply causation, and it would
be wrong to simply blame secularization for the ills of liberal democracies based on these observations. After all, populism, nationalism,
and illiberal politics are also features of highly religious societies, and
it suffices to look to India's Hindu nationalism or right-wing populism
in Catholic Poland to recognize the potential nexus between religious
traditionalism and populist authoritarianism. Yet the prominence or

even exacerbation of nationalist populism, hyperpartisanship, and social polarization in rapidly secularizing societies suggests that the demise of religion is not a silver bullet for the beast of partisanship and extremism, nor a tonic that will lead to a more rational, moderate, and compassionate politics either. Instead, there is reason to believe that while the retreat of religion may assuage some social conflicts, it is likely to exacerbate others. Thus, in lieu of the old religious culture wars we may find ourselves confronted with a new secular identity politics that is no less virulent, divisive, or judgmental but lacks religion's potential to become a source of social capital, prophetic criticism, and self-reflection. Two recent developments illustrate this risk.

First, the rise and nature of new postreligious political movements on the left and the right, which are more secular but often also ideologically much more radical and which increasingly supplant religiously motivated movements as agenda-setters in their coalitions. At first glance, this may appear counterintuitive, in particular to many observers of right-wing politics. After all, Donald Trump's overwhelming success among white evangelicals or European populists' explicit use of Christian symbols seem to suggest that right-wing populism really is driven by white Christian nationalism. Moreover, one could argue that claims about the rise of a religiously fueled populist Right do not necessarily stand in contradiction to the demographic weakening of the religious Right, since the very decline of religion may have led to a siege mentality and reactionary cultural backlash. However, while such a mentality may indeed have led many religious conservatives to jump on the right-wing populist bandwagon, there is good reason to believe that the latter's engine is primarily fueled by the rise of a new secular Right.

This is particularly obvious in Europe, where closer scrutiny reveals not only that right-wing populist supporters there are disproportionately irreligious but also that underneath right-wing populists' superficial commitment to Europe's "Judeo-Christian identity," these parties often pursue highly secular policy agendas. The French RN, for instance, has made a hardline secularist interpretation of *laïcité* a centerpiece of their agenda and now promotes increasingly far-reaching bans of religious expression from the public sphere. Meanwhile, Germany's AfD has called for its party members to leave the churches, for clergy to be prohibited from intervening in political debates, for religious education in schools to be abolished, for theology faculties to be defunded, and for the church-friendly settlement of "benevolent neutrality," which Böckenförde sought to defend, to be abolished in favor of a stricter separation of church and state. In addition, right-wing populists across the board clash with church doctrines not only on questions around race relations and immigration but also on social issues like gay marriage or abortion, as Europe's far-right groups have embraced more socially liberal positions in an attempt to present themselves as defenders of a "modern Western lifestyle" against "backward" Islam.

Within the European electorate this political divergence is mirrored by a growing schism between the old religious Right and the new secular Right. The former is largely composed of the churchgoing and more educated middle classes, committed to socially conservative church teachings on abortion and gay marriage, but also with more openness toward immigration, and attached to conservative or Christian Democratic parties. By contrast, the new secular Right typically consists of disenchanted working-class voters, who combine more "progressive" attitudes on social issues with cultural nativism and authoritarian tendencies. Its supporters tend to have less allegiance to church teachings and look more favorably on right-wing populist policies. In Europe, this schism expresses itself empirically through an electoral "religion gap" in support for right-wing populist parties, whereby church attendance is often one of the strongest empirical predictors for *not* voting for right-wing populist parties.

In the United States, by contrast, there is no such clear divide between the old religious and the new secular Right, as both have rallied behind Donald Trump. However, a closer analysis of Trump's campaign and early core supporters still reveals a significant shift in the balance of power within the Republican coalition toward a more secular brand of conservatism. For instance, GOP grassroots supporters under Trump have become less and less characterized by "suburban mothers" who organize themselves in church halls to defend their children's rights to a Christian education or push for higher moral standards in politics. Instead, fringe movements like the alt-right, groups like the Proud Boys, and ill-defined conspiracy theories like QAnon, all of which are much more secular in outlook, have become increasingly influential. (In some cases, particularly among alt-right movements, there has been a shift not so much to secularism as to attempts to revive the pre-Christian religious traditions of European paganism.) Similarly, the Republican electorate has gradually shifted from affluent (and largely religious) suburbs to the (increasingly secularized) white working class.

While there is still significant overlap between America's old religious and new postreligious Right, survey data also show important differences between the two in terms of attitudes, suggesting a steady rapprochement between the situations in Europe and the United States. For instance, while conservative Christians have remained strongly opposed to gay marriage and abortion, but have become increasingly more open toward immigration (increasing, for instance, their support for citizenship for undocumented immigrants from 28 percent in 2011 to 37 percent in 2018), Trump's secular supporters have moved in the opposite direction. They have hardened their views on race and immigration but show comparatively less concern about LGBT rights or abortion. Alt-right figures openly discuss their frustration over the "problem" of religious conservatives' refusal to countenance abortion for nonwhite infants. With scholars stressing that among conservatives "religious participation may have a moderating effect on politics, particularly on matters of race, immigration, and identity," the secularization of the Right may be heralding a more virulent form of racial or identitarian politics.

This trend has also been amplified by the further secularization of the Left, which has led to a similar focus on identitarian issues, albeit in the opposite direction. As the *Economist*'s Lexington column recently pointed out,

> The most avowedly secular Democrats – well-educated "woke" liberals – are also the likeliest to moralise. Their Puritanical racial and gender politics sit in a long tradition of progressive Utopianism. . . . Yet these new Puritans of the left, though (or perhaps because) they are more secular than earlier progressives, are far more extreme. Their view of social justice has no place for forgiveness or grace.

While perhaps counterintuitive, this observation is supported by recent electoral data as well as by my own research findings from over 130 interviews with political and religious leaders in the United States, Germany, and France. For instance, during my conversations with Democratic officials in the United States, many senior figures stated that the most radical voices in favor of "wokism," "cancel culture," or race- and gender-focused identity politics came from white, secular, upper-middle-class liberals. By contrast, interviewees argued that, for instance, African Americans—who also happen to be by far the most religious part of the Democratic coalition—were often much less concerned with cultural tribalism and "woke" activism than with a pragmatic espousal of social justice, health care, and better wages. Emblematically, just 3 percent of Hispanic Americans use the "woke" term "Latinx" to describe themselves. It is, therefore, perhaps no surprise that the moderate and pious Catholic Joe Biden rode to the Democratic nomination on the support of African Americans, while being often vehemently opposed by many secular white liberals.

These trends on the American left seem to be mirrored in Europe. Here, traditional working-class parties have largely abandoned not only connections to unions and references to class solidarity but also to the influences of Christian social doctrine, in favor of a focus on multiculturalism, environmentalism, and woke social activism, with racial discourse that often seems imported from America. The picture is complicated by the fact that English and Continental working-class parties had their origins not just in Christian social teaching but also in explicitly atheistic communist ideas; nevertheless, the overall trend is clear. As in America, this shift has coincided with a fundamental remaking of these parties' demographic outlook: traditional constituencies of blue-collar and union voters and even immigrant communities have gradually been replaced by well-educated, white, upper-middle-class liberals. A 2017 survey in Britain showed, for instance, that 77 percent of Labour Party members were middle class, nearly half lived in London or affluent southern England, and 57 percent were college graduates. Similarly in France, sociologists like Pascal Perrineau have observed the social and cultural gentrification—*embourgeoisement*—of the French Left. That embourgeoisement was, again, paralleled by the end of religious influence on the left; of course the French Left had anticlerical origins, but especially in the second half of the twentieth century it had a very powerful Catholic wing (*cathos de gauche*) centered on figures like Jacques Delors or even François Mitterand himself. But no more. Secularization, and the subsequent rise of new postreligious political movements, have hence fundamentally reshaped the focus, strategy, and policy agendas of both the political Right and Left.

A second and perhaps even more profound way in which secularization may have inadvertently contributed to a more polarized political culture and the rise of illiberal nationalism is through the erosion of religion as a source of social capital, prophetic criticism, and self-reflection. Sociologists like Harvard's Robert Putnam have long emphasized the importance of religion as a key source of social capital, especially among disadvantaged parts of the population. In the United States, for instance, nearly half of all associational membership has traditionally been church-related, half of all personal philanthropy has been religious in character, and half of all volunteering has occurred in a religious context. This has been particularly important for otherwise disadvantaged working-class communities as, unlike many other sources of social glue, religious communities are freely accessible and have historically facilitated social cohesion and mobility by cutting across class divides and political parties.

Moreover, in the form of what has come to be known as civil religion, at least a vague form of quasi-Protestant belief has also provided a shared sense of belonging, common symbols, and a source of prophetic criticism for America's religiously, politically, and racially diverse society. Civil religion of some sort has historically been prevalent in most societies, from Athena's patronship of Athens to the United Kingdom's established church, but it has received particular attention in the American case because it has proved so successful in forging unity out of diversity. US presidents and civil-society leaders alike have routinely appealed to America's civil-religious tradition in order to bridge social divides and hold the nation accountable to its own higher principles. Joe Biden's inauguration speech, in which he praised the healing power of faith for a divided nation, cited St. Augustine, appealed to Americans to hold true to the nation's higher ideals, and led the nation in silent prayer, was only the most recent prominent expression of this tradition.

However, as secularization rapidly advances in the United States and other Western nations, religion's ability to serve as a source of inclusive collective identity, social capital, and prophetic criticism is faltering. Biden's references to faith in his campaign and inauguration speech drew criticism from the secular Left, which perceived it as being too religious. At the same time, it largely failed to reach Trump supporters, many of whom seemed to set greater store by the neopagan "QAnon Shaman" with his Viking helmet than by Biden's invocation of the Christian saint. Recent scholarship also suggests that the much-lamented malaise of America's white working class may be tightly linked to the steep decline of social connectedness, employment, marital stability, and cultural conservatism in the wake of rapid secularization. As the American Enterprise Institute's Tim Carney argues, "The woes of the white working-class are best understood not by looking at the idled factories but by looking at the empty churches."

Combined with the rise of more secular and more radical left-wing and right-wing movements, this crisis of civil religion (or civilly effective religion) and social connectedness returns Western societies to the profound predicament Böckenförde diagnosed almost six decades ago: namely the question of how a liberal society can define community and the common good over profound differences and build a unifying political culture in the increasing absence of shared narratives, symbols, institutions, and values. To be sure, secularization and the decline of religion are only a part of this puzzle. Globalization, rapid ethnic change, the technological transformation of work, and the economy have equally undermined traditional pillars of civil society, eroded senses of belonging and identity, bred division and resentment, and led to new political schisms and reconfigurations. However, historically, faith communities and a shared (civil-)religious tradition have served as a social buffer, cultural lubricant, and political bridgebuilder in such periods of upheaval. Without them Böckenförde's dilemma reemerges more powerfully than ever. The postreligious politics of the Left and Right have shown limited promise in healing a fragmented culture, providing social capital, or facilitating critical self-reflection. Democracy after God appears to be in for a rough ride. ⚘

May 21, 2021

THE SMALL MAGAZINE PROJECT

ELAYNE ALLEN

As the year-long project that has been Breaking Ground*'s pub-lic-facing publishing comes to an end, we encourage our readers and the community we have built to explore other publica-tions—many of which publish* Breaking Ground*'s community of writers, and several of which (*Comment, Mere Orthodoxy, Plough, New Polity*) are also edited by* Breaking Ground*'s editors. Elayne Allen, below, offers a graceful and inspiring overview of the landscape of humanist and Christian humanist "little magazines." There's a whole world out there. Dive in!*

WHEN ONE SURVEYS the landscape of public discourse, exas-peration is often the most appropriate response. Political rivals seem more interested in hurling philippics at each other than debating society's most urgent questions. Imperious sneering at adversaries' weakest arguments is the defining posture of the day.

Amid the cacophony of today's disjointed discourse, there are a few magazines with modest circulations but hefty intellect that offer a refreshingly countercultural approach to public dialogue. In November 2020, *The Point* magazine published *The Opening of the American Mind,* an anthology of essays it had published between 2010 to 2020. Founded in 2009, *The Point* pins this pithy but

ELAYNE ALLEN is a research assistant at the American Enterprise Institute and an alumna of Hudson Political Studies, the Hertog Foundation, and the John Jay Insti-tute. Follow her on Twitter @Elaynethepain.

lofty self-description: "A magazine founded on the suspicion that modern life is worth examining." *The Opening* is a book well worth reading—not just because it's a delightful snapshot of *The Point*'s intellectual dexterity, but also because it offers a window into the political significance of the small-magazine project in general.

Other publications that I would classify alongside *The Point*, though each with its distinct tone, are: *The Hedgehog Review*, which has no discernable political leaning but aims to understand and propose remedies for the malaise of the modern age; *Plough*, a Christian magazine that sometimes tilts left, but sans political zeal, preferring to ask "the big questions"; most recently, *The Lamp*, which touts "consistent undiluted Catholic orthodoxy" and publishes a rich banquet of content. Of course, other high-caliber publications fit the bill too: *National Affairs*, *The New Atlantis*, *Mere Orthodoxy*, *Comment*, and plenty more.

The unifying feature of these publications is, I think, that they betray the intellectual habits of minds liberally educated: philosophically nimble engagement with the chosen material; detachment from ideological and partisan argumentation; and, above all, desire to understand the truth of the matter at hand. As Jon Baskin and Anastasia Berg, the editors of *The Opening of the American Mind*, point out in their introduction, *The Point*'s intellectual project bears striking resemblance to the goals of humanistic education. (By humanistic, I do not refer to the philosophical movement called "humanism," but to the liberal arts, which, roughly speaking, are disciplines focused on the basic questions of existence.) They observe that, over the course of a lifetime, everyone inevitably confronts reality's labyrinth of philosophically fraught choices: "what to eat, where to work, how to vote, whom to love or what to worship."

The book greets its readers with a bracing assortment of essays. Authors bring a liberally-educated tenor to a broad range of issues: race, #MeToo, today's literature, right-wing neo-reactionary politics. Describing their vision for *The Point*, Baskin and Berg write, "To create a public space that could do justice to the adventure of the American mind—in its full diversity and vitality—meant allowing our writers to go wherever their experience would take them." They continue, "It meant publishing liberals and conservatives, philosophers and activists, Marxists and Catholics, New Yorkers and Midwesterners."

The Point's general tone is intellectually self-aware and hospitable to sound thinking from politically various voices, a trait it shares with other humanistic publications. In his essay "Tired of Winning," Baskin describes his life working in communications for a progressive think tank. Working there meant you were "on the side of reality" and that "there were no questions, only answers." His job required him to "package those answers as appealingly as possible" and "exist completely within the confines of this self-congratulatory stupor." Partly driven by his distaste for such work, Baskin then recounts his discovery of new and intellectually serious leftist magazines: *n+1, Jacobin, The Baffler*, and others. But he quickly realized that even these magazines, however probing, were limited to the confines of their ideological horizons. For the most politically diehard publications, the intellectual's job is merely to "aid the activist" because "writing just is a form of messaging."

The Point, on the other hand, attempts "to conduct a conversation about modern life that includes but is not limited by political conviction." Baskin continues, "Our political conversation today suffers from hardly anything so much as a refusal of anyone to admit the blind spots and weaknesses of their ideas, the extent to which they fail to tell the whole truth about society or even about their own lives." *The Point* grasps the inevitable intellectual limits of political argumentation. This awareness leads them to run pieces that are unconventional for mainstream intellectual publications – see, for example, a recent essay in which Cistercian monk and Catholic integralist Edmund Waldstein reflects on celibacy as a path to experience God's love more deeply. Or Agnes Callard's often zany but always edifying column.

Readers might wonder how Christian publications like *Plough* or *The Lamp* can participate in this humanistic endeavor if they bring prior theological commitments to their ideas. While it might seem that dogma is incompatible with intellectual openness, Christianity (when it's truest to itself) embraces worldly wisdom in its full vibrance. In *The Love of Learning and Desire for God: A Study of Monastic Culture*, Jean Leclercq describes the tender affection with which medieval monasteries regarded secular sources of knowledge. Leclercq's sparkling line captures their attitude: "The literature of this world can be an ornament of our souls as well as of our style, if we but know how to direct it to the worship of God." Furthermore, intellectual openness does not demand total skepticism on all philosophical matters. During a recent book event for *The Opening*, Jonny Thakkar noted that *The Point* has no definitive political position, but seeks writing that is intellectually challenging. There are surely philosophical limits to what counts as challenging within contemporary discourse. Like *The Point*, Christian humanist publications eschew definitive political positions but, unlike *The Point*, embrace defined theological parameters – with delightful results.

So what's special about the humanistic publications, Christian or not, if they cultivate the same intellectual virtues as liberal education? Are publications like *The Point* and *The Lamp* merely outposts or extensions of liberal education that simply reach different audiences? Not exactly. Unlike the academy, humanistic publications have a public mission as their primary focus. Academic work, particularly in the liberal arts, requires temporary suspension from everyday concerns and the political debates of the day. Elizabeth Corey has written in *National Affairs* that the disinterested attitude (an essential ingredient of liberal learning) "demands a quieting of the self and its interests in order to enter into the intellectual and moral worlds of other people who may be quite unlike us in terms of geography, history, and outlook." Zena Hitz observes in *Lost in Thought: The Hidden Pleasures of an Intellectual Life* that the intellectual life involves total (if temporary) retreat from the world.

When academic work is truest to itself, it is not responding to the news, and it resists being politicized. Good academic work requires stepping away from the heat of contemporary debates. Peer-reviewed periodicals usually lack direct bearing on current events; they contribute to academic dialogue within segmented research havens. The primary goal of scholarly journals is not to inform public debate but to contribute to a highly specialized academic discussion. Of course, scholarly work is often pregnant with lessons for present-day political debates, and of course scholars themselves have political positions, but unless they are corrupt, scholars' primary aim is not to inform public debate.

By contrast, Baskin and Berg write that *The Point*'s intellectual mission involves "leaving the library stacks – and every other enclave of settled opinion – and confronting the pandemonium of the American mind in its multiple manifestations: in contemplating and reading but also at work and at home, in love, in protest and at play." *The Point*'s vision of the American mind "is not a mind bred in isolation to rule or instruct its fellow citizens but one driven out into the world by its curiosity." *The Point*'s writers and editors receive simultaneous instruction from, on the one hand, worldly events and daily experiences, and on the other hand the great lineage of humanistic thought that dwells on reality's fundamental, unchanging truths. The humanistic magazine converses with the world, sometimes offering guidance, other times listening – but its defining aim is to contribute to public discourse. It is a bridge, in a way, between the active and contemplative lives.

These dual reservoirs of the humanistic magazine generate a hybrid form of dialogue – one that doesn't require temporary suspension of one's political and philosophical commitments, as liberal learning does, but embraces them. But it embraces them in a way that is chastened by the very humanistic tradition that it draws from. As Berg and Baskin point out in the introduction, "The writers in this collection signal their opposition to the prevailing assumption that political commitment is incompatible with a desire for dialogue, self-reflection or self-criticism." Yet humanistic magazines deploy the full intellectual excellence and humility that liberal learning instills. Such publications are the rare meeting ground where philosophical gaze and practical toil come to a truce and sit down for coffee.

In this way, humanistic journals have marvelous democratic potential. One can join a community of readers and writers without toils of enrollment, relocation, or unthinkable tuition. If, say, an aerospace engineer, rap legend, homemaker, or barista is too busy for full-time intellectual work, humanistic publications can nourish his or her mind during moments of leisure, however brief.

This intellectual practice is profoundly important for both public life and personal flourishing, and one of the things that the tradition itself implies is that these two are in fact linked. When someone reads a humanistic publication, her mind and spirit are fed by the deep wells of *ressourcement* while her practical reason is still engaged with public matters and the concerns of her political moment. The humanistic journal's community of readers and writers considers political matters with utmost depth (entering into conversation with the great texts and thinkers of the past) and breadth (welcoming input from personal experience, their fellow citizens, and the contemporary social landscape). Baskin and Berg write, "Only through dialogue with our fellow citizens – only by continually opening ourselves to their criticism, instruction and difference – can we credibly claim to maintain an open mind." Humanistic journals, clearly distinct from both unadulterated intellectual activity on the one hand and mere partisan punditry on the other hand, fulfill a peculiar social role.

At the heart of such publications, I think, is an unspoken belief that politics need not be a realm of pure power, but can sometimes obey reason and conform to truth and justice; that conversation, beauty, and friendship can be roots of political order. By infusing public debate with reflection and academic rigor, humanistic journals attempt to both learn from and elevate political discourse beyond itself – pushing politics past its natural cycles of cynicism. The publications actively test the question posed by Alexander Hamilton's *Federalist* No. 1 about whether polities can be guided by "reflection and choice, or whether they are forever destined to depend for their political constitutions on accident and force." Jonny Thakkar remarked during *The Opening* book event that, in *The Point*'s early years, he and his fellow editors realized they needed to defend two related ideas at the heart of the magazine's mission. The first, he said, is "that intellectual life didn't always have to be disciplined to political ends." The second is that "political life can be enriched by genuine intellectual exploration."

The uncomfortable truth about humanistic publications is that, despite their democratic potential, they remain stubbornly niche. It can be hard to see how political life is "enriched" by humanistic publications if few people read them. But a crucial rejoinder can be culled from *The Point*'s capacious intellectual project. A defining trait of small humanistic publications is that they are free from political missions. Even as they study the "pandemonium of the American mind," their aim isn't to democratize the intellectual life, if that means to persuade massive numbers of people that what they really want to be doing is reading essays by Cistercian monks. Rather, as noted above, it is to cultivate intellectual sobriety for readers who crave it, even when popular taste prefers scornful takedowns. And that sobriety can through these journals become available to those who are not college educated, or (as *The Point* staff member and author Joseph Keegin has described) who have complicated relationships to the world of academia, as well as those whose membership in the guild is more straightforward.

In the readership of these magazines, in the events that they offer, even (at least occasionally) in the Twitter threads about the pieces, those who want to be part of a conversation like this can find each other. Amid an intensely polarized era, when more and more of life becomes politically sorted, humanistic publications' committed readership reveals a stubborn urge to find wisdom. As writer and editor Adam Keiper recently noted, magazines do what Substacks cannot: "With strong editorial leadership, a magazine can lift writers to produce better work than they could on their own and can help readers learn things they did not already know they cared about." Their audiences may be small, but the sense of wonder that lives on their pages resonates with an unchanging part of the human spirit.

Humanistic publications offer philosophical and literary texture to reality's inevitable moral complexity. Becca Rothfeld recently wrote in *Liberties* journal about "sanctimony literature," a perfect inverse of the writing cultivated by the humanistic magazine. The defining mark of sanctimony literature is its barren moral imag-ination, wherein virtue resides exclusively on the political plane. The height of sanctimony literature's ethical drama involves unin-tended self-caricature: outspoken communists, activists attending ICE protests, rants about capitalism's universal destruction, and so on. What sanctimony literature fails to do is what the humanistic magazine achieves: in Rothfeld's words, "the intellectual excitement of trying to answer the exceedingly complicated question of what a morally serious person should be like." Humanistic publications eschew juvenile portraits of the moral life, whether progressive or conservative, and instead prefer to plumb the depths of the human heart and the strange world we live in. These publications have dared to seek illumination amid the flux of confusion that no ideology can adequately paper over. For those unsated by trite fiction and pandering commentary, the humanistic publication promises abundance.

It's unclear whether the state of discourse today is worse than it's ever been. The shift to digital communication seems to have deteriorated dialogue by abbreviating it and incentivizing factionalization. At best, social media mirrors the dismal state of debate, unflattering as it is. If America's social order continues to careen down such a path, it would be difficult not to conclude that "accident and force" are the governing principles of our politics. But humanistic journals offer a third way, not sealed off from politics, nor mired in partisan bickering. So long as publications like *The Point* have a stake in discourse, there is reason to hope in our public life. ⚘

BREAKING GROUND

Christian Civic Humanism for a World Renewed

SUSANNAH BLACK

> Behind many a story of tyranny lies collusion between oppressor and oppressed, a community that prefers to accept a shrunken public realm rather than pay the price of discerning and articulating complex truth in public.
>
> —Oliver O'Donovan, *The Ways of Judgment*

OLDHAM'S MOOT

IN HIS BOOK *The Year of Our Lord 1943*, Alan Jacobs describes "the Moot," a group established in 1938 by J. H. Oldham, following an international ecumenical conference on "Church, Community and State" that had met in Oxford in July 1937. Oldham "sought to mobilise a movement of both thought and action engaging with society on the basis of Christian faith," and over the next ten years, Oldham's Moot regularly convened a group of Christian and Christian-adjacent public intellectuals, among them T. S. Eliot, John Baillie, Donald MacKinnon, Alec Vidler, Michael Polanyi, and Karl Mannheim. The purpose of the Moot was to "cultivate a profound Christian humanism in the public life of their society." "One can waste a great deal of time, in the present world," wrote Eliot,

> by disagreeing with people whose thought is really irrelevant to one's own thinking. . . . What is valuable is the formulation of differences within a certain field of identity. . . . These are the

people worth disagreeing with, so to speak. This I think we have in the Moot, and this we ought to keep.

Michael Polanyi said that these discussions "changed our lives." Jacobs discusses the Moot and other thinkers close to it: C. S Lewis, Simone Weil, Richard and Reinhold Niebuhr, W. H. Auden.

As Anne and I have pursued this *Breaking Ground* project over the last year, Jacobs's book has been a lurking presence in our minds. Could we, we wondered, face a crisis not simply as something to be survived, but as an occasion for courageous and imaginative, future-oriented reflection and planning? What, we wondered, was this year revealing about who we were? What exactly is this culture of ours? And how can we pursue a world that is better than the one we left behind in March of 2020?

NEXT STEPS

We've spent this year commissioning pieces that have brought a Christian-humanist lens to those areas of our common life especially touched by the always-interesting 2020–21 news cycle: political po-larization; the fragmentation of social trust; the nature, use, and abuse of political authority; the possibility of solidarity between races and classes; the isolation and disembodiment that the pandemic seems to have so intensified; the horror of the way we treat our elders and the possibility of a renewal of the virtue of filial piety on a culture-wide level; the promises and dangers of medical technology. We tried to be responsive without being reactive. We tried to be practical, even as we sought to understand some of the deeper currents at work rather than propose a litany of policy prescriptions.

And in doing all this we have somehow attracted an extraordi-nary network of people and organizations, a network I do not see paralleled elsewhere. Theologically orthodox, these groups and indi-viduals – American, English, and Canadian – are otherwise varied in their political approaches, theological stream, civil sphere, and civic mission. Thus they are also varied in the audiences they serve.

We find ourselves now with a body of work and an institutional structure that deserve stewardship. And the challenges that remain are stark. Our public discourse seems caught in purity tests and cancellation; we have systematically refused what Oliver O'Donovan has called our basic duty to each other:

> not, as such, the obligation of a subject specifically, but the obligation of a member of society, something owed to the neighbor before anything is owed to the ruler. This is the duty to preserve the public truth of social engagements by exercising candor in the public realm, a candor which necessarily includes appraisal of the conduct of political authority. . . . Yet free speech can only be encouraged, not conferred, for free speech is a participation in the word of God, not a privilege which one form of constitution may confer, another refuse. Neither is it a "right" that one citizen may claim, another forgo. That would imply that only the private citizen who exercised it had an interest in it, whereas candor is of the greatest importance for the public realm itself. Candor is simple public duty, often underperformed, often performed badly, out of simple reluctance to take responsibility for the truth on which the community depends.

This is the duty that the *Breaking Ground* network will seek to promote. We believe that there is a great need for just such a network to help Christians working in various areas of society to think through and make decisions for action that draw from the deepest wells of the Christian-humanist tradition.

And just what is this tradition? Christian humanism, born out of the ferment of the Renaissance, combined the Quattrocento's renewed interest in classical scholarship and the nature and possibilities of humanity with a profound commitment to the reality and centrality of the Christian faith. Influencing both the Protestant Reformation and the Counter Reformation, it fostered an explosion of scholarship, imaginative and didactic writing, ethical reflection, investigation of the natural world, visual art and architecture, music and education, as well as new social forms and the renewal of personal piety. In its civic form, it sought to bring these goods into the public sphere, shaping political structures and the minds of rulers, as well as bringing new honor and responsibility to the office of the citizen.

This is the tradition from which we've drawn inspiration and sought to water for a new bloom in our time. So what's next? Well, for one thing, while our public-facing publishing venture is wrapping up, the *Breaking Ground* network of institutions and the leaders stewarding them will continue to meet together to have these conversations; I encourage you to follow the work of, and consider becoming involved with, any one or more of our partner organizations.

I encourage you also to seek out the conversation we have been having in these pages where it is continuing: in *Comment*, *Plough*, and The Trinity Forum, and also in the pages of a new crop of humanist and Christian humanist "little magazines" so ably described by Elayne Allen in her piece in these pages.

What are these magazines for? Above all they are institutions that serve as bridges between our contemplative and active lives: between the leisure that is the basis of culture and the practical reason aimed toward action that we must all use as we make choices in our private lives as family members and economic actors, and in our public lives as citizens.

These magazines also serve as hubs around which communities form: that dense network of friendships and conversations, writers and editors, scholars and churchmen, community shepherds and organizational leaders. This symphony, this mosaic, is the Christian-humanist public sphere.

THE PUBLIC CALLING

This is not, we believe, an optional extra for human life and Christian discipleship. It is inappropriate for us to fail to participate in public life. Becoming a Christian means being able to be, more effectively, what humans always were supposed to be, what Adam was made to be, and what his progeny should have been after him: rulers under God over the created world, rulers of our own lives and households, full participants with full responsibility in the human project.

And as both the Hebrew and Greek strands of our tradition testify, that project is in essence a political one: We are political animals. To be confined only to private life, to getting and spending or to the good of our households, as important as these things are, is to be only half human. Set free by Christ, we should not act like slaves who are denied responsibility for the *res publica*, the public thing. Made part of his ruling family, we should not act like private citizens.

This does not of course mean that all are called to hold public office. As O'Donovan puts it,

> The duty of public candor is not a duty of public office alone. Subjects who hold no public office may discharge it by the way they tackle their business in the public realm, look to safeguard the common good in their commercial engagements, articulate and discuss the common good with those they deal with, not isolating themselves by technical narrowness or professional mystique, by advocating, justifying, listening to others' advocacy and justification, seeking a common understanding and approach to common tasks, avoiding the sins of rhetorical exaggeration and administrative impatience.

But we are all called to be civic agents, to lead in the spirit of Elijah and risk in the model of Paul. And this will require a very different sort of public engagement—and private support—than the models of recent memory.

THE OPPOSITIONAL STANCE

One of the things that *Breaking Ground* has addressed extensively over the last year, and that we must now push forward in grappling with, is the way that Christianity has conducted itself in politics.

Evangelicalism has done great good in the world, both the movement as it began in the eighteenth century in Great Britain, and the revival of that movement in the second half of the twentieth century in the United States. But the more recent version has had a culture problem, which is really an authority problem.

This new American evangelicalism understood itself as fundamentally not at the center of power or of intellectual life: it was made up, largely, of non-mainstream people who were not in the mainline churches and who wanted to reject the oppositional culture of fundamentalism without rejecting the tenets of the faith. It always had the uneasy sense that this might not be possible; it always had the flavor of attempting to create a just-as-good-as-secular-culture culture, to prove to the mainstream that it was not like its embarrassing funda-mentalist uncles. It did not perceive itself as having authority.

This culture of supplication gave rise, in reaction, to certain problems among many of the evangelicals who supported Trump. It also gave rise to certain problems in anti-Trumpian evangelicalism. In both cases, there was a fundamental unease with power, a fun-damental inability to perceive oneself as having authority: a kind of addiction to victimhood, to being the underdog.

This, combined with the pathologies in our political culture at large, has created four distinct political distortions. First, some Christians now perceive Christianity as little more than an interest group among other interest groups, the religious-industrial complex that jockeys and seeks rent alongside lobbyists from, say, the oil and gas industry – one that seeks "favors" from the state. Second, in an attempt to rebuke this squeamish instrumentalism we see a growing affection for the suggestion that political involvement at all, let alone state support for churches, is bad for the church – as Nilay Saiya suggested recently in the pages of *Christianity Today*. (Saiya cannot seem to imagine a kind of Christian relationship to politics that is not as an interest group.) And then there is a third thing happening: a preemptive self-alienation, a bunker mentality or willingness to cry persecution, which prevails all too frequently on the right. Fourth, we see a desire to distance oneself from those "other" Christians, the embarrassing conservative ones, such that we can preserve our sophisticated relationships, our pristine calling to translate from the sacred to the secular, our Christian cosmopolitanism.

CHRISTENDOM IN A PLURALIST SOCIETY

This all seems, frankly, sad and unnecessary. It's just not the way normal human politics is ordinarily done, nor is it the way human culture is normally made. It's perfectly possible to have an orthodox Christianity that understands itself to be at the center of making hu-man culture, while interacting with non-Christians and their cultural products who are also at the center, and with a grounded sense of political responsibility: because that's just what's actually true. And it's not as though this is the first time this has happened. This is the story of the roots of the church, of St. Paul in the agora, of St. Augustine in his study, of Hellenic philosophy and Judaic theology, of Roman playwrights and Hebrew prophets.

The work that *Breaking Ground* has been a part of is simply this work: continuing the work of Oldham's Moot, of that midcentury Christianity which itself has roots that, age by age, reach back to the very beginnings of our faith, of our civilization, of the world that God created and redeemed and that we are called to form and fill.

The thing is, this is all very natural. Our culture is inescapably woven together with Christianity. Whatever cultural work we do, whatever political projects we pursue, whatever scholarship we do, whatever art we make is in profound continuity with the past five thousand years of mainstream human cultural life. It is (one might gently point out) the secularists who are out of place, using words and ideas whose origins they do not know, living and working in buildings built by those who share our faith. They too, though, are carrying out Adam's task, aided by common grace, and if we somehow think that we can't or shouldn't work in cooperation with them toward the good – tell that to Aquinas, as he cooperated with Aristotle. We don't need to be anxious. We just need to carry our work forward.

The anxiety that refuses to do this, and which gives rise to all four distortions of Christian political life I mentioned above, has a particular name. Its name is pusillanimity. It is thinking oneself less able, with less authority, than one in fact has. It is being self-marginalizing, self-emasculating.

Pusillanimity must be refused: it is in fact a vice, though one often disguised as the virtue of humility. It must be refused in part because those who are pusillanimous are dangerous: they don't believe they really have authority, and so they can only imagine using power for their own private gain, or for irresponsible schemes, and they are afraid of losing it. Like a rageaholic who screams because he feels he is unheard, if they do have power they may hurt others with it through not knowing their own strength; if the pusillanimous person is a Christian in a pluralist society, he may forget the actual purpose of politics and seek to govern for the benefit of

Christians *as a kind of interest group*, as opposed to the general good. This is a recipe for disaster in a person and in a state.

MAGNANIMITY

The corresponding virtue to the vice of pusillanimity is, of course, magnanimity.

How can we claim, as Christians, that magnanimity is anything but one of what St. Augustine called the "splendid vices" of the pagans? Aristotle defined μεγαλοψυχία, *megalopsychia*, greatness of spirit, as "claiming much and deserving much." This sounds impossible to square with humility, and with being followers of the Lord, who "did not regard equality with God as something to be grasped."

But St. Thomas tells us that, indeed, magnanimity is a virtue. He gives it a subtle twist, however—and with that twist he throws the whole of human life into proper shape. "Magnanimity," he writes,

> by its very name denotes stretching forth of the mind to great things. . . . Since a virtuous habit is denominated chiefly from its act, a man is said to be magnanimous chiefly because he is minded to do some great act. . . . An act is simply and absolutely great when it consists in the best use of the greatest thing.

John Witherspoon, certainly familiar with Aquinas's rescue of this virtue, preached a sermon to the 1775 Princeton graduating class that is one of the most thoughtful and thorough treatments of Christian magnanimity that I know of. As we seek to mend what has gone wrong in the relationship of Christianity to our public life, and to move forward in our public calling, I can think of few better guides.

His text was from 1 Thessalonians: "For you know how, like a father with his children, we exhorted each one of you and encouraged you and charged you to walk in a manner worthy of God, who calls you into his own kingdom and glory."

The virtue of magnanimity, says Witherspoon, is what leads men

> to attempt great and difficult things, to aspire after great and valuable possessions, to encounter dangers with resolution, to struggle against difficulties with perseverance, and to bear sufferings with fortitude and patience.

THE MAGNANIMOUS MULTITUDE

Witherspoon also, in a way, "democratizes" that most undemocratic of virtues, as Christianity itself democratizes Aristotelian *eudaimonia*, opening its gates to women, to slaves, to the sick and the poor and those otherwise sadly lacking in an Athenian private income or a Roman latifundium.

We are to live according to our station (he would say) but in every station, we may live nobly. I'd push back against what sounds like the more rigid aspects of this formulation: an auto mechanic's daughter may obviously get a philosophy doctorate; a banker's son may read too much Wendell Berry and apprentice himself to a farmer. But his point remains, and that point is at its best not different from Freddie deBoer's in his recent *Cult of Smart*: there are different kinds of ways of living a good human life, and not everyone need aim at a tenure-track position at an Ivy.

Magnanimity will spur us to greatness but keep us from a mean grasping, as well as from having contempt or bitterness toward those whose place in life is not ours. It will not create pride or overweening ambition, but will make men "active and zealous in the duties of that place in which they already are." Each of us, by our rational nature, our descent from Adam and reception of the creation mandate to make civilization, has a high enough birth to exercise this virtue – or to fail in it. Each of us, by our adoption in Christ, has been given an even greater scope. "When a prince, or other person of the first order and importance in human life," Witherspoon says,

> busies himself in nothing but the most trifling amusements, or arts of little value, we call it mean, and when any man, endowed with rational powers, loses them through neglect, or destroys them by the most groveling sensuality, we say he is acting below himself. The contrary of this, therefore, or the vigorous application of all our powers, and particularly, the application of them to things of moment and difficulty, is real magnanimity.

Nor will magnanimity drive us to refuse obedience, refuse the call of just authority. It is not the magnanimous soul that says "no gods, no masters." In his *Letter to the Duke of Norfolk*, John Henry Newman writes that we must seek to vanquish that mean, ungenerous, selfish, vulgar spirit" which is a corruption of our nature, and which,

> at the very first rumour of a command, places itself in opposition to the Superior who gives it, asks itself whether he is not exceeding his right, and rejoices, in a moral and practical matter to commence with scepticism.

Nor will it lead us to refuse to recognize excellence not our own: this is not self-aggrandizement but very nearly its opposite. Magnanimity has room for others, for their good, for a delight in their excellence. It is above all not envious. Because it has this spaciousness in it, it is entirely compatible with – even requires – humility, and the willingness to be delighted by the world; indeed, St. Thomas tells us that humility and magnanimity are paired virtues, each according to right reason helping us to act well, with wisdom, in the world.

THE DUTY OF DESIRE

Magnanimity defeats irony-poisoning and the cynicism that keeps us from full engagement with life. Pusillanimity is closely related to the vice of acedia, of the boredom or apathy that refuses to be interested in the interesting, or to acknowledge or treat the worthwhile as worthwhile. In *The Last Battle*, the tide has turned: Eustace has fought off two Calormene soldiers who have kept a group of Dwarfs captive. "Well struck!" King Tirian says. "Now, Dwarfs, you are free. Tomorrow I will lead you to free all Narnia. Three cheers for Aslan!" But the Dwarfs refuse – they refuse both to believe that they are really freed, that there is an Aslan to follow, and they refuse the call of high service, to help free others. "We've been fooled once, and we're not going to be fooled again. . . . The Dwarfs are for the Dwarfs." This cynicism is what magnanimity refuses.

Witherspoon goes so far as to say that in fact it is *only* those who have received the gospel who can be truly magnanimous: that only in Christianity can greatness be wedded to goodness, and classical arete to the theological virtues. His reasons for this are striking. "A great mind," he says, has great capacities of enjoyment as well as action. . . . The large and increasing desires of the human mind, have often been made an argument for the dignity of our nature, and our having been made for something that is great and excellent.

Witherspoon—and Christianity itself—offer an answer to desire, and to suffering, remarkably different from the Classical Good Life Emergency Backup Philosophy (i.e., stoicism) does. Stoicism teaches us to desire less, to accept loss and death. Christianity teaches no such thing.

The greatness and excellence that we properly desire with the desire that is part of magnanimity—what human ambition could satisfy this? What empire could quench our thirst? What noble deed could be noble enough? Above all, what human task of city-building is glorious enough to satisfy our desire—unless that task is caught up in the building of the new Jerusalem? And what ruler is glorious enough to satisfy our desire for someone glorious to follow—unless that Ruler is the King of Kings?

Too, it is only Christian magnanimity that contains within itself the best medicine against the danger of magnanimity's distortion into pride: What do we have that we have not received? All that we have, the very image of God in us, is a gift. We will not refuse to perform Adam's civilizational and regal task, but we will never forget that we rule by gift-right, and by adoption.

META-VIRTUE

We must aim, Witherspoon says, at what is *really* valuable, to do the *most* good, and in that exercise all the skill, all the courage, and all the diligence that we can. But skill, courage, and diligence alone are not enough—else, he says,

> a rope-dancer might be a hero: Or if any person should spend a whole life, in the most unwearied application of accumulating wealth, however vast his desires, or however astonishing his success, his merit would be very small.

To be magnanimous is to aim to do not a little good in the world, but a great deal of good, and to have those powers to actually get that good done. This is not a matter of personal gifts precisely: one may be naturally gifted in many ways, but fail to improve these gifts. Magnanimity is the virtue that leads one to want to cultivate the other virtues, to want to become virtuous, to want to become powerful and effective in doing good. It is in that way a kind of meta-virtue, or sum of the virtues.

And to be both accountable and effective, the magnanimous person must not be a lone wolf. We must seek counsel, seek those friends who will check us if we slip into pride, and seek to be part of groups – like the Moot – that will draw us together with those who will challenge us when we should be challenged, who will help us and whom we can help, who will remind us that the reality of politics is, and always remains, friendships. These groups, formal and informal, which the jurist Johannes Althusius, writing in 1603, called *collegia*, are, along with natural families, the basic building blocks of our social world. The network that they form as they overlap and interpenetrate is what we call civilization. One might think of it as the root structure along the bank of time, channeling the power of its flow and preventing its dissipation into impotence, or its rage in a flood.

And in all of this, magnanimity must never conflict with other virtues. As Witherspoon reminds us,

> The object of our desires must be just as well as great. Some of the noblest powers of the human mind, have often been exerted in invading the rights, instead of promoting the interest and happiness of mankind. . . . Our desires ought to be governed by wisdom and prudence, as well as justice.

THE TRIBE OF THE EAGLE

It is a sobering warning. Witherspoon was, after all, part of that founding generation of whom Lincoln, in his Lyceum address, said that they sought to make their names great in establishing a country to test the "capability of a people to govern themselves." Whether or not one believes that the founding generation was magnanimous in the full Christian sense of the virtue as Witherspoon describes it, and whether or not the war they fought was just, the rest of Lincoln's warning Witherspoon would most heartily have echoed:

It is to deny, what the history of the world tells us is true, to suppose that men of ambition and talents will not continue to spring up amongst us. And, when they do, they will as naturally seek the gratification of their ruling passion, as others have so done before them. The question then, is, can that gratification be found in supporting and maintaining an edifice that has been erected by others? Most certainly it cannot. Many great and good men sufficiently qualified for any task they should undertake, may ever be found, whose ambition would inspire to nothing beyond a seat in Congress, a gubernatorial or a presidential chair; but such belong not to the family of the lion, or the tribe of the eagle. What! think you these places would satisfy an Alexander, a Caesar, or a Napoleon? – Never! Towering genius distains a beaten path. It seeks regions hitherto unexplored. – It sees no distinction in adding story to story, upon the monuments of fame, erected to the memory of others. It denies that it is glory enough to serve under any chief. It scorns to tread in the footsteps of any predecessor, however illustrious. It thirsts and burns for distinction; and, if possible, it will have it, whether at the expense of emancipating slaves, or enslaving freemen.

This kind of greatness, Witherspoon would say, is precisely the pagan counterfeit of the real thing. But it gestures toward that real thing.

SELF-COMMAND AND THE PUBLIC GOOD

So how does this play out in our lives? Witherspoon gets specific. "Religion calls us to the greatest and most noble attempts, whether in a private or a public view." In private, in the interior of self-command, is true greatness. As Solomon wrote, "He that is slow to anger, is better than the mighty, and he that ruleth his spirit, than he that taketh a city." This is a matter of, as Winthrop says, resisting "corrupt and sinful passions," but it is also a matter of *directing* one's passions. The *rule* of one's spirit is not its quenching, and the harnessing of one's spiritedness to the real good of oneself and one's community, is the real battle, and he who achieves it has conquered truly. It is an embarrassing fact of our culture that the language of self-rule has been replaced with the language of self-management: every man his own HR department.

In public, "every good man is called to live and act for the glory of God, and the good of others. Here he has as extensive a scene of activity, as he can possibly desire." What we have been given, in Christianity, is something truly worthwhile – to glory in God and to build his kingdom. Compared to this, to build what Witherspoon calls "altars to our own vanity," seems the real pusillanimity. We are like knights who serve a truly great king, one who is worthy of every possible exertion and hazard we can bring to his service. We should pity those who, though they are in some ways magnanimous, don't have the gift of a proper aim, a proper ambition, for their magnanimity. Part of being magnanimous is having something truly worthwhile to *do*, and that, he says, is what the pagans did not have.

IN PURSUIT OF THE COMMON GOOD

How is this related to politics, and to the public sphere? Here we must turn from John Witherspoon to Charles de Koninck, and his dispute with Jacques Maritain.

Maritain is, along with Lewis and Sayers and Eliot, one of Jacob's key figures. De Koninck did not make the cut, though he should have. In his discussion of their debate, Chad Pecknold notes again that strangeness which Jacobs notes, and which Anne and I found so inspiring in our work at *Breaking Ground*: "It may seem odd that a theoretical dispute would emerge amid world war, but it's precisely in times of crisis that people find urgent incentives to re-examine first principles."

It was, indeed, in the year of our Lord 1943 that de Koninck published his essay "On the Primacy of the Common Good against the Personalists." In it, he criticizes the idea, popularized by Maritain, that the individual human person is the fundamental unit of society, and that the primacy of the human person provided the best check against the totalitarianisms of Right and Left then in the process of shredding the world.

This is not the case, says de Koninck. The common good is not the collection of the private goods of individuals, which, if put to it, we could enjoy alone: a piece of birthday cake, a cellphone. Rather, common goods are those that we can only enjoy with each other: the good of being a daughter, a wife, a mother. The good of being a friend. Common good has, as its glue, love, and the exchange of justice and friendship that makes us truly human. As de Koninck points out,

> The good of the family is better than the singular good, not because all the members of the family find in it their singular good: the good of the family is better because, for each of its individual members, it is also the good of the others.

We experience the love of our families, and our love for our families, as a delight. But it is a delight that is profoundly unlike the delight we have in cake, or even in private aesthetic experience. When I love my brother, I don't just enjoy his company—though I do. I also desire his good, very deeply, and even if somehow I weren't able to have his company, I would never lose the desire for his good. And it is a love that perfects us, that makes us better—it can't help but do so.

TO SEEK THE CITY'S GOOD

We all feel this instinctively to be true: we've experienced it, at least to some degree. What de Koninck reminds us of is that fundamentally politics is about the same thing, the same exchange of love and justice—of what Johannes Althusius, writing in 1603, referred to as "symbiotic *ius*." Political love, the political common good, is less cozy than familial love, and does not replace it—but it is the same kind of thing, though grander and more stately. Our love of our polity—our city, our nation, the community of nations—and our care for these public bodies, and the public good, also perfects us, drawing us out of ourselves, drawing us to great things. As Pecknold writes,

> God made the world good—and very good. His goodness is diffused throughout the whole of creation. So the greater the common good, the more goodness it communicates, and the greater our love should be for that good—up the scale of goodness to God himself, who is the uncaused cause of all goodness.

What does it mean to love the city's good? De Koninck quotes St. Thomas:

To love the good of the city in order to appropriate it and possess it oneself does not make a good politician, for it is thus that the tyrant too loves the good of the city, in order to dominate it, which is to love himself more than the city: in fact it is for himself that he desires the good, not for the city. But to love the good of the city that it might be preserved and defended is truly to love the city, and it is that which makes a good politician, so much that, with an eye to conserving and augmenting the good of the city, he exposes himself to danger and neglects his private good.

To love its good is of course to will that it be good. "'My country, right or wrong,'" as Chesterton says, "is a thing that no patriot would think of saying. It is like saying, 'My mother, drunk or sober.'" Of course one does not cease to love, but one wills that one's mother be sober, one's country be just.

Because the love of the city, the pursuit and experience of the political common good, is one of the things – like the love of one's family – that perfects us. It was for the sake of the Jews also and not just for the sake of the Babylonians that God, through Jeremiah, commanded them, "Seek the welfare of the city where I have sent you into exile, and pray to the LORD on its behalf, for in its welfare you will find your welfare." Even out of Jerusalem, they were political animals. Even before we enter into the new Jerusalem, so are we.

And though here we have no abiding city . . . neither, let us remember, did the ancients. Polybius wrote that at Roman funerals, honored statesmen of the past, those who had done great good for their city, were represented by men of like height to them, wearing masks that resembled them, whose good deeds for the city were recounted beginning with the most ancient. "By this means," he wrote,

by the constant renewal of the good report of brave men, the celebrity of those who performed noble deeds is rendered immortal, while at the same time, the fame of those who did good service to their country becomes known to the people and a heritage for future generations. But the most important result is that young men are thus inspired to endure every suffering for the public welfare in the hope of winning the glory that attends on brave men.

And that was the best spur on offer for Roman magnanimity: if you exerted yourself for the sake of the Eternal City to great deeds, perhaps (accounts differed) your shade would have a high rank in the Elysian fields, and a young man might wear a mask of your face while your deeds were recited before the assembly. But your shade is not exactly you, any more than the mask is you.

We have not just a better spur, but a better spur *even on Roman terms*. Allowing our citizenship in our own cities here to prepare us for and open us into our citizenship in the new Jerusalem: that is food for the magnanimous soul indeed. "Do you not know that we are to judge angels? How much more, then, things pertaining to this life!" This is St. Paul's exasperated cry against pusillanimity. And we seek the praise not only of our descendants, but of God himself.

Witherspoon says that he is not "able to conceive any character more truly great than that of one, whatever be his station or position, who is devoted to the public good under the immediate order of Providence . . . he complains of no difficulty and refuses no service, if he thinks he carries the commission of the King of Kings."

In the order of nature, the greatest good we can do is to serve God by serving each other, by seeking the true political common good. This is not as high a good as performing the spiritual acts of mercy, or fulfilling the Great Commission. But it is a good we neglect at our peril. We ought no more to refuse it than we ought to refuse to care for the members of our own household, or of the household of faith.

GRAY-MARKET PUBLIC SPHERE

And so we are called to the public sphere. But the public sphere we must operate in is, for Christians, a bit of a gray market these days. Secularization has meant that when we speak of public things in public places, bringing God into the picture can often be tricky.

But we will not close ourselves off from or take a hostile attitude toward "secular society" or the public world: this is the world that God has given us, and dismissing it or refusing to take part, or attempting to create a parallel "Christian public sphere" is not what we ought to do.

And so the institutions and publications that are *Breaking Ground*'s successors will foster what is notably lacking in our society: good conversation. Ironically, the humanist vision of debate and reason and charity – rejected even by some Christians as a cucked approach to a world at war – is what we can offer the secular world now. We can engage in truly good argument – not simple-minded own-the-libs free-speechism – like the *Daily Caller* – and not the low-temperature, vaguely posthuman and fundamentally materialist debates of *Quillette*.

Rather, we will foster levelheaded but passionate and interesting debates and writing in the Christian humanist tradition, keeping humanism and even the best aspects of liberalism alive (though founded on pre-liberal principles) when they have been abandoned by both the left and the post-Christian right.

And in our habits of conversation, our charitable reading of each other, our honesty and willingness to remain in conversation with those with whom we disagree, we must model for the increasingly polarized secular world what a public discourse looks like that does not rest on accusation, bad-faith readings, guilt by association, cancellation, and the blandest of contemporary certainties.

THE SUCCESS OF THE FAILURES

What did the men and women of Oldham's Moot do? According to Jacobs, not much. They did not carry out on England a Christian version of the reconstruction of society that, for example, the United States carried out on Japan in the postwar years.

But Jacobs underestimates their work. They reshaped our public sphere as Christian intellectuals. We still live in the mental world they made, and our institutions reflect this: we are still building what they imagined.

We need to become members of that public sphere and carry it on, making our own good-human work in a time when the Christian and secular worlds seem further and further apart, and in an age when Christianity, at least conservative Christianity, will (it seems likely) be ever more aggressively shut out of the public sphere because of its association with Trump. We must not give up normal, sunlit institutions where we can still have access to them – the universities, the mainstream press, nonprofits, philanthropy – but we must press on even where we can't.

If we are called to the part of public service that is fostering and engaging in public conversation, it should not and cannot matter whether Christians are in the ascendency culturally, any more than someone who is called to a private life can only fulfill his duties when there's a bull market. If you're called to private life, you'll do your best in whatever market there is. And if you know your work, and you understand the world, you'll know that markets shift, and fortunes change, and the point is to do the work that is yours.

What keeps a man or woman who is called to public life out of it is exile – literal exile, Seneca's exile, or Dante's. None of us is in exile from our earthly polity. As long as we are able, what we're called to do is to take responsibility, no matter what the current circumstances. That is our job. We can't wait for more less-difficult or more-straightforward times in which to express that political love. There are no other people who are ours, and no other time. And these things, too, are gifts. ✿

BEHOLDING GROUND

*Tracing Reality's Shattering to Illuminate
a Still More Excellent Way*

ANNE SNYDER

*"Have you understood all these things?" Jesus asked. The disciples
said to him, "Yes." And he said to them, "Therefore every scribe
who has been trained for the kingdom of heaven is like a master of
a house, who brings out of his treasure what is new and what is old."*
—Matthew 13:51–52

*I have found the most compelling repairs are the ones that make
themselves visible, that leave evidence of the breakage and also of
the imagination by which the breakage becomes transformed. Such
repairs are always provisional, imperfect, and ongoing. Like a
nest, they involve continual mending. They ask for a willingness to
keep remaking what is perpetually at risk of falling apart. It is this
remaking by which a home, and a life, may come: not in spite of
what has gone before, but because of it.*

—Jan Richardson,
Sparrow: A Book of Life and Death and Life

THIS ENTIRE PROJECT was born out of an ache.

It was an ache of wanting birth to stanch the flow of death.

It was an ache of watching institutions that I love shudder in
dread of shuttering as the lockdowns took their early swipes.

It was an ache of sensing that my own nation was at its weakest
state in its brief yet storied history, weakened in all the things

that allow a collective to endure a global wallop and stay standing: social trust and goodwill, respect for authority (with that authority then stewarding its legitimacy with honor and an eye for service), a shared identity and agreed-on origin story, civic maturity that puts the life of the whole ahead of oneself. It was an ache of doom before still further fragmentation, a doom of dread that a common vision of reality itself was evaporating.

I suppose at some instinctive level *Breaking Ground* was born also from the ache of an artistic brain trained to pay attention to the currents that run beneath the surface of shock and havoc, and to find there hints of revelation. I knew early that I needed multitudes of others smarter and differently skilled than I for this sort of societal scuba dive to come up clear (thank you, Susannah Black! thank you, contributors!); the question was how to gather when "Scatter!" was the order of the day.

Thanks to the agility of digital tools, and to the awakened sense among many institutional leaders that the old way of doing things on one's own would not cut it in the face of the interconnected social earthquake that was steamrolling our days, gather we did, albeit with fewer gigabytes blessing our communion. This platform publicly launched just hours after the first memorial service was held for George Floyd one year ago, and as I said in the gray twilight of what would become the violent summer of 2020, "*Breaking Ground* is first and foremost an act of hope."

It was an act of hope that the church might yet prove itself agile in the face of widespread suffering, and that a public space for reflection, conversation, and yes, skilled disagreement, too, could hasten helpful action. It was an act of hope that amid our society-wide need for energy and creativity, the technocratic and utilitarian would be tutored by the moral and the humane. It was an act of hope that today's Christian minds might be prepared to light the kind of candle for vigil and next steps that a post-Christian society like ours might still recognize in the vestiges of buried longing. And it was an act of hope that a still-potent, still-faithful God was working and shifting and creating in our global upheaval, if only we could develop the patience to see.

But how to see, exactly? And with whom? How could we be confident that what we were seeing and naming was real, and not simply our own glass?

I have neither the philosophical nor neuroscientific chops to dissect the nature of reality: Is it a question? Is it subjective? But answering the above triad with care has been *Breaking Ground*'s high calling and, in a year of epistemological rupture, our thorny task. For it turns out that reality, like suffering, is iconoclastic: Each new drama shatters our preconceived notions of what's actually going on, what works and what's effective, what the categories for our understanding should be, what the questions are that we should be asking, and, most painfully for so many this last year, who our tribe actually is (or ever was). This shattering builds into a redefining process that can be as exhausting as it is indiscriminate, challenging individuals, institutions, whole nations, a generation.

What we tried to do here, in this pilot year of a conversational exploration and, hopefully, longer-term community, was dive into these trenches with you and trace in real time the contours of those shards so sharply disrupting our common life. We looked at the abject failure of our politics to stop mass death, a failure superseded only by the failure of our own Christian community to meet the moral opportunity presented by the nation's awakening to the realities of ongoing racial injustice – a failure of clarity, unity, and grace that ceded the floor to the pagan poles. We reflected on the renewed attention so many of us have found ourselves paying to proximate goods: the household, the family, the neighbor, the village. We named the weakening authority of expertise and sought a more capacious understanding of wisdom worth following, and how to cultivate cultural receptivity to such wisdom. We debated justice's relationship to peace and vice versa as our streets shook, and revisited what unity in a polis even is. And so much more.

Woven through all the unmaskings of this year, of course, was the final crumbling of a narrative of self-sufficiency that has proved to be as false to the way we are wired as it is destructive to the tomorrow we need to build. Somehow, in the very paradox of social isolation, I think we've all finally realized that we cannot secure ourselves. As Walter Brueggemann said so softly in the first of six contemplations that set the tone for this whole endeavor, we can only be secured by someone who is faithful to us. We need someone to hear us, which in turn demands that we continually train to become the kinds of people worthy of another's need to be heard and seen. This includes our neighbor. This includes God.

And this is where we land. The central task facing our society as we exit the Covid-19 pandemic and return to some semblance of physical normalcy is to build a common vision of reality. We happen to be living through an institutionally neutered moment, when people are choosing totalizing explanations based on the psychic rewards of belonging to a particular group. It's increasingly yielding extremists, but—and here's my hope—it's also squeezing out a chastened remnant. And it's this remnant I'd like to speak to as we close.

It may be too late to build a common vision of reality, and it may never have existed in the first place; but without it, the system of relationships that we know as "society" will continue to disintegrate. "Common" does not mean complete; it is God, the ultimate iconoclast, who alone has that perch. But my hope is that those tethered to his love might yet be moved to create spaces like this one, on and off the page, for honest reflection, dialogue, imagination, and especially grace. For it is in the neighbor's face that we behold God's face, it is in the neighbor's pain that we find our assumptions softened and our numbness dispelled, and it is in the neighbor's story that our own story is tutored, shaping, as we perceive and listen and learn to love, the ground for us to stand on, and for us to build once more. ⚘

457

INDEX

ABOUT COMMENT

IF CHRISTIANITY is going to reclaim its collective witness in the West, an alliance must be built between elite and commoner, scholar and practitioner, black and white, able-bodied and disabled, immigrant and indigenous, young and old. If the church is to draw closer to God's heart and revive her force in history, her way will be one of suffering, sacrifice, atonement, and humility. She will love despite fear, count the cost, and consider it joy. She will be bridging, beatitudinal, and broken.

This is the vision of *Comment*. Published by Cardus, a think tank devoted to renewing North American social architecture across the spheres of our common life, *Comment*'s writers are animated by 2,000 years of Christian social thought as they probe some of the deepest fractures – and invitations – in that life today.

We navigate an era rife with division, distrust, powerful moral narratives attempting to cancel each other out, widespread institutional weakness, and insecurity. People in silos defined by group identity and fortified by ideological allegiance have lost the ability to converse with one another, and the historical middle space where exciting collaborations, neighborly virtue, and pragmatic hope typically flourish has faded from public consciousness.

Civic and organizational leaders are struggling to stand in the gap to protect this increasingly fragile space. As this anthology attests, this struggle has only gotten fiercer since 2020. The intensified heat of our cultural contest, and the loneliness experienced by those struggling to sustain vocations of healing and social renewal, calls for a visionary weaving of Christian social thought, practice, and institutional forces.

Comment is taking on this vital work. Bridging the worlds of thinker and doer and attracting voices from across the spectrum of civic experience and Christian expression, the magazine is composing a multi-part harmony to reweave our social and moral fabric.

Will you join us?

Subscribe to *Comment* at commentmag.com.

ABOUT PLOUGH

THIS BOOK has cast a dramatic spotlight on realities that many long wished to ignore. What answers does Christianity give to these and other pressing challenges of our day? How can we advance justice, live sustainably, educate our children, use technology wisely, and build a culture of life? Can Jesus' radical teachings in the Sermon on the Mount be put into practice?

Plough is a quarterly magazine for people eager to explore these important questions. It pledges allegiance to neither the left nor the right. Instead, *Plough* aims to challenge and inspire readers of every persuasion to pursue a practical way of faith with integrity and enthusiasm. As our founding editor, Eberhard Arnold, wrote more than a century ago, *Plough*'s mission is "to proclaim living renewal, to summon people to deeds in the spirit of Jesus, to spread the mind of Christ in the social distress of the present day, to apply Christianity publicly, and to testify to God's action in current events."

This is an ambitious mission. That's why *Plough* draws on contributors from diverse faith traditions such as Cornel West, Pope Francis, N. T. Wright, Edwidge Danticat, Rowan Williams, Liz Bruenig, Shane Claiborne, Christian Wiman, Stanley Hauerwas, Bill McKibben, David Bentley Hart, Shadi Hamid, and Susannah Heschel. Each issue pairs fresh contemporary voices with insights of great thinkers of the past such as Dorothy Day, Dietrich Bonhoeffer, Eugene Debs, Thomas Aquinas, Soren Kierkegaard, Teresa of Avila, Oscar Romero, Thomas Merton, and Simone Weil.

Plough draws together people who, though diverse, hold a common conviction that the gospel isn't an impossible ideal – it's a way of life. Connect with thousands of others around the world who share this vision by joining the extraordinary network of engaged thinkers and doers who make *Plough* one of Christianity's most exciting meeting places today.

Join this living network.

Subscribe to *Plough* at plough.com.